THE POLITICS OF NATIONAL MINORITY PARTICIPATION IN POST-COMMUNIST EUROPE

T0383711

EAST WEST INSTITUTE

New York Prague Moscow Kyiv Brussels Košice

The EastWest Institute is an independent, not-for-profit organization working to defuse tensions and conflicts that threaten geopolitical stability while promoting democracy, free enterprise, and prosperity in Central and Eastern Europe, Russia, and other states of Eurasia. The EastWest Institute operates through a network of affiliated centers, including New York, Prague, Moscow, Kyiv, Košice, and Brussels, and was formerly known as the Institute for EastWest Studies.

For more information, please contact us at:

EastWest Institute
700 Broadway, Second Floor
New York, NY 10003
Tel (212) 824-4100, Fax (212) 824-4149
Website: http:/www.iews.org
E-mail: iews@iews.org

THE POLITICS OF NATIONAL MINORITY PARTICIPATION IN POST-COMMUNIST EUROPE

STATE-BUILDING, DEMOCRACY, AND ETHNIC MOBILIZATION

JONATHAN P. STEIN, EDITOR

EASTWEST INSTITUTE

Routledge
Taylor & Francis Group

LONDON AND NEW YORK

First published 2000 by M.E. Sharpe

Published 2019 by Routledge
2 Park Square, Milton Park, Abingdon, Oxon OX14 4RN
52 Vanderbilt Avenue, New York, NY 10017

Routledge is an imprint of the Taylor & Francis Group, an informa business

Library of Congress Cataloging-in-Publication Data

The politics of national minority participation in post-communist Europe : state-building,
democracy, and ethnic mobilization / by EastWest Institute ; edited by Jonathan P. Stein.
    p.cm.
    Includes bibliographical references and index.
    ISBN 0-7656-0528-7 (alk. paper)
    1. Europe, Eastern—Politics and government—1989– 2. Europe, Eastern—Ethnic
relations. 3. Minorities—Europe, Eastern—Political activity. 4. Post-communism—Europe,
Eastern. I. Stein, Jonathan P. II. EastWest Institute (New York, N.Y.)

DJK51 .P66 2000
323´.042´08900947—dc21   00-05935

ISBN 13: 978-0-7656-0528-3 (hbk)

CONTENTS

CONTRIBUTORS

Jonathan P. Stein is a research associate at the EastWest Institute's Prague Centre.

Carlos Flores Juberías is a professor of law at the University of Valencia.

Janusz Bugajski is Director of East European Studies at the Center for Strategic and International Studies in Washington, D.C.

Neil J. Melvin is a professor of government at the University of Leeds.

Nenad Zakošek is an associate professor of political science at the University of Zagreb.

James Pettifer is a research fellow of the European Research Institute, University of Bath, UK.

Ivan Ilchev is a professor of history at the University of Sofia.

Michael Shafir is an analyst at Radio Free Europe/Radio Liberty, Prague.

Erin Jenne recently completed a Ph.D. in political science at Stanford University.

Jack Snyder is a professor of political science at Columbia University.

FOREWORD

Since the end of the Cold War, there has been no shortage of reminders of the terrible consequences of ethnic conflict. As we have seen in the Balkans and around the globe, in a matter of days and weeks, peoples can be relegated to abject human misery and whole societies set back decades in their quest for a better life. The gap between the prosperous nations and those whose economies are unable to grow becomes wider. Visions of democracy, prosperity and cooperative inter-state relations remain but dreams. Wherever inter-ethnic tensions are high or where they can easily be inflamed by politicians, the path to power is shortened for extremist forces, who typically maintain control by quashing internal dissent, hijacking the economy for the benefit of political cronies, and provoking conflict with neighboring states.

While this tendency has been widespread throughout the developing world, post-communist Europe has provided an environment particularly conducive to authoritarian nationalism. The post-communist transition has witnessed the emergence of weak states that are incapable of ensuring security for their citizens and migration patterns and border changes that have left territorially concentrated minorities outside "their" states, all of which is exacerbated by a deep economic malaise. Insecurity and instability, coupled with the collapse of official Communist ideology, have created fertile ground for opportunistic political leaders to mobilize long-standing and deep-seated ethnic rivalries for their own political gain. Profiteers have been successful in exploiting these conflicts for financial gain. The wars of Yugoslav succession and the recent devastation endured by the peoples of Kosovo and Serbia provide only the most tragic examples of ethnic nationalism's destructive potential.

Elsewhere in post-communist Europe, the absence of state-organized or state-sponsored ethnic violence has not meant an absence of ethnic conflict, but has merely kept it largely out of the view of Western publics. Nevertheless, constitutional provisions assigning symbolic precedence to ethnic majorities, restrictive language laws, exclusionary citizenship measures, biased electoral systems, the denial of cultural rights to ethnic minorities, and failure by officials to curtail localized violence are frequent features of the post-communist political landscape. Wherever they are present, they have represented an ongoing threat to democratic consolidation, aided forces hostile to economic reform, impeded integration into Euro-Atlantic institutions, and damaged the fragile confidence-building processes necessary to building lasting regional stability. Even leaders with clearly demonstrable track records of being in the European democratic tradition have demonstrated their willingness to use ethnic politics to enhance their power or attempt to stay in power.

As part of its efforts to promote democracy, economic transformation, and security throughout central and eastern Europe as well as in Russia and the states of Central Asia and the Caucasus, the EastWest Institute (EWI) has placed the need to study and address ethnic conflict within post-communist polities at the center of its concerns. The present volume, generously funded by the Carnegie Corporation of New York, grew out of the EWI's Program on Managing Ethnic Conflict, an initiative established at the very outset of the post-Cold War era to develop innovative methods for reducing the fear and mistrust between ethnic majorities and minorities that can derail positive social and political change. This volume follows a highly successful volume the Institute published in 1993, Minorities: The New Europe's Old Issue. The Institute's projects in South Eastern Europe, including the Task Force on the future of the Federal Republic of Yugoslavia, address the issues dealt with in this volume as Europe seeks to transform its southeastern part into a secure, stable, democratic, and prosperous region.

The recurring crises in the Balkans have, however, tended to obscure from view promising developments elsewhere in central and Eastern Europe over the past decade. In the latter half of the 1990's, Estonia and Latvia responded to the prolonged engagement of western institutions, including non-governmental organizations such as the EWI, by gradually adopting frameworks for extending citizenship to their Russophone minorities. Ethnic Hungarian minorities played a key role in allying with democratic forces to dislodge populist authoritarian regimes in Romania and Slovakia. At the same time, Bulgaria's Turkish minority integrated politically with liberal forces to defeat a post-communist government that had led the country to the brink of economic collapse. Clearly, close examination of these states' experiences can provide invaluable lessons for promoting stability and reconstruction in the Balkans.

Nevertheless, the course of post-communist transformation remains exceptionally fluid, and ethnic groups' mutual mistrust and recrimination will continue to endanger the gains made so far. It is our hope, therefore, that the present volume will assist students of the region, leaders, and policy makers in familiarizing themselves with the problems of political accommodation confronted by multi-ethnic post-communist states, as well as encouraging further attention to the obstacles that remain to be overcome. The Board of Directors of the EastWest Institute is proud to sponsor the publication of this series and welcomes comments and suggestions from its readers.

John Edwin Mroz
President and Founder, EWI

István Gyarmati
Senior Vice President, EWI

ACKNOWLEDGMENTS

The gestation of this book has been unusually long, which may, alas, be the inevitable price to be paid when contributors are scattered far and wide, and when a volume's incubator is as extraordinarily dynamic and fast-changing an organization as the EastWest Institute (EWI). The volume was originally conceived by Robert W. Mickey, who, after his departure from the EWI, continued to make many important contributions to its realization. For his patience (and prodding), I must also express my profound gratitude to Stephen B. Heintz. During Stephen's term as Executive Vice President of the EWI and Director of its Prague Centre, his leadership, energy, and intellectual depth set an example that was nothing short of inspiring, and I remain honored by his friendship and camaraderie. Istvan Gyarmati of the EWI and Vasil Hudák, the current Director of the Prague Centre, read the entire manuscript and provided valuable comments. Nevertheless, the contents of the book remain solely the responsibility of the editor and authors. They should not be construed as reflecting the views of either the EWI or the Carnegie Corporation of New York.

I also benefited greatly from suggestions made by my editor at M.E. Sharpe, Patricia Kolb, which have made this a more thematically cohesive and, I hope, accessible volume than it otherwise would have been. Prior to his departure into the New Economy, Scott Rogers provided reliable administrative (and moral) support as the Institute's Director of Publications. In the book's latter stages, Natasha Randall stepped coolly into the breach, copyediting the manuscript and coordinating its final preparation with admirable professionalism. Scott Tennant's typesetting skills are also gratefully acknowledged.

Finally, I must also thank my long-time friend and partner, Vladěna Steinová, for helping me in innumerable ways to keep everything in its proper perspective. An altogether different sort of debt is owed to my brother, Ethan, whose company I shared for the last time shortly after taking on this project. To him is owed the incalculable debt of memory, and it is to that sustaining memory that this volume is dedicated.

Jonathan P. Stein
May 11, 2000

1

NATIONAL MINORITIES AND POLITICAL DEVELOPMENT IN POST-COMMUNIST EUROPE

Jonathan P. Stein

Over the past decade, the assertion of ethnic identity has dominated much of the politics of post-communist central and eastern Europe and the former Soviet Union. During the period of Soviet state-building and later during the Cold War, this region, extremely diverse ethnically both within and across neighboring states, was marked by a rigid channeling of political participation that attempted uniformly to suppress officially unsanctioned demands and modes of expression, including those emerging from ethnic cleavages. With the collapse of communism, however, there has been a dramatic expansion of distinctively ethnically-focused political action, ranging from ethnic voting to ethnic cleansing. Clearly, the recognition, cultivation, and assertion of ethnicity is now unbound from the strictures of the recent past.

But exactly in what sense is the high salience of ethnic group identities and their claims upon the state a response to the demise of communism? On one level, ethnicity "unbound" seems to be in keeping with conventional wisdom. Observers often assume that the mobilization of ethnicity as the primary cleavage of post-communist social and political conflict is inevitable, a thesis that comes in both vulgar and analytically more sophisticated variants. In its vulgar form, communist repression is seen as having placed latent ethnic antagonisms in a "deep freeze." According to this view, significant portions of the region's populations managed covertly to bear their ethnic identities—intact, unaffected, and primary—across two or more generations, resolved and prepared to seize the first available opportunity to settle old accounts with ethnic foes. Thus, the post-communist "thaw" reactivated a host of dormant group conflicts, border disputes, and primordial or ancient "tribal" hatreds.[1]

Stated in such a reductionist manner, this view has been widely challenged by scholars who locate the "necessity" of post-communist ethnopolitics in the collapse or weakening of states whose stability depended on the political monopoly of a single party. To be sure, historical grievances may contribute to shaping the form ethnopolitics assumes.[2] Yet ethnic categories provide an attractive template for building new states or strengthening old ones not because they express some underlying condition *sub specie aeternitatis*, but because they are relatively fixed and are thus easily identifiable by actors within emerging polities and potential challengers who have been excluded from them. One need not have well-developed state institutions to frame the distinction between friend and foe or collective self and other; in their absence, "groupness" itself becomes a highly valued resource, the more so as individuals perceive increasing threats to their economic and physical security. Thus, ethnopolitics fills the ideological and institutional vacuum left by the collapse of the party-state.[3]

Clearly, there is much to recommend focusing on the structural context of nation-state building, for in many respects, the dynamics of the region's ethnic conflicts are similar to those found in the postcolonial developing world, which have themselves exhibited remarkable similarities.[4] Recognition of these similarities is reflected in renewed attention to the influence of the international environment on ethnic conflict within states, particularly the relational dynamic between ethnic minorities, their external homelands (or "kin states"), and the "home states" in which they reside.[5] Such similarities also form the premise for efforts to come to grips with the successes and failures of (non)intervention by intergovernmental organizations and other interstate actors.[6] All of this suggests that ethnic conflicts, while informed by the past, are more usefully thought of as eminently rational political struggles over the future.[7]

This volume shares many of the assumptions and analytical foci of the rationalist approach to ethnopolitics, recognizing that it is precisely the primordial concern with communal solidarity, the preservation and expression of collective identity, and the allocation of group prestige that provides politicized ethnicity with its profound mobilizational power and gives competing claims their zero-sum character.[8] Indeed, because rational and primordial motivations usually operate simultaneously within ethnic communities, and because the state is the primary locus of the material and symbolic power for which they strive, there often seem to be precious few brakes on ethnicity's momentum as a political force. In the absence of external hegemony, internally weak multi-national states, such as those that emerged from communism, face the threat of disintegration into smaller parts, only to produce unstable successor states that are themselves wracked by ethnonational conflict. Ethnicity "unbound" can seem to resemble a machine that goes of itself, fueled by the dismal Hobbesian logic of a culturally homogenizing war of all against all.

But from the perspective of this volume's contributors, ethnicity "unbound" connotes something quite different, for its contemporary political importance in much of the region, while undeniably conditioned by structural factors, has been far from inevitable and uniform. Rather, given the numerous ways in which political participation and contestation have been organized, the relative salience of ethnic cleavages and the consequences of their mobilization require a good deal of explanation. Moreover, ethnic categories, even those operative in the region's most heated pairings of ethnic majorities and minorities, are often more malleable than many scholarly observers and policymakers recognize. Indeed, as the first decade of post-communism comes to a close, it is not at all obvious that ethnic identity must or will remain among the central motive forces of social and political conflict. On the contrary, perhaps the most important lesson to be drawn from this volume is that ethnicity, as it has functioned in post-communist politics, is best considered "unbound" by explanations that are all too often freighted with teleological assumptions.

The varied contours of ethnopolitics in post-communist Europe require a conception of ethnic conflict that is not restricted to organized intercommunal violence. In fact, notwithstanding the widespread attention it has received as human tragedy or international security threat, and despite the extremely high stakes for national minorities implied by the formation of 22 new states in post-communist Europe and the former Soviet Union, inter-ethnic violence has remained exceedingly rare.[9] This does not mean that ethnic relations within these states are typically harmonious or that cultural heterogeneity has not significantly affected their ability to consolidate democratic regimes and develop the institutional coherence required for urgent tasks such as economic reform. It is no accident that of the five post-communist countries invited in July 1997 by the European Union to begin "fast-track" accession negotiations, four—the Czech Republic, Hungary, Poland, and Slovenia—most closely approximate the nationalist ideal of congruent ethnic and political boundaries, while the fifth (Estonia) achieved a similar result at independence through the proxy of ethnically exclusive citizenship.[10]

Organized, and especially militarized, violent ethnic conflict is often sufficient to undermine a state's efficacy, if not its viability, but it is not necessary to such an outcome, as the peaceful dissolution of Czechoslovakia most plainly demonstrates. Ethnic conflict is therefore best defined as describing a broad range of circumstances in which different ethnic groups inhabiting the same state's territory maintain antithetical goals regarding the degree of public recognition and autonomy accorded to them by the political system. Thus understood, differences in the determinants, degree, and form of conflict, and in the ability of domestic and international actors to manage it, can more readily be identified and analyzed. At the same time, and of equal importance to scholars and policy makers concerned with the prospects for democratic consolidation in the region, the contributors to this volume collectively attempt to provide a deeper understanding of the complicated interplay between ethnic conflict and post-communist regime transition.

The chapters include a comparative analysis of post-communist electoral systems, an examination of nationalist ethnic majority parties, five country-specific case-studies, an exploration of the politics of the region's Roma population, and a concluding chapter that evaluates options for ethnic conflict management by domestic- and international-level actors. The focus of these studies is limited in two important ways. First, and most obviously, the volume's geographic scope is largely contained to post-communist Europe and the Baltic successor states of the former Soviet Union. The decision to forgo treatment of the extremely complex ethnopolitics within what is now the Commonwealth of Independent States (CIS) reflects not only a pragmatic concern with what a single volume can feasibly achieve, but also the marked gap in political development within the post-communist world. Compared with central and eastern Europe and the Baltic states, the CIS is uniformly characterized by far lower state institutional capacity, dramatically poorer democratic performance, higher susceptibility to external threats, and weaker receptiveness to western influence.[11] As James Pettifer's chapter demonstrates, some of these distinctive macro-political features have played a central role in shaping ethnic relations also in Albania.

Similarly, while western Europe is clearly experiencing an ethnic "revival" as it accelerates simultaneous processes of integration and regionalization,[12] the causes and consequences of ethnic conflict in the East are sufficiently distinctive to merit separate attention. The region's pre-communist history, the legacy of communist rule, and the vagaries of the exceptionally uncertain and fluid post-communist context all caution against a continent-wide analysis, at least until the politics of ethnicity in central and eastern Europe, like the region's political regimes more broadly, exhibit more settled patterns that are better understood.

Second, the country case studies focus almost exclusively on political interactions between ethnic majorities and the largest of each country's ethnic minorities, despite the presence in each of these states of other ethnic minorities of varying sizes. The rationale for this is not an ethnic minority's size, however, but rather its "ethnicness," that is, the degree of its consciousness as a distinct collectivity and the extent of its political organization to maintain itself as such. It is politically conscious and organized ethnic minorities' demands concerning past and present treatment, their mobilization within or against the political system to realize these demands, and the political system's response to this mobilization that are of most serious consequence both domestically and internationally. In short, these are the ethnic minorities whose modes of political participation shape the establishment of either civic and inclusive or ethnically defined and exclusive polities.

The remainder of this introduction examines several themes that emerge in the individual chapters and attempts to situate them within current theorizing about ethnicity and post-communist political change, occasionally referring to cases from the region that are not included among the country studies. An important caveat is in order, however. While there are many common factors shaping post-communist ethnopolitics, the manner in which they operate is often difficult to tease out. In some cases, they seem to fuel or exacerbate ethnic conflict, while in others they appear to reflect or be caused by ethnic conflict itself. *A la* Tocqueville, indirect effects often seem more important than direct effects, and dependent and independent variables are frequently difficult to distinguish.[13] It may be helpful, therefore, to think of these relationships in terms of a process of *structuration* in which political institutions established by a set of agents affect social attitudes and identities, which in turn potentially lead to further institutional change.[14] Above all, the variations on the themes discussed below point to the contemporary fluidity of political outcomes and the explanatory and predictive limitations analysts must confront. While they do highlight a number of useful lessons for policymakers, they also underscore the need for caution, circumspection, and a healthy dose of skepticism toward any proposed policy response.

Historical Legacies, Path-Dependency, and Feedback Mechanisms

In recent years, scholars have emphasized the importance of placing historical and institutional legacies at the center of theorizing about political, social, and economic change.[15] Social scientists have thus begun to develop more systematic understandings of the manner in which attention to temporally linked sequences and feedback processes can improve the study of large-scale change, highlighting in particular the self-reinforcing properties of such processes.[16] Beginning from often highly contingent starting points, political, social, and economic interactions produce outcomes that feed back on themselves, narrowing over time the range of further possible outcomes.

This approach is particularly useful in examining the domestic sources of ethnopolitics in the post-communist context, for it sheds important analytical light on a phenomenon that appears in several of the contributions to this volume, namely the tendency of majority-minority interactions to spiral towards political marginalization of the minority. Two factors underpinning this sequential process merit attention. First, the historical legacies that communist rule bequeathed to political institutions, actors, and identities serve to prod ethnopolitics along certain paths and not others. A second and related domestic "path-setting" factor highlighted by many of the contributors is the definition of statehood embraced by post-communist constitutions.

The Leninist Legacy

Ken Jowitt has powerfully described the debilitating social, cultural, and political legacies of "Leninist" rule for post-communist politics: intense privatism and ingrained patterns of dissimulation, fragmented personal and public identities, the absence of an established successor elite, and the lack of widely shared standards of legitimacy with which to sanction reconstituted political authority.[17] Moreover, Leninist regimes served in certain respects to sustain key elements of pre-communist traditional political cultures that further impede the adoption of democratic norms and practices—an important theme in James Pettifer's contribution to this volume.[18] What concerns us foremost here, however, are the consequences for multiethnic post-communist states of emulating, to varying degrees and for varying periods of time, Soviet nationality policies, and the sudden shift from no effective electoral participation to universal suffrage in an environment where partisan loyalties are undeveloped, interest groups are non-existent, and economic issues loom large.

All multinational communist states attempted to shore up their stability by exploiting their ethnic diversity, using means ranging from the development, promotion, and cooptation of ethnic minority elites (e.g., Albania, Bulgaria), to the provision of autonomous territories for larger ethnic minorities (e.g., Romania until 1968, Kosovo and Vojvodina in the Serbian republic of Yugoslavia), to the grandest experiment of all, ethnoterritorial federalism (the Soviet Union, Yugoslavia, and Czechoslovakia).[19] None of the states in this last category still exists, two of them have been the site of a great amount of bloodshed, and the survival of many of their successor states is by no means guaranteed.[20]

For post-communist political actors in states that adopted ethnoterritorial institutional arrangements, this experience remains the dominant frame for viewing majority-minority relations. Governing elites belonging to today's ethnic majorities frequently were yesterday's minorities in federal states.[21] Moreover, following the collapse of communism, what previously had been merely formal constitutional provisions, such as the right of federal units to secede or extravagantly high legislative supermajority requirements, could be exploited to gain independence either by design or, as in the case of Czechoslovakia, by default.[22] Now facing their own "national problem," these elites perceive all demands for territorial autonomy, partner–nation status, or federal arrangements as a slippery slope to secession—precisely because it is one that their own ethnic constituencies slid down. Simply put, ethnic majority elites in the Baltics, Croatia, Macedonia, Slovakia, and elsewhere "know better," and their lessons have not been lost on neighbors, such as Romania, that never knew full-scale ethnofederalism.

The second legacy issue is an acute form of the problem addressed by Samuel Huntington in his classic work on politics in the developing world: the lagging capacity of existing political institutions to respond to the rapid expansion of participation by newly mobilized social forces.[23] Given that the capacity to extract societal resources (i.e., an effective taxation bureaucracy), a monopoly of the legitimate means of violence, and effective administrative control mechanisms are all necessary to a state's survival, the debility of post-communist public agencies, high levels of crime and corruption, unstable and ineffective governments, and uncertain relations between constitutional branches represent a serious cause for concern. Most importantly, the crucial element of social and political stability for Huntington, well-institutionalized parties capable of channeling popular mobilization, aggregating divergent societal preferences, and providing coherence to legislative and executive action, are also largely absent from much of the post-communist landscape. In contrast to most post-authoritarian countries, where old parties were successfully resurrected after the lifting of repression, post-communist party systems have arisen almost entirely *de novo*, with even communist successor parties "new" to the extent that they must attract authentic popular support and have been no less prone to fragmentation than other parties.[24]

The establishment of new parties in post-communist polities is made problematic by what Juan Linz and Alfred Stepan call "the relative flatness of the landscape of civil society."[25] While rich with status distinctions of considerable political importance, communist party-states embraced as their *raison d'être* the suppression of socioeconomic class distinctions and autonomously articulated interests and identities. Weakly organized societies, on this view, impede the rapid institutionalization of parties, leaving would-be elites without stable electoral constituencies and thus with a strong incentive to establish catch-all parties that appeal to more easily identifiable regional and ethnic identities.

This view is not without its critics, however. Herbert Kitschelt, for example, points out that what he calls the categorical "tabula rasa" view fails to account for variations in the region's party systems and implausibly assumes that a decade hence, voters remain unable to comprehend their economic interests.[26] Nevertheless, while Kitschelt does find examples of relatively successful parties arrayed programmatically along more traditional socioeconomic cleavages, of the countries he studies, only Bulgaria is marked by politically salient ethnic differences—and there, as Ivan Ilchev's chapter shows, declining salience has been due in large part to Turkish emigration. Clearly, marketization and closer ties to the West have introduced new socioeconomic cleavages, issue dimensions, and political attitudes. However, these changes have proceeded furthest precisely in those states where politically mobilized ethnic minorities—and thus a "stateness" threat to the central, coordinating authority required to formulate and implement the policies necessary to bring them about—are absent.[27]

Indeed, even where formal democratic procedures are upheld, political actors threatened by the transition from a command to a market economy have good reason to perpetuate the perception of a stateness threat. Particularly where organized opposition to the old regime was weak and antireform communist elites formed barely reconstructed successor parties that gained power following the first democratic elections, the combination of inchoate socioeconomic classes and economic dislocation has been met by ethnonationalism as a tactical means of diverting mobilization around competing economic interests and agendas.[28] As Janusz Bugajski's chapter demonstrates, cronyism in privatization, slowness in liberalizing prices, and rampant clientilism are encouraged and exploited by nationalist ethnic majority parties, which favor a high level of dirigisme precisely in order to maintain control over the ethnic distribution of public benefits. Not surprisingly, therefore, they have served as "flank" parties and often as coalition partners of reactionary leftist-populist parties with roots in the old regime, a pattern that has marked post-communist politics to varying degrees in Bulgaria, Croatia, Romania, Serbia, and Slovakia.[29] Together, these forces mobilize the most vulnerable segments of the population—industrial workers, the elderly, the less educated, and rural inhabitants—around real or imagined internal and external threats to national survival, thus lowering the *traceability* of political responsibility for economic malaise.[30]

Ironically, in some cases, such as the Russian-speakers of Latvia and the Albanians of western Macedonia, the exclusion of minorities from public employment as a result of job discrimination or language requirements has served to push them more quickly into the private sector, where they often prosper. However, privatization can also exacerbate economic discrimination, as Erin Jenne's chapter on the Roma points out. Most importantly, however, economic uncertainties amplify all groups' fears concerning the future and their place in it, potentially resulting in more radical policy demands by ethnic minorities and thus raising overall levels of ethnic tension. For example, demands for minority-language universities reflect in part the fear that non-university graduates will be shut out from higher-status employment opportunities. Yet such demands also feed ethnic majority fears that minorities are attempting to develop parallel and eventually separate societies rather than joining or acceding to majority state-building designs.

Ethnicity and Constitutional Symbolism

A fundamentally important institutional consequence of the establishment of entirely new parties is that between 1990 and 1993, most of the countries in the region adopted new constitutions or radically revised existing ones.[31] Constitutional framers typically committed themselves to the usual basket of western principles: representative democratic institutions, guarantees of individual rights, some form of judicial review, civilian control of the military, social welfare rights, and protection of private property. However, most of the constitutions adopted by multiethnic post-communist states share another important feature that directly reflects the legacy of communist nationalities policies: preambles that define statehood in national-cultural, rather than civic-territorial, terms.[32] The state's basis in popular sovereignty is, in other words, established in a few brief phrases, while its symbolic "ownership" is simultaneously transferred to the dominant ethnic group.

The degree to which such definitions have structured ethnic conflict cannot be overestimated, for they introduce a chronic blurring of the distinction between the "normal" politics played out within an established constitutional framework and the "extraordinary" politics aimed at altering that framework.[33] Simply put, for ethnic minorities seeking equal status with the "state-bearing" nation, politics remains stuck in an extraordinary mode, with profound implications for social and political stability. Indeed, wherever constitutions proclaimed the dominant ethnic group's symbolic ownership of the state, politically mobilized ethnic minorities opposed their ratification, reflecting the irrelevance at moments of political founding of standard hermeneutic practice, according to which preambles are considered "formally symbolic rather than legally binding" as compared to provisions contained in the constitution's "operative text."[34] For, despite inclusion of "civic" provisions in the text, the preamble "states and reinforces constitutional nationalism," establishing *de facto* permanent second-class citizenship for non-members of the dominant group—in some cases preserving communist constitutions' practice of explicitly categorizing non-members by ethnicity.[35]

At issue in this founding conflict is group status. Yet, as Donald Horowitz notes, "[w]hereas material advancement can be measured both relatively and absolutely, the status advancement of one ethnic group is entirely relative to the status of others."[36] Thus, nationally defined statehood reifies precisely those political claims that are least amenable to bargaining, negotiation, and compromise. Moreover, as the country studies detail, such constitutional symbolism has been used by legislators, jurists, and administrators to interpret provisions concerning public use of minority languages, minority-language education, and local government in ways molded to fit the aspirations of the national group in whose name the state has been created. Similarly, in Albania, Bulgaria, and Romania, ethnic majority actors attempted to interpret vague provisions concerning the legal status of ethnic minority-based parties in the light of preambles to deprive them of the right to electoral participation.

Michael Shafir's chapter on the Hungarian minority in Romania offers a particularly trenchant analysis of how these constitutional politics establish a destabilizing feedback mechanism. The more broadly applicable lesson is that as the status accorded to minorities is perceived as threatening their longterm domination by the ethnic majority, politically mobilized minorities frame their demands in response to it, pressing for firm guarantees of linguistic, cultural, and educational rights. Combined with their initial opposition to the constitution, this lends credibility to arguments that they are disloyal to the state, which in turn may weaken moderates within the ethnic majority. The ethnic majority's intransigence then provokes increasingly desperate and radical demands as ethnic minority moderates similarly lose influence, reinforcing the political salience of ethnicity and the electoral incentives that follow from it. Eventually, as has happened with Albanians in Macedonia and Kosovo, an ethnic minority may entirely reconcile itself with the repudiation of the civic state and accept nothing less than partner-nation status, territorial autonomy, or outright independence.

The Role of New Political Institutions

Obviously, constitutions structure and channel political power in explicit as well as symbolic ways, while quasi-constitutional features of post-communist political systems can have similarly important effects on the quality of ethnic relations. The role of four such institutional influences interests us here: electoral systems, parliaments, presidents, and devolution of political power to municipal and regional administrations.

As Carlos Flores Juberías's chapter shows, a variety of post-communist electoral paradigms for ethnic minority participation have been established. For the region's larger minorities—those that can mobilize sufficient support to surpass electoral thresholds—proportional representation has ensured regular parliamentary representation. However, whether helping or hindering the electoral prospects of ethnic minority parties through the use of thresholds, districting, ballot laws, or other devices, none of these states' electoral legislation comprehends the crucial distinction between representation "in the tangible but narrow sense of legislative office holding" and in the "broader sense of incorporating [an ethnic group's] concerns and interests in the calculations of politicians belonging to a variety of groups."[37] Thus, while party list proportional representation has led to party proliferation and the need for *seat pooling* to create coalition governments, in no case has electoral legislation provided incentives to construct multiethnic governing coalitions through *vote pooling* encouraged by schemes such as the single transferable vote or alternative vote models of proportional representation.[38] In the absence of such incentives, not only have multiethnic governing coalitions been extremely rare, but where they have emerged, as in Romania following the 1996 general election or Slovakia after the 1998 elections, there has been little of the electorally motivated moderation of party positions that would make their persistence, and lasting accommodation, more likely.

Regardless of the initial choice of electoral systems, however, it was virtually inevitable, given the absence of institutionalized political parties, that parliaments would become the dominant institutional site of ethnic conflict following the first competitive elections after the fall of communism. Even where "bottom-up" mass movements formed in opposition to the old regime, their fragmentation and recrystallization as ideologically distinct, electorally viable parties invariably occurred through the "top-down" formation of parliamentary factions.[39] And, while electorally successful ethnic minority parties typically gained stable constituencies and maintained relatively high levels of party discipline from the outset, the electoral incentives for ethnic majority party-builders to sharpen ideological distinctions, together with the path-setting legacy issues discussed in the preceding section, tended to exacerbate rather than mitigate ethnic tension. This was reflected, particularly in the first electoral term, in the projection nationwide of divisive parliamentary debates among ethnic elites, opposition to ethnic minority parties' proposals, and charges of disloyalty owing to legislative agendas dominated by non-negotiable symbolic issues such as anthems, seals, and the design of flags and banknotes. As Nenad Zakošek's chapter on Croatia demonstrates, in such circumstances walkouts by outvoted and outmaneuvered minority parties could have especially tragic consequences.[40]

Notwithstanding strong criticism of presidential as opposed to parliamentary regimes in recent years,[41] it is plausible that directly elected presidents may ameliorate some of the conflict-generating consequences of democratization described above. Once in office, directly elected presidents may have relatively more autonomy from partisan considerations than presidents elected by parliaments, using their popular mandate to override the more corrosive effects on ethnic relations of party formation and competition. Moreover, presidents that are empowered not only symbolically through direct election but also constitutionally relative to prime ministers and parties may be even better situated to carve out political space for managing tensions.

Outcomes in individual cases are, however, too unruly to draw firm conclusions regarding such institutional effects, while more contingent factors such as statesmanship and political relations between presidents and prime ministers appear (at least so far) to play a more important role.[42] The indirectly elected Lennart Meri of Estonia, despite swearing a constitutional oath of office that obliges the president to fulfill his or her duties "for the benefit of the Estonian people,"[43] supported the establishment of a presidential round-table on ethnic relations which has been the most successful of those in the region precisely because of his moral authority and political will. Yet attempts by the indirectly elected former president of Slovakia, Michal Kováč, to use his office to develop similar back channels of interethnic compromise quickly ran aground after Prime Minister Vladimír Mečiar, whose minority government lost a no-confidence vote initiated by Kováč in March 1994, returned to power six months later following early elections. Meanwhile, former president Ion Iliescu of Romania demonstrated that even where a directly elected president is precluded from political party membership, he may nonetheless exercise his role as a national, rather than a state, guardian.

The tendency of directly elected presidents to view themselves as representing the dominant ethnic group (and to be perceived this way by minorities) may become even more pronounced in cases where constitutionally strong presidents are permitted to continue as political party leaders. This seems particularly true of presidents such as Franjo Tudjman or Slobodan Milošević of Croatia and Serbia, respectively, whose parties consolidated themselves in power through the waging of ethnonationalist war. Moreover, as with the lack of incentives for interethnic accommodation in parliamentary electoral law, nowhere in post-communist Europe are directly elected presidents, whether strong or weak, constitutionally or statutorily obliged to win the support of a minimum proportion of ethnic minority votes. Nevertheless, the record on ethnic mediation of even directly elected, strong post-communist presidents is by no means unambiguous. In Macedonia, which excludes the president from holding a political party appointment, Kiro Gligorov made very effective use of the constitutionally mandated Council for Inter-Ethnic Relations, whose members the president is empowered to appoint.

Finally, efforts to consolidate democratic rule in post-communist Europe have been premised on commitments by state actors to devolve previously highly centralized power to local and regional authorities. There are three respects in which this issue has been influenced by, and has affected, ethnic relations. First, in many cases devolution has been delayed by concerns that it would mean *de facto* territorial autonomy for autochthonous minorities.[44] To the extent that democratic consolidation requires some degree of self-governance by previously impotent local political units, the braking effect of ethnopolitics is obvious. Second, and conversely, the refusal to enhance local self-rule has led several autochthonous minorities to radicalize their demands and press for territorial autonomy, as this seems the only alternative in the face of unwilling central governments. Third, in some cases, notably the ethnically mixed city of Cluj in Transylvania, national politicians with a strong local power base who are intent on exacerbating ethnic tensions have foiled efforts by more moderate ethnic majority elites to develop state-wide policies that adequately address ethnic minority concerns.

The International Context: Kin States, Home States, and Interstate Actors

The international context in which post-communist ethnopolitics is played out can be characterized quite simply: uncertain, dangerous, and fraught with misperceptions. Most post-communist states lack effective security guarantees, while the West's feckless response to the wars of Yugoslav succession and turmoil in the Caucasus has done little to assuage their leaders. Unless and until they build sufficient institutional capacities, they are "weak states" internationally, and the politically emergent nations that "own" them will remain fearful of external threats and internal fifth columns.[45] At stake is more than territory: external challenges to these nations' statehood typically entail a threat to their cultural survival or unity as well. As James Pettifer's chapter points out, persistent Greek claims to Northern Epirus are premised on a rejection of a distinct Albanian ethnicity and heritage. Similarly, Bulgarian irredentism's challenge (so far rhetorical) to Macedonia's statehood rests on rejection of "Macedonianness," as have Greek efforts to isolate the new state diplomatically. Finally, with many home states also kin states to ethnic minorities elsewhere, the international environment is one in which behaviors are likely to be misunderstood, opportunities for actors to distort their significance plentiful, and potentialities for conflict strong.

Kin State Behavior

Presently, most post-communist kin states are unable and unwilling to employ aggressive, irredentist policies. However, influential actors within kin states—government officials and agencies, political parties, media outlets, religious and charitable organizations, commercial firms, and other nongovernmental organizations—often play an important role in framing and supporting demands by home state minorities. These actors may be motivated by one or more of a variety of factors: the level of ideological commitment to ethnic solidarity, the electoral interests of office-seeking elites, and the presence or absence of effective external incentives to comply with the preferences of international actors.[46]

Official kin state behavior thus falls along a spectrum that can include varying levels and combinations of material support for home state minorities, resettlement assistance, initiatives in international fora, and bilateral contacts with home state governments. At the extreme end of intervention, kin states may back favored home state political forces more or less openly by promoting leadership rifts or taking advantage of them when they emerge. For example,

Albania sanctioned provocateurs to distribute leaflets in western Macedonia in 1994 mocking the moderate wing of the ethnic Albanian Party of Democratic Prosperity and used state-controlled satellite media in an effort to convince ethnic Albanians of the need to replace their "ineffective" leadership.[47] The chapters by Neil Melvin and James Pettifer addressing, respectively, the role of Russian nationalist forces in fomenting anti-independence sentiment in the Baltics and the destabilizing influence in southern Albania of Greek Orthodox clergy in northern Greece, provide similarly telling examples of the importance of non-state (or quasi-state) actors.

Home State Responses

Post-communist home states commonly interpret kin state behavior as hostile, that is, intended to increase the propensity of minorities to embrace, and ultimately attempt to realize, secessionist aims. Their own weakness and the absence of international security guarantees magnify home states' fear that kin states will increase the benefits and lower the costs for ethnic minorities to challenge their territorial integrity. Of course, some kin state behaviors engender more outrage than others. Donations of textbooks are less troublesome than donations to political parties, which, unsurprisingly, are viewed by home states as a grave violation of their sovereignty. Aside from direct and sustained involvement with home state minorities, forms of intervention likely to be perceived as aggressive can include public pronouncements endorsing, for example, demands by ethnic kin that they be granted "partner-nation status."[48]

Beyond protesting to intergovernmental organizations, home states may respond by punishing, or threatening to punish, ethnic minorities on the ground. They may withhold or rescind implementation of policies to protect minority interests or attempt to demobilize minority political actors through legal changes, while pressure from domestic sources such as increased countermobilization of ultranationalist groups may push more moderate officials to undertake these and other measures and to adopt tougher positions when negotiating with kin states. Finally, home states may attempt to rebuff their own ethnic minorities' kin states by embracing a kin state role themselves. Thus, Vladimír Mečiar's government repeatedly countered Hungary's attempts to defend its ethnic kin in southern Slovakia by accusing Hungary of pursuing assimilationist cultural "genocide" against the tiny Slovak minority in Hungary.

Interstate Actors

In view of these dynamics, an array of interstate actors has attempted to contain and resolve conflict and reduce the potential for its emergence. The field of intergovernmental organizations (IGOs) includes NATO, the European Union (EU), the Organization for Security and Cooperation in Europe (OSCE, formerly the CSCE), the Council of Europe (CoE), and the United Nations (UN). In addition, several relatively influential non-governmental organizations (NGOs) disseminate information, pressure home states and kin states, and work to enhance efforts at preventive diplomacy. Finally, there are "Great Power" states that wield disproportionate influence over decision-makers in the region, acting directly on government officials and ethnic minority leaders, as well as indirectly through their dominant positions in IGOs.[49]

The set of policies these actors have cobbled together has been uneven in several respects. The response of Germany, the United States and IGOs to the Yugoslav secession crisis of 1990–1992 and, later, to the war in Bosnia, revealed that the actors themselves do not always share common interests and goals, occasionally pursuing contradictory policies with disastrous results.[50] Moreover, their influence on regional actors has varied greatly. In some cases, states' behavior has been altered significantly by their desire to join IGOs such as the EU and NATO. Yet this approach has worked to a more limited degree in the case of the CoE, admission to which was tied to acceptance of Recommendation 1201, a series of conceptually muddled blandishments concerning ethnic minority local self-governance adopted by the Council's Representative Assembly. Their interpretation was left to home states' jurists and politicians, who unanimously rejected any construal of its ambiguous provisions that might underwrite the notion of collective rights.[51]

At the same time, the incentive of western integration has in some cases been a double-edged sword. Shafir demonstrates how the Romanian government's relations with Hungary and its treatment of the country's Hungarian minority improved while Romania was under consideration for inclusion in the first wave of eastward expansion by the EU and NATO, only to deteriorate following exclusion. This raises the question of just how "deep" changes in state behavior resulting from international incentives and pressure really are. As Nenad Zakošek's chapter points out, while modification of Croatia's constitution to include more generous and ameliorative provisions for Croatia's ethnic Serb population was the result of "successful" international pressure on Croatian officials in 1991, this did nothing to prevent the forced exodus of

Serbs that has since rendered the provisions irrelevant. On the contrary, cases such as Croatia, Serbia, and Slovakia suggest that international "imperialism" can contribute to mobilizing ultranationalist forces.[52]

While the limitations of international pressure described above mainly concern efforts to influence home state behavior, international actors may be more effective in dissuading post-communist kin states from exacerbating conflict situations. The incentive of integration with the West is perhaps the decisive factor underlying the quieter line adopted by Hungary's Horn and Orban government following the nationalist assertiveness of Joszef Antall's first post-communist government. While Greece's membership in the EU and NATO has shielded it from international pressure and enabled Greek elites effectively to block unfavorable policies, Albania's heavy dependence on EU financial assistance and military assistance from the U.S. make it especially susceptible to such pressure. Albania's early aggressive moves on behalf of its ethnic kin in Macedonia and Kosovo were effectively halted by the international community, although recent support from Albania for separatist rebel forces in Kosovo may be an indication that the Albanian state's extremely weak institutional capacities are likely to render international leverage ineffective to the extent that officials are unable to implement *any* policy consistently.[53] Similarly, despite early dire predictions, the West's relations with Russia in the 1990s have been marked by remarkable success in preventing destabilizing official Russian behavior *qua* kin state. Since many of the region's larger minorities (Albanians, Hungarians, and Russians) are dispersed across many home states, successful efforts to improve kin state behavior may have a powerful multiplier effect in ameliorating ethnic tensions.

An important component of the international community's success in influencing kin state behavior has been its emphasis on urging kin state/home state pairs to sign bilateral basic treaties. Historical precedents, including the German–Danish treaty, the settlement between Austria and Italy over South Tyrol, and the more recent German–Polish and German–Czech treaties, suggest that bilateral pacts can be effective in dampening the potential for conflict, independent of the possibility that the signing of a treaty itself suggests reduced levels of tension. Such treaties reduce long-term uncertainty regarding standards of minority treatment, codify cooperation on issues related to compliance and monitoring, define and regulate acceptable forms of kin state behavior (for example, cultural exchange and border cooperation), and thus weaken radicals among home state minorities. Perhaps most importantly, they signify the kin state's unambiguous recognition of the home state's sovereignty and territorial integrity.[54] While the main problem in the post-communist context remains compelling states to sign on the dotted line, the record of such treaties concluded thus far—particularly Hungary's treaties with Romania and Slovakia—is somewhat encouraging.

Finally, a related factor shaping ethnic relations domestically, as well as helping to manage disputes between kin states and home states, is the array of international legal instruments developed by the UN, the CoE, and the OSCE. These instruments' provisions recognize individual rather than collective rights, which are thus conferred upon members of cultural groups rather than upon the groups themselves. While this distinction can lead to conceptual and legal confusion, as the CoE's Recommendation 1201 illustrates, these instruments nonetheless hold out the promise of giving ethnic grievances a more stable cast. In the case of home states, recourse to international law offers predictable limits to the types of claims kin states may make concerning their ethnic kin abroad. For minorities themselves, rights discourse provides a patina of moral legitimacy with which to apply political leverage from a position of weakness, and may even serve an educative function in polities unaccustomed to constitutionalism and the rule of law. However, precisely because rights operate as "gag rules" that categorically exclude specified types of claims from political discourse, it is also worth worrying about the potentially problematic long-term effects of habitually invoking them.[55] That is, "rights talk" may ultimately render majority-minority conflicts less amenable to resolution, as it has with political contestation over cultural issues in the West, to the extent that it operates to suppress politically-derived alternatives for managing ethnic relations in the future.[56]

The Ethnic Minority Party

As we have seen, the motor of post-communist ethnopolitics is the confluence of ethnic groups' fears about the future and electoral competition in a context of weak state capacities and uncertain national identities. Thus, understanding the causes and consequences of ethnic minorities' political mobilization lies at the heart of this book. The effect of incentives for ethnic majority political actors to aggravate ethnic tensions, in turn shifting the balance of power within minority communities toward more radical leaders and demands, suggests that in some cases ethnic relations will worsen. As in Kosovo, some of the politically volatile situations that result can be expected to lead to violent confrontations. There is, of course, no reason to expect this depressing logic to be ineluctable and universal. On the contrary, the salience of ethnic cleavages can be expected to diminish, and other, more politically tractable, cleavages to be mobilized, to the extent that "stateness" problems are overcome, whether through channels established by international incentives and pressure, domestic statecraft, or, as is most likely, a combination of the two. The prospects for this, however, are not comprehensible without a better understanding of the minority political organizations that compete for power.

Common Features

Throughout the region, ethnic minority parties represented in parliaments resemble what Shafir calls "holding companies" for the range of interests within ethnically bounded communities. In the limiting case of the Hungarian community in Romania, the Hungarian Democratic Federation of Romania (UDMR) serves as an organizational umbrella for a broad array of voluntary and professional associations and entities, as well as ideological tendencies that typically parallel those expressed in separate parties among the ethnic majority. Usually, a single party dominates, or, as in Slovakia, a highly stable, well-integrated coalition of parties has emerged. Their membership and constituencies are coeval with the minority's population, electoral mobilization is unproblematic, and turnout becomes akin to a census.[57] Politically disciplined constituencies are mirrored by politically disciplined party organizations. Despite a wide range of preferences among minority voters and elites, the party or coalition is united in its legislative behavior, typically voting *en bloc* even on non-ethnic issues.

Arrayed along the dimension of tactics and goals, from cooperation with ethnic majority parties to secession, all of the region's ethnic minority parties have experienced rifts among moderates and radicals, with the latter gaining significant influence. Nevertheless, despite often severe internal disagreements, they have been highly successful in blocking the entry of intra-group competitors. Where new parties have been formed, they usually have been successfully marginalized. There are two major political consequences of these communities' ability to maintain the authority of single parties or party-like coalitions. First, their political power remains less diluted than it would be otherwise, particularly given electoral laws that penalize smaller parties. Second, it impedes the formation of cross-ethnic coalitions, as moderate minority leaders are unable to peel off activists and voters and join forces with moderate ethnic majority parties.[58]

While it thus seems clear that ethnic minority parties have organized and electorally mobilized their constituencies with a high degree of discipline, this begs an important question: *Why ethnic parties in the first place?* Why were ethnic minority elites and activists unable or unwilling to establish permanent channels of political participation with like-minded ethnic majority political forces from the outset of the old regime's demise? And why has this situation remained virtually unchanged even after party systems have crystallized to the point that ideological affinities with ethnic majority parties are much clearer? Two answers emerge from the country studies and from the discussion so far.

First, with the decay of the old regime's repressive capacity, ethnic minority elites established their own organizations, whether political or non-political. In some cases, these organizations were set up as human-rights advocacy groups (Albania's *Omonia*, for example). In others, they developed in order to articulate and defend ethnic minority interests through electoral contestation, but in coordination with umbrella opposition movements (Slovakia, Romania, the Baltics). Once established, however, non-party organizations transformed themselves into parties, and all ethnic minority parties were eventually forced to compete separately due to the exclusionary rhetoric and policy positions adopted by ethnic majority elites among reactionary ex-communist and opposition groupings. In still other cases, ethnic parties were founded with the clear aim of contesting local and national elections alone in anticipation of the likely mobilization of nationalist political forces (Bulgaria, Croatia, Macedonia). But in all cases, the initial development of separate organizational entities narrowed considerably the possibilities for future cross-ethnic political organization.

Second, policy preferences on ethnic issues diverge widely enough that cross-ethnic parties, coalitions, and alliances have been exceedingly rare and even more difficult to sustain. Majority parties with whom ethnic minority parties agree on non-ethnic issues often part company on a range of ethnic issues, from the distribution of symbolic goods (official language status, the use of national symbols) and material goods (regional development plans, the allocation of resources and power to sub-national governments) to macro-level conflicts over group status and state "ownership," usually contested through constitutional politics. Moreover, given the absence of electoral incentives that would benefit moderate forces, even when these preferences do not differ much, the electoral liabilities of cross-ethnic cooperation have been perceived as prohibitively high. Smaller liberal parties in Latvia, Romania, and Slovakia, for example, have chosen to coordinate political and electoral activities with minorities at best on a limited *ad hoc* basis. Those parties that unambiguously devote themselves to interethnic accommodation (Janis Jurkins' Harmony for Latvia is a rare example) do not survive or hold power for long.

The Character of Ethnic Minority Demands

That mobilized minorities have organized in a common manner and have faced similar structural constraints is clear. But it is a mistake to assume that all of them, absent these constraints, would seek to establish civic polities based on equal and universal citizenship rights within a defined territory. Western observers eager to point out the obvious illiberalism of ethnically defined statehood often overlook this fact, and to some extent the myth of minority virtue has been reinforced by minorities' own embrace of the discourse of rights. However, that today's majority oppressors were yesterday's oppressed minorities should caution us against believing that today's minorities are somehow automatically predisposed to greater liberalism than those now adopting ethnically exclusionary policies. In the case of Romania, Shafir argues that ethnic Hungarians moved toward a national conception of the polity only after their civic conceptions were rejected by ultra-nationalist Romanian elites. He argues cogently that Hungarian political radicalization was a consequence, rather than a cause, of their political marginalization. However, among Albanians in Kosovo and western Macedonia, among Serbs in Croatia, and among various groups of Russian-speakers throughout the former Soviet Union, the call for ethnic autonomy during the post-communist period came quickly. These demands are understandable given the institutional legacies and dynamics of constitutional politics described above, yet it is necessary to acknowledge the independent effect they have had on ethnic relations.

In this respect, the distinction between large and small minorities becomes more important. Smaller minorities (Vlachs, Germans, Pomaks, Armenians, Roma, and others) have in many cases been granted the means of cultural autonomy through state-funded educational provisions, cultural facilities, and the like, and in some cases have been offered guaranteed—albeit token— parliamentary representation. Larger, and especially geographically concentrated, minorities, in contrast, are more likely to define, and to be perceived by ethnic majority actors as defining, ethnic autonomy in territorial terms.[59] While cultural versus territorial definitions of autonomy are at the core of internal party splits between ethnic minority moderates and radicals, their proponents differ mainly over the scope of decision-making powers to be sought in those geographic regions in which they dominate numerically. Yet these regions are themselves typically ethnically mixed, with many of their urban areas "ruralized" by large influxes of ethnic majority peasants *cum* workers under communist-era industrialization and population policies that were intentionally designed to promote greater homogenization of culturally mixed territory. Unsurprisingly, areas with large concentrations of minori-ties—often adjacent to kin state frontiers—have therefore been marked by higher levels of activity by nationalist majority parties in the name of ethnic majorities threatened by a loss of status and power at the local level.[60]

The symbolic corollary to large minorities' demand for autonomy is the demand for "partner-nation" status, which has been articulated by Hun-garians, Serbs, Albanians, and some communities of Russian-speakers. In practical terms, this status connotes joint decision-making with the ethnic majority on major issues (such as membership in interstate alliances); reform of institutions, from electoral systems to legislatures to executives, in order to privilege the larger minority; proportional ethnic representation in public agencies; and a host of other public policy provisions, symbolic and material, which are thought to follow from this status.[61] Clearly, this vision of shared state "ownership" by *nationally defined* citizens departs considerably from the civic notions of collectively exercised individual rights that animate the operative and proposed legal instruments promulgated by IGOs such as the Council of Europe and the OSCE. On the contrary, "partner-nation" status is much closer to power-sharing concepts advanced by Arend Lijphart and others under the heading of "consociational democracy."[62] That this approach is illiberal in the name of stability is self-evident; that its require-ment of highly disciplined constituencies discourages democratic practices within ethnic groups is also clear. As Carlos Flores Juberías's analysis of the Dayton Accord's constitutional proposals for Bosnia suggests, what remains surprising is its staying power, given a two-decade understanding that the very conditions required for the success of consociational arrangements obviate the need for them.[63]

Policy Implications

In one sense, this volume is straightforwardly concerned with the conse-quences of ethnic majorities' numerical superiority over politically mobilized ethnic minorities. The significance of numbers is clear from ethnic minorities' justifications for claims to special status, as well as from the adoption of quasi-consociational arrangements even where, as in Croatia, they were soon rejected in practice. It is similarly reflected in ethnic majorities' fears of ethnodemo-graphic trends and political contestation of how these are measured, with the Macedonian census in 1994, for example, requiring more international observers than were dispatched to monitor its elections.[64] The relative numerical balance of majorities and minorities is, in Donald Horowitz's words, "an indication of whose country it is," and it translates through ethnically-based parties directly into political power.[65]

In these circumstances, domestic elites and international actors face several conceptual difficulties in developing policy responses appropriate to encouraging multiethnic democracy. First, the historical lessons of Leninism's constitutional legacy with respect to nationality suggest little more than pitfalls to be avoided, but which in most cases have not. Moreover, many of the region's elites do not perceive as role models western counterparts who hector them regarding the political practices that follow from national definitions of statehood. On the contrary, nationalist governments frequently resort to *tu quoque* tactics, invoking a morally equalizing argument well captured in one western scholar's admonition to his colleagues that "for many, a few months' intensive reexamination of Anglo-American experience would be more valuable than as many years devoted to immediate examination of Soviet nationalities."[66]

Second, concepts fundamental to developing long-term policies to ameliorate ethnic tension have failed to provide much assistance in structuring political discourse. Minorities often propose public policies that few (including their drafters) understand. For example, Shafir demonstrates the conceptual incoherence of "communitarian autonomy" proposed by the UDMR, and shows how its incoherence was in part the result of the requirements of compromise within an increasingly divided party. Of course, conceptual ambiguity can have healthy political consequences: the "implied contract" nature of much legislation is useful in overcoming disagreements and uncertainties that may result in immobilism.[67] However, weak states that are deeply divided ethnically resemble internally the international environment.[68] In post-communist Europe, proposals built on concepts that are prone to misinterpretation are likely to remain "essentially contested" and thus to invite actors to hedge their bets by imputing worst-case intentions when they are advanced by ethnic opponents.[69]

The lack of definition in the region's political cultures and institutions of the rule of law in general, and of complex concepts such as "rights" in particular, similarly impedes political action, apart from that of committed nationalists and political entrepreneurs seeking to capitalize on ethnic tensions. International actors such as the Council of Europe have made matters no clearer by imposing on new members Recommendation 1201, whose vague and incomplete language provides ammunition for all sides and clarity for none. Unfortunately, it is symptomatic of the problems international actors face in sequencing their policies. Short-term problems require quick responses, but policymakers have done an inadequate job of guarding against the possibility that these may freeze in place otherwise fluid ethnic categories and thus maintain the political salience of ethnicity to the detriment of long-term conflict management. Erin Jenne's chapter on the Roma goes even further, suggesting that this may produce the unintended consequence of mobilizing unorganized ethnocultural groups to claim the mantle of nationhood itself.

This returns us to a point raised at the outset: ethnic identities tend to be more fixed relative to those of class, but are less so in absolute terms than many observers acknowledge. The Roma, as Jenne notes, are a notoriously difficult category; it is unclear, for example, which individuals seek or "objectively" deserve the label. Neil Melvin demonstrates the political consequences of the fluidity of "Russianness" among non-Estonians and non-Latvians and how, particularly in Latvia, political contenders responded to relatively porous sociocultural boundaries between Russians and Latvians by reinforcing them, thereby ethnicizing politics to the detriment of civic outcomes. Similarly, Ivan Ilchev illustrates the race to claim the Pomaks, ethnically Slav Muslims, as ethnic kin by both Turkish and ethnic Bulgarian political parties. Even among majority ethnic groups, ethnic categories can lose their sharpness at the edges. As Pettifer observes, political divisions and mutually exclusive kinship ties among the Ghegs and Tosks in Albania mediate the Albanian/Greek conflict and complicate policy responses to asymmetries in regional development. In an environment where elites and individuals are still determining who is who, puzzling over policy approaches becomes even more difficult.

The point here is not that ethnic conflict results from conceptual and identity-driven misunderstandings. Opposing ethnopolitical forces comprehend their situation remarkably well, anticipating each other's moves and responding accordingly. Thus, the key concern for policymakers should be to gain a thorough understanding of their predicament. Overall, the region's ability to "unbind" itself from ethnicity and to develop civil polities is obscured by a powerful paradox. Civil polities historically have depended on strong states. Liberal democracy has historically followed, not preceded, effective political institutionalization, or, as Huntington put it, "[a]uthority has to exist before it can be limited."[70] Weak polities, such as those in postcommunist Europe, find it easier to structure political competition around ethnocultural cleavages. How, then, can they avoid reifying the resultant conflict and construct civic polities while simultaneously developing the state capacities necessary to support them? In the volume's concluding chapter, Jack Snyder offers some provocative suggestions along these lines.

Notes

1. For a widely-read and influential example of this argument, see Robert D. Kaplan, *Balkan Ghosts: A Journey Through History* (New York: Vintage Books, 1994).

2. Stephen Van Evera, "Hypotheses on Nationalism and the Causes of War," in Charles A. Kupchan, ed., *Nationalism and Nationalities in the New Europe* (Ithaca: Cornell University Press, 1995), pp. 136-57, esp. 147-51.

3. Barry Posen, "The Security Dilemma and Ethnic Conflict," in Michael Brown, ed., *Ethnic Conflict and International Security* (Princeton: Princeton University Press, 1993), pp. 103-24; Ernest Gellner, "Nationalism in the Vacuum," in Alexander J. Motyl, ed., *Thinking Theoretically About Soviet Nationalities* (New York: Columbia University Press, 1992), pp. 243-54. See also David Ost, "The Politics of Interest in Eastern Europe," *Theory and Society*, vol. 22, no. 3 (1993), and Jack Snyder, "Nationalism and the Crisis of the Post-Soviet State," in Brown, *Ethnic Conflict and International Security*, pp. 79-102.

4. Donald L. Horowitz, *Ethnic Groups in Conflict* (Berkeley: University of California Press, 1985).

5. For a classic exposition, see Myron Weiner, "The Macedonian Syndrome: An Historical Model of International Relations and Political Development," *World Politics*, vol. 23, no. 4 (July 1971), pp. 665-83. See also Donald L. Horowitz, "Irredentas and Secessions: Adjacent Phenomena, Neglected Comparisons," in Naomi Chazan, ed., *Irredentism and International Politics* (Boulder: Lynne Rienner Publishers, 1991), pp. 9-23. For the post-communist context, see Rogers Brubaker, "National Minorities, Nationalizing States, and External National Homelands in the New Europe," in his *Nationalism Reframed: Nationhood and the National Question in the New Europe* (New York: Cambridge University Press, 1996). Recent related collections include Michael E. Brown, ed., *International Dimensions of Ethnic Conflict* (Cambridge: MIT Press, 1996), and David A. Lake and Donald Rothchild, eds., *The International Spread of Ethnic Conflict: Fear, Diffusion, and Escalation* (Princeton: Princeton University Press, 1998).

6. See, for example, Abram Chayes and Antonia Handler Chayes, eds., *Preventing Conflict in the Post-Communist World: Mobilizing International and Regional Organizations* (Washington, D.C.: Brookings, 1996), and Konrad Huber and Robert W. Mickey, "Defining the Kin State: An Analysis of its Role and Prescriptions for Moderating Its Impact," in Arie Bloed, ed., *The Role of Bilateral Treaties in Regulating Minority Rights* (Amsterdam: Martinus Nijhoff, 1998).

7. See, for example, Robert H. Bates, "Modernization, Ethnic Competition, and the Rationality of Politics in Contemporary Africa," in Donald Rothchild and Victor A. Olorunsola, eds., *State Versus Ethnic Claims* (Boulder: Westview Press, 1983); David D. Laitin and James D. Fearon, "Explaining Inter-Ethnic Cooperation," *American Political Science Review* vol. 90, no. 4 (Dec. 1996), pp. 715-735. See also Ronald Rogowski, "Causes and Varieties of Nationalism: A Rationalist Account," in Edward A. Tiryakian and Ronald Rogowski, eds., *New Nationalisms of the Developed West* (Boston: Allen and Unwin, 1985), pp. 87-108.

8. Walker Connor, *Ethnonationalism: The Quest for Undertsanding* (Princeton: Princeton University Press, 1994); Joseph Rothschild, *Ethnopolitics: A Conceptual Framework* (New York: Columbia University Press, 1981).

9. See Laitin and Fearon, *op. cit.*, p. 716. The authors note that in only one of the Soviet Union's fourteen non-Russian successor states (Moldova) has there been violent conflict between Russians and the titular nationalities for which these states (formerly union republics) are named. Similarly, ethnic violence between Russians and titulars has occurred in only two of the

sixteen former autonomous republics within the current Russian Federation (Chechnya and Tuva). The incidence of ethnic violence between the forty-five non-Russian minorities and titulars in the fourteen non-Russian successor states is even lower, occurring in just two cases. See also John R. Bowen, "The Myth of Global Ethnic Conflict," *Journal of Democracy*, vol. 7, no. 4 (October 1996), pp. 3-14.

10. For this definition of nationalism, see Ernest Gellner, *Nations and Nationalism* (Ithaca: Cornell University Press, 1983), p. 1. NATO membership also was offered the same month to three of these states—the Czech Republic, Hungary, and Poland.

11. For a survey of the evidence, see Juan J. Linz and Alfred Stepan, *Problems of Democratic Transition and Consolidation. Southern Europe, Latin America, and Post-Communist Europe* (Baltimore: Johns Hopkins University Press, 1996), pp. 445-52. See also Ian Bremmer and Ray Taras, *New States, New Politics: Building the Post-Soviet Nations* (Cambridge: Cambridge University Press, 1997). For public opinion data that confirm this geographic division in terms of support for democratic norms and values, see Richard Rose and Christian Haerpfer, *Change and Stability in the New Democracies Barometer. A Trend Analysis, Studies in Public Policy*, no. 270 (Glasgow: Centre for the Study of Public Policy, 1996), and Charles Gati, "The Mirage of Democracy," *Transition*, vol. 2, no. 6 (March 22, 1996) pp. 6-12.

12. For an early examination of this phenomenon, see Anthony Alcock, Brian Taylor, and John Welton, eds., *The Future of Cultural Minorities* (London: St. Martin's Press, 1979).

13. See Jon Elster's exposition of Tocqueville's causal argumentation in his *Political Psychology* (Cambridge: Cambridge University Press, 1993).

14. On structuration, see Anthony Giddens, *Central Problems in Social Theory: Action, Structure and Contradiction in Social Analysis* (Berkeley: University of California Press, 1979). For application of the concept in political science, see Alexander E. Wendt, "The Agent-Structure Problem in International Relations," *International Organization*, vol. 41, no. 3 (Summer 1987), pp. 225-70 and David Dessler, "What's at Stake in the Agent-Structure Debate?," *International Organization*, vol. 43, no. 3 (Summer 1989), pp. 441-73.

15. See, for example, Peter B. Evans, Dietrich Rueschemeyer, and Theda Skocpol, eds., *Bringing the State Back In* (Cambridge: Cambridge University Press, 1985). Historical institutionalism is developed theoretically in Sven Steinmo, Kathleen Thelen, and Frank Longstreth, eds., *Structuring Politics: Historical Institutionalism in Comparative Analysis* (New York: Cambridge University Press, 1992). For reviews of the field, see Peter A. Hall and Rosemary C. R. Taylor, "Political Science and the Three New Institutionalisms," *Political Studies*, vol. 44 (1996), pp. 936-957, and Ellen Immergut, "The Theoretical Core of the New Institutionalism," *Politics and Society*, vol. 26, no. 1 (March 1998), pp. 5-34.

16. See W. Brian Arthur, *Increasing Returns and Path Dependence in the Economy* (Ann Arbor: University of Michigan Press, 1994); Douglass C. North, *Institutions, Institutional Change, and Economic Performance* (Cambridge: Cambridge University Press, 1990); Paul Pierson, "When Effect Becomes Cause: Policy Feedback and Political Change," *World Politics*, vol. 45, no. 4 (July 1993), pp. 595-628; and Paul Pierson, "Increasing Returns, Path Dependence, and the Study of Politics," *American Political Science Review* (forthcoming, 2000).

17. Ken Jowitt, *New World Disorder. The Leninist Extinction* (Berkeley: University of California Press, 1992), ch. 8.

18. Ibid., ch. 4. On communist "neo-traditionalism" and its implications for the ongoing transitions, see also Grzegorz Ekiert, "Democratization Processes in East Central Europe: A Theoretical Reconsideration," *British Journal of Political Science*, vol. 21 (Fall 1991), pp. 289-313. The effects of neo-traditionalism are particularly revealing in Slovakia, where the geo-

graphic distribution of support for Vladimír Mečiar's populist-nationalist Movement for a Democratic Slovakia, dominated by former communists, is far more closely correlated with support in the inter-war period for Andrej Hlinka's authoritarian Slovak People's Party than it is with regional unemployment. See Jonathan Stein and Mitchell Orenstein, "Dileme izgradnje demokratske države u Slovačkoj," *Politička misao* (Zagreb), vol. 33, Nos. 2-3 (1996), pp. 121-51.

19. For the definitive analysis of these policies, see Walker Connor, *The National Question in Marxist-Leninist Theory and Strategy* (Princeton: Princeton University Press, 1984). For an excellent treatment of the factors underpinning eastern European communist parties' initial strong support among many national minorities, see R.V. Burks, *The Dynamics of Communism in Eastern Europe* (Princeton: Princeton University Press, 1961).

20. Yugoslavia now exists as a "confederation" of Serbia and Montenegro. Thus, it shares only the name of the pre-1991 state.

21. This is not to say that indigenous ethnic elites under communism did not support existing federal arrangements on instrumental grounds, for which the center provided strong material incentives. In much of the Soviet Union itself, notably the Baltic republics, this was the case until *demokratisatsiia* and *glasnost* undermined indigenous elites' monopoly of mobilizational resources and empowered counter-elites pressing a more primordialist ethnic agenda. See Philip G. Roeder, "Soviet Federalism and Ethnic Mobilization," *World Politics*, vol. 43, no. 2 (January 1991), pp. 196-232.

22. See Rogers Brubaker, "Nationhood and the National Question in the Soviet Union and Post-Soviet Eurasia: An Institutionalist Account," *Theory and Society*, vol. 23, no. 2 (1994), pp. 47-78. See also Reneo Lukic and Allen Lynch, *Europe from the Balkans to the Urals. The Disintegration of Yugoslavia and the Soviet Union* (Oxford: Oxford University Press, 1996). On Czechoslovakia's post-1989 constitutional paralysis and subsequent elite-brokered dissolution, see Eric Stein, *Czecho/Slovakia: Ethnic Conflict, Constitutional Fissure, Negotiated Breakup* (Ann Arbor: University of Michigan Press, 1997).

23. Samuel Huntington, *Political Order in Changing Societies* (Yale University Press, 1968).

24. Barbara Geddes, "A Comparative Perspective on the Leninist Legacy in Eastern Europe," *Comparative Political Studies*, vol. 28, no. 2 (July 1995), pp. 239-74.

25. Juan J. Linz and Alfred Stepan, "Political Identities and Electoral Sequences: Spain, the Soviet Union, and Yugoslavia," *Daedelus*, vol. 121, no. 2 (Spring 1992), p. 132.

26. See Herbert Kitschelt, "Post-Communist Democracies: Do Party Systems Help or Hinder Democratic Consolidation?," paper presented at the Conference on Democracy, Markets, and Civil Societies in Post-1989 East Central Europe, May 17-18, 1996, Center for European Studies, Harvard University, and Herbert Kitschelt, "Formation of Party Cleavages in Post-Communist Democracies, *Party Politics*, vol. 1, no. 3 (1995), pp. 447-72.

27. For a prescient analysis of the patterns of party competition emerging from such factors, see Geoffrey Evans and Stephen Whitefield, "Identifying the Bases of Party Competition in Eastern Europe," *British Journal of Political Science*, vol. 23, no. 3 (1993), pp. 521-48. On the priority of established "stateness" to effective political and economic reform, see Linz and Stepan, *Problems of Democratic Transition and Consolidation*.

28. See V. P. Gagnon, Jr., "Ethnic Nationalism and International Conflict: The Case of Serbia," *International Security*, vol. 19, no. 3 (Winter 1994), pp. 130-67. See also Tim Snyder and Milada Vachudová, "Are Transitions Transitory? Two Types of Political Change in Eastern Europe Since 1989," *East European Politics and Societies*, vol. 11, no. 1 (Winter 1997), pp. 1-35.

29. Flank parties are defined as "ethnically based parties surrounding a multiethnic coalition and typically espousing ethnically more extreme positions than the coalition, with its mixed

support, is able to do." Donald L. Horowitz, *A Democratic South Africa?* (Berkeley: University of California Press, 1991), p. 167. In post-communist Europe, where multiethnic coalitions are the exception, nationalist flank parties may be better understood as parties that press a primordial ethnic agenda on entrepreneurial politicians for whom ethnopolitics is more clearly instrumental to realizing other political or economic interests.

30. For a valuable exposition of political traceability, see Douglas Arnold, *The Logic of Congressional Action* (New Haven: Yale University Press, 1990).

31 Geddes, "A Comparative Perspective on the Leninist Legacy in Eastern Europe," pp. 258-59.

32. For a partial review of this trend, see Robert Hayden, "Constitutional Nationalism in the Former Yugoslav Republics," *Slavic Review*, vol. 51, no. 4 (Winter 1992), pp. 654-74. See also Julie Mostov, "Democracy and the Politics of National Identity," *Studies in East European Thought*, vol. 46, no. 1 (1994), pp. 9-31 and Robert W. Mickey, "Citizenship, Status, and Minority Political Participation: The Evidence from the Republic of Macedonia," in Gerd Nonneman, Tim Niblock, and Bogdan Szajkowski, eds., *Muslim Communities in the New Europe* (London: Ithaca Press, 1996), pp. 53-74.

33. For this distinction, see Bruce Ackerman, *We the People* (Cambridge: Harvard University Press, 1991).

34. Hayden, "Constitutional Nationalism in the Former Yugoslav Republics," p. 657.

35. *Ibid.*, p. 658, Mostov, "Democracy and the Politics of National Identity," pp. 16-17. On the political significance of naming ethnic groups in public law, see also Carlos Flores Juberías's and Nenad Zakošek's chapters in this volume.

36. Horowitz, *Ethnic Groups in Conflict*, pp. 223-24.

37. Horowitz, *A Democratic South Africa?*, p. 165.

38. *Ibid.*, ch. 5 and Horowitz, *Ethnic Groups in Conflict*, pp. 628-51.

39. See generally Attila Ágh, ed., *The Emergence of East Central European Parliaments: The First Steps* (Budapest: Hungarian Centre of Democracy Studies Foundation, 1994).

40. A second, albeit derivative, factor in the failure of parliaments to mitigate ethnic conflict may be their own low level of institutionalization—a lack of qualified non-partisan research staff, poor communication with constituents, the absence of normatively binding rules of decorum, and so forth. For a good summary description of these shortcomings, see William H. Robinson and Francis Miko, "Parliamentary Development Assistance in Central Europe and Former Soviet Union: Some Lessons from Experience," in Lawrence D. Longley, ed., *Working Papers on Comparative Legislative Studies* (Appleton, Wisc.: Research Committee of Legislative Specialists, International Political Science Association, 1994), pp. 409-28.

41. Juan J. Linz and Arturo Valenzuela, eds., *The Failure of Presidential Democracy* (Baltimore: Johns Hopkins University Press, 1994).

42. This may be true of the role of presidents in post-communist democratization more generally. See Ray Taras, ed., *Post-Communist Presidents* (Cambridge: Cambridge University Press, 1997). See also Thomas A. Baylis, "Presidents Versus Prime Ministers: Shaping Executive Authority in Eastern Europe," *World Politics*, vol. 48, no. 3 (1996), pp. 297-323.

43. *Constitution of the Republic of Estonia*, art. 81.

44. Delays have come about either by failure to enact constitutionally required statutes on local and regional governance or by refusal to implement existing legislation.

45. See Joel S. Migdal, "Strong States, Weak States: Power and Accommodation," and Joan Nelson, "Political Participation," both in Myron Weiner and Samuel P. Huntington, eds, *Understanding Political Development* (Boston: Little, Brown, 1987).

46. This last factor may, of course, be epiphenomenal: for example, the desire to secure greater international relief assistance in the case of Albania, or European Union and NATO membership in the case of Hungary, is likely to be premised on the interest of kin state officials in winning re-election.

47. Similar assistance came from the ethnic Albanian-dominated Kosovo province of Serbia. See Robert W. Mickey, "Macedonia: Unstable in a Stable Way," *Transition*, vol. 1, no. 1 (1995), pp. 36-40.

48. The Foreign Ministry of Hungary's first post-communist government backed this proposal. Stephen Engelberg and Judith Ingram, "Now Hungary Adds Its Voice to the Ethnic Tumult," *New York Times*, January 25, 1993.

49. Economic forces constitute an additional, albeit nonpurposive, "actor" in the international context that greatly affects ethnopolitics. As the Albanian and Bulgarian case studies demonstrate, regional economies have profoundly affected migratory patterns to reorder the dynamics of kin state/home state relations. For a thorough discussion of these issues, see Myron Weiner, ed., *International Migration and Security* (Boulder: Westview Press, 1993).

50. See Ivo H. Daalder, "Fear and Loathing in the Former Yugoslavia," in Brown, ed., *The International Dimensions of Internal Conflict*, pp. 35-68. For an excellent account of the fateful influence of these actors' contradictory interests and aims in setting and carrying out policy towards Bosnia, see the series of articles by Mark Danner in *The New York Review of Books* November 20, December 4, and December 18, 1997; February 5, February 19, March 26, and April 23, 1998.

51. Recommendation 1201's vagueness on the issue of collective rights may be the chief reason it was made binding only on new admissions to the Council, not on existing member states.

52. On this point, see Claus Offe, "Ethnic Politics in East European Transitions," in his *Varieties of Transition: The East European and East German Experience* (Cambridge: MIT Press, 1996), p. 75.

53. Moreover, as James Pettifer's chapter argues, Albania's official behavior over the long term is likely to remain indeterminate until a wider and more permanent Balkan settlement is reached.

54. See generally Bloed, ed., *The Role of Bilateral Treaties in Regulating Minority Rights.*

55. Stephen Holmes, "Gag Rules or the Politics of Omission," in Jon Elster and Rune Slagstad, eds., *Constitutionalism and Democracy* (Cambridge: Cambridge University Press, 1988), pp. 19-58.

56. Mary Ann Glendon, *Rights Talk: The Impoverishment of Political Discourse* (New York: The Free Press, 1991).

57. For a discussion of this phenomenon in ethnically divided postcolonial polities, see Horowitz, *Ethnic Groups in Conflict*, pp. 326-30.

58. Obviously, such ethnic "outbidding" occurs among ethnic majorities as well. Bugajski notes, for instance, that Franjo Tudjman's ruling Croatian Democratic Community, declared itself to be "the most Croatian of all parties." In general, these dynamics closely resemble those affecting the multiethnic coalitions, alliances, and parties described in Horowitz, *ibid.*, pp. 365-440.

59. Russians, Hungarians, Serbs, and Albanians within home states are thus also more likely to argue that their own minority status should be sharply distinguished from that of smaller cultural groupings, which have indeed often been over-represented in governmental nationalities commissions and other special-bodies in order to dilute the influence of minorities viewed as more "threatening" by nationalist elites. For a useful discussion of the distinction between cultural and territorial autonomy, see Brubaker, "Nationhood and the National Question in the Soviet Union and Post-Soviet Eurasia: An Institutionalist Account," pp. 55-56.

60. Indeed, nationalist ethnic majority parties have done very well precisely in those electoral districts that comprise the massive communist-era housing estates on the fringes of such "ruralized" cities as Bratislava and Cluj. See Gyorgy Enyedi, "The Transition of Post-Socialist Cities," *European Review*, vol. 3, no. 2 (1994), pp.171-82.

61. See Mickey, "Citizenship, Status, and Minority Political Participation: The Evidence from the Republic of Macedonia."

62. See, for example, Arend Lijphart, *Democracy in Plural Societies* (New Haven: Yale University Press, 1977).

63. For an early demonstration of the tautology of the consociational approach, see Eric A. Nordlinger, *Conflict Regulation in Divided Societies*, Occasional papers in International Affairs, no. 29 (Cambridge: Center for International Affairs, Harvard University, 1972). For a similar critique of Lijphart's consociational proposals for South Africa, see Horowitz, *A Democratic South Africa?*, ch. 5.

64. Mickey, "Macedonia: Unstable in a Stable Way," pp. 38-39.

65. Horowitz, *Ethnic Groups in Conflict*, p. 194.

66. John Armstrong, "The Autonomy of Ethnic Identity: Historic Cleavages and Nationality Relations in the USSR," in Alexander J. Motyl, ed., *Thinking Theoretically about Soviet Nationalities* (New York: Columbia University Press, 1992), p. 33.

67. Kenneth Shepsle, "Congress Is a 'They,' Not an 'It:' Legislative Intent as Oxymoron," *International Review of Law and Economics*, vol. 12 (1992), pp. 239-56.

68. Posen, "The Security Dilemma and Ethnic Conflict."

69. W.B. Gallie, "Essentially Contested Concepts," *Proceedings of the Aristotelian Society*, vol. 56 (1956), pp. 167-98.

70. Huntington, *op. cit.*, p. 8.

2

POST-COMMUNIST ELECTORAL SYSTEMS AND NATIONAL MINORITIES: A DILEMMA IN FIVE PARADIGMS

Carlos Flores Juberías

Introduction: The Dilemma of Popular Sovereignty and Ethnic Pluralism

Following the demise of state socialism in Europe, the reconstruction of citizenship has been the most fundamental point of departure for political institutional change, and also its most problematic aspect. Following an era in which the distribution of status, resources, and opportunities was largely dependent on conformity with prescribed orthodoxy, and state power was essentially unconstrained by effective mechanisms of public accountability, the new regimes' constitutions proclaimed ideals long embedded in most western texts—above all, popular sovereignty, equality before the law, and protection of fundamental rights. Yet, having quickly abandoned the thesis of the leading role of the Communist Party and the formally privileged position of the proletariat, the terms and meaning of citizenship have been conditioned by high levels of ethnic mobilization in much of the region. At the public-institutional and legal levels, this is perhaps most visible in many of these states' electoral systems.

To be sure, every post-communist east European constitution has enshrined the principle of popular sovereignty in a relevant portion of its text. Most do so by opening their first chapter with a solemn proclamation that sovereignty resides in "the people."[1] A few have augmented this assertion with one of national or multinational collective identity.[2] But even those successor states created by, or as a by-product of, extremely conflictual internal nationalist tendencies—e.g., Croatia and the former Federal Republic of Yugoslavia—or

that have similarly stressed the "national" dimension of their statehood—
e.g., Slovenia, Slovakia, and Macedonia—have not hesitated to introduce
within or alongside such proclamations an endorsement of the principle that
"the people," defined as *citizens,* are the source of all state power.[3]

In every case, too, this proclamation has been joined by a set of rules—
ordinarily placed among those constitutional provisions dealing with basic
rights, but in several cases even among provisions defining the structure of
and relations between governmental branches—outlawing invidious discrimination in the exercise of political power. In the Czech Republic's constitution, for example, the list of impermissible bases for encroachment on the
principle of civic equality—"gender, race, color, language, belief, religion,
political or other persuasion, national or social origin, membership in a
national or ethnic minority, property, birth, or other status"[4]—risks redun-
dancy rather than the possibility of lacunae.

A direct consequence of these regimes' embrace of popular sovereignty and
civic equality has been the parallel constitutionalization—also in a manner
familiar to western democracies—of the free exercise of parliamentary deputies'
mandates. Thus, notwithstanding the democratic convention of identifiable
government and opposition alignments—supported, particularly in parliamentary regimes, by party discipline—the limits of the representative function
are ultimately defined by adherence to the existing legal order and the individual deputy's conscience. And, because official discrimination is constitutionally impermissible, an important corollary is that the people's representatives, through whom popular sovereignty is realized, are typically obliged to
serve the community as a territorially-defined whole rather than any given
nationally- or functionally-defined segment of it.[5]

But is it possible to reconcile popular sovereignty and civic equality with
the revival of political self-consciousness on the part of ethnonational
majorities and minorities residing within the same territorial boundaries?[6] As
in other times and places, this dilemma is politically salient throughout post-
communist Europe because the conditions that give rise to it are empirically
pervasive. How, then, can the ideal of a unitary citizenry presupposed by post-
communist constitutions be realized when "the people" in most of these new
states happen to be a multinational reality?[7]

It should be emphasized at the outset that the apparently zero-sum nature
of the dilemma—either undivided popular sovereignty and civic equality or
official acknowledgment and representation of group difference—tends to
dissolve in the face of actual practice. For, while the proscription of discrimination based on a citizen's ethnic origin seems to be an essential feature of

the modern democratic state, positive public provision for ethnocultural plurality has historically been an equally fundamental hallmark of such states, one that has often served to sustain an overarching sense of identity and loyalty.[8] Even in the United States, one of the world's most majoritarian liberal democracies, the view that "prejudice against discrete and insular minorities may be a special condition, which tends seriously to curtail the operation of those political processes ordinarily to be relied upon to protect minorities," expressed in the famous footnote four of Justice Stone's opinion in *United States v. Carolene Products Co.*, has become a pillar of political freedom.[9]

Nevertheless, the protection envisaged by Justice Stone is intended to defend an official definition of the polity in which ethnicity remains an essentially private matter left to voluntary associations. It is the freedom and opportunities of individual minority group members, not the right of distinct sub-cultures to corporate political representation, that is recognized and protected in public law in the United States, a principle that has remained largely untouched either by voting rights doctrine or by administrative quotas aimed at promoting diversity in education and employment.[10] And it is precisely this distinction that provides a useful analytical vantage point from which to examine and classify how post-communist European regimes have confronted the question of how to regulate ethnic minority political participation. Five general approaches can be discerned in the institutional frameworks established by these regimes' constitutional provisions, statutory legislation, and/or governmental decrees:

- opposition to participation by ethnic minorities as such;
- official neutrality towards ethnicity;
- active support and facilitation of effective competition by ethnic minority parties;
- formal guarantees of political representation; and
- ethnic territorialization, an institutional culmination of guaranteed representation in extreme form.

The aim of this chapter is mainly taxonomic. Therefore, no attempt will be made to contribute directly to debates among legal and political theorists regarding the level and type of protection owed to ethnic minorities,[11] although certain normative implications that follow from the analysis provided here will be addressed in the conclusion. However, before proceeding further, two additional points must be noted. First, the five models used to classify individual cases are necessarily heuristic, their purpose being to assess whether and to what extent a particular regime's institutional framework establishes a special status for ethnic minority parties relative to other political contenders. Second, in some cases, the regime's classification is not obvious from explicit legal provisions, but instead must be inferred by comparing the institutional framework with the degree of ethnic heterogeneity and the political-historical context of particular ethnic minorities' presence within the state. For both reasons, it is necessary to begin by examining how ethnic minority–based parties could be expected to fare in the absence of special provisions designed to affect their status, for the normal operation of any *generally applicable* electoral framework is bound to have a profound effect on outcomes.

Institutional Frameworks of Minority Representation

Because ethnic minorities constitute a class of a more general feature of political life, it is reasonable to assume that under democratic conditions proportional representation will better serve their interests than majority rule. Of course, pure proportionality is an unattainable ideal, "a model which real things resemble in various degrees but which is never duplicated in reality."[12] All such systems limit in various ways the principle that the share of seats awarded to a party should be equal to its share of the popular vote, primarily through choices about the geographical shape and magnitude (i.e., number of seats) of electoral districts, electoral thresholds, seat-allocation formulas, and legislative size.[13] Bearing this in mind, however, the more perfectly proportional a system is, the more hospitable it will be for minorities, whether they are ideologically-based and relatively open-ended or constituted by relatively fixed ethnocultural cleavages. Thus, statewide—or at least large-magnitude—electoral districts; low electoral thresholds; adoption of minority-friendly seat-allocation formulas such as Hare rather than d'Hondt;[14] and relatively large legislatures are among the features most likely to enhance the representation of minorities, including ethnic minority political parties, in parliaments.

Of these features, electoral thresholds are usually the most significant determinant of minorities' political fortunes.[15] Indeed, quite apart from whether or not ethnicity is the primary basis of a party's organization and programmatic appeal, the consequences of electoral thresholds in the unsettled context of post-communist politics can be profound. In the June 1992 Czechoslovak parliamentary elections, for example, three Czech parties, one Slovak party, and one Czech-Slovak two-party coalition, all of them pro-federal, were kept out of both houses of the Federal Assembly despite receiving near or above 4 percent of the vote each, thus significantly influencing the political composition of the Czechoslovak parliament and government at a decisive—indeed, fateful—moment in the state's history. Each of the entirely or partially proportional parliamentary electoral systems analyzed here features a threshold, ranging from 3 percent for individual parties in Croatia and Romania, 4 percent in Albania, Bulgaria, Latvia, Lithuania, and Moldova, and 5 percent in the Czech Republic, Slovakia, and Poland (and for all electoral contenders in Russia), to incrementally higher thresholds of 7, 8, 9, 10, and even 11 percent (the Czech Republic) for multi-party coalitions.[16] For ethnic minority–based parties, especially important variables include whether such thresholds operate at the national level; whether they are set at a level that comes close to the minority's share in the overall population of the state; and whether they are raised significantly for electoral coalitions, thereby impeding cooperation between minority parties of whatever type.

However, a proportional electoral system is not necessarily the only or best means of heightening representation of ethnic minorities. Where ethnic minorities are heavily concentrated in a particular geographical area, a majoritarian electoral system with appropriately drawn district boundaries can be equally hospitable to such groups, if not more so.[17] Albania and Bulgaria, among others, fall into this category; in both countries, ethnic minority parties did well under majority rule on the two occasions—Albania in 1992 and Bulgaria in 1990—when elections were held under a mixed proportional-majoritarian electoral system.[18] But neither can it be ignored that pure majority rule, especially in single-member districts, does little to foster party formation and presents especially serious obstacles to the creation of minor political parties, thus doing more harm than good over the long term to ethnic minorities' prospects for independent political representation.[19]

This does not mean that proportional representation, even with accessible thresholds, offers the best assurance to ethnic minority parties, for several other features of such systems are highly significant in determining a party's level of representation and influence. In particular, requirements that parties present a large number of signatures to qualify for inclusion on the ballot; an obligation to field candidates in a large number of districts in order to be eligible to put up separate national lists where this is a possibility; restrictions on free media access applied to parties that field candidates in only a small number of districts; the exclusion of smaller parties from public financing of campaign and operational expenses; and disfranchisement of citizens living outside the country are only a few examples of procedural burdens that may weigh especially heavily on ethnic minorities. As we shall see, the extent to which such provisions are applied, together with the framing of more general electoral rules and their modification with respect to ethnic minority parties, divides the eastern European regimes into analytically distinct paradigms of ethnic minority political participation.

Opposing Ethnic Minority Representation

Only two states in the region, Albania and Bulgaria, have straightforwardly opposed the representation of ethnic minorities as such while otherwise granting members of these minorities full and immediate citizenship and political rights.[20] Both countries have resorted to identical legal strategies, have taken action in fairly similar political situations, and have been equally unsuccessful in realizing their aims with respect to their primary targets for exclusion. The Russian Federation, on the other hand, has voiced no explicit commitment to political exclusion of ethnic minority parties; but, at least with respect to its most powerful legislative institution, the State Duma, it has been far more successful in achieving this goal in practice.

In Bulgaria, a prohibition against ethnic minority representation was implemented prior to the 1991 elections through provisions contained in the July 12, 1991, Constitution and in the August 20, 1991, Electoral Law.[21] Article 11.4 of the Constitution mandated that "there shall be no political parties established on ethnic, racial or religious lines, nor parties which seek the violent usurpation of state power," while article 12.2 specified that "citizens' associations, including trade unions, shall not pursue any political objectives, nor shall they engage in any political activity which is in the domain of the political parties." Accordingly, the Electoral Law limited candidate nominations and electoral campaigning to political parties that, in registering, did not violate article 11 requirements.

Unable to field candidates unless they transformed their civil association into a political party, ethnic Turk political leaders of the Movement for Rights and Freedoms, the main target of these provisions, were obliged to seek party registration, which they did simply by renaming themselves the Party of Rights and Freedoms (DPS).[22] This move was first challenged before a regional court and then before the Supreme Court, both of which ruled against the DPS. However, the Central Election Commission agreed in its September 11, 1991, decision—although by an extremely narrow vote—to accept the validity of the Movement's original 1990 registration and to recognize its old name and ballot colors for the 1991 elections. This ruling was then appealed by the post-communist Bulgarian Socialist Party (BSP) to the Constitutional Court, which ruled in favor of the DPS on the grounds that the party was open to support, membership, and votes from nonethnic Turk citizens, and that it in fact stood for basic constitutional values entitled to protection, namely educational, linguistic, and cultural rights. However, the Court's decision was announced only after DPS candidates were forced to run as independents in the election, and the DPS remains an exception in Bulgaria, as no other ethnically- or religiously-based party has since been allowed to register.[23]

Notwithstanding the Bulgarian Constitutional Court's vindication of the DPS's right to compete politically, however, other provisions of the 1991 Electoral Law seriously impaired its electoral prospects. In particular, articles 11 and 12 placed restrictions on voting rights of Bulgarian citizens living abroad. While these provisions were stated in general terms and thus formally affected all citizens regardless of their ethnic origin, their main target was quite obviously the DPS, the most likely political agent of the sizable number of ethnic Turks who had migrated to Turkey since 1989. While the DPS nonetheless managed, with 7.55 percent of the popular vote, to improve upon its 1990 results in the 1991 elections, its share slipped significantly to 5.44 percent in 1994. However, this may have been due less to disenfranchisement than to the DPS decision, following a fallout with the Union of Democratic Forces–led government in late 1992, to form a government coalition with the BSP despite the latter's previous challenge to its legality and its predecessor's notorious campaign, launched in 1984, aimed at forced assimilation of the Turkish minority. In 1997, the DPS decided to run in a coalition with several other parties that gained a combined 7.6 percent of the popular vote and 19 parliamentary seats.[24]

In the case of Albania, article 12 of the 1992 Law on Elections for the People's Assembly allowed citizens to run for parliament either as representatives of political parties and coalitions or as independent candidates.[25] This apparently harmless paragraph was initially aimed at preventing the various "transmission belt" social organizations created under the old regime by the communist Workers' Party from fielding candidates, a practice that the previous electoral legislation—drafted in 1990 before the transition had really begun— still allowed.[26] However, the provision was officially interpreted in accordance with the July 25, 1991, Law on Political Parties, which excluded from registration "parties [established] on a religious, ethnic or regional basis." Thus, the official Albanian strategy was virtually identical to that pursued in Bulgaria, with a ban on registration of ethnically-based political parties accompanied by a prohibition on any other type of civil association—necessarily including ethnic minority-based organizations—from fielding candidates in elections.

In Albania, this approach was clearly aimed against *Omonia*, a social organization representing the ethnic Greek minority in the southern districts of the country that had run a very distant third in the 1991 elections, obtaining just five of 240 seats.[27] *Omonia*'s initial attempt to register as a political party following enactment of the Law on Elections was thus blocked on the grounds that it was an ethnically-based grouping that fell under the ban established by the Law on Political Parties. However, faced with domestic and international pressure—the latter coming mainly from the Greek government—the Ministry of Justice ultimately accepted the registration of a Party for Defense of Human Rights, which was simply *Omonia* broadened slightly to admit some ethnic Albanians into its ranks under a name that, like the DPS in Bulgaria, couched the party's ethnic appeal in a universal idiom.[28] Yet harassment of Greek minority candidates did not end there: the new party reported many abuses and irregularities in the districts in which it fielded candidates, and the two seats it gained in the new parliament, already an anomalously low total given that its vote increased from a negligible 0.73 percent to 2.9 percent in 1992, were granted only after a series of interventions by the courts.[29]

In contrast to Albanian and Bulgarian *de jure* efforts to keep ethnic minority parties out of their parliaments, the Russian Federation's electoral rules have realized this outcome by being framed in an apparently more neutral, procedural manner. Elections to the State Duma—the lower, and more powerful, chamber of the Russian legislature—are regulated by provisions contained in the Federal Constitution, the Federal Law on Basic Guarantees of Electoral Rights of Citizens of the Russian Federation, and the Federal Law on Elections of the State Duma of the Federal Assembly of the Russian Federation. Yet no prohibition or restrictions against ethnically-based parties can be found in any of these legal texts.[30] The sole substantive provision dealing explicitly with ethnic groups, article 29.2 of the constitution, merely bans the dissemination of propaganda asserting racial or national superiority and forbids provocation of racial or national hatred; it thus cannot plausibly be understood as excluding the representation of ethnic minority parties.

Nevertheless, at least three provisions contained in the Law on Elections effectively negate any possibility that ethnic minority-based forces could gain representation in the Duma. In establishing who is entitled to take part in elections, article 32 defines an eligible organization as "an all-Russian public association established in the manner stipulated by federal laws," thus implying that only "all-Russian" parties are to be allowed to compete in elections. The impact of this provision on ethnic minority parties becomes clear in light of Chapter VI's requirement that no less than 200,000 voters' signatures be presented in support of a federal list of candidates, with the proviso that "no more than seven percent of the required total number of signatures" may be collected in the same subject of the Russian Federation.[31] This makes it impossible for an ethnic minority party—or, for that matter, *any* regionally- or locally-based organization—to run for any of the 225 seats allotted on a proportional basis, as only forces substantially organized in at least fifteen to twenty federal units can fulfill this legal requirement.[32] Finally, the 5 percent statewide electoral threshold similarly forecloses the possibility that any ethnic minority-based party might gain parliamentary representation.

Thus, the Russian electoral system, although not explicitly opposed to representation of ethnic minorities as such, in fact poses so many impediments to effective political participation by ethnic minority-based parties that it should be classified as more hostile towards their effective representation at the statewide level than the systems in place in either Albania or Bulgaria. While it is true that ethnic minorities are represented in the Russian Parliament's upper house, the Federation Council, this must be weighed against the weakness of this body. The fact remains that despite Russia's extremely diverse and strongly territorial ethnic composition, not a single ethnic minority-based party is represented in the current Duma, just as none was represented during the previous electoral period.[33]

Overlooking Ethnopolitics

Attempts at establishing ethnically neutral electoral frameworks can be found in those post-communist states where ethnic cleavages have not been mobilized prior to and during party system formation and strictly ethnic appeals play little or no role in domestic politics. But such frameworks have also been adopted within a cluster of countries where sizable ethnic minorities *have* been politically mobilized and where strong nationalist tendencies are present among the ethnic majority as well. In these cases, constitutional and legislative framers have chosen official neutrality towards ethnicity in their electoral systems as the best strategy for avoiding protracted and perhaps state-threatening conflict.

Among the first set of cases, the Czech Republic is the best and perhaps only "pure" example. The constitution's preamble identifies the state in wholly non-ethnic terms with "We, the citizens of the Czech Republic," and neither the constitution nor the electoral law contains a single provision intended to deny, enhance, or guarantee corporate political representation of ethnic minorities.[34] Similarly, in the mere two articles devoted to "Rights of National and Ethnic Minorities" in the Charter of Fundamental Rights and Freedoms, only cultural, educational, and linguistic rights are mentioned.[35] Yet, to the extent that the Czech Republic has been able to pursue a policy of strict compliance with the principles of non-discrimination and individual equality before the law, this is due not merely to its high degree of ethnic homogeneity. Particularly with respect to the 315,000 Slovaks (3.1 percent of the population), who constitute by far the largest ethnic minority, political mobilization, as in the United States, appears to be attenuated by the fact that they are immigrants lacking an historical territorial basis who have *freely chosen* to settle and remain in the Czech Republic and for whom identification with the Czech state has thus been relatively unproblematic.[36]

Included in the second set of cases are those countries, namely Ukraine, Macedonia, and Belarus, that have retained the first-past-the-post electoral system based on single-member districts inherited from the *ancien regime*.[37] In addition to, and perhaps intentionally reinforcing, whatever formal principles of civic equality these states have enshrined in their fundamental legal texts, this type of system offers far fewer opportunities for varying electoral formulae in a way that would either hinder or facilitate representation of ethnic minorities as such. Nevertheless, as has been demonstrated in Macedonia, at least one powerful, if crude, institutional device—namely, gerrymandering— exerts a more concentrated effect on ethnic minority representation within such electoral systems than is the case with proportional representation—in the limiting case casting doubt on official neutrality itself.[38] A related caveat, as suggested above, is that because this type of system is also far more likely to present a serious impediment to party formation, it may contribute to ethnic peace at the price of slow democratic consolidation.[39] Indeed, particularly where such a system is combined with presidentialism, it is highly vulnerable to manipulation by an authoritarian leader, as has been shown most clearly in Belarus.[40]

Where proportional representation has been adopted, the most prominent example of a consciously neutral approach to ethnicity in response to high levels of ethnic mobilization is that taken by Moldova. The October 14, 1993, Law on Elections to Parliament—the country's first post-communist electoral legislation—envisaged multimember districts, seat allocation via the d'Hondt formula, and a 4 percent threshold at the statewide level.[41] However, when electoral districts were established only a few days later, state officials found themselves confronted by a highly consequential dilemma. If district boundaries were drawn according to ethnic settlement patterns—which essentially would mean the creation of discrete constituencies in the conflict-ridden regions of the Transdniester and Gagauzia—the electoral boycott threatened by separatist forces in these areas would probably fail to gain widespread support, but at the risk of giving anti-system forces institutional leverage for building a territorially-defined base. On the other hand, if the authorities deliberately ignored ethnic realities by creating mixed districts and diffusing the ethnic Russian and Gagauze population among ethnic Moldovans, this would likely be regarded as an outright provocation that might easily motivate separatist forces to seek independence with renewed vigor.[42] Eventually, the so-called "Resolution on Procedure for Enacting the Law on Elections to Parliament," adopted on October 19, 1993,[43] squared the circle by creating a single, statewide constituency, allowing ethnically-based parties to maximize their gains while diluting the impact of a boycott and severing any possible link—at least from a legal perspective—between specific parties and regions. Thus, precisely because of the exceptionally high salience of ethnicity, the Moldovan electoral system has turned out to be perhaps the most ethnically blind in all of post-communist Europe.

Supporting Ethnic Minority Representation

An intermediate strategy, halfway between ignoring ethnic diversity in electoral rules and guaranteeing the representation of ethnic minorities as such, is the one followed by Poland and Hungary—not coincidentally two of the countries in which ethnic conflicts are most marginal to domestic politics—and, for a short period, by Lithuania. In these three cases, we find clauses in electoral legislation that support—but do not grant—representation of ethnic minorities in parliament and local governments, either by significantly loosening the requirements for fielding candidates or through other exemptions from the generally applicable electoral rules, with the aim in both instances being to make it easier for ethnic minority candidates to win seats. The first practice can be found in the Polish electoral laws of 1991 and 1993, while the second appears in the Hungarian legislation regulating local elections, in the 1992 Law for the Election of the Lithuanian Seimas, and, again, in the 1993 Polish electoral law.

Under article 63 of the 1991 Law on the Elections to the Polish *Sejm*, candidates could be nominated within their constituencies by "voters, political parties and organizations, and social organizations, who and which establish for this purpose national or local electoral committees."[44] However, in order to have the list accepted by the relevant committee, article 69.4 required nominations to be supported "by personal signatures of at least 5,000 voters residing in a given electoral district," although by gathering at least 50,000 signatures nationwide, a party would be entitled to field candidates in every constituency in the country regardless of the number of signatures collected in any particular district (article 70.1). Meanwhile, in order to field a national list, article 76.2 required parties to have previously registered its lists in no less than five constituencies.

However, in the case of ethnic minority party candidates, these requirements were eased substantially. According to article 70.2, organizations representing national minorities could enjoy the advantage provided by article 70.1—that is, fielding candidates in any district of the country—provided they were able to gather just 20,000 signatures, while according to article 76.3, an ethnic minority organization was entitled to field a national list "regardless of the number of district lists of candidates it has registered."

When the 1991 law was amended in May 1993, the most significant changes were aimed at reducing the high degree of proportionality that had characterized the 1991 system and at making it more difficult for smaller parties to field candidates at the district and national levels. With respect to the level of proportionality, the new law introduced a threshold of 5 percent for individuals and 8 percent for coalitions for seats gained at the district level, and increased the threshold for individual parties to 7 percent for access to any of the 69 seats allocated from the national list. Regarding the requirements for fielding candidates, the new law reduced the required number of signatures per district to 3,000, but made it necessary for parties to field candidates in at least half of the country's 52 districts in order to be allowed to put up a national list.[45]

As in 1991, however, the 1993 law treats ethnic minority organizations differently.[46] The most obvious and decisive advantage is set forth in article 5: ethnic minority organizations can choose to be exempted from either the 5 percent threshold for obtaining seats at the district level or from the 7 percent threshold for obtaining seats from the national list, which, if enforced, would block all of them from gaining any representation in the parliament given individual ethnic minorities' share of the total population. Similarly, article 91.3 waives the general requirement that lists be presented in 26 districts in order to field a national list of candidates, instead requiring national minority organizations to present lists in only 5 districts throughout the country. However, the law does not exempt such parties from the general requirement of including in the national list only citizens previously registered as candidates in district lists, which is tantamount to requiring that they present as many as 69 candidates throughout the country and thus campaign in many more districts than any ethnic minority in Poland could possibly cover. As a result, no ethnic minority group was able to present a national list for the September 1993 elections;[47] their representatives—four ethnic German deputies and one senator—were elected exclusively from district lists.[48]

Provisions contained in the Hungarian 1990 Local Elections Law were identical in intent to Polish practice. Law LXIV/1990 was an absurdly complex piece of legislation, establishing different electoral systems for smaller towns, larger cities, and the capital, with directly elected mayors in some cases but not in others.[49] Among its confusing requirements, however, Chapter XI contained three articles exempting ethnic minority candidates from electoral rules applicable to other candidates. Article 48.2 established the right of ethnic minority candidates to appear as such—i.e., as members of a discrete community—on the ballot, and even to write their name and the name of the organization they represent in both Hungarian and their own language, while article 48.3 required that Hungarian public television and radio set aside airtime for ethnic minority organizations "on the last day of the electoral campaign."

The most significant provisions of the Hungarian legislation, however, were contained in articles 49 and 50. Under article 49, an ethnic minority candidate who did not succeed in an election conducted by majority rule and multiple vote was nonetheless elected if he won at least two-thirds the votes obtained by the last elected candidate.[50] Under article 50, when elections were held using party lists and proportional representation,[51] the first candidate in any given ethnic minority slate would also be elected provided that his list won at least two-thirds the number of votes obtained by the last ordinarily elected candidate. In both cases, the number of city council members consequently increased by one.

Finally, although the provisions concerning ethnic minorities in the 1992 Law on Elections to Lithuania's *Seimas* amounted to less than a couple of lines, their effect deserves to be taken into consideration.[52] The electoral system adopted was a mixed one: half of the deputies were elected on the basis of a two-round majority system in single-member districts (articles 8 and 75), while the other half—70 of 141 seats—were proportionally distributed nationwide using the Hare quota and a 4 percent threshold (articles 8 and 76). The only provision that specifically referred to ethnic minorities, contained in article 76, exempted ethnic minority organizations from the 4 percent threshold, thereby allowing them to obtain a seat simply by achieving the Hare quota (number of valid votes/number of available seats, i.e., one-seventieth of the national vote).

The application of this exemption in the 1992 elections allowed the Union of Poles of Lithuania to double its representation in the *Seimas:* besides the two seats obtained in single member districts located in two areas with a sizable Polish community, the party got two more seats from the portion awarded by proportional representation, despite having received a mere 2.07 percent of the vote.[53] However, this feature of the Lithuanian electoral system did not survive very long. In June 1996, during the run-up to a new round of national elections, the *Seimas* adopted a series of amendments to the electoral law that raised the electoral threshold from 4 percent to 5 percent—and to 7 percent for coalitions—while abolishing the exemption for national minority parties.[54]

Granting Ethnic Minority Representation

Ethnically-defined electoral systems in post-communist Europe, as elsewhere, assume one of two broad forms, characterized either by guaranteed representation of ethnic minorities within unitary institutions or by federal constitutional arrangements and, under the most unstable variant, separate, ethnically-based party systems. Included in the first group are the electoral systems introduced in Romania beginning with an executive decree of March 14, 1990, in Croatia—at least for a short period—by the August 1992 electoral law, and in Slovenia by the March 1992 electoral law.[55] Each of these country's constitutions and/or electoral legislation expressly recognizes particular ethnic minorities, which, regardless of their size or the strength of their electoral support, are assured a minimum number of seats in the lower house of the legislature and, in some cases, in local representative bodies as well, with each group retaining the right to enlarge its representation by fielding candidates for additional seats under the generally applicable electoral rules.

In Romania, article 4.1 of the executive decree stated that the proportional system introduced by the decree was itself the foremost guarantee of fair representation of all ethnic minorities in parliament. Nevertheless, article 4.2 also guaranteed that "organizations representing national minorities registered on the date of adoption of this Executive Decree which did not manage to receive the number of votes needed to obtain a seat in the Chamber of Deputies . . . would be granted one deputy."[56]

In Romania's initial multi-party elections in May 1990, only three ethnic minority organizations managed to obtain representation on the strength of their popular support. The Hungarian Democratic Federation of Romania (UDMR) received almost one million votes, and, with 29 deputies and 12 senators, became the major opposition party in the first democratic parliament.[57] The Democratic Forum of Germans of Romania and the Roma Democratic Union of Romania, with vote totals below 1 percent, obtained one seat each. However, after applying article 4.2, nine other ethnic minority organizations—those established by Armenians, Bulgarians, Greeks, Lipovenians, Poles, Serbs, Czechs and Slovaks, Turks, and Ukrainians—were each granted a single seat (the Jewish organization did not participate).[58]

Prior to the September 1992 elections, however, the 1990 decree was replaced by Law No. 68/1992, which severely limited the degree of proportionality but retained the automatic grant of a single seat in the Chamber of Deputies to registered ethnic minorities, among other reasons because it had in the meantime been guaranteed by the December 1991 Romanian Constitution.[59] Nevertheless, the law's framers were able to limit this guarantee on the justification that the constitution deferred to statutory law on the manner in which it should be implemented. These limitations came in two forms. Article 4.2 stipulated that a national minority would be granted representation only if its candidates "have obtained throughout the country at least five per cent of the average number of validly expressed votes throughout the country for the election of one deputy," while article 4.4 excluded from the guarantee any ethnic minority organization which contested the elections as fully or partially integrated components of coalitions with other political forces. Although the effect of the first clause was insignificant, the second appears to have reflected the ruling party's growing fear of attempts at unification among opposition forces.[60]

Indeed, a major disincentive to inter-ethnic party-building was already established by article 59 of the constitution, which stipulates, *in fine*, that "citizens of a national minority are entitled to be represented by one organization only," a provision that amounts to a constitutionally embedded channeling of political identity for a substantial portion of Romania's citizenry. The parliamentary bylaws similarly require that all ethnic minority deputies who have received their mandates through the provisions of article 59 of the constitution form unitary parliamentary factions, again curtailing both intra-ethnic political pluralism and ethnic majority-minority coalitions. Only the UDMR, having obtained its representation under the generally applicable electoral rules, has been eligible to form its own factions.

Following the 1992 elections, which no ethnic minority organization contested as a member of a coalition with other parties, 13 extra deputies, representing the nine already existing national minority organizations plus the Democratic Union of Muslim Tatars in Romania and the Italian Community of Romania (both of which registered only after the 1990 elections), obtained seats in the Chamber of Deputies as a result of the guarantee. The Germans and the Roma also benefited from guaranteed representation in 1992, as only the UDMR obtained seats on the strength of its popular support this time around. The Jewish community, which in 1990 did not field candidates and in 1992 withdrew them, as well as the Albanian community (which was late in organizing) did not obtain representation until the 1996 election.

In Croatia, the system introduced by the short-lived August 1992 electoral law was similar to that in Romania insofar as it guaranteed a minimum level of representation in the lower house of the *Sabor* to all officially recognized ethnic minorities. However, the Croatian system also acknowledged the existence of an especially numerous and significant minority—the Serb community—and granted it not just a single "testimonial" parliamentary mandate, but seats proportional to its share of the overall population, although the form of this acknowledgment in the wording of the relevant provision also reflected the Serbs' uncertain status within the state. Article 10.2 of the House of Representatives Electoral Law expressly named and granted a single seat to each of four "national" communities: Hungarians, Italians, and, as in Romania, omnibus ethnic minorities—in this case one comprising Czechs, Slovaks, Russians, and Ukrainians, and another composed of Germans and Austrians. Along with this clear attribution of status, however, article 10.1 stated that "members of ethnic and national communities or minorities with a share of the population of the Republic of Croatia exceeding 8 percent as per the population census from 1981, shall be entitled to be represented in the Parliament proportionally to their respective participation in the overall population in the manner provided by this Law." Of course, there was no ethnic minority other than the Serb community (which comprised 11 percent of the population prior to the war) that qualified under article 10.1, nor, since the provision referred only to the 1981 census, could there be in the future. The ambiguity of the article, therefore, could only be understood as a deliberate means of avoiding use of the word "Serb" in a major piece of Croatian legislation.

The system established by the 1992 Electoral Law was a mixed one in which 60 seats were proportionally allocated among party lists in an at-large national district with a 3 percent threshold (article 24), while the remaining 60 seats (plus the four allotted to ethnic minorities) were allocated through plurality vote to individual candidates in single-member districts of approximately equal size (article 23). Article 23.3 mandated the creation of four special electoral units for Hungarians, Italians, Czechs-Slovaks-Russians-

Ukrainians, and Germans-Austrians, although it deferred definition of their main features to a subsequent "Law on Electoral Units for the House of Representatives of the Parliament of the Republic of Croatia."

For the Serb community, however, the procedure was bound to be more complicated. In principle, Serb candidates could run either as independent candidates, members of purely Serb parties or movements, or members of any existing multiethnic political force. If, through the operation of the ordinary electoral rules, a sufficient number of ethnic Serb candidates were elected, no further procedures would be necessary. But if ethnic Serbs were not elected to the House in a number sufficient to match their share of the overall population—which in 1992 meant 13 deputies—then rules contained in article 26 were to be applied. In particular, article 26.1, repeating the intentionally ambiguous wording noted above, stipulated that "the number of the representatives of the House of Representatives shall increase up to the number which is needed for the required representation to be attained, and the members of a certain community or a minority, who have been put up on the state list, but have not been elected, shall be considered as elected representatives in the order corresponding to the proportional success of each individual list in the elections" (emphasis added). If the predetermined number of representatives still could not be attained, article 26.2 mandated that the president call by-elections within 60 days of the date of the first session of the newly elected House in as many special electoral units as required.

When put into practice for the August 1992 elections to the *Sabor*'s House of Representatives, the requirements of the Law on Electoral Units were fulfilled by awarding seats to eight non-elected Serb candidates—two from the Croatian People's Party, and three each from the Social Democratic Party of Croatia and the Serbian People's Party.[61] However, by the time of the 1995 elections, the original features of the system were no longer in operation, reflecting the severe reduction in the size of the Serb community following the Croatian government's seizure of the autonomous Serb-dominated regions of Western Slavonia and Krajina. These military operations were memorialized in a broader change in the electoral system, with the provision benefiting the Serb community drastically modified to grant only three seats elected in special districts. Moreover, while the mixed features of the existing system were maintained, the sizes of the two factions were changed in favor of greater proportionality: 80 seats would be proportionally elected, while only 28 seats would be awarded in single member districts. Yet this was accompanied by a significant rise in the electoral thresholds—to 5 percent for individual parties, 8 percent for two-member coalitions, and 11 percent for larger groupings.[62]

For the January 2000 elections, a new election law passed on October 29, 1999 reduced still further the guarantees and political leverage of the Serb community. The new law provided a mere five seats for representatives of all ethnic minorities, allocating only one for the Serbs, one each for Hungarians and Italians, one for Czechs and Slovaks, and the fifth for members of the Austrian, German, Ruthenian, Ukrainian, and Jewish minorities, all of them to be elected in special districts.[63] However, in compliance with the constitutional principle of voting equality, the law allowed members of the ethnic minority communities to decide whether to vote in these special districts or as ordinary citizens voting for the lists established in their constituencies. In the case of the Serb community, only 27,789 of 168,606 registered voters cast their ballots in the special electoral district.[64]

The case of Slovenia is similar to the two cases described above insofar as ethnic minorities are guaranteed a presence as such in parliament, but the country is distinguished by privileging only certain minorities in this way and in *inverse* relation to their share of the total population. Thus, article 80 of the 1991 Constitution proclaims the right of the Hungarian and Italian minorities to seats in the 90-member lower house—the National Assembly—of the parliament.[65] Yet Hungarians and Italians—although historical inhabitants of the current territory of Slovenia—are the smallest minorities in the country, numbering less than 12,000 members. According to the 1991 census, their share in the population (0.43 and 0.16 percent, respectively) is smaller than that of Croats (2.76 percent), Serbs (2.44 percent), Muslims (1.37 percent), and even self-proclaimed Yugoslavs (0.63 percent).[66] The fact that the constitution grants seats in the National Assembly only to these two ethnic minorities is even more anomalous given that Slovenia has one of the world's very few corporatist upper houses—the National Council—in which local, economic, and social interests are autonomously represented. This body would seem to be much better suited to separate representation of ethnic minorities than the National Assembly.[67]

In accordance with the constitutional mandate, article 2.3 of the 1992 Electoral Law recognized that "the Italian and Hungarian minorities have the right to elect one delegate each," and consequently created a sort of parallel electoral system comprising several exceptions from the generally applicable electoral rules. Thus, Italian and Hungarian minority representatives would be elected exclusively by members of these communities (article 8) in "special constituencies . . . formed in the territories inhabited by the Italian and Hungarian minorities" (article 20), i.e., Koper/Capodistria for the Italian community and Murska Sobota for the Hungarian community. In these constituencies, special electoral boards for the supervision of elections are formed (article 25), and parties can field candidates by gathering the required number of voters' signatures only from members of the ethnic community (article 36). As only one representative is elected by each community, the electoral formula is also different from the otherwise proportional one, being majoritarian with a multiple preferential vote and with by-elections conducted whenever an ethnic minority representative's mandate ceases before the National Assembly is dissolved.[68]

Ethnicity as the Basis of Political Representation

The most radical approach to guaranteeing parliamentary representation of ethnic minority-based organizations is found in those countries that have made ethnic cleavages the ultimate basis of political competition by maintaining the communist regimes' adoption of ethnic pluralism as a territorial principle. Included in this group are the former Czechoslovakia, the former and current Yugoslavia, Bosnia-Herzegovina, and the Russian Federation. In these cases, we find federal states composed of territorial units defined along ethnic lines and bicameral legislatures with seats in the lower house distributed on a proportional basis and equal representation of the federal units in an upper house.[69] Accordingly, with the exception only of the Russian Federation, whose lower house excludes ethnic minority-based parties, political representation at the statewide level in these countries is (or was) fully channeled through ethnic composition, with electoral competition occurring within discrete ethnic boundaries and elected deputies ideally sitting in federal parliaments as representatives of Slovaks, Montenegrins, Chechens, and so forth.

Of course, in an area of the world where ethnic diversity is endemic, ethnic federalism has rarely approached this ideal state of affairs. With the exception of the Czech Republic, no current or former federal units in fact approach ethnic homogeneity, and in only Estonia and Latvia were voting rights initially limited to inhabitants belonging to the titular ethnic group. Thus, deputies in the Czechoslovak House of Nations elected within the Slovak Republic did not represent ethnic Slovaks exclusively; representatives in the Russian Federation Council from Tatarstan do not represent ethnic Tatars without also representing the republic's ethnic Russians; and Serbia does not send only ethnic Serbs to represent the republic in the federal legislature. While ethnicity has been the decisive factor in drawing the borders of federal units in each of these cases, citizenship still determines who is entitled to political representation.

Nevertheless, because federalization originally preceded rather than followed democratization in these cases, the institutionalized commitment of such states to ethnoterritorial units left them extremely vulnerable to outright collapse when rapid political mobilization of their populations finally occurred (Czechoslovakia, pre-war Yugoslavia, and the Soviet Union). Conversely, their survival would have been or currently is dependent on *de facto* political domination by one of the constitutive ethnic groups (Czechs in Czechoslovakia, Serbs in the former and current Yugoslavia, and Russians in the Soviet Union and the Russian Federation), thus virtually ensuring a high degree of authoritarianism. And, because none of the post-communist federations adopted ethnic disfranchisement, the problems this commitment poses for both state-building and democratization have been most severe where no ethnic group constitutes a majority or at least a large plurality of the overall population, a situation that is well-illustrated by both pre- and post-war Bosnia-Herzegovina.

In Bosnia-Herzegovina's first competitive elections in December 1990, the population voted almost exclusively along ethnic lines, thus producing a parliament composed mainly of ethnically-based parties in which the strength of each party corresponded very closely to the size of the ethnic community it represented.[70] Moreover, the constitutional order included a collective presidency very much in the spirit of the still-existingYugoslav Federal Presidency, containing two Muslims, two Serbs, two Croats, and a seventh member representing all other ethnic groups, with each set of leaders elected exclusively by members of their respective ethnic communities.[71] finally, these constitutional arrangements and the composition of the parliament also led to the fragmentation of the cabinet and higher administrative echelons along ethnic lines.

Despite the tragic experience of the war, or perhaps because of it, the outcome of the ongoing peace process has been the reconstruction of Bosnian institutions in accordance with territorialized ethnicity. The November 1995 Dayton Peace Agreements signed by representatives of the three contending factions contain a number of annexes, including a draft Constitution for Bosnia and Herzegovina.[72] The constitution's twelve articles propose a set of institutions for the new state comprising, *inter alia*, a bicameral parliament, a collective presidency, a cabinet, and a constitutional court. Each is constructed on the basis of the existing ethnic divisions and is thus entirely dependent on maintaining exact inter-ethnic parity in order to ensure the cooperation necessary for the day-to-day operation of government.

Thus, the House of Peoples of the Parliamentary Assembly comprises fifteen members, five designated by the *Republika Srpska* National Assembly, five by the Croat delegates to the Federation of Bosnia and Herzegovina legislature, and five by the Muslim delegates. Following similar criteria, two-thirds of the 42 members of the House of Representatives are to be directly elected from the territory of the Muslim-Croat Federation, with the remaining one-third elected from the territory of Republika Srpska (article IV).[73] Regarding the executive, article V creates a collective presidency composed of a Bosniak (Muslim), a Croat, and a Serb, with each directly elected by the citizens in each of the two entities of the state.[74] Similarly, no more that two-thirds of the cabinet ministers may be citizens of the Muslim-Croat Federation, while deputy ministers should necessarily belong to a different community than that of the prime minister. Finally, four of the nine constitutional court justices are to be appointed by the Muslim-Croat Federation's legislature, another two by the Republika Srpska legislature, and the remaining three by the European Court of Human Rights, which is to choose non-citizens either of the republic or any neighboring state (article VI).

Not surprisingly, the sources of disequilibria under such a system are ubiquitous. To offer just a few examples, a quorum in the House of the Peoples will require the presence of at least three Bosniak, three Croat, and three Serb delegates (article IV.1.b); the governing functions in each house will be performed by a Chair and two Deputy Chairs who should belong to different ethnic communities and rotate posts periodically (article IV.3.b); a vote by two-thirds of any ethnic group's representatives against any measure will be sufficient to veto it (article IV.3.d), while even a simple majority may do so by declaring the measure to be "destructive of a vital interest" of its community and thereby forcing its referral to the Constitutional Court (article IV.3. e and f); and dissolution of the House of the Peoples requires a vote of the majority of at least two of the three groups of representatives.

In essence, the Constitution of Bosnia and Herzegovina drafted in Dayton envisages a set of parliamentary, executive, judicial, military, and even financial institutions entirely constructed on the principle of ethnicidentification and whose realization is therefore entirely dependent on inter-ethnic cooperation. The paradox, of course, is that this attempt at complete political regulation of inter-ethnic relations is premised on the idea that the peaceful and spontaneous inter-ethnic relations required to implement it are no longer possible.

Conclusion

Legal frameworks for electoral competition in eastern Europe currently treat ethnic minority parties in very different ways, with the five paradigms examined in this chapter ranging from more or less obvious attempts to exclude ethnic minorities as such from political life to facilitation and even guarantees of a voice in statewide institutions. On the other hand, functional homogeneity and adherence to the principles of equality before the law and non-discrimination on ethnic grounds, or, more commonly, the dangerously high political salience of ethnicity, have led other countries to overlook the issue, officially treating ethnic minority-based parties no differently than any other political grouping.

Clearly, the political relevance of an ethnic minority—its size, degree of self-consciousness, level of mobilization, support from neighboring states, and, in the latter case, inter-state relations—profoundly affects how it is treated by the existing electoral legislation. Yet the relationship is often an inverse one: the more politically relevant an ethnic minority, the more likely it is that the electoral system will, in some measure, challenge its ability to compete, while the more insignificant and non-threatening it is, the greater the likelihood that the legal framework will include at least a few mechanisms aimed at supporting it or even granting it a minimum level of representation.[75] And the likelihood that the latter paradigm—essentially one of "testimonial" participation—will be adopted appears to be heightened where a state has itself mobilized ethnicity by fashioning its identity around that of its ethnic majority.

However, it may be impossible to draw definitive conclusions about the status of an ethnic minority solely on the basis of how it is treated by the electoral framework. The extent to which an electoral system facilitates or hinders an ethnic minority party's ability to be represented in parliament is certainly an important indicator of an ethnic minority's capacity to pursue and defend its interests. But other issues, including linguistic, educational, and cultural rights, along with the material resources necessary to exercise these rights effectively, are equally important—and perhaps more so given their obvious significance in determining whether, when, and to what extent an ethnic minority is able to mobilize politically. Indeed, highly publicized and apparently generous mechanisms for political representation of ethnic minorities may in some cases provide a smokescreen for cooptation of a minority's leadership and demobilization of its social base.

Of course, the oppositional paradigm that challenges ethnically-based parties' legality or relegates them to political oblivion by introducing insurmountable requirements for effective political participation does not merit a positive assessment, as it is typically the hallmark of an authoritarian regime. Nevertheless, the paradigm of facilitation, and even more so those adopted by several East European countries in order to guarantee representation of ethnic minority parties, raise serious problems of their own for a democratic political order. Two types of arguments may be made against such paradigms.

The first argument is founded on the principled claim that any form of electoral "affirmative action" that awards ethnic minority political groupings with privileges denied to others violates basic democratic principles of non-discrimination and equality before the law. The objection here is not to differential treatment for a particular social group *per se*, as this would be acceptable in other domains of public life, such as education, cultural provision, or even welfare expenditure. Rather, the objection centers on the introduction of special privileges in a particular domain—political participation—in which scrupulous respect for equality is crucial, perhaps especially because, in the context in which such privileges have been introduced, the values of equality and non-discrimination are frequently not yet widely assumed and deeply embedded.

The second type of argument centers on a more "realist" assessment of the undesirable political consequences that are likely to follow from such paradigms, all of which have become manifest in varying degrees in the cases examined here. Facilitating electoral competition by ethnically-based parties or granting them parliamentary representation *ex ante* encourages the creation of such parties, indirectly promotes confrontation rather than alliances with parties representing non-ethnic ideologies, tends to reduce the presence of ethnic minority candidates in non-ethnically-based parties (and thus the latter parties' interest in problems pertaining to ethnic minorities), discourages political pluralism within ethnic minority communities, and generates a perception of ethnic minorities and their representatives as exogenous and problematic elements of a country's political life. Moreover, the presence of a large number of minorities of varying size and political relevance may, as in the cases of Romania and possibly Croatia, give authorities greater leeway in artificially "equalizing" the status of each by creating a set of vocal yet domesticated and state-dependent ethnic representatives to neutralize the influence of those considered to pose a greater threat.

Of course, it should be emphasized again that neither of these arguments means that ethnic minority-based parties should be discouraged, much less banned. Rather, as Arend Lijphart has argued, the issue, particularly important for democratizing regimes, is one of self-determination versus pre-determination of collective political actors.[76] At the same time, however, several cases examined here—the Russian federation being perhaps the leading example—demonstrate that, considered by itself, Lijphart's preferred mechanism for ensuring self-determination, proportional representation, will be insufficient to achieve this goal if the procedural minutiae of such systems—the political relevance of which vary from case to case—operate to circumvent it. More importantly, as the case of Bosnia-Herzegovina illustrates, the fact that ethnic segmentation is self-determined provides no guarantee that a power-sharing system, or even the maintenance of statehood itself, will be a viable outcome.

Still, viewed from the perspective of the analysis of electoral systems provided here, Lijpart's central point—that the most reasonable strategy for protecting ethnic minorities in a way that is neither discriminatory nor manipulative is one based on a high degree of self-determination—is surely correct. Beyond the initial selection of collective actors, this would entail a sincere push for increased political engagement, particularly through existing inter-ethnic political forces, but it would also not be limited to statewide legislative institutions. Rather, it would include, for example, greater local and regional empowerment, as well as an ensemble of grass roots-initiated special-purpose consultative bodies that can complement the representative role of parliaments by providing a forum for airing political issues that are especially relevant to a particular community.

An instance of such a strategy is Hungary's Local Elections Law, whose discrimination in favor of ethnic minorities, while still normatively problematic, is surely preferable to its realization at the state-wide level—a possibility that was in fact considered but ultimately rejected.[77] Given much of eastern Europe's thin tradition of citizenship, only such concrete steps—all of which are geared towards insulating the core of the political system from centrifugal ethnic mobilization—seem capable of institutionalizing the principle "that government is or ought to be instituted for the common benefit, protection, and security of the people, nation or community."[78]

Appendix:
Current Ethnic Minority Representation in Post-Communist Parliaments

Country, Last Election	Party	Ethnicity	% Votes	Seats (% of Total)
Albania, 1997	Human Rights Unity Party (PMDN)	Greek	2.8	4 (2.5)
Belarus, 1995	None	—	—	—
Bosnia-Herzegovina, 1998	Coalition for a Unified and Democratic BiH (KCDBiH), comprising the Party of Democratic Action (SDA) and Party for BiH (SBiH)	Bosniak Muslim	32.7	17 (40.4)
	Croatian Democratic Union of BiH (HDZBiH)	Croat	11.2	6 (14.2)
	New Croatian Initiative (NHI/HKDU)	Croat	2.2	1 (2.3)
	Sloga (comprising SNS, SPRS, SNSD)	Serb	12.0	4 (9.5)
	Serbian Democratic Party (SDS)	Serb	9.1	4 (9.5)
	Serbian Radical Party RS (SRSRS)	Serb	6.6	2 (4.7)
	Radical Party RS (RSRS)	Serb	1.5	1 (2.3)
Bulgaria, 1997	Movement for Rights and Freedoms (DPS) within the Union for National Salvation (ONS)	Turkish	7.6	19 (7.9)
Croatia, 2000	Serbian People's Party (SNS)	Serb	n.a.	1 (0.7)
	Hungarian Democratic Community of Croatia (DZMH)	Hungarian	n.a.	1 (0.7)
	Independent	Italian	n.a.	1 (0.7)
	Croatian Peasant Party (HSS)	Czech/Slovak	n.a.	1 (0.7)
	Alliance of Ruthenians and Ukrainians	Ruth./Ukr.	n.a.	1 (0.7)
Estonia, 1999	Estonian United People's Party (EURP)	Russian	6.1	6 (5.9)
Hungary, 1998	None	—	—	—
Latvia, 1998	Party of Latvia's Russian Citizens	Russian	1.2	0 (0.0)
Lithuania, 1998	Election Action of Lithuania's Poles (LLRA)	Polish	3.0	2 (1.4)
	Alliance of Lithuanian National Minorities (LTMA)	Misc.	2.4	0 (0.0)
	Lithuanian Russian Union (LRS)	Russian	1.6	0 (0.0)
Macedonia, 1998	Party of Democratic Prosperity (PDP), Democratic Prosperity Party of Albanians (PDPA), and People's Democratic Party (NDP)	Albanian	19.3	25 (20.8)
	Democratic Party of Turks in Macedonia (DPTM), Party for the Total Emancipation of Romanies in Macedonia (PCERM), Party for Democratic Action of Macedonia (SDAM), and Democratic Progressive Party of Romanies in Macedonia (DPPRM), together with the Socialist Party of Macedonia (SPM)	Turkish Romany	4.7 n.a.	2 (1.6)
	Union of Romanies in Macedonia (SRM)	Romany	n.a.	1 (0.8)
Moldova, 1998	None	—	—	—
Poland, 1997	German Social and Cultural Society of Upper Silesia (TSKSNO)	German	n.a.	2 (0.4)
Romania, 1996	Hungarian Democratic Union of Romania (UDMR)	Hungarian	6.6	25 (7.2)
	Union of Armenians of Romania (UAR)	Armenian	n.a.	1 (0.2)
	'Brastvo' Comm. of Bulgarians in Romania (CBBR)	Bulgarian	n.a.	1 (0.2)
	Greek Union of Romania (UER)	Greek	n.a.	1 (0.2)
	Italian Community of Romania (CIRI)	Italian	n.a.	1 (0.2)
	Comm. of Russian Lipovenians of Romania (CRLR)	Russian	n.a.	1 (0.2)
	Union of Poles of Romania 'Dom Polski' (UPR)	Polish	n.a.	1 (0.2)
	Democratic Union of Serbs in Romania (UDSCR)	Serb	n.a.	1 (0.2)
	Democratic Union of Slovaks and Czechs in Romania (UDSCR)	Czech/Slovak	n.a.	1 (0.2)
	Democratic Union of Muslim Tatars in Romania (UDTTMR)	Tatar	n.a.	1 (0.2)
	Democratic Union of Turks in Romania (UDTR)	Turkish	n.a.	1 (0.2)
	Union of Ukrainians in Romania (UUR)	Ukrainian	n.a.	1 (0.2)
	Democratic Forum of the Germans of Romania (FDGR)	German	n.a.	1 (0.2)
	Party of the Roma (PR)	Romany	n.a.	1 (0.2)
	Cultural Union of Albanians in Romania (UCAR)	Albanian	n.a.	1 (0.2)
	Federation of Hebrew Communities in Romania (FCER)	Jewish	n.a.	1 (0.2)

Russia, 1999	None	—	—	—
Slovakia, 1998	Hungarian Coalition Party (SMK/MKP)	Hungarian	9.1	15 (10.0)
Slovenia, 1996	n.a.	Italian	n.a.	1 (1.1)
	n.a.	Hungarian	n.a.	1 (1.1)
Ukraine, 1998	None	—	—	—
Yugoslavia, 1996*	Vojvodina Hungarian Union	Hungarian	1.9	3 (2.1)
	Vojvodina Coalition	Hungarian	1.3	2 (1.4)
	Sandzak's List	Muslim	1.4	1 (0.7)

Note: Only ethnically based parties (or parties committed to the defense of specific ethnic minorities) are listed. Where bicameral legislatures exist, only the lower house is included.

*The Democratic League of Kosovo, the main organization representing Kosovo Albanians, refused to participate in the election.

Notes

1. See , for example, art. 1.2 of the 1991 Bulgarian Constitution ("The entire power of the State shall derive from the people"); art. 2.2 of the reformed Hungarian Constitution ("In the Republic of Hungary all power resides in the people exercising its sovereignty through its elected representatives as well as directly"); and art. 2.1 of the 1994 Moldovan Constitution ("National sovereignty belongs to the people of the Republic of Moldova, who exercise it directly or through representative bodies in the manner established by the Constitution").

2. See, for example, art. 3 of the 1993 Russian Constitution ("The multinational people of the Russian Federation shall be the vehicle of sovereignty and the only source of power in the Russian Federation").

3. See art. 1.2 of the 1990 Croatian constitution ("Power in the Republic of Croatia emanates from the people and belongs to the people as a community of free and equal citizens"); art. 8.1 of the 1992 FRY constitution ("In the Federal Republic of Yugoslavia, power shall be vested in the citizens"); art. 3 of the 1991 Slovenian constitution ("In Slovenia, supreme power is vested in the people. Citizens exercise that power directly, and most notably, at elections"); art. 2.1 of the 1992 Slovak constitution ("The power of the state is vested in the citizens who shall exercise it directly or through their representatives"); and art. 2.1 of the Macedonian constitution ("Sovereignty in the Republic of Macedonia derives from the citizens and belongs to the citizens"). But note the more exclusionary organic conception of popular sovereignty contained in art. 2.1 of the Romanian constitution ("National sovereignty resides with the Romanian people"), while art 4.1 similarly proclaims that "The State foundation is laid on the unity of the Romanian people."

4. Art. 3.1 of the Charter of Fundamental Rights and Freedoms (annexed to the 1992 Czech constitution). See also the similar wording of art. 14 of the 1991 Slovenian Constitution ("Everybody in Slovenia is guaranteed equal human rights and basic liberties, without respect to nationality, race, sex, language, religion, political or other convictions, marital state, birth, education, social status or any other personal circumstances. All are equal before the law"), and art. 12 of the 1993 Estonian Constitution ("All persons shall be equal before the law. No person may be discriminated against on the basis of nationality, race, color, gender, language, origin, religion, political or other beliefs, financial or social status or other reasons"). Even Romania's constitution, despite its proclamation of exclusive national sovereignty, contains a similar clause at art. 4.2 ("Romania is the common and indivisible homeland of all its citizens, without any discrimination on account of race, nationality, ethnic origin, language, religion, sex, opinion, political adherence, property or social origin").

5. See, for example, art 67 of the Bulgarian Constitution ("1. Members of the National Assembly shall represent not only their constituencies but the entire nation. No Member shall be held to a mandatory Mandate. 2. Members of the national Assembly shall act on the basis of the Constitution and the laws and in accordance with their conscience and convictions"); art. 66 of the 1991 Romanian Constitution ("1. In the exercise of their mandate, Deputies and Senators shall be in the service of the people. 2. Any imperative mandate shall be null"); art. 21 of the Albanian Constitutional Law ("It is the duty of a deputy to the People's Assembly to serve the people and the homeland conscientiously"); and art. 70.1 of the 1998 Albanian constitution ("Deputies represent the people and are not bound by any obligatory mandate"). Similarly, the Constitution of the Czech Republic requires that deputies and senators take a vow contained in art. 23 (3. "I promise allegiance to the Czech republic. I promise upon my honor to exercise my mandate in the interest of all the people and according to the best of my knowledge and conscience"), while art. 26 stipulates that "Deputies and Senators shall exercise their mandate personally in accordance with their vow, without being bound, in doing so, by any orders."

6. For the purposes of this essay, I will assume the definition of ethnic minority set forth in art. 2.1 of the Convention for the Protection of Minorities adopted by the Committee of Ministers of the Council of Europe following the proposal issued by the European Commission for Democracy Through Law on February 8, 1991. An ethnic minority is thus "a group which is smaller in number than the rest of the population of a state, whose members, who are nationals of the state, have ethnic, religious or linguistic features different from those of the rest of the population, and are guided by the will to safeguard their culture, traditions, religions and languages." An essentially identical definition is the one proposed by Prof. Capotorti in his role as a special rapporteur for the United Nations Subcommittee on Human Rights. See UN Doc. E/CN 4/sub. 2/385 rev. 1, p. 102. On this issue, see Mitja Zagar and Ales Novak, "La protección de las minorías nacionales en la Europa Central y del Este a través del Derecho Constitucional e internacional," in Carlos Flores Juberías, assoc. ed., *Derechos y libertades en las nuevas democacias de la Europa del Este, Humana Iura*, 8/9 (1998/1999), pp. 19-69 (esp. pp. 27-34).

7. The literature on this aspect of ethnic minority protection in Eastern Europe from a comparative perspective is not especially abundant, however. See, for example, Sergio Bartole, "Partecipazione politica e tutela delle minoranze nell'esperienza delle nuove democrazie dell'Europa centro-orientale," in Fulco Lanchester, ed., *La legislazione elettorale degli Stati dell'Europa Centro-Orientale* (Milan: Dott. A. Giuffrè Editore, 1995), pp. 125-45; Florence Benoît-Rohmer and Hilde Hardeman, "The Representation of Minorities in the Parliaments of Central and Eastern Europe," *International Journal on Group Rights* 2:2 (1994), pp. 91-112, and Bernard Owen, "Political Representation of Minorities: Integration or Segregation," CSCE ODHIR Bulletin, vol. 1, no. 2 (Spring 1993), pp. 1-5.

8. See Arend Lijphart, *Democracy in Plural Societies. A Comparative Exploration* (New Haven: Yale University Press, 1977).

9. 304 U.S. 144 (1938). See also John Hart Ely, *Democracy and Distrust* (New Haven: Yale University Press, 1980).

10. See Michael Walzer, "Pluralism: A Political Perspective," in Stephen A. Thernstrom, ed., *The Harvard Encyclopedia of American Ethnic Groups* (Cambridge: Harvard University Press, 1980), pp. 781-87, reprinted in Will Kymlicka, ed., *The Rights of Minority Cultures* (Oxford: Oxford University Press, 1995), pp. 139-54.

11. For recent work in this area, see, for example, Robert McKim and Jeff McMahan, *The Morality of Nationalism* (New York and Oxford: Oxford University Press, 1997), and the articles collected in Kymlicka, *The Rights of Minority Cultures*.

12. Douglas W. Rae, *The Political Consequences of Electoral Laws* (New Haven: Yale University Press, 1967), p. 29.

13. See Rein Taagepera and Matthew Soberg Shugart, *Seats and Votes. The Effects and Determinants of Electoral Systems* (New Haven: Yale University Press, 1989); Rae, *The Political Consequences of Electoral Laws,* and Arend Lijphart et al., *Electoral Systems and Party Systems. A Study of Twenty-Seven Democracies, 1945-1990* (Oxford: Oxford University Press, 1995), pp. 21-39.

14. While seat-allocation formulae are the most obscure and difficult to understand element of proportional representation systems (particularly as they are amenable to a seemingly infinite array of modifications), the implications of this choice are especially consequential for minor parties. Essentially, what is at issue is the extent to which the formula comprehends residual votes in setting the "cost" of seats, since the importance of residual shares, i.e., the number of votes exceeding the quota needed for each additional seat, will be proportionately greater the smaller the party. See Rae, *The Political Consequences of Electoral Laws,* pp. 28-39.

15. On electoral thresholds — their size, operation, and consequences — see Taagepera and Shugart, *Seats and Votes,* pp. 133-35, and Lijphart et al., *Electoral Systems,* pp. 25-30.

16. In all cases, the thresholds operate at the state-wide level, and in a few of them, e.g., Estonia and Poland, they are complemented with additional thresholds for surplus or national list for district list mandates.

17. On the different types of majoritarian systems, see Taagepera and Shugart, *Seats and Votes, passim,* and Lijphart et al., *Electoral Systems,* pp. 16-21.

18. See Robert Austin, Kjell Engelbrekt, and Duncan Perry, "Albania's Greek Minority," and Wolfgang Höpken, "Die Wahlen in Bulgarien–ein Pyrrus Sieg für die Kommunisten?," *Südost-Europa,* vol. 39, nos. 7-8 (1990), pp. 429-57.

19. On this widely discussed topic, see the seminal article by Maurice Duverger, "The Influence of Electoral Systems on Political Life," *International Social Science Bulletin,* vol. 3 (1951), pp. 314-52. See also the broader and more recent studies in Arend Lijphart and Bernard Grofman, eds., *Choosing an Electoral System: Issues and Alternatives* (New York: Praeger, 1986), and Bernard Grofman and Arend Lijphart, eds., *Electoral Laws and Their Political Consequences* (New York: Agathon Press, 1986).

20. The proviso of full and immediate membership in the polity thus eliminates from consideration the most exclusionary cases: the refusal of Estonia and Latvia to grant their large Russian minorities immediate, full, and unconditional citizenship. While both states have moved to ease their citizenship rules along more inclusionary lines in recent years, this problem necessarily lies beyond the purview of this chapter, because electoral regimes regulate how citizens' votes are cast, counted, and translated into parliamentary seats, not who qualifies as a citizen. On the Russian minorities in these states, see Neil Melvin's chapter in this volume. See also Benoît-Rohmer and Hardeman, "The Representation of Minorities," p. 102-07; Jeff Chinn and Lise A. Truex, "The Question of Citizenship in the Baltics," *Journal of Democracy,* vol. 7, no. 1 (January 1996), pp. 133-47; Dzintra Bungs, Saulius Girnius, and Riina Kionka, "Citizenship Legislation in the Baltic States," *RFE/RL Research Report,* vol. 1, no. 50 (December 1992), pp. 38-40; Bart Driessen, "Slav Non-citizens in the Baltics," *International Journal on Group Rights,* vol. 2, no. 2 (1994), pp. 113-38; and H. J. Uibopuu, "Dealing with Minorities—A Baltic Perspective," *The World Today,* vol. 48, no. 6 (June 1992), pp. 108-09. Valuable case studies of individual Baltic countries include George Ginsburg's, "Lithuanian Citizenship Issues: The Temptations of 'Purity,'" *The Parker School Survey of East European Law,* vol. 2, no. 9 (November-December 1991), pp. 9-10; Richard J. Krickus, "Latvia's 'Russian Question,'"

RFE/RL Research Report, vol. 2, no. 18 (April 1993), pp. 29-34; and Vello A. Pettai, "Shifting Relations, Shifting Identities: The Russian Minority in Estonia After Independence," *Nationalities Papers,* vol. 23, no. 2 (June 1995), pp. 405-12.

21. See *Constitution of the Republic of Bulgaria,* in International Institute for Democracy, *The Rebirth of Democracy. 12 Constitutions of Central and Eastern Europe* (Strasbourg: Council of Europe Publishing, 1996), pp. 10-47, and "Bill for Elections of National Assembly Members, Municipal Councilors and Mayors [enacted August 20, 1991]," in Stephen B. Nix, ed., *Election Law Compendium of Central and Eastern Europe* (Kyiv: IFES/ACEEEO, 1995), pp. 40-56.

22. On the DPS, see S. Riedel, "Die türkische Minderheit im parlamentarischen Systems Bulgarien," *Südost-Europa,* vol. 42, no. 2 (1993), pp. 100-24, Klaus Schramayer, "Die bulgarische Parteien," *Südost-Europa,* vol. 43, nos. 6-7 (1994), pp. 336-60, and Ivan Ilchev's chapter in this volume.

23. For two contrasting views on the issue, see Snejiana Botusciarova, "La legislazione elettorale in Bulgaria," in Fulco Lanchester, ed., *La legislazione,* pp. 267-80, and Rumyana Kolarova and Dimitr Dimitrov, "Electoral Law in Eastern Europe: Bulgaria," *East European Constitutional Review* vol. 3, no. 2 (Spring 1994), pp. 50-55.

24. On the successive Bulgarian parliamentary elections, see Stephen Ashley, "Elections in Eastern Europe: Bulgaria," *Electoral Studies,* vol. 9, no. 4 (1990), pp. 312-18; Dobrinka Kostova, "Parliamentary Elections in Bulgaria, October 1991," *The Journal of Communist Studies,* vol. 8, no. 1 (1992), pp. 196-203; Georgi Karasimeonov, "Parliamentary Elections of 1994 and the Development of the Bulgarian Party System," *Party Politics,* vol. 1, no. 4 (October 1995), pp. 579-89; and Richard Crampton, "The Bulgarian Elections of 19 April 1997," *Electoral Studies,* vol. 16, no. 4 (1997), pp. 560-63.

25. See "Law on Elections for the People's Assembly of the Republic of Albania [enacted February 4, 1992]," in Nix, *Election Law Compendium,* pp. 14-24. The mixed system introduced by this law was substantially reformed on February 1, 1996, by a new law which essentially enhanced its majoritarian features, raising thresholds and reducing by 15 the number of seats allocated proportionally from the national list.

26. See "Loi Electorale d'Albanie du 13 novembre 1990 (No. 7423)" in Bernard Owen and Halina Opolska, *La re-invention democratique. Les premieres elections en Europe de l'Est* (Paris: Association Francaise de Science Politique, 1991), pp. 1-29.

27. See Bogdan Szajkowski, "The Albanian Election of 1991," *Electoral Studies,* vol. 11, no. 2 (1992), pp. 157-61.

28. On the Albanian-Greek conflict, and the problems posed by the Greek minority in Albania, see Louis Zanga, "Albanian-Greek Relations Reach a Low Point," *RFE/RL Research Report,* vol. 1, no. 15 (April 10, 1992), pp. 18-21, Robert Austin, Kjell Engelbrekt, and Duncan Perry, "Albania's Greek Minority," *RFE/RL Research Report,* vol. 3, no. 11 (March 18, 1994), pp. 19-24, and James Pettifer's chapter in this volume.

29. Hans-Joachim Hoppe, "Demokratischer Machtwechsel in Albanien," *Osteuropa,* vol. 42, no. 7 (July 1992), pp. 609-20. The Party for Defense of Human Rights obtained three seats in 1996, and four seats in 1997.

30. See *Constitution of the Russian Federation,* in International Institute for Democracy, *The Rebirth of Democracy,* pp. 359-92. For the Electoral Law, see Nix, *Election Law Compendium,* pp. 269-94.

31. On the main features of the Russian electoral system, see Carlos Flores Juberías, "*Vybory* '95: las elecciones del 17 de diciembre a la *Duma* estatal de la Federación Rusa," *Cuadernos Con-*

stitucionales de la Cátedra Fadrique Furió Ceriol 13 (1995), pp. 157-65.

32. Romania introduced a rather similar system by means of the April 26, 1996 Law on Political Parties, though given the ethnic structure of the country it is unlikely to produce such devastating effects on ethnic minority representation. With the intention of limiting "party inflation," the new law requires parties seeking registration to prove an enrollment of at least 10,000 members, local branches in at least 15 counties, and no less than 300 members in each county. The Hungarian Democratic Federation of Romania (UDMR), the most significant ethnic minority party in the country (and the only one that has not required the benefit of guaranteed representation), already has branches in 19 counties, making it unlikely that the new provisions will jeopardize its legal status. See Michael Shafir, "Political Engineering and Democratization in the New Law on Political Parties," *Transition*, vol. 2, no. 14 (July 12, 1996), pp. 60-63.

33. On developments in the Russian party system and Duma, see Matthew Wyman, Bill Miller, Stephen White, and Paul Heywood, "The Russian Elections of 12 December 1993," *Electoral Studies*, vol. 13 (1994), pp. 254-71; Ian McAllister and Stephen White, "Democracy, Political Parties and Party Formation in Post-Communist Russia," *Party Politics*, vol. 1, no. 1 (1995), pp. 49-72; and Flores Juberías, *"Vybory '95."*

34. For the text of the constitution, see Gisbert H. Flanz, "The Czech Republic" in Albert Blaustein and Gisbert H. Flanz, eds., *Constitutions of the Countries of the World* (Dobbs Ferry, N.Y.: Oceana Publications, 1993), and "Law of the Czech National Council of 28 August 1990, on Elections to the Czech National Council," in Nix, *Election Law Compendium*, pp. 86-98.

35. See Mahulena Hosková, "Die Charta der Grundrechte und Grundfreiheiten der CSFR," *Europäische Grundrechte Zeitschrift*, vol. 18, nos. 16-17 (1991), pp. 369-74 and pp. 397-402, and Helmut Slapnicka, "Das tschechoslowakische Verfassungsprovisorium," *Osteuropa Recht*, vol. 4, no. 91, pp. 269-70 and pp. 275-85. An English-language version of the text can be found in the *Bulletin of Czechoslovak Law*, vol. 30, nos. 1-2 (1991), pp. 11-28.

36. See Walzer, "The Politics of Pluralism," pp. 142-44. It should be pointed out, however, that many of those counted as Slovaks in the most recent census in 1991 are Roma, who have been disproportionately affected by highly controversial measures aimed at preventing them from obtaining citzenship following the breakup of Czechoslovakia on January 1, 1993. As with the Russian minority in Estonia and Latvia, consideration of these measures is beyond the scope of this chapter. See Office of the United Nations High Commissioner for Refugees, *The Czech and Slovak Citizenship Laws and the Problem of Statelessness* (February 1996).

37. See "Law of Ukraine on Election of Peoples' Deputies of Ukraine [enacted November 18, 1993, as amended on December 22, 1994]," "[Macedonian] Law on Election and Recall of Representatives and Assemblymen" (repealed by a new set of laws in July 1998), and "Law of the Republic of Belarus on Elections to the Deputies to the Supreme Council of the Republic of Belarus [enacted October 27, 1989, and amended December 1994]," in Nix, *Election Law Compendium*, pp. 346-59, pp. 192-202, and pp. 26-38.

38. It should also be pointed out that, despite assurances of civic equality, the Macedonian constitution's preamble contains the strongest endorsement of ethnically-defined national sovereignty of the three countries ("Macedonia is established as a national state of the Macedonian people"). Even so, the sheer concentration of ethnic Albanians in the Western part of the country has assured significant representation, while post-electoral formation of inter-ethnic government coalitions has helped maintain a degree of political stability. See Rober W. Mickey, "Unstable in a Stable Way," *Transition*, vol. 1, no. 1 (January 30, 1995), pp. 38-41, and Robert W. Mickey and Adam Smith Albion, "Success in the Balkans? A Case Study of Ethnic Relations

in the Republic of Macedonia," in Ian M. Cuthbertson and Jane Leibowitz, eds., *Minorities: The New Europe's Old Issue* (Institute for EastWest Studies, 1993).

39. This point is emphasized in Stephen B. Heintz and Oleksandr Pavliuk, *Securing Sovereignty: Ukraine's First Five Years of Independence* (Institute for EastWest Studies, 1997), p. 16.

40. See, generally, Juan J. Linz and Arturo Valenzuela, eds., *The Failure of Presidential Democracy* (Baltimore: Johns Hopkins University Press, 1994). See also Ustina Markus, "A War of Referenda in Belarus," *Transition*, vol. 2, no. 25 (December 13, 1996), pp. 12-15.

41. See "Law on Elections to Parliament [enacted October 14, 1993]," in Nix, *Election Law Compendium*, pp. 204-18.

42. See Jeff Chin and Steven D. Roper, "Ethnic Mobilization and Reactive Nationalism: The Case of Moldova," *Nationalities Papers*, vol. 23, no. 2 (June 1995), pp. 291-327, and William Crowther, "La construcción de las instituciones democráticas en Moldavia," in Carlos Flores Juberías, ed., *Las nuevas instituciones políticas de la Europa Oriental* (Madrid: CEC/IVEI, 1997).

43. "Resolution on Procedure for Enacting the Law on Elections to Parliament," in *Republic of Moldova Parliamentary Elections. February 27, 1994* (Washington, D.C.: IFES, 1995), pp. I/29-I/31.

44. See "Law on Sejm Elections [enacted July 3, 1991]," in Nix, *Election Law Compendium*, pp. 220-42, and David McQuaid, "The 'War' over the Election Law," *RFE/RL Report on Eastern Europe*, vol. 1, no. 31 (August 2, 1991).

45. See Louisa Vinton, "Poland's New Election Law: Fewer Parties, Same Impasse?," *RFE/RL Research Report*, vol. 2, no. 28 (July 9, 1993), pp. 7-17, and Elzbieta Morawska, *Poland*, unpublished manuscript on file at the University of Chicago Center for the Study of Constitutionalism in Eastern Europe.

46. For a brief assesment, see Jan Wawryzniak, "La legislazione elettorale in Polonia," in Lanchester, *La legislazione elettorale*, p. 181.

47. For a comparison of the 1991 and the 1993 elections, see Marian T. Grzybowski, "Parliamentary Elections in Czech and Slovak Republics and in Poland, 1991-1993: In Search of an Adequate Electoral System," *paper presented at the XVI IPSA World Congress in Berlin*, August 21-25, 1994, and Paul G. Lewis, "Party Development and Political Institutionalization in Post-Communist Poland," *Europe-Asia Studies*, vol. 46 (1994), pp. 777-99.

48. In contrast, under the less restrictive 1991 law, the representation of ethnic minorities in the Sejm was more than three times larger: the German Minority got seven seats, the Movement for Silesia's Autonomy got two, and one seat each was obtained by the Association of Podhele Residents, the Eastern Orthodox Party, the Wielopolska Region and Poland Party, and the Electoral Coalition of the Piast Ethnic Group. On the political significance of the German minority in Poland, see Tomasz Kamusella, "Asserting Minority Rights in Poland," *Transition*, vol. 2, no. 3 (February 9, 1996), pp. 15-18, and Tomasz Kamusella and Terry Sullivan, "The Germans in Upper Silesia: The Struggle for Recognition," in Karl Cordell, ed., *Ethnicity and Democratisation in the New Europe* (London: Routledge, 1999), pp. 169-81.

49. See "Loi No. LXIV de l'an 1990 sur les élections des députés locaux des collectivitès locales et des Maires," in Owen and Opolska, *La re-invention democratique*, pp. 40-65, and Carmen González Enríquez, "Las elecciones generales y locales húngaras de 1990," *Revista del Centro de Estudios Constitucionales* 9 (1991), pp. 225-50.

50. The majority-rule, multiple-vote system was used to elect all councilmen in cities with under 10,000 inhabitants and one-half of all councilmen in cities with over 10,000 inhabitants as well as in the 22 districts of the capital.

51. This was the system used to elect the remaining councilmen in cities with more than 10,000 inhabitants and in the capital.

52. "Law on Elections to the Seimas [enacted July 9, 1992]," in Nix, *Election Law Compendium*, pp. 164-75.

53. On the October 1992 elections, see Sauļius Girnius, "The Parliamentary Elections in Lithuania," *RFE/RL Research Report*, vol. 1, no. 48 (December 4, 1992), pp. 6-12.

54. *OMRI Daily Digest*, June 28, 1996.

55. See "Décret-Loi pour les élections présidentielles et législatives," in Owen and Opolska, *La re-invention démocratique*, pp. 1-29; "The Law on the Elections of Representatives in the Parliament (Sabor) of the Republic of Croatia," in Nix, *Election Law Compendium*, pp. 58-67; and "Law on Elections to the Chamber of State [National Assembly, enacted March 10, 1992]," *op. cit.*, pp. 332-44.

56. On the 1990 Romanian electoral system, see Daniel Nelson, "Romania," *Electoral Studies*, vol. 9, no. 4 (1990), pp. 355-66.

57. On the UDMR, see Michael Shafir's chapter in this volume.

58. These organizations were the Union of Armenians of Romania, the Bulgarian Union Banat-Romania, the Greek Union of Romania, the Community of Russian Lipovenians of Romania, the Union of Poles of Romania 'Dom Polski,' the Democratic Union of Serbians and Krashovanians in Romania, the Democratic Union of Slovaks and Czechs in Romania, the Turkish Democratic Union of Romania, and the Union of Ukrainians in Romania. On the first competitive elections in Romania, see, *inter alia*, Tom Gallagher, "Romania. The Disputed Election of 1990," *Parliamentary Affairs*, vol. 44, no. 1 (1991), pp. 79-93, and Nelson, "Romania."

59. "Law No. 68/1992, on Election to the Chamber of Deputies and the Senate [enacted July 15, 1992]," in Nix, *Election Law Compendium*, pp. 244-63.

60. See Michael Shafir, "Romania's New Electoral Laws," *RFE/RL Research Report*, vol. 1, no. 36 (September 11, 1992), p. 25.

61. See Mirjana Kasapovic and Nenad Zakošek, "Elections and the Emerging Party System in Post-Socialist Croatia," paper presented at the XVI IPSA World Congress in Berlin (August 1994).

62. See *Narodne Novine* 68/1995, and Nenad Zakošek, "The Emergence of a New Parliament in an Unfavourable Environment: Croatian Parliament 1990-1996," paper presented at the RCLS International Conference on the New Democratic Parliaments: The First Years, Ljubljana-Portoroz, June, 1996.

63. See Law on the Election of Representatives of the Croatian National Parliament, *http://www.sabor.hr*.

64. For the election results, see *http://www.izbori.hr*. The new law also significantly altered the electoral system's basic traits, transforming the existing mixed formula into a purely proportional one, introducing ten 14-member districts (plus another two special districts for ethnic minorities and Croats living abroad), and a 5 percent threshold.

65. For an English version of the relevant constitutional articles concerning ethnic minorities, complemented by other important legal provisions, see Vera Klopcic and Janez Stergar, eds., *Ethnic Minorities in Slovenia* (Ljubljana: Institute for Ethnic Studies/Information Bureau of the Republic of Slovenia, 1994), pp. 40-69.

66. See Klopcic and Stergar, *Ethnic Minorities in Slovenia*, p. 8.

67. The small size of the National Assembly, moreover, gives both communities exceptionally strong influence relative to ethnic Slovenes. While the ratio of citizens to representatives is

roughly 22,000/1 nationwide, it is 8,500/1 for the Hungarian minority and 3,000/1 for the Italians. This disproportionality is further magnified by the fact that, unlike in Croatia, ethnic Italians and Hungarians may also participate in the election of the rest of the lower house, in effect giving them a double vote.

68. See Franc Grad, "The Slovene Electoral System," in Lanchester, ed., *La legislazione elettorale...*, op. cit., pp. 245-67, and Klopcic and Stergar, *Ethnic Minorities in Slovenia*, op. cit., pp. 22-23.

69. In the former Czech and Slovak Federal Republic, each republic was entitled to 75 seats in the 150-member House of the Nations. In the Federal Republic of Yugoslavia, both Serbia and Montenegro send 20 representatives to the Chamber of the Republics, despite the fact that Serbia's population is 17 times larger than Montenegro's. In the Russian Federation, the Federation Council is composed of two representatives from each of the 89 federal units — 21 republics, six *krai*, 49 *oblasts*, two federal cities, one autonomous *oblast*, and 10 autonomous districts.

70. Bosnia's population at the time was already overwhelmingly self-identified in ethnic terms: 40 percent Muslim, 32 percent Serb and 18 percent Croat. The Muslim-based Democratic Action Party (SDA) received 41.2 percent of the vote, the Serbian Democratic Party (SDS) 34.5 percent, and the Croatian Democratic Union (HDZ) 20.7 percent. See John B. Allcock, "Yugoslavia," in Bogdan Szajkowski, ed., *New Political Parties of Eastern Europe and the Soviet Union* (Harlow: Longman, 1992).

71. For the collective Presidency, Muslim candidates Fikret Abdic and Alija Izetbegovic obtained 44 percent and 37 percent of the vote, respectively; Serbs Nikola Koljevic and Biljana Plavsic, 25 percent and 24 percent; and Croats Stjepan Kljuic and Franjo Boras, 21 percent and 19 percent. Ejup Ganic was elected to represent all other ethnic communities. See Allcock, "Yugoslavia," op. cit.

72. See "The Dayton Bosnia Peace Agreement," *http://www.oscebih.org/documents/docs.htm*.

73. The constitution's wording is confusing at times, reflecting the highly unwieldy state structure envisaged. Thus, the "Federation of Bosnia and Herzegovina" is the territory jointly inhabited by the Muslim and Croat communities and the *Republika Srpska*. The Federation and the "*Republika Srpska*" are "entities," and it is the aggregation of both that creates "The Republic of Bosnia and Herzegovina."

74. The Bosnian electoral law can be found at *http://www.oscebih.org/documents/docs.htm*. For the results of the 1998 presidential and parliamentary elections, see *http://www.oscebih.org/98results/el98-results.htm*.

75. A factor clearly affecting the way this axiom operates is when an ethnic minority's political relevance derives from inter-state relations, in which case the quality of these relations, and the power and incentives represented by the neighboring state, may be determinative of the treatment the minority receives. At one pole, this certainly appears to be the case with Slovenia's generous provisions for its Italian minority, while the other pole may be represented by the hostile treatment by Slovakia of its much larger Hungarian minority (although primarily only at the level of linguistic rights and cultural provision) until Vladimír Meciar's government lost power in 1998.

76. Arend Lijphart, "Self-Determination versus Pre-Determination of Ethnic Minorities in Power-Sharing Systems," in David Schneiderman, ed., *Language and the State: The Law and Politics of Identity* (Montreal: Les Editions Yvon Blais, 1991), pp. 153-65. Reprinted in Kymlicka, *The Rights of Minority Cultures*, pp. 275-87.

77. Edith Oltay, "Hungary Passes Law on Minority Rights," *RFE/RL Research Report*, vol. 2,

no. 33 (August 20, 1993), pp. 57-61. It should also be noted that the absence of guaranteed representation has not prevented the Hungarian National Assembly from being a rather ethnically diverse body. During the first parliament (1990-1994), the parties represented in the Assembly contained eight ethnic Germans, two Roma, one Jew, one Armenian, one Pole, one Slovak, and one Croat, with the Alliance of Free Democrats being by far the most ethnically diverse of the parliamentary factions. See Benoît-Rohmer and Hardeman, "The Representation of Minorities," p. 110.

78. *The Virginia Declaration of Rights*, Sec. 3.

3

NATIONALIST MAJORITY PARTIES: THE ANATOMY OF ETHNIC DOMINATION IN CENTRAL AND EASTERN EUROPE

Janusz Bugajski

The emergence of political pluralism in eastern Europe has also heralded the rebirth of ultra-nationalism. Although its exponents have differed in their origins, programs, social bases, and impact on political developments in the region, they have also shared certain fundamental characteristics. These include the centrality of the notion of the state as an ethnically-based unit, a suspicion of democratic institutions and of unbridled freedom of expression, a preference for administrative unitarism and centralism, and maintenance of a high degree of state intervention in the economy in order to regulate the ethnic composition of control over production and distribution. In its most extreme or developed forms, ultra-nationalism resembles fascism, marked by a xenophobic disdain of other nations, support for authoritarian political arrangements verging on totalitarianism, and a mystical emphasis on the "organic unity" between a charismatic leader, an organizationally amorphous movement-type party, and the nation.[1]

It is useful to distinguish at the outset between tolerant nationalism and conflictive or ultra-nationalism. In its broadest sense, nationalism may be positive or negative, defensive or aggressive, and future-oriented or backward-looking. It may contain both rational and irrational elements, be internally consistent or contradictory, and be prone to cycles of intensity and passivity.[2] On the positive side, nationalism, or more precisely, "patriotism," may be a cohesive and motivating force in asserting a group's identity and regaining elements of sovereignty or statehood.[3] It may foster pride in a shared history, instill a sense of communal loyalty, and mobilize societies for a common purpose in reconstruction and development. During traumatic periods of rapid change, national identity, with all its symbolic, ritualistic, and cultural attributes, provides an anchor of stability and predictability.[4] Nationalism is a collectivist ideology insofar as it legitimates the pursuit of group interests, but it is not necessarily xenophobic or reactionary. Indeed, during the nineteenth century, it was advocated by leading intellectuals to undermine autocratic states and was closely linked with political and economic liberalism.

Nationalism becomes a negative force when, by strictly defining the boundaries of a community, it generates a pronounced anti-liberal and ethnocentric bias, asserting the superiority of one group's culture, language, and religion while denigrating outsiders as inferior and contemptible. In such cases, nationalist leaders, in seeking to forge a single political unit, deliberately define and exclude alien elements, operating on the axiom that a perceived foreign or domestic threat is necessary to provide the sense of cohesiveness that unites a "people." The persecution of minorities by newly independent nations may also be a form of aggressive compensation for their own prior subjugation, whether at the hands of leaders of current domestic minorities or foreign elites. In either case, the political style of this brand of nationalism typically emphasizes fears of domination, absorption, or extinction, and thrives on the social psychology of victimization and the blaming of "others" as culprits—whether these are minorities or neighboring majorities.[5]

Yet the appeal of ultra-nationalism is also in many cases *residual*, particularly in territorially well-established states where more moderate variants or alternative ideologies fail to generate sufficiently strong feelings of loyalty and enthusiasm. Here, ultra-nationalists typically employ anti-communism to attack their opponents, particularly liberals, social democrats, and ethnic minority parties, with the communist label used loosely to imply that Jews, minorities, and foreign powers are manipulating the political system. Furthermore, ultra-nationalist parties are in these cases often protest parties, benefiting from widespread anger and frustration with political inefficacy and economic dislocation; hence, their popular constituencies invariably include disaffected youths and economically vulnerable workers.[6] They are also more likely to gain a foothold within states, whether old or new, that contain large and potentially more threatening minorities, especially where the ethnic cleavage structures competition for scarce resources, and where cultural or religious differences are exacerbated by deep-rooted historical grievances. In such circumstances, numerous issues can provoke hostility and confrontation, including questions of language, education, and cultural policy, immigrant versus native status, and the allocation of political power, status, and material assets.[7]

Several factors determine whether democratization or the loosening of authoritarian political controls temper or aggravate ethnic conflicts and engender xenophobic parties. These include the speed at which ethnic issues are recognized as important, the size and strength of ethnic groups, the ethnic composition of the previous regime and its opponents, the policies of leaders of the main ethnic groups, and the presence or absence of external ethnic allies.[8] While it may be true that, as a result of the history of nationalism in the region, "every nation in central and eastern Europe is beset by a deep fear about its survival,"[9] it seems equally clear that many of these variables are strongly affected by widespread disorientation resulting from the sheer severity of post-communist social and economic disruption. If economic reforms fail to bring rapid and visible benefits to sizable segments of the populace, ultra-nationalists, even if they do not come to power, can exploit popular frustrations and apply pressure on fragile governments through both parliamentary and extra-institutional means.[10]

The communist past, no less than the turbulent present, has also conditioned these variables by inuring citizens to forms of political intercourse that prescribe simplistic solutions to complex problems and clear-cut contrasts between correct and incorrect policies. In such circumstances, social and political interactions have been highly vulnerable to polarization, with irreconcilable ethnic foes supplanting class enemies in a political cosmology which itself owes much to the key elite actors drawn to nationalist politics: provincial intellectuals, especially historians and writers who previously propagated communist ideology, local *apparatchiks* with little to gain from the separation of politics and economics, and state enterprise managers whose interest in securing ownership or continued subsidies (or both) can be justified in terms of national interests.[11] Moreover, for much of the region, habituation to a polity that subordinates ethnicity to citizenship has been impeded by authoritarian traditions of more ancient provenance, revived by reactionary forces whose cultural affinity for ascriptive hierarchies and hostility toward political pluralism cannot be regarded as being merely instrumental to the pursuit of material gain.

Given this mix of structural conditions, social actors, and cultural impulses, the nationalist organizations that have emerged among the majority nations of central and eastern Europe have taken on various hues. Some are fairly obvious proxies for the disempowered communist apparatus, while others have been created by former anti-communist nationalist dissidents. Whatever the case, their focus on national and ethnic questions has typically preempted the articulation of clear socioeconomic programs and stable forms of political contestation.[12] Where nationalist majority parties have come to power, a more or less *ad hoc* and even romantic approach to economic matters is apparent, with successes credited to the unique qualities of the nation and its "pro-national" leaders, and setbacks blamed on the conspiratorial machinations of "international capital" and its domestic allies. Yet, to the extent that a traditional, left-right political spectrum determined by socio-economic ideologies has been cross-cut by national cleavages, this merely serves to indicate processes of change and development that are more fundamental than either democratization or economic reform.

To understand the scope and significance of nationalist politics in post-communist Europe, this chapter will examine the origins, structure, leadership, goals, constituencies, governmental representation and influence on official policies of the most significant nationalist majority parties in a cross-section of states. The assessment will focus on six countries where nationalist parties and organizations have played an important role in gaining state independence, fueling conflicts with domestic ethnic minorities, and/or exacerbating tensions with neighboring states: Slovakia, Romania, Bulgaria, Croatia, Macedonia, and Albania.

Slovakia

Following the Czechoslovak "velvet revolution" in November 1989, federal authorities were soon confronted by the reemergence of Slovak aspirations for national autonomy.[13] The leaders of the civic-oriented Public Against Violence (VPN) in Slovakia and its Czech counterpart, Civic Forum, initially believed that democratization and decentralization would prove sufficient to hold the federation together. Instead, the lifting of communist political controls allowed autonomist and separatist forces to gain ground in Slovakia and sparked competition among the new Slovak parties that focused principally on the symbolic politics of national emancipation and the constitutional implications of a formal declaration of sovereignty.[14]

The most successful pro-autonomy grouping, the Movement for a Democratic Slovakia (HZDS), split off from the pro-federalist VPN in March 1991. Led by Vladimír Mečiar, who was removed as the republic's prime minister the following month by the pro-federal leadership of the Slovak National Council, the HZDS program ranked Slovak national concerns above all other issues. The party adopted an increasingly anti-federal position, cognizant of the popular appeal of Slovak autonomy and competition from other, more radical nationalist groups. By March 1992, Mečiar's party had become the strongest political force in Slovakia with an estimated 40 percent support in public opinion polls. The HZDS program called for immediate declaration of Slovak sovereignty and the adoption of a Slovak constitution, yet also supported creating a confederation with the Czech Republic, a vague but shrewd recipe given that opinion polls also indicated that a majority of Slovaks favored preserving a common state with the Czechs. Support for the HZDS was highest in the industrialized areas of western and central Slovakia, where Mečiar's national-populist program gained the backing of state enterprise managers and workers threatened by economic rationalization. His evident anti-Hungarian stance and opposition to autonomy for the Hungarian minority concentrated in southern Slovakia also allowed him to find a *modus vivendi* with more radical ultra-nationalist elements.

The HZDS captured 37.26 percent of the vote in the June 1992 elections and missed winning an absolute majority in the Slovak National Council by only two seats, gaining 74 of 150 mandates. Mečiar's victory led to Slovak independence by default following failed negotiations with the adamantly pro-federal Czech prime minister, Václav Klaus, in the summer of 1992, and a timetable for separation was agreed. Slovakia formally attained independence on January 1, 1993, with Mečiar at the head of a minority government and HZDS member Michal Kováč installed as president by the National Council the following month.[15] Mečiar and the HZDS have remained the strongest political force in Slovakia, winning a new four-year term in October 1994 in early elections precipitated by the collapse of his first post-independence government the previous March. Significantly, he had lost the support of virtually all HZDS co-founders, including President Kováč, who had hoped to maintain a liberal course of development following a loosening of relations with the Czechs. This led to the HZDS's radicalization, with Mečiar forming a "red-brown" coalition government with two small extremist parties, the far left Association of Slovak Workers (ZRS), and the neo-fascist Slovak National Party (SNS), and creating a politically loyal economic elite through control of privatization and offers of sector- and firm-specific benefits. Yet his government's increasingly authoritarian policies toward domestic opponents in general and the Hungarian minority in particular generated mounting international condemnation, leading to NATO's decision in 1997 to exclude Slovakia from its eastward expansion and the European Union's decision the same year to postpone accession negotiations.[16] Although the government parties were soundly defeated by a strongly "pro-European" grand coalition in the September 1998 elections, with the EU in December 1999 inviting Slovakia to begin accession negotiations, the new administration was forced to impose economic austerity measures. While this was unavoidable given the fiscal irresponsibility and lack of microeconomic restructuring under the Mečiar government, it has also maintained the HZDS as the country's single most popular party with around 25 percent support.

The second largest Slovak party that veered toward national separatism, the Christian Democratic Movement (KDH), was founded in February 1990 by Ján Čarnogurský, a former dissident who was released from prison during the revolution. The KDH quickly developed into the VPN's strongest competitor, emerging from the June 1990 elections as the second most popular Slovak party. It joined the ruling federal coalition with the Civic Forum and the VPN and supported the adoption of a constitutional amendment in December 1990 that ceded many of the federation's powers to the two republics. The KDH initially supported preserving the federation, but wished to base it on an inter-republican treaty, likewise raising the issue of sovereignty. Despite its official support for preserving the federation, the KDH allied itself with Slovak nationalist parties in the Federal Assembly in vetoing propositions for a referendum on the country's future constitutional setup. Indeed, Čarnogurský proclaimed his ultimate goal to be the gradual dissolution of Czechoslovakia.

Drawing explicitly on the tradition of the inter-war Catholic populist leader Andrej Hlinka, the KDH began to adopt a more nationalist orientation, advocating a Czechoslovak confederation and a "sovereign and equal" Slovakia. The KDH's growing image as a defender of Slovak rights was reflected in its increasing popularity. After recasting its program in a more nationalist fashion, it became the strongest political force at the local level, gaining 27.5 percent of the vote in local elections in November 1990. Following the VPN split in March 1991, the KDH became the strongest political force in the Slovak National Council, holding 31 seats. However, the KDH's support for Mečiar's removal as republic prime minister, and the dilution of its confederationist stance under pressure from its federalist coalition partners, greatly diminished the KDH's popularity.

Internal factionalization within the KDH became evident by early 1992. With the party leadership supporting the Czech and Slovak federalist parties' push for de-communization, a policy that was in part aimed explicitly at thwarting Mečiar and the HZDS, the Slovak Christian Democratic Movement (SKDH) emerged as an overtly separatist wing, and formally split off in March 1992. Led by Ján Klepáč, deputy chairman of the Slovak

National Council, the SKDH attracted four members of the Slovak government, 11 KDH deputies in the Slovak National Council, and five of the KDH's 25 Federal Assembly deputies. However, the new party failed to distinguish itself from the plethora of other small nationalist parties and, lacking the HZDS's strong base among the old communist *nomenklatura,* attracted only 3 percent of the vote in the June 1992 elections, fading from the political scene following a similarly poor showing in 1994.[17]

The KDH itself fared poorly in the June 1992 elections, receiving only 8.88 percent of the vote, less than half its total in 1990, and gaining just 18 seats in the Slovak National Council. Distrustful of the HZDS's commitment to democracy, its parliamentary deputies voted against ratification of the Slovak constitution in September 1992. Indeed, while it has maintained a deeply conservative Catholic and pan-Slav orientation, it has remained steadfast in its defense of political democracy, opening its candidate list to a small civic liberal party in the 1994 elections, opposing the Mečiar government's draconian anti-Hungarian language law in November 1995, and playing a key role in forging the broad coalition of democratic opposition parties that defeated the HZDS in 1998.

The most radical nationalist organization, the Slovak National Party (SNS), was established in February 1990. During early 1990, public support for the SNS climbed significantly. By late spring, it was polling 20 percent, although the party gained a more modest 14 percent of the vote in the first free elections in June 1990, finishing third in the elections to the Slovak National Council with 22 seats, while gaining 15 seats in the Federal Assembly. However, its popularity then dropped substantially by the November 1990 local elections, in which it received only 3 percent of the vote. This decline appeared to be the result of internal conflicts and competition with other nationalist groups, particularly as the KDH, the Party of the Democratic Left (former Communists), and VPN deputies who supported Mečiar began to adopt nationalist positions.

The SNS organized street protests in support of immediate independence and against alleged Czech domination and Hungarian subversion. Contending that all national minorities in Slovakia had to respect the sovereignty of the Slovak nation, it supported stripping the Hungarian minority of language rights at a time when even Mečiar was reluctant to go this far. While the KDH identified with the conservative Catholic corporatism of the inter-war Slovak autonomy movement, the SNS explicitly endorsed the full-fledged clerico-fascist regime of the Nazi-allied wartime Slovak puppet state, and openly advocated the rehabilitation of its president, Jozef Tiso, who was executed for war crimes in 1947. The SNS supported the declaration of Slovak sovereignty that had been pushed unsuccessfully by nationalist groups in March 1991, and obtained 7.93 percent of the popular vote and 15 Slovak National Council seats in the June 1992 general elections. Its center of support was in Bratislava, where its share of the vote was 17 percent, and in some ethnically mixed southern and western districts. Following independence, the SNS split into moderate and ultra-nationalist factions, with the moderates abandoning the party and uniting with the breakaway HZDS factions. Under the leadership of the militant Ján Slota, the rump SNS, backed by remnants of the SKDH, has since 1994 become completely dependent on its alliance with the HZDS for retaining political influence.[18]

Slovak nationalists also revived *Matica slovenská* (Slovak Motherland), a national-cultural association whose origins date back to the years of Hungarian occupation under the Hapsburg Empire, and whose mission was to preserve Slovak culture against increasing Magyarization.[19] By the end of 1992, *Matica slovenská* had significantly expanded its membership and influence. In August 1992, its General Assembly elected Jozef Markuš as chairman and issued a program calling for Slovak independence. It claimed to have 400 local branches, a membership of some 140,000, and over 600,000 sympathizers. The association, reported to have extensive influence among the nationalist Slovak intelligentsia, emphasized the importance of strengthening Slovak culture and education, and established extensive publishing ventures. *Matica slovenská*'s program focused on "deformations" in Slovak education caused by decades of communist and Czech influence. It would therefore strive to rebuild the educational system and cultural life in a "national spirit" and cooperate closely with all relevant government organs.

As a programmatic corollary, *Matica slovenská* campaigned against Slovak "denationalization," clearly alluding to demands by Hungarians for more extensive collective rights. Working with the SNS in 1990, *Matica slovenská* drafted a version of a new language law that made Slovak the country's exclusive language in all administrative affairs and public communications. In April 1993, *Matica slovenská* issued a statement claiming that Slovak language, culture, and identity were dying out in southern Slovakia as a result of Hungarian activism. It accused ethnic Hungarian political parties of creating an atmosphere of "national, cultural, and existential insecurity" in mixed areas and opposed all efforts at local autonomy in Hungarian areas as a violation of the "cultural and territorial integrity" of the republic. It proposed to the National Council that the law on local self-government be amended; ethnic Slovaks evidently had to be ensconced in all leading positions in public administration to eliminate opportunities for Hungarian discrimination. Having obtained a high level of state funding as well as strong support from Slovak emigrés, *Matica slovenská* has remained at the forefront of Slovak nationalism, providing the ideological and conceptual underpinnings for virtually all anti-minority measures.

Indeed, the constitutional preamble's proclamation that the state's establishment represented the will of "We, the Slovak nation" had been a staple of earlier drafts produced by *Matica slovenská*. Ethnic Hungarian members of the Slovak National Council unanimously opposed the constitution's ratification in September 1992, arguing that it failed to guarantee the identity and self-government of minorities or allow for the creation of territorial "self-administrative" entities that would satisfy Hungarian aspirations for cultural autonomy. Indeed, the constitution explicitly declared that the rights of ethnic minorities could not endanger Slovak sovereignty and territorial integrity, a provision that was viewed by Hungarians as particularly vulnerable to abuse. Similarly, they pointed out that only "national organizations" could be formed by ethnic minorities, a provision that could potentially be construed to enable the dissolution of ethnic minority parties. Hungarian deputies unsuccessfully proposed a constitutional amendment to guarantee the right to develop one's national, ethnic, linguistic, or cultural identity, while banning any activities that lead to assimilation.[20]

Hungarian leaders also claimed that the constitution offered no legal guarantees for the use of minority languages in dealing with the authorities. Language rights had initially been defined by the language law enacted by the Slovak National Council in October 1990, which represented a compromise between ethnic Hungarian leaders and *Matica slovenská*.[21] The law declared Slovak the official language of the Slovak Republic while entitling members of an ethnic minority that constituted 20 percent of the population in an administrative district to use their language in official proceedings. There was, however, no stipulation requiring state officials to be proficient in minority languages. The application of the law also resulted in Hungarian names no longer being registered in birth registers, invalidated moves toward restoring Hungarian appellations for municipalities, and abolished bilingual street signs. It also permitted officials to refuse to conduct marriage and funeral services in Hungarian.

Following Slovakia's admission to the Council of Europe in June 1993, Bratislava came under international pressure to alter some of its minority rights legislation.[22] In May 1994, the interim administration formed by a broad opposition coalition after the fall of Mečiar's government sought to expand minority language rights to include bilingual signs and registration of Hungarian birth names. It also attempted to amend the existing legislation on Slovakia's administrative set-up, which Hungarian organizations feared would "minoritize" the Magyar population in five new districts. Both measures were sharply condemned by *Matica slovenská* along with other nationalist groups and were subsequently rejected as the HZDS, the SNS, and a few nationalist deputies within the coalition parties voted against them.[23] Moreover, while a long-delayed bill permitting bilingual road signs in towns where ethnic Hungarians comprise at least 20 percent of the population was adopted in July 1994, all of the provisions governing the use of minority languages were replaced by the 1995 law—initiated by the SNS—after the HZDS returned to power. While its enforcement was sporadic at best, the new law made Slovak the only permissible language in all official proceedings, as well as in many other spheres of daily life. Despite pledges to the Council of Europe and the Organization for Security and Cooperation in Europe, a supplementary law on minority languages—also mandated by the constitution—was not adopted until 1999, after the new government, which includes the main Hungarian party, assumed power.[24]

Romania

Since early 1990, a host of ultra-nationalist organizations have been established in Romania. Some were a continuation of the "national communist" orientation of the Ceausescu regime, while others were new incarnations of pre-war and wartime fascist movements drawing support from sections of the population disillusioned with economic reform and seeking a strong authoritarian government. As in Slovakia, an alliance between these two tendencies developed in the first post-communist years as the centrist and civic-oriented alternatives failed to establish firm support among Romanian voters. And, like Slovakia, nationalist majority parties lost influence or were swept directly from power following a critical "re-democratizing" election, the country's most recent, in November 1996, with the country's main ethnic minority-based party, the Hungarian Democratic Federation of Romania (UDMR) joining the government.[25]

One of the most significant nationalist groupings, the Party of Romanian National Unity (PUNR), was established shortly before the May 1990 elections with evident links to the communist *nomenklatura*. The PUNR claims to represent the interests of the ethnic Romanian population in

Transylvania and is decidedly anti-Hungarian in its orientation. Thus, the party has opposed all efforts at establishing administrative-territorial enclaves in the region, and PUNR leaders have persistently advocated the reunification of the country within its historical boundaries and called for a renewal of the "spiritual unity" of Romanians.

The PUNR captured 4.9 percent of the vote and gained 16 mayorships in the February 1992 local elections, as compared to 2.12 percent in the May 1990 parliamentary elections. The leading institutional actor of the transition, President Ion Iliescu's National Salvation Front (FSN), which itself had deep roots in the Ceausescu regime, formed electoral coalitions with the PUNR in several Transylvanian counties. Most notably, the PUNR won control of the large Transylvanian city of Cluj-Napoca, where ethnic Hungarians constitute about 25 percent of the population, with party leader Gheorghe Funar becoming mayor. In the September 1992 parliamentary elections, the PUNR captured 7.71 percent of the popular vote and received 30 lower house seats and 14 senate seats, indicating a dangerous swing toward ultra-nationalism among a significant portion of the Romanian population.[26]

The Greater Romania Party (PRM) was established in May 1991 by a group of journalists writing for *Romania Mare*, a popular nationalist magazine founded in June 1990. The PRM's leaders included the magazine's chief editor, Corneliu Vadim Tudor, who is believed to have links with the Ceausescu regime's secret police, the Securitate. The PRM is a strictly hierarchical organization, in many ways resembling the defunct Romanian Communist Party, and is widely viewed as the most nationalistic and chauvinistic political group in Romania. At the outset, the party claimed that Romania's national unity and sovereignty were threatened internally and externally, and it denounced the FSN government for its inability to combat the danger.[27] In the September 1992 elections, the PRM captured 3.8 percent of the vote, gaining 16 deputies to the lower house of parliament and six senators. The PRM disseminated propaganda asserting that the Hungarian minority was plotting to dismember Romania, and at the party's first congress in March 1993, Tudor demanded a crackdown on the UDMR. Tudor has also praised Ceausescu for being a Romanian patriot and described the 1989 revolution as an "armed attack" against the country by Hungary and the former Soviet Union.

The Socialist Labor Party (PSM) was formed in November 1990 and drew its support from former Ceausescu loyalists with strong nationalist orientations. Indeed, the party is viewed as the legal successor to the defunct Romanian Communist Party. The PSM garnered 3.03 percent of the vote in the September 1992 parliamentary elections and gained 13 seats in the Chamber of Deputies and five senate seats. Together with the PUNR and the PRM, the PSM assured the government, led by the main formation to emerge from the FSN, Iliescu's Party of Social Democracy in Romania (PDSR), of a parliamentary majority after the 1992 elections. The PDSR initially tried to keep them at arm's length so as not to appear overtly nation- alistic, denying them positions in the cabinet while avoiding early elections lest they exploit popular dissatisfaction with economic conditions to score significant gains. In particular, the authorities tried to keep the largest na- tionalist group, the PUNR, confined to Transylvania, where it remained tied to a local Romanian elite fearful of Magyar encroachment on its privileges. Nevertheless, while Bucharest increasingly feared that Funar was building an independent national power structure out of Bucharest's reach, the PUNR, followed by the PRM and the PSM, began rotating through the government itself in various combinations from August 1994 until August 1996.[28]

Smaller groups include the radical rightist Movement for Romania, created in December 1991 by Marian Munteanu, a former leader of the Bucharest University Students' League who gained renown for his opposition to Iliescu's FSN government. Munteanu cast himself as the champion of the "New Generation" betrayed by developments since the 1989 revolution, and he attacked other nationalist groups for their ties to the communist past. In its program, the Movement praised Christian mysticism and collectivism, while criticizing liberalism and social democracy for contradicting the "cultural and spiritual nature" of the Romanian people. It avowed the linguistic, cultural, and religious unity of the Romanian nation and its superiority among European peoples, and advocated cooperation with other Orthodox Christian countries and with Romanian emigrés willing to defend the country's national interests. The Movement issued its own publications, set up a "Veterans Corps," and reportedly received funds from Romanian neo-fascists in the West.[29] In fact, in addition to its ideological links to the pre- war Fascist organization, the Romanian Legionary Movement (or Iron Guard), the Movement's internal structure—no elected leadership and enforced consensus based on discipline and obedience—replicated the Legionnaire cell organizations. However, the Movement withered after May 1993, when government officials condemned the revival of the "Legionary phenomenon" in Romania and singled out Munteanu's group as the prime culprit.

The New Christian Romania Party, founded in May 1992 as an openly neo-Fascist organization, similarly viewed itself as a continuation of the

Iron Guard. It claimed several hundred members and revered the Iron Guard's leader, Corneliu Codreanu, as a national hero deserving of sainthood. The party staged several public meetings in Bucharest, seeking to bridge the gap between older fascists and a younger generation of activists disillusioned with post-Ceausescu developments. The Bucharest Municipal Court was sharply criticized by democratic parties for allowing the NCRP to organize, as it allegedly contradicted constitutional provisions banning the formation of extremist political groups. Yet several similar ultra-rightist groupings have operated during the past few years. Like the parties and groups described here, many were believed to have close ties with former *Securitate* agents and Ceausescu loyalists seeking to benefit from populist, nationalist, and xenophobic sentiments among broad segments of the Romanian population.[30]

Finally, bearing a certain organizational resemblance to Slovakia's *Matica slovenská*, *Vatra Romaneasca* (Romanian Cradle) was established in February 1990 with Radu Ceontea as its elected chairman and Iosif Constantin Dragan, a former Iron Guardist who financed numerous extremist activities, made honorary president at *Vatra's* second national conference in June 1991. Like *Matica slovenská*, *Vatra Romaneasca* defined itself as a "socio-cultural and civic organization" with no ambitions of becoming a political party, claiming a membership of four million by early 1992. Nevertheless, again like *Matica slovenská*, it coordinated its efforts with nationalist parties, in this case primarily the PUNR, calling Romanian nationalism the necessary response of a small country "under pressure from a united Europe, an internationalized world, and the dilution of national culture."

Unlike *Matica slovenská*, however, the very establishment of *Vatra Romaneasca* was an avowed response to that of the UDMR, which it considered to be "a communist successor party" and a threat to Romanian unity. *Vatra Romaneasca* leaders asserted that ethnic Hungarians should have no special rights in Transylvania, claiming that they currently enjoyed a privileged position. *Vatra Romaneasca's* nationalist ideas allegedly influenced the judicial system in the area, and the PUNR and *Vatra* also reportedly benefited from high-level military support, especially from the Romanian Third Army based in Transylvania. During the 1992 election campaign, *Vatra Romanaesca* representatives regularly visited military bases, and films produced by it were shown to recruits. As a result, PUNR candidates obtained a high share of votes on military bases throughout Transylvania.

Developments generated by the rapid emergence of these groups represented a sharp deterioration vis-à-vis an initial revolutionary phase marked by cooperative efforts between Romanian and Hungarian activists. Various repressive policies were abandoned by the NSF government, the Hungarian population was legally permitted to establish its own political organizations, and far-reaching concessions were granted in cultural and educational affairs. But relations between the new administration and the Hungarian minority began to worsen in the first months of 1990. Hungarian spokesmen charged that the anti-Ceausescu revolution had been hijacked by neo-communists who were thwarting the emergence of a democratic system, and President Iliescu was quickly accused of tolerating extremist anti-Hungarian nationalist forces in Transylvania in order to mobilize and shore up popular support. Hungarian leaders also charged that the authorities undertook a systematic campaign to place NSF loyalists throughout public institutions, including local government, schools, and the legal system, and to eliminate ethnic Hungarians from influential positions.[31] In what was viewed as a further provocation by Hungarian leaders, in March 1993 Bucharest announced the appointment of two ethnic Romanian prefects in the Magyar-majority counties of Harghita and Covasna. Vlad Adrian Casuneanu, the Covasna prefect, admitted to being a member of *Vatra Romaneasca*, leading to vehement protests by local Hungarians. Observers believed that the government had acceded to the demands of nationalists in the appointment of Romanian prefects, in return for their continuing parliamentary support.

In these circumstances, Hungarian leaders quickly began insisting on the introduction of a new law on national minorities to regulate the legal status of minority groups. Although the position of minorities had improved substantially after the revolution, many of the gains were considered reversible because they lacked firm legal safeguards. In November 1991, a new constitution was adopted by a two-thirds parliamentary majority prior to its submission for public approval. Hungarian deputies voted against the proposed text, arguing that the constitution did not mention the rights of national minorities, but simply provided an exhaustive list of prohibitions. For example, at any administrative level, members of a national minority could not use their mother tongue, even if they formed an overwhelming local majority. And, while the constitution did not prohibit Hungarian-language education, nor did it specify the degree to which such education was allowed.

As in Slovakia, ethnic Hungarian leaders were chary of leaving these determinations to statutory law given constitutional articles that defined the country as a "unitary national state" with prohibitions on activities deemed to be "separatist," and feared that such provisions could also provide a constitutional underpinning for a future ban on ethnic-based parties. Indeed, aside from widespread opposition among Romanian parties to any notion of Hungarian autonomy, whether cultural or territorial, the threat of a ban on minority-based political organizations has been a recurrent one, appearing most recently in April 1996.[32]

Given his power base in Transylvania's ethnic Hungarian metropole, Funar has contributed most to escalating ethnic tensions. He has enacted various restrictions on the Hungarian minority, including bans on bilingual shop signs and street names, and prohibitions on freedom of assembly and bans on cultural and educational activities. In June 1994, he caused a furor by initiating archeological excavations in the center of Cluj around the statue of the Magyar King Mathias in order to "prove" Romanians' historical claim to the city. Hungarian leaders viewed this as a political provocation, consistent with Furar's threat to erase Cluj's Hungarian heritage. According to some critics, the PUNR was deliberately stirring ethnic tensions in Transylvania because its popular support had slipped, and it wanted to quash the planned treaty between Budapest and Bucharest. Thus, it sought to elicit a strong Hungarian reaction, re-ignite tensions, and revive support for the nationalists.[33] Indeed, while the opposition-led government that took power with UDMR participation in November 1996 has marginalized most of the ultra-nationalist groups, Funar and the PUNR remained in control of Cluj, ensuring that efforts directed toward easing ethnic relations remained troubled.[34]

Bulgaria

The Committee for the Defense of National Interests has been the most active Bulgarian nationalist group since the onset of democratization, serving as an umbrella organization for several nationalist parties and claiming some 40,000 members. Under the chairmanship of parliamentary deputy Dimitar Arnaudov, its main goals were to protect the "territorial integrity" and "ethnic space" of Bulgaria by including all "patriotic Bulgarians," regardless of their political orientation. To achieve this objective, the Committee attacked the agendas of any organization viewed as threatening the integrity of the Bulgarian state. Its principal target was the Movement for Rights and Freedoms (DPS), the largest organization representing ethnic Turkish interests. The Committee challenged the DPS's right to participate in the political process, claiming that the group harbored separatist intentions. In July 1990, the Committee planned several strikes in the Kurdzhali region of southeastern Bulgaria, where Turks comprised over 70 percent of the population at the time and where the Committee claimed to have a strong base. The protests were directed against the awarding of parliamentary seats gained by the DPS and the introduction of Turkish-language schooling.

Bulgarian nationalist forces attempted to benefit from difficult economic conditions and political uncertainty. In November 1990, as the Socialist government faced massive social unrest and mounting political opposition, nationalist groups in the Razgrad area in northeastern Bulgaria, inhabited by large numbers of Turks, declared an "independent Bulgarian republic." They refused to recognize Sofia's authority in the region because the government had purportedly displayed too much leniency toward the Turks. Protests were staged against the restoration of Turkish family names, and nationalist leaders called for acts of civil disobedience to counter alleged Turkish radicalism. The Committee and other groups opposed giving Turks national minority status, as this would have allegedly threatened the state's integrity. The Razgrad Republic was renamed the Association of Free Bulgarian Cities, linking several towns containing large Turkish minorities. A civil parliament was to be formed to counterbalance the National Assembly, which the Committee accused of betraying Bulgaria's national interests. In recognition of mounting tensions fueled by the nationalist initiative, Bulgaria's president, Zhelu Zhelev, appeared on national television to appeal for calm. Following his intervention, the Free Cities campaign subsided.

Suspicions persisted that the Committee and other radical national associations were created, supported, and financed by local activists of the post-communist Bulgarian Socialist Party (BSP), whose legal predecessor had orchestrated a brutal assimilation campaign directed against the Turkish minority from 1984 until 1989. An indication of these cordial ties was the forging of a pre-election alliance in October 1991 between the Socialist Party and five nationalist groupings. Committee delegates then met in February 1992 and voted to dissolve the group, creating instead a new party, the National Democracy Party, which adopted a more moderate agenda focusing mainly on national and social issues. Dimitar Arnaudov, who also served as deputy chairman of the Fatherland Party of Labor, was appointed to chair the new party.[35]

The Fatherland Party of Labor, which included former members of the local communist *nomenklatura,* served as the political wing of the Committee. Party ideologists claimed that Bulgaria contained only one ethnic group and that the Turks were in reality forcibly converted Bulgarians misled by radicals promoting pan-Turkic objectives. In this scenario, Bulgaria stood on the front line against Muslim penetration into Europe. While the Fatherland Party and other ultra-nationalist groupings obtained less than 1.5 percent of the vote in the October 1991 elections to the Grand National Assembly, they claimed to possess an extensive infrastructure and to benefit from substantial sympathy in mixed population areas. Moreover, although they were not a potent political force, with BSP support they could cause a great deal of localized tension and pressure parliamentary deputies to pay heed to their demands.

Some small xenophobic Bulgarian parties have focused their attention on combating other minorities. The Christian Democratic Party led by Orthodox priest Georgi Gelemenov declared "war" on the Roma and sought to provoke conflicts in Plovdiv and other cities by using local skinhead gangs. In December 1993, several Roma groups issued an open letter demanding a ban on all "fascist" parties and organizations, including the Gelemenov group. Roma leaders were also critical of the Bulgarian media for disseminating Gelemonov's views.[36] Bulgarian nationalists have also clustered around irredentist Macedonian organizations, including a resuscitated Internal Macedonian Revolutionary Organization (VMRO), which does not accept the permanent independence of the new Macedonian state. If ethno-political conflicts were to escalate in Macedonia in the wake of the Kosovo conflict, Bulgarian nationalism and irredentism could undergo a significant resurgence and conceivably radicalize domestic politics, especially in the event of Serbian, Greek, or Albanian intervention against Skopje.

Although nationalist parties in Bulgaria failed to instigate widespread communal conflict, their protests and initiatives had some resonance in the legislature and among the population at large. In particular, their campaigns against ethnic Turkish political representation complicated the democratization process. The new Bulgarian constitution provided that "No organization shall act to the detriment of the country's sovereignty and national integrity, or the unity of the nation, nor shall it incite racial, national, ethnic, or religious enmity, while article 11 prohibited the registration of political parties based on 'ethnic, racial, or religious lines.' " While these stipulations avowedly served to protect the Bulgarian state, they were frequently cited by nationalists to undermine the rights of minorities. Nationalist organizations capitalized on widespread ethnic Bulgarian fears of Turkish subversion and applied pressure on government organs to outlaw all ethnic-based associations on the grounds that they were politically motivated and therefore "anti-state."

The main Turkish organization, the Movement for Rights and Freedoms (DPS) was singled out in this regard. In August 1991, the Sofia City Court decided that a political party formed by the DPS was unconstitutional, as it was ethnically based, and could not participate in the upcoming elections. The DPS claimed that it was not founded on ethnic principles and that it harbored no separatist or autonomist ambitions. In September 1991, the Supreme Court banned the Rights and Freedoms Party (the political wing of the DPS) from participation in the general elections on the grounds that it propounded an exclusivist ethnic and religious platform. Nonetheless, the DPS itself and various Turkish cultural and social organizations were not prohibited from functioning, and the DPS competed legally in the second general elections in October 1991.[37]

The absence of a clear-cut official language policy left the question of teaching Turkish as an optional course in elementary schools open to various interpretations. Nationalists held the view that Bulgarian, as the country's official language, should be the only language offered to Bulgarian citizens. Many ethnic Turks felt that Turkish should become part of the Bulgarian school curriculum so that their mother tongue would continue to be used by future generations. When the National Assembly prepared to vote on the issue in February 1991, tensions soared and the Committee for the Defense of National Interests, in conjunction with other nationalist groups, formed a Bulgarian National Union and organized protests in a dozen cities. They declared that Slav Bulgarian parents should keep their children away from school until Turkish was taken off the curriculum. The Union specifically opposed the introduction of optional Turkish-language classes in schools attended by large numbers of Muslims, depicting this as the Turkification of Bulgarian education.

The wave of protests subsided when the National Assembly voted to postpone the introduction of Turkish as an optional subject during the 1991 school year, a move condemned by Turkish leaders as unconstitutional. The beginning of the school year in September 1991 was marred by boycotts led by minority organizations in some Turkish areas. Subsequently, the National Assembly passed laws prohibiting the teaching of minority languages in state schools. This essentially anti-Turkish legislation was proposed by nationalist deputies and drew overwhelming support from the BSP parliamentary majority. However, the new Bulgarian government decreed that ethnic minority pupils in municipal schools could receive instruction in their native languages as an optional subject for a few hours a week, thus resisting nationalist pressures, which were not officially revived when the BSP returned to power in 1994. Indeed, the diminution of the ethnic Turkish population since then as a result of substantial migration to Turkey, coupled with the DPS's consequent need to join an electoral coalition with small ethnic Bulgarian political parties prior to the 1997 election, further undercut the appeal and influence of ultra-nationalism.[38]

Croatia

The Croatian Democratic Community (HDZ) dominated Croatian politics from the run-up to independence in 1991 until January 2000, when, as in Slovakia and Romania, nationalist forces and their ultra-nationalist allies were swept decisively from power by parties (and voters) eager to embrace a "pro-European" profile. Billing itself as the "most Croatian of all parties," the HDZ was established in February 1989 while Yugoslavia was still extant. It presented itself as the singular alternative to the old Yugoslav structure, and its program called for outright national sovereignty. Led by the former Titoist army general and ideologist of the 1971 Croatian nationalist movement, Franjo Tudjman, the HDZ drew support from across the political spectrum, which it was able to translate into an overwhelming victory in the April 1990 elections. Out of 356 seats in the Croatian Assembly, the HDZ gained 206.[39] From the outset, the HDZ claimed nearly half a million members with branches around the country, while much of its organizational apparatus, despite Tudjman's dissident past, was simply appropriated from the League of Communists.

Until early 1991, Tudjman engaged in protracted negotiations within the federal presidency on restructuring relations among the six republics. Zagreb[40] maintained that Croatia and Slovenia were paying the lion's share of the state budget and remained concerned over growing centralizing trends in Belgrade. However, even before the breakdown of negotiations over a new confederal arrangement, Croatia made important strides toward secession. The Tudjman administration began to purge Serb and Yugoslav loyalists from the bureaucracy and security forces, restored Croatia's historical state symbols, and held a plebiscite on independence in May 1991, in which the overwhelming majority of voters opted for sovereignty.

Croatia's second multi-party elections to the lower house of parliament, the Chamber of Deputies, and at the presidential level took place in August 1992. However, they were marred by instances of intimidation, HDZ control over the mass media, irregularities in election procedures, incomplete voter registries, and the fact that elections could not be conducted in Serb-held territories. Tudjman was reelected president for a five-year term with 56.73 percent of the vote. The HDZ maintained its dominant position in the Chamber of Deputies, gaining 85 of 136 seats with 43 percent of the popular vote. In elections held for the upper house in February 1993, the HDZ retained a nearly two-thirds majority, although defeats in certain opposition strongholds, including Split, Rijeka, and Osijek, stripped the party of its aura of invincibility. Nonetheless, the HDZ performed well in municipal elections, particularly in areas directly affected by the war. Because of its broad umbrella nature, the HDZ managed to marginalize or neutralize the more extremist neo-fascist parties, including the Croatian Party of Rights, which openly sought to rehabilitate the wartime fascist (*Ustaša*) state.

However, the HDZ also incorporated ultra-nationalist factions, particularly Herzegovinian Croats, which had an increasingly powerful impact on party and state policy as Tudjman consolidated his control of both.[41] This was already clear following the 1992 general elections with the appearance of a growing rift in the HDZ between a conservative nationalist faction, led by Deputy Prime Minister Vladimir Seks and Defense Minister Gojko Susak, and a more centrist-liberal wing. The latter, led by former Yugoslav president and speaker of the lower house Stipe Mesić, and Josip Manolić, speaker of the upper house, called for the curtailment of party interference in the country's media. Observers believed that the liberal faction would probably attract three times the number of voters as the conservatives. In April 1994 Mesić and Manolić founded the Croatian Independent Democrats (HND), which was joined by 18 parliamentarians, thus briefly threatening the HDZ's majority in the house. The HND charged Tudjman with being an autocrat pandering to ultra-nationalist Herzegovinan Croats who, although outside Croatia's recognized international borders, played an integral role within the party.

Nevertheless, it quickly became clear that the HND, which at the time was the only plausible challenger to confront the HDZ since independence, would not assume a significant role. Its center-left populism, while potentially capable of generating widespread appeal, was quickly devalued by the tainted pasts of Manolić, a former Communist and HDZ security boss, and Mesić, who was implicated in several HDZ privatization scandals.[42] However, in 1997, Mesić and a part of the HND membership joined the Croatian People's Party (HSS), giving him an opportunity to distance himself further from his HDZ past. It was from this position that he was elected president in February 2000 following Tudjman's death in December 1999.

Clearly, the monolithic stature and longevity in power of the HDZ and President Tudjman owed much to the protracted war following the dissolution of the Yugoslav federation, which represented a level of authentic threat to the state's existence and a concomitant need to centralize power that set Croatia apart from the other cases examined here. For precisely this reason, however, it is important to emphasize the causal link between Croatian nationalism and the war itself, especially given the powerful structural and historical conditions that made that link so strong in the Yugoslav case.[43]

When the HDZ was swept into power, it occasioned considerable alarm among the Serb minority and, indeed, the party made little effort to acquire the support of the large Serbian population. On the contrary, as Tudjman and his associates sought to transform nationalist sentiments into electoral backing, they made many inflammatory statements. By 1988, Belgrade's propaganda machine had already begun to focus Serbs' attention on the atrocities of the wartime Croatian Ustaša regime. Thus, when the HDZ reintroduced the traditional checkerboard insignia, the Šakovnica, as Croatia's national emblem, its display was easily depicted as evidence of the revival of the fascist Independent State of Croatia, which was responsible for the murder of several hundred thousand Serbs.[44] The Zagreb authorities simultaneously declared the Latin alphabet to be the country's official script and removed signs bearing the Cyrillic script, an action widely viewed as an unnecessary provocation. Serb leaders also charged that non-Croats were being pressured to abandon their home villages. Many local Serbs, keenly sensitized to the bloody episode of Ustaša rule, perceived these acts to be the first steps in the reintroduction of a Fascist regime.

The political and military insurrection of Serbs in the Krajina region appeared to be fully supported by the Serbian authorities in Belgrade. During 1990, the Yugoslav People's Army, which was increasingly becoming a tool of the Slobodan Milošević's Serbian regime, actively began to support rebel Serbs in Croatia whose leaders were calling for autonomy. Serbia's intervention on behalf of the insurgents caused the authorities in Zagreb to view the Krajina Serbs more as puppets of Serbia than as Croatian citizens with legitimate concerns about their future status. As a result, the Tudjman government was reluctant to engage in serious negotiations and was especially unwilling to discuss the question of territorial autonomy, a concession that Zagreb calculated would fuel "Greater Serbian" irredentist pressures and destabilize the Croatian regime.

The impasse in negotiations, rapid moves toward independence, the deliberate fanning of ethnic divisions by both Belgrade and Zagreb, and active planning by Milošević to truncate Croatian territory led to full-scale conflict. Serbia promptly accused the Croatian government of imposing a state of siege in minority areas. It also charged Zagreb with anti-Serb discrimination and of creating an "ethnocracy" along war-time Ustaša lines. In fact, purges in the old Communist apparatus in Croatia displaced many Serbs who held prominent positions in the defunct system, which Serbian media depicted as a racist design to turn Serbs into second-class Croatian citizens. The Croatian president himself came under severe criticism for concentrating too much power in his hands and for enacting various restrictions in the mass media. Zagreb justified such measures as temporary but essential to preserving unity during a national emergency, especially in the face of mounting pressure and threats from Belgrade.

In February 1991, as the Serb-Croat conflict escalated, the Serb National Council in Knin declared the independence of Krajina from Croatia. The legality of the move was not recognized by Zagreb. During the summer and fall of 1991, Serb insurgents fighting against the poorly armed Croatian National Guard gained control over about a quarter of Croatian territory. By December 1991, over 5,000 deaths were reported in the fighting, countless thousands were injured, and over a quarter of a million refugees fled or were expelled from the conflict zones. With the expiration of the EC-brokered Brioni moratorium, in October 1991 the Croatian parliament restated the republic's independence and negated all federal laws and Yugoslav jurisdiction in Croatia.

In order to obtain diplomatic recognition, the Croatian authorities moved to provide stronger guarantees of minority rights. Certain assurances were contained in Croatia's new constitution, which declared all of Croatia's constituent nationalities as equal, and their members were guaranteed freedom to express their nationality and language. Nonetheless, serious concerns remained that the document was not explicit enough in institutionalizing minority rights and insuring against the domination of political life by ethnic Croats. Serb leaders charged that it was not forthright enough in recognizing the collective rights of the Serb minority. The issue of political or territorial self-determination was not clearly enunciated. Such omissions were condemned by Serb leaders as a deliberate negation of specifically Serb interests and an indication of growing Croatian repression.

In May 1992, the Croatian parliament ratified a Constitutional Law of Human Rights and Freedoms and the Rights of National and Ethnic Communities or Minorities. This legislation institutionalized the special position of minorities, with emphasis on the Croatian Serbs. The objective was to amplify those provisions in the Croatian constitution that dealt with the rights of minorities to cultural autonomy. The Constitutional Law guaranteed a special self-governing status for the Knin and Glina districts, proportional representation for all minority groups that comprised more than 8 percent of the population, and the right to special education in one's own language.[45] The legislation would assign to Serbs almost complete internal governance of the two Krajina districts, including the authority to police, raise taxes, and run local courts, schools, and the media. The system of proportional representation required that Serbs be represented in parliament in numbers commensurate to their share of the population, thus ensuring that Serb deputies would have at least 12 percent of Sabor seats. However, the law was largely irrelevant as long as Serb guerrillas refused to surrender their territories.

President Tudjman repeatedly made it clear that Croatia would not countenance any diminution of its territory. Ultimately, for the government and opposition alike, there could be no peace without the reintegration of the Krajina region. The United Nations Protection Force (UNPROFOR), established by the UN Security Council in January 1992 in four areas of Krajina, stood as a buffer between Croatian and Serb forces, thus preventing Croatia from taking military action to regain these areas. While observers calculated that Zagreb's military position remained too weak to launch any major offensives, the UNPROFOR force proved unable to carry out its mandate of restoring the pre-war demographic structure and compelling Serb militias to disarm. As a result, there was a growing impatience among both the Croatian leadership and the opposition parties over the presence of the UN force, which simply froze Serbian military gains in place. Thus, with no ultimate resolution in sight, the final disposition of the Krajina was ultimately decided when Croatia achieved the capability to assert its sovereignty over the region by military force, driving out virtually the entire Serb population in August 1995.[46]

Zagreb also attempted to manipulate citizenship and naturalization criteria in order to prevent Bosnian refugees from settling permanently in Croatia. A strict immigration policy was instituted: to obtain citizenship an applicant had either to be married to a Croatian citizen, be born within the territory of Croatia, or be a Croatian emigrant. Moreover, applicants were required to prove at least five years of continuously recorded residence, know the Croatian language and Latin alphabet, and demonstrate "that they respected the legal order and customs in the Republic of Croatia."[47] The naturalization process remains lengthy and allows for the possibility that individuals can be rejected on the basis of subjective judgments. These ambiguous criteria have ensured that officials can interpret the policy arbitrarily in order to further the state's ethnic homogenization and in particular to deny citizenship to Serbs. On the other hand, the victory by the Social Democratic Party/Croatian Social Liberal Party (SDP/HSLS) coalition and Mesić's subsequent election as president may prove to be a watershed. The new government has begun cooperating with the International War Crimes Tribunal for the Former Yugoslavia (it had been inconceivable to Tudjman and HDZ governments that Croats could be guilty of war crimes), and the new administration's emphasis on European integration implies significant strengthening of the country's minority rights provisions.

Macedonia

Several nationalist parties demanding Macedonian statehood were established during 1990 in the face of the mounting crisis of the Yugoslav state.[48] The most important of these, the Internal Macedonian Revolutionary Organization — Democratic Party for Macedonian National Unity (VMRO-DMPNE), held its founding congress in June 1990. The party's platform called for a "spiritual, economic, and ethnic union of the divided Macedonian people and the creation of a Macedonian state." Although it renounced the terrorist heritage of the pre-Second World War VMRO, the VMRO-DMPNE leadership pledged to continue its political traditions and called for the recognition of Macedonian ethnic minorities by neighboring states. Although VMRO-DMPNE leaders appeared to depart from the pre-War VMRO's traditional pro-Bulgarian orientation by ostensibly favoring a sovereign Macedonia with no changes to the republican constitution, its critics asserted that the organization was "supremacist" and in the service of "Greater Bulgarianism," while some VMRO factions in fact expressed far more ambitious irredentist objectives, seeking the union of all Macedonian territories in Yugoslavia, Bulgaria, and Greece. VMRO activists also claimed that the territorially compact Albanian minority, which comprises 22.9 percent of the population, was a subversive element in Macedonian society, pointing to Albanian leaders' support of their ethnic kin's pro-independence movement in Kosovo to accuse them of planning to tear away Macedonia's western regions, which would then be annexed to Albania.

VMRO-DMPNE has been led by Ljupco Georgievski since his initial election as chairman in April 1991. In the first multi-party elections in November-December 1990, VMRO-DMPNE gained 37 of the 120 National Assembly seats, surpassing all other parties but remaining unable to form a government on its own. Georgievski became vice-president of Macedonia after the 1990 ballot but resigned in 1991 to indicate his party's dissatisfaction with what it regarded as President Kiro Gligorov's political weakness in negotiations with Greece over the name of an independent Macedonian state, perversely accusing Gligorov of being a Serb agent while VMRO-DMPNE itself adopted a strong pro-Bulgarian position.

After months of bitter dispute, the Kljusev government lost a vote of no-confidence in July 1992 due to its failure to gain widespread international recognition for the state and halt Macedonia's economic decline. A broad-based coalition government took over in September 1992 after VMRO-DMPNE was given the opportunity to form a government but proved unable to elicit sufficient parliamentary support. Branko Crvenkovski, a member of the post-Communist Social Democratic Union of Macedonia (SDSM), eventually assembled a weak coalition with the Reform-Liberal Party (now simply the Liberal Party—LP), and the two ethnic Albanian parties, the Party of Democratic Prosperity (PDP) and the smaller Democratic Party of Albanians (DPA). As a result, the staunchly anti-communist and anti-Albanian VMRO-DMPNE went into opposition.[49]

By the end of 1992, VMRO-DMPNE boasted a membership of some 150,000 people, with branches in every region of the country as well as ten sections abroad among Macedonian exiles. It also established a youth organization. However, because of factional disputes, the number of VMRO-DMPNE seats in parliament was reduced to 35 over the course of 1991-1992. VMRO-DMPNE deputies continued to criticize the government on both national and socio-economic grounds. They claimed that the governing coalition had failed to ensure Macedonia's international recognition and internal security while pursuing an essentially Communist economic agenda. VMRO-DMPNE has also periodically staged nationalist rallies in Skopje and other large cities to mobilize its supporters.

Almost from the outset of the old regime's demise, however, VMRO-DMPNE began splintering into several competing groupings, including the Democratic Party, VMRO-United, and VMRO-Patriotic Party, in addition to several parliamentary factions at odds with the leadership. This substantially weakened the impact of the strongest nationalist tradition in Macedonia. Vladimir Golubovski, who left VMRO-DMPNE as a result of political and personal disputes, founded the most viable breakaway group, the VMRO-Democratic Party, which was formally established in Ohrid in January 1991. With the collapse of Yugoslavia, VMRO-DP adopted a staunchly pro-independence program and attacked the republican government for pursuing "an indulgent policy toward the Albanians." Like VMRO-DMPNE, VMRO-DP has been consistently critical of Albanian activists' persistent demands for autonomy, arguing that any such arrangement would truncate Macedonia and leave the country exposed to renewed foreign domination. As a result, it attained some influence among Slavs in western Macedonia who remain fearful of Albanian militancy, particularly the Albanians' demand that the constitution, which defines Macedonia as a "national state of the Macedonian people," be amended to include the Albanians as a "constitutive" nation. This demand remains unfulfilled, as it is viewed by Macedonian nationalists as a precursor to eventual ethnic federalization.[50] The VMRO-DP, in turn, has been accused of adopting a militant pro-Bulgarian position and of favoring eventual unification with Bulgaria.

Prior to the general elections in November 1990, the Movement for Pan-Macedonian Action (MPMA), VMRO-DMPNE, the Peoples Party, and a number of smaller nationalist organizations formed a Front for Macedonian Unity in order to gain a sizable block of seats in the National Assembly and counter the electoral success of the reform Communists and the ethnic Albanian PDP and DPA. In its program, the loosely organized Front called for a sovereign Macedonia and proposed forging a united platform against the SDSM and the Albanian parties. The MPMA failed to gain seats in the November 1990 elections, receiving barely 3.2 percent of the popular vote. Much of its nationalist appeal was captured by the better-organized VMRO-DMPNE. Nonetheless, the MPMA did gain representation in almost half of the local *opstina* councils. Following the ballot, the MPMA expanded its organization, and by early 1993 it claimed branches in 31 districts, with a membership of 20,000 people, and a bourgeoning youth wing.

VMRO-DMPNE has remained an important force in the Macedonian party system, and its key nationalist assumption, enshrined in the constitution, that the state "belongs" to the ethnic majority, remains politically unassailable. The practical impact of this political symbolism was perhaps most powerfully demonstrated by repeated clashes in 1994 and 1995 between the government and the Albanians over the establishment of an Albanian University in Tetovo, with rioting in early 1995 that left one Albanian dead.[51] Indeed, in early 1997, VMRO-DMPNE officially supported protests against Albanaian-language tuition staged by Macedonian students at the University of Skopje's Pedagogical Faculty, on the grounds that it violated the constitution.

Nonetheless, despite, or perhaps precisely because of, pervasive fears among ethnic Macedonians of the Albanians' loyalty to the young state, as well as because of significant western pressure for the maintenance of territorial integrity as a condition of recognition, the SDSM, the LP, and the small Socialist Party continued to solicit ethnic Albanian inclusion and even over-representation in each cabinet.[52] Although the Albanian parties have not gained their key demands on re-defining Macedonian statehood, they have been able to secure expanded Albanian-language educational provision at the primary and secondary levels and have continued to accept participation in each government lest a more radically anti-Albanian coalition be arrayed against them.

This appears to be a fragile but promising balance. In fact, it is a balance that has been continued by VMRO-DMPNE itself since its victory in the October 1998 parliamentary elections. VMRO-DMPNE's support had declined in elections held in 1994 and 1996, prompting Georgievski to downplay nationalist themes and focus the party's campaign on the parlous state of Macedonia's economy, which had been badly eroded by mismanagement, the authorities' inability to attract foreign investment, and, most importantly, international sanctions against neighboring Yugoslavia. Indeed, unlike Slovakia, Romania, and Croatia, where nationalist forces gained power before being marginalized by sweeping opposition victories, VMRO-DMPNE's long years in opposition appear to have tempered its radicalism. Georgievski used the formation of a new government to undermine other party leaders, reducing its executive committee from 20 to 14 members. Most importantly, although the PDP, the SDSM's coalition partner, was excluded from the cabinet, Georgievski included the ethnic Albanian DPA, which had undergone a considerable measure of de-radicalization of its own. In justifying the move to his own nationalist supporters, Georgievski declared that "the Republic of Macedonia has the firm determination to [abandon] Balkan standards and become a creator of stability in the region and beyond, and thus to stop being a subject of concern [to] the international community."[53]

At first glance, a government including the most nationalist ethnic Macedonian and Albanian parties does not appear to be a recipe for stability. Yet the arrangement benefits precisely from the fact that each party's stature as the most hard-line of their respective ethnic groups' political forces implies an absence of organized challengers that could assail their compromises. In addition, a crucial element of VMRO-DPMNE's de-radicalization had been its formation of the Coalition for Changes with the liberal Democratic Alternative (DA). As Georgievski put it, the coalition united "two parties, two structures of people who not so long ago had different, often conflicting, ideologies and considerations." This, according to Georgievski, made the VMRO-DPMNE/DA coalition "a kind of national reconciliation and [offers] the possibility for greater flexibility [with regards to the] political differences within the Macedonian national body."[54]

Albania

Following the collapse of Communist rule, Albania did not develop any sizable explicitly nationalist organizations. Nevertheless, a few small extremist parties have operated in the country.[55] The Albanian National Unity Party was registered in March 1991 under the chairmanship of Idajet Beqiri. Its program has included calls for the creation of a pan-Albanian confederation encompassing all territories inhabited by Albanian majorities in Yugoslavia, Macedonia, and Greece. Party leaders demanded that Tirana take a more forthright role in support of the rights of ethnic Albanians in the Kosovo region of neighboring Serbia (where Albanians make up about 90 percent of the population), and they recognized Kosovo's declaration of independence in September 1991. The party voiced its readiness to work with all political organizations whose goals were to "protect Albanian national interests," inside and outside the country.

Observers believed that the party included many former hard-line Communists who were seeking to capitalize on nationalist sentiments among the population. Although they openly sought to "recover" Albanian territories from neighboring countries, party leaders claimed that they did not propose forcible reintegration. Membership has remained small, although latent support within other political parties is often claimed. Indeed, although the party failed to win seats in the general elections of March 1992, receiving under 1 percent of the national vote, the major Albanian parties, the Democrats and Socialists, also contained deputies, members, and sympathizers who have voiced militant nationalist sentiments. The Democrats have periodically purged the more radical elements but remain concerned about charges of being anti-national.

The Motherland Political Association was founded in July 1991. Its leadership has worked in a close alliance with the Albanian National Unity Party, declaring their main goal to be the creation of a pan-Albanian confederation in the Balkans. Thus, both groups quickly allied themselves with the Kosovo Patriotic and Political Association, focusing much of their attention on the demand that Tirana take a more active role in supporting Albanian interests in Kosovo. Several other explicitly nationalist and irredentist organizations have also surfaced. These included a resuscitated *Balli Kombetar* (National Front), the major anti-Communist resistance group during World War II, and the monarchist Legality Movement, which maintained links with Albanian exiles. Disaffected nationalist members of the Democratic Party formed a new Democratic Party of the Right in late 1993 and sought to build a broader coalition with like-minded factions.

Although ultra-nationalist influence in Albania has continued to be restrained, economic hardship coupled with regional instability could provide it with wider public resonance and give increasing prominence to nationalist sentiments within the mainstream Albanian parties. On the other hand, like Macedonia, it is more likely that the country's deep dependence on western assistance, particularly reconstruction aid in the aftermath of the profound civil breakdown in early 1997, will compel the major parties to keep ultra-nationalist and irredentist forces in check. This is especially true in the wake of the Western military intervention in Kosovo in 1999, during which Albania was used as a NATO staging area, with NATO's continued presence in the region placing a powerful constraint on irredentist aims.

In fact, the main source of ultra-nationalist Albanian parties has been the position of the Greek minority, which has provided a focus for both autonomist demands among the minority and xenophobic reactions among the ethnic majority. In 1991, a draft constitution was presented to parliament. According to article 7, Albania "respects the generally accepted principles and norms of international law, and recognizes the guarantees provided by international law to minorities." However, article 8 of the document elicited strong criticism from the Greek minority, as well as from international organizations and human rights groups. It declared that political parties and organizations could not be created on the basis of nationality or ethnicity; it also barred political organizations of a "fascist or racist character, or those that by their program and activities threaten to overthrow by force the constitutional order, against the independence and territorial integrity of the country." Greek leaders raised serious objections to stipulations prohibiting the formation of minority political organizations. They claimed that such provisions violated the right of minorities to express their political will and limited their participation in the country's political life.[56]

Although the Greek organization *Omonia* gained five seats in the March 1991 general elections, controversy over the participation of ethnic-based parties culminated in the formulation of a new electoral and political party law that prohibited parties based on ethnic or regional criteria. The draft of the election law submitted in January 1992 initially contained an article allowing for the participation of ethnic-based parties and was welcomed by the Conference on Security and Cooperation in Europe (CSCE) and other multinational bodies. This legislative amendment was partly a result of CSCE intervention, which impressed on the Albanian authorities their obligation to abide by Helsinki principles when drafting the law. But after a serious dispute in the National Assembly over the role of ethnic-based parties, there was a last-minute change in article 13 that effectively disqualified *Omonia* from participating in the elections. This move, backed by nationalist politicians, enraged

Greek activists and led to vehement protests by Athens. The election controversy was partially eased when the Albanian government agreed to register the Greek-based Unity Party for Human Rights and permitted it to stand in the March 1992 parliamentary elections. The new party succeeded in gaining two seats to the newly constituted National Assembly. But the election campaign itself was marred by conflicts, as some Albanian officials charged that irredentist Greek organizations were campaigning for the Unity Party and distributing campaign literature printed in Greece.

As tensions mounted between Athens and Tirana during 1993 and 1994, nationalist politicians benefited from the turmoil to press for various anti-minority measures, including crackdowns on *Omonia* gatherings and propaganda activities. Although neither President Sali Berisha nor the Democratic Party government could be accused of xenophobic extremism, they sought to avoid accusations of pandering to Greek ambitions or neglecting Albanian national interests. Hence, the trial and conviction of five *Omonia* activists in September 1994 on charges of espionage and arms smuggling could be interpreted as a vindication of Tirana's fears of Greek subversion as well as a public relations exercise by the authorities to maintain public support and remove the threat of an ultra-nationalist resurgence. Indeed, the political neutralization of Albanian nationalists was instrumental in reducing tensions between Athens and Tirana in succeeding months, when the "*Omonia* five" were released on probation and bilateral talks yielded a Greek crackdown on the terrorist Northern Epirus Liberation Front, an irridentist group which operated from Greece and which Albania had long claimed benefited from Greek official indifference if not tacit support.[57]

Conclusion

Nationalist majority parties have mushroomed throughout eastern Europe since the disintegration of centralized Communist political control, but their significance for government policy at central, regional (or republican), and local levels has varied. These groups can be tentatively placed into three broad categories, based on their size, program, influence, and impact on state policy. The preceding description and analysis has provided some specific examples of their profile and position in the region's transitional political systems.

The most far-reaching effect has been evident in the former federal states of Czechoslovakia and Yugoslavia, where *independence-oriented* nationalist forces helped the constituent republics achieve state sovereignty and subsequently determined or heavily influenced legislation concerning the status of ethnic minorities and relations with neighboring states. These are political parties and umbrella national movements that have primarily pressed for the sovereignty or outright independence of federal republican units via electoral competition, employing ethnic identity to mobilize public support. In contrast to political forces that premise support for independence on the maintenance of a democratic regime (for example, the KDH in Slovakia), independence-oriented nationalists have tended to be chauvinistic or xenophobic, as their definition of the state's character, if not of citizenship itself, does not extend beyond the majority ethnic group. Such parties characteristically manipulate ethnic divisions to ensure their electoral success and predominance in government following the attainment of independence and veer toward authoritarian politics. Pertinent examples include the Movement for a Democratic Slovakia and the Croatian Democratic Community.

A second group, *radical nationalists*, comprises xenophobic and chauvinistic political groupings whose activities are premised solely on the repression of any manifestations of minority self-organization and political representation. While such groups are usually small and localized, in some cases they act as guardians of the ethnic power structure, playing a useful role as allies of more moderate nationalist ruling parties by deflecting popular attention from pressing economic problems and undermining democratic parties that are programmatically oriented toward addressing them. Some of these organizations have evidently been promoted and financed by elements of the former Communist *nomenklatura,* while others have been formed by disaffected former dissidents with populist and xenophobic inclinations. Examples of such parties include the Party of Romanian National Unity, the Greater Romania Party, the Committee for the Defense of National Interests and the Christian Democratic Party in Bulgaria, the Slovak National Party, and the Croatian Party of Rights. The most extremist neo-fascist groups have advocated violence and have either forged links with skinhead gangs or established their own paramilitary detachments.

Unlike conventional parties or movements, *ethnonationalist* cultural organizations focus their attention on the preservation and promotion of the "national community" by defining themselves as standing above all partisan political agendas and socio-economic programs. However, as such groups' activities are invariably based on the assumption of a chronic threat to national survival, whether from internal or external sources, they cooperate quite closely with radical nationalist parties. Indeed, their members and leading activists tend to be intellectuals who seek to provide the ideological underpinnings and nationwide informational and organizational networks necessary for the effective legitimation and widespread manifestation of anti-minority, anti-liberal, and anti-foreign sentiments. The most influential examples of such organizations are *Matica slovenská* in Slovakia and *Vatra Romaneasca* in Romania.

These three categories are certainly neither exhaustive nor mutually exclusive, and other groups may be radicalized if ethnic relations become polarized, which is most likely if the demands of ethnic minorities escalate or if there are clear external threats to the survival or territorial integrity of the state. The impact of such movements on political life is clearly contingent upon the extent of democratic institution building, economic stabilization, market reform, administrative decentralization, and the recognition of minority rights in a range of endeavors and representative bodies. Public dissatisfaction and disengagement from the political process could also allow radical parties to increase their support base and electoral impact.

Undoubtedly, as in much of western Europe, ultra-nationalist and neo-fascist parties will occupy a position on the fringes of the political system. In most instances, they will remain divided and compete for the radical vote and the most "patriotic" national program. A more significant danger in parts of post-communist Europe is the deliberate manipulation and aggravation of ethnonational relations by clientilist quasi-authoritarian parties that benefited from leading their countries to independence and have now lost power. The Croatian and Slovak examples are important cases in point. At the same time, faced with pressures from neighboring states and/or the militant stance of some of their domestic ethnic kin, even a reasonably moderate and tolerant administration may become radicalized or adopt anti-minority measures. Developments in Albania and Macedonia may yet prove to be particularly instructive in this regard. Additionally, the impact of small ultra-nationalist parties in parliamentary bodies needs to be carefully scrutinized, as in divided legislatures they can assume the role of power brokers and inject militancy into government policy, as the cases of Romania and Slovakia have demonstrated.

Democratic consolidation in all east European states remains dependent on the construction of stable and representative parliamentary structures and procedural regularity within administrative institutions, with both based on a constitutional system in which ethnicity does not determine the quality of citizenship. Clearly, some states have registered faster progress than others in these essential areas. The cases examined in this chapter are those that have been particularly susceptible to ultra-nationalist diversions and authoritarian politics that impede the development of tolerant, pluralistic democratic regimes and societies. Their histories suggest caution when assessing whether the indisputably positive developments of recent years in particularly vulnerable states such as Slovakia, Romania, and Croatia represent genuine breakthroughs to democratic consolidation or mere interludes preceding the next authoritarian temptation.

Notes

1. See Trond Gilberg, "Ethnochauvinism, Agrarian Populism, and Neo-Fascism in Romania and the Balkans," in Peter H. Merkl and Leonard Weinberg (Eds.), *Encounters with the Contemporary Radical Right* (Boulder: Westview, 1993), pp. 95-110, and András Körösenyi, "Revival of the Past or New Beginning? The Nature of Post-Communist Politics," *Political Quarterly*, vol. 62, no. 1 (January-March 1991), pp. 52-74.

2. See Woodrow J. Kuhn's, "Political Nationalism in Contemporary Eastern Europe," in Jeffrey Simon and Trond Gilberg (Eds.), *Security Implications of Nationalism in Eastern Europe* (Boulder: Westview, 1986), pp. 81-107; and Orlando Patterson, *Ethnic Chauvinism: The Reactionary Impulse* (New York: Stein and Day, 1977).

3. See Anthony D. Smith, "The Origin of Nations," *Ethnic and Racial Studies*, vol. 12, no. 3 (July 1989), pp. 340-67.

4. For an analysis of the significance of ethnicity along these lines, see Cynthia H. Enloe, *Ethnic Conflict and Political Development* (Lanham, NY: University Press of America, 1986).

5. See Robert A. LeVine and Donald T. Campbell (Eds.), *Ethnocentrism: Theories of Conflict, Ethnic Attitudes, and Group Behavior* (New York: John Wiley and Sons, 1972); and Vamik D. Volkan, *The Need to Have Enemies and Allies: From Clinical Practice to International Relationships* (Northvale, N.J.: Jason Aronson Inc., 1988); see also Katherine Verdery, "Nationalism and National Sentiment in Post-Socialist Romania," *Slavic Review*, vol. 52, no. 2 (Summer 1993), pp. 196-97.

6. For a valuable overview, see Ronald Linden, "The Appeal of Nationalism," and G.J. Brown, "The Resurgence of Nationalism," in *Radio Free Europe/Radio Liberty Research Report*, vol. 2, no. 24 (June 14, 1991). These features suggest some clear parallels between post-communist nationalism and ultra-nationalist resurgence in western Europe. See Hans-Georg Betz, *Radical Right-Wing Populism in Western Europe* (London: Macmillan, 1994).

7. See Dan Landis and Terry Boucher, "Themes and Models of Conflict," in Jerry Boucher, Dan Landis, and Karen Arnold Clark (Eds.), *Ethnic Conflict: International Perspectives* (Newbury Park, CA: Sage, 1987), pp. 18-31.

8. For a valuable analysis, see Renee de Nevers, "Democratization and Ethnic Conflict," *Survival*, vol. 35, no. 2 (Summer 1993), pp. 31-48.

9. George Schopflin, "Aspects of Language and Ethnicity in Central and Eastern Europe," *Transition*, vol. 2, no. 24 (November 29, 1996), p. 9.

10. Thomas S. Szayna, "Ultra-Nationalism in Central Europe," *Orbis: A Journal of World Affairs*, vol. 37, no. 4 (Fall 1993). See also Thomas S. Szayna, *Ethnic Conflict in Central Europe and the Balkans: A Framework and U.S. Policy Options* (Santa Monica: Rand, 1994).

11. Verdery, "Nationalism and National Sentiment in Post-Socialist Romania," pp. 189-90.

12. For a compelling discussion of the dangers to democracy that follow from working-class mobilization along non-class lines in Eastern Europe, see David Ost, "Labor, Class, and

Democracy: Shaping Political Antagonisms in Post-Communist Society," *Working Papers on Transitions from State Socialism* #93.3 (Cornell University, Mario Einaudi Center for International Studies, 1993).

13. For an excellent analysis of Czech-Slovak relations up to the period immediately preceding 1989, see Carol Skalnik Leff, *National Conflict in Czechoslovakia: The Making and Remaking of a State, 1918-1987* (Princeton: Princeton University Press, 1988).

14. See Jiří Pehe, "The Inevitable Divorce," *Freedom Review*, vol. 23, no. 6 (November-December 1992). For an exhaustive analysis of constitutional politics during this period, see Eric Stein, *Czecho/Slovakia: Ethnic Conflict, Constitutional Fissure, Negotiated Breakup* (Ann Arbor: University of Michigan Press, 1997).

15. See Jiří Pehe, "Czechs and Slovaks Prepare to Part," RFE/RL, *Research Report*, vol. 1, no. 37 (September 18, 1992), Jan Obrman, "Cechoslovakia's New Governments," *RFE/RL, Research Report*, vol. 1, no. 29 (July 17, 1992), and Jifií Pehe, "The New Slovak Government and Parliament," *RFE/RL Research Report*, vol. 1, no. 28 (July 10, 1992).

16. See Sharon Fisher, "Domestic Policies Cause Conflict with the West," *Transition*, vol.2, no. 19 (September 20, 1996), pp. 56-61. Of the five post-communist associate members with which the EU declined to begin formal accession negotiations in March 1998, Slovakia was the only candidate excluded solely on political grounds.

17. See Jiří Pehe, "Slovak Nationalism Splits Christian Democratic Ranks," *RFE/RL, Research Report*, vol. 1, no. 13 (March 27, 1992), and Sharon Fisher, "Tottering in the Aftermath of Elections," *Transition*, vol. 1, no. 4 (March 29, 1995), pp. 20-25.

18. On these splits and realignments, see Milan Niã, Jan Obrman, and Sharon Fisher, "New Slovak Government: More Stability?," *RFE/RL Research Report* vol. 2, no. 47 (November 26, 1993), pp. 24-30.

19. This account draws on material collected by *Matica slovenská* in *Tri roky obnovenej älenskej základne Matice slovenskej, 1990-1992* (Liptovský Mikuláš: TeLeM, 1994); *Valne Zhromazdenie Matice slovenskej*, 1992, Bratislava, 33/1992; the *Second Memorandum of Slovaks From Southern Slovakia*, adopted at the April 1993 *Matica Slovenská* meeting in Surany, Slovakia; and *Tri roky Matice slovenskej*, 1993-1995 (Martin: Matica slovenská, 1996).

20. Consult the Constitution of the Slovak Republic, published in *Hospodarské Noviny*, Prague, September 11, 1992, in *FBIS-EEU-02-179-S*, September 15, 1992, and *Hungarians in Slovakia*, Information Bulletin, September 1992, compiled on behalf of the ethnic Hungarian political movement Coexistence, Bratislava.

21. See Jan Obrman, "Language Law Stirs Controversy in Slovakia," *RFE/RL, Report on Eastern Europe*, vol.1, no. 46 (November 16, 1990); and Georg Brunner, "Minority Problems and Policies in East-Central and South-East Europe," *International Issues*, vol. 1, no. 3 (1992).

22. See Alfred Reisch, "Slovakia's Minority Policy Under International Scrutiny," *RFE/RL, Research Report*, vol. 2, no. 49 (December 10, 1993).

23. For details see *CTK*, Prague, May 16, 1994, FBIS-EEU-94-096-A, May 17, 1994.

24. See Sharon Fisher, "Making Slovakia More 'Slovak,' " *Transition* vol. 2, no. 24 (November 29, 1996), pp. 14-17.

25. See Michael Shafir's chapter in this volume.

26. On the origins of the PUNR and its ally, Vatra Romaneasca, see Dennis Deletant, "The Role of *Vatra Romaneasca* in Transylvania," *RFE/RL, Report on Eastern Europe*, vol. 2, no. 5 (February 1, 1991).

27. See *Romania Mare*, May 17,1991, and *Adevarul*, Bucharest, May 17,1991, both in *FBIS-EEU-91-103*, May 29,1991.

28. For a detailed chronology, see Don Ionescu and Michael Shafir, "Romanian Government Reorganized," *RFE/RL, Research Report*, vol. 3, no. 11(March 18, 1994), Michael Shafir, "Ruling Party Formalizes Relations with Extremists," *Transition*, vol. 1, no. 5 (April 14, 1995), Michael Shafir, "Anatomy of a Pre-Election Political Divorce," *Transition*, vol. 2, no. 2 (January 26, 1996), pp. 45-49, and Michael Shafir, "A Note on the Breakup of the Government Coalition," *Transition*, vol. 2, no. 20 (October 4, 1996), p. 29.

29. See Michael Shafir, "The Movement for Romania: A Party of 'Radical Return,'" *RFE/RL, Research Report*, vol. 1, no. 29 (July 17, 1992).

30. See *Romania Libera*, December 1, 1992; and Michael Shafir, "Growing Political Extremism in Romania," *RFE/RL*, Research Report, vol. 2, no. 14 (April 2, 1993).

31. See the interview with Bela Marko, UDMR President, "Changes in the Administration or a Nationalist Diversionary Game," 22, Bucharest (April 8-14, 1993), in *JPRS-EER-93-047-S*, May 28, 1993.

32. See Michael Shafir, "Political Engineering and Democratization in New Law on Parties," *Transition*, vol. 2, no. 14 (July 12, 1996), pp. 60-63.

33. See "The Dramatic Hours of Kolozsvar Archaeological Excavations to Start Today," *Nepszabadsag*, Budapest, June 22, 1994, *FBIS-EEU-94-139*, July 20, 1994; and Michael Shafir, "Ethnic Tension Runs High in Romania," *RFE/RL, Research Report*, vol. 3, no. 32, (August 19, 1994). On the eventual signing of the bilateral treaty with Hungary, see Michael Shafir, "A Possible Light at the End of the Tunnel," *Transition* vol. 2, no. 19 (September 20, 1996), pp. 29-32.

34. This seems all the more true given that declining support for Funar's party was confirmed in the election. See Michael Shafir, "Opting for Political Change," *Transition*, vol. 2, no. 26 (December 27, 1996), pp. 12-16.

35. See Kjell Engelbrekt, "Nationalism Reviving," *RFE/RL Report on Eastern Europe*, vol. 2, no. 48, 29 November 1991; and the "Official Announcement on the Dissolution of the Nationwide Committee for Defense of National Interests and the Founding of a National Defense Party," *Presluzhba Kurier*, Sofia, 19 February 1992, in FBIS-EEU-92-038, 26 February 1992.

36. Stoyan Tsvetkov, "Racists and Gypsies," *Kontinent*, Sofia, 3 January 1994, *FBIS-EEU-94-004*, 6 January 1994, and *RFE/RL Daily Report*, no. 1, 3 January 1994.

37. On the failure of official efforts to prohibit the DPS from electoral competition, see Carlos Juberías Flores's chapter in this volume.

38. On these more recent developments, see Ivan Ilchev's chapter in this volume.

39. See Milan Andrejevich, "Croatia Goes to the Polls," *RFE/RL, Report on Eastern Europe*, vol. 1, no. 18 (May 4, 1990), pp. 33-37.

40. Valuable background information can be found in Milan Andrejevich, "Croatia Between Stability and Civil War (Part 1)," *RFE/RL, Report on Eastern Europe*, vol. 1, no. 37 (September 18, 1990), and Part 2 in *RFE/RL, Report on Eastern Europe*, vol. 1, no. 39 (September 28, 1990).

41. See Marinko Culic, "Herzegovinian Croata Steer Croatian Politics," *Transition*, vol. 2, no. 14 (July 12, 1996), pp. 31-32.

42. See Patrick Moore, "Changes in the Croatian Political Landscape," *RFE/RL, Research Report*, vol. 3, no. 22 (June 3, 1994), and Patrick Moore, "Dashed Hopes, Endless Conflict," *Transition*, vol. 1, no. 1 (January 30, 1995), pp. 23-28.

43. For background conditions, see Ivo Banac, *The National Question in Yugoslavia: Origins, History, Politics* (Ithaca: Cornell University Press, 1984), Pedro Ramet, *Nationalism and Federalism in Yugoslavia: 1963-1983* (Bloomington: Indiana University Press, 1984), Stephen

Burg, *Conflict and Cohesion in Socialist Yugoslavia* (Princeton: Princeton University Press, 1983), Ante Čuvalo, *The Croatian National Movement, 1966-1972* (New York: East European Monographs, 1990), and A. Ross Johnson, *The Role of the Military in Communist Yugoslavia: An Historical Sketch* (Santa Monica: Rand Corporation, 1978). The account of the breakdown of Yugoslavia that follows draws on Lenard J. Cohen, *Broken Bonds: The Disintegration of Yugoslavia* (Boulder: Westview, 1993), Branka Magaš, *The Destruction of Yugoslavia* (London: Verso, 1993), and James Gow, *Legitimacy and the Military: The Yugoslav Crisis* (New York: St. Martin's Press, 1992).

44. The same could be said of the subsequent introduction of the *kuna* as the new currency in May 1994. Although this was the ancient name of Croatian money, it was also the name of the currency used by the *Ustaša* regime.

45. See Republic of Croatia, *Constitutional Law of Human Rights and Freedoms and the Rights of National and Ethnic Communities or Minorities in the Republic of Croatia,* Zagreb, December 1991.

46. See Patrick Moore, "An End Game in Croatia and Bosnia?," *Transition,* vol. 1, no. 20 (November 3, 1995), pp. 6-12.

47. Svetlana Vasovic-Mekina, "Slovenia and Croatia: How to Become a Citizen: State as Prison," Vreme, Belgrade, March 8, 1993, in *FBIS-EEU-93-065,* April 7, 1993.

48. For background information, see Milan Andrejevich, "Macedonia's New Political Leadership," RFE/RL, *Report on Eastern Europe,* vol. 2, no. 20 (May 17, 1991); and Duncan Perry, "The Macedonian Question Revitalized," *RFE/RL, Report on Eastern Europe,* vol. 1, no. 34 (August 24, 1990).

49. See Duncan Perry, "The Republic of Macedonia and the Odds for Survival," *RFE/RL Research Report,* vol. 1, no. 46 (November 20, 1992).

50. In fact, a "Belgian" solution has from the outset been one of the Albanians' principal demands, and a successful referendum on territorial autonomy organized by the Albanian parties in January 1992 was declared illegal by the Macedonian authorities. See Perry, *ibid.* For the full text of the Macedonian constitution see *Nova Makedonija,* Skopje, November 25, 1991, in *JPRS-EER-92-016-S,* 10 February 1992.

51. See Duncan Perry, "On the Road to Stability—Or Destruction?," *Transition,* vol. 1, no. 15 (August 25, 1995), pp. 40-48.

52. Perry, *ibid.,* Stefan Krause, "Moving Toward Firmer Ground in Macedonia," *Transition,* vol. 3, no. 2 (February 7, 1997), pp. 45-46, and Fabian Schmidt, "From National Consensus to Pluralism," *Transition,* vol. 1, no. 4 (March 29, 1995), pp. 26-30.

53. See International Crisis Group, "Macedonia: New Faces in Skopje," January 8, 1999, *http://www.intl-crisis-group.org/projects/sbalkans/reports/mac06main.htm.* Georgievski also emphasized that the previous cooperation between the SDSM and PDP had made a "large contribution" in this respect.

54. *Ibid.*

55. Some information on Albanian ultra-nationalist organizations can be found in *Tirana Radio Network,* September 24, 1991, in FBIS-EEU-91-188, September 27, 1991; and Robert Austin, "Albania," *RFE/RL Research Report,* vol. 3, no. 16 (April 22 1994).

56. See the Albanian entries in the *Country Reports on Human Rights Practices for 1992 and 1993,* Department of State, Washington D.C., U.S.

57. See Marianne Sullivan, "Mending Relations with Greece," *Transition,* vol. 1, no. 15 (August 25, 1995), pp. 11-16.

4

THE POLITICAL PARTY AS NATIONAL HOLDING COMPANY: THE HUNGARIAN DEMOCRATIC FEDERATION OF ROMANIA

Michael Shafir

The Hungarian Democratic Federation of Romania (UDMR) was established on Christmas Day, 1989, three days after a week of violent demonstrations and street-fighting culminated in the fall of Nicolae Ceausescu's twenty-five-year dictatorship.[1] Both its founders and mass base overwhelmingly supported the revolution, and sought from the outset to link political democratization in Romania as'a whole with the recovery of cultural rights systematically eroded since the late 1950s by Gheorghe Gheorghiu-Dej's "national" communism and its xenophobic elaboration under Ceausescu. During this period, Romania had broken not only with the Comintern, but also with the Soviet development model based on institutionalization, co-optation, and control of minority ethnicity, replacing it with a strategy of agressive Romanianization through gerrymandering, internal migration, and repression of Hungarian-language education. The small Mures Autonomous Magyar Region, a faithful application of the Soviet model's territorial basis, was weakened legally and administratively, and finally eliminated in 1968.[2] As a project of cultural standardization and political assimilation, however, Romanian national communism was a failure. The Hungarians, even many of those in the Romanian Communist Party (PCR) retained their language and identity, and the UDMR quickly emerged as an effective political alternative to the National Salvation Front (FSN), the ruling legislative and executive body established and led by former Ceausescu allies who spearheaded his overthrow, trial by a military court, and execution.

While the composition of the FSN leadership suggests a palace coup assisted by a popular uprising, the uncertainty of the revolution's nature and outcome nonetheless temporarily united Romanian and Hungarian anti-Ceausescu forces.[3] So cooperative were relations during and immediately after December 1989 that a few prominent members of the UDMR joined the FSN Council, the Front's highest body, among them Karoly Kiraly, a former high-ranking PCR official who had resigned in protest over the Party's anti-Hungarian policies; Laszlo Tokes, the UDMR's honorary chairman and a Reformed Church minister who led the Timisoara demonstrations that sparked the revolution; and Geza Domokos, a former PCR Central Committee member and director of the Kriterion publishing house, who became the UDMR's first elected chairman.

On January 5, 1990, the FSN "solemnly declared" that it would "guarantee individual and collective rights and freedoms for ethnic minorities." It stressed that the "sad inheritance left behind by the dictatorship" made it necessary to elaborate these guarantees as a matter of constitutional law, and promised to establish a Ministry for Ethnic Minorities. "The blood shed in common" during the revolution, the FSN proclaimed, "has shown that the policy of hate-mongering based on the chauvinistic policy of forced assimilation, as well as the successive attempts to defame neighboring Hungary and the Hungarians of Romania, could not succeed in breaking the confidence, friendship and unity between the Romanian people and the national minorities."[4]

Of course, the UDMR's very existence was proof that ethnic political mobilization had not been relegated to the past, and that stable democratic rule would thus depend not on hortatory affirmations of unity, but on the strength and durability of inter-ethnic political alliances. But the idyll was short-lived. In the space of six years, ethnic polarization has left the UDMR isolated and virtually powerless within Romanian politics, leading it to adopt an increasingly anti-system stance. Its institutional development merits scrutiny because it not only reflects how political interaction with the ethnic majority has defined Hungarians' conception of their relationship to the Romanian polity, but because it underscores the political radicalization that has undermined democratic consolidation in other post-communist states as well. The first section supports the assumption that the UDMR serves as a proxy for the Hungarian minority as a collective social actor by analyzing the party's support among Hungarian voters, its composition, and its organizational structure. Each reflects as well as conditions the increasing political distance between Romania's two main ethno-national groups, which is examined in greater depth in the second section. Here, shifts in UDMR strategy and tactics are traced to disputes over the constitutional definition of the Romanian state and the official cultural policy that has followed from this definition. The final section considers the internal dynamics and changing balance of power within the UDMR, which are associated with the development of its current conception of communal autonomy.

Electoral Performance, Composition, and Organization

Both national elections held up to the time of this writing attest to the high salience of ethnicity in structuring Hungarians' political loyalties. In the first free elections in May 1990, the UDMR received 7.2 percent of the popular vote for the Senate and 7.23 percent of the vote for the Assembly (later Chamber) of Deputies, sufficient to place second in a field of eighty-three parties dominated by the FSN, which won decisive majorities in both houses and 85 percent of the vote for its presidential candidate, Ion Iliescu. Similarly, in September 1992, the UDMR gained 7.59 percent of the vote for the Senate and 7.46 percent of that for the lower house.[5] Its share of the vote in both elections was thus nearly identical to the 7.1 percent of Romania's 23.2 million citizens identified as Hungarian in the 1992 census.[6] Equally significant in this regard is the absence of any serious intra-ethnic competition. The Socialist Magyar Party, founded in early 1993, has gained very little support for the "socialist option" that its leader, Janos Fazekas, once a deputy prime minister under Ceausescu, claims has been neglected by the UDMR. Nor has Kalman Kiss's Hungarian Free Democratic Party succeeded in mobilizing opposition to what it regards as the UDMR's ethnic "extremism." On the contrary, Kiss is widely viewed as a puppet of Iliescu's Party of Social Democracy in Romania (PDSR), which emerged following a March 1992 split within the FSN between Iliescu and then-Prime Minister Petre Roman (who now heads the Democratic Party-National Salvation Front—PD-FSN).[7]

In both elections, the UDMR benefited from party list proportional representation (PR), enabling it to gain parliamentary representation well above that guaranteed to national minorities by the electoral law.[8] And while some Romanian nationalists have proposed replacing PR with single-member districts, thereby making it unlikely that the UDMR could win seats anywhere but the two counties with a Magyar majority, the other parliamentary parties, driven by their own electoral calculus, have rejected such a change.[9] On the other hand, after joining the government in late 1994, the anti-Hungarian Party of Romanian National Unity (PUNR) proposed raising the electoral threshold to 8 percent for two-party lists and 10 percent for those comprising three or more parties, a scheme which, as we shall see, could conceivably be applied to the UDMR.[10] A similar but weaker provision of the existing law which raises the current 3 percent threshold by 1 percent for each additional member of an electoral coalition (up to 8 percent) was not applied to the UDMR in 1992, but remains subject to interpretation.

By 1992, the Romanian party system had begun to crystallize, and an alliance of opposition parties called the Democratic Convention of Romania (CDR) placed second behind Iliescu's PDSR, receiving slightly over 20 percent of the vote for both houses of parliament. The UDMR had also joined the CDR, but it was agreed from the outset that it would run on separate lists in both national and local elections. In the latter contests, held in February 1992, it won 2,681 of 38,946 local council seats and elected 161 of the country's 1,340 mayors,[11] posting its best results in Harghita and Covasna counties, where the Magyar population forms, respectively, 84.6 percent and 75.2 percent of the population.[12] However, the UDMR's calls for greater autonomy, now backed by local political strength, exposed the CDR to government accusations of aiding Hungarian irredentism, further weakening the UDMR's remaining ties to Romanian parties. The final break came in February 1995, immediately after the government coalition expanded yet again to include, in addition to the PUNR, the similarly nationalist Greater Romania Party (PRM) and the Socialist Labor Party (PSM).[13]

The UDMR's political marginalization has not affected its success as a mass organization with widespread popular backing. By its May 1991 congress, it reported a membership of 533,000, roughly one-third of the entire Hungarian population, a figure that has since increased to approximately 600,000.[14] A 1993 poll of ethnic Romanians and Hungarians revealed that 66.7 percent of the latter had a "very good" or "good" opinion of the UDMR, although supporters expressed far less satisfaction with the UDMR's positions on economic and social matters than on the defense of collective rights. Loyalty to the UDMR, it would seem, reflects Hungarian voters' emphasis on inter-ethnic relations and their hostility toward the post-1992 government coalition, whose extreme nationalist members met with the highest levels of disapproval.[15]

The relative importance of such environmental factors may, of course, hold serious implications for the UDMR in the future. In a follow-up survey conducted in early 1995, two Hungarian respondents in five agreed that "the UDMR defends its own party interests, rather than those of the electorate," four times more than in the 1993 poll, while the UDMR's overall approval rating among Hungarian voters dropped to 53.5 percent.[16] Yet this may simply be a further reflection of the incompatibility of ethnic mobilization with coherent aggregation of Hungarian voters' diverse non-ethnic interests. As Geza Szocs, a former Senator, described the Federation's role at its Second Congress, the UDMR is the Hungarian minority's "lawyer, economic adviser, messenger, confessor and psychiatrist."[17] Thus, to the extent that representation of material interests continues to be viewed as presupposing secure ethnic boundaries and subordinate to their defense, a decline in approval will not necessarily translate into a decline in electoral support.

To be sure, traditional socio-economic ideologies have a strong institutional voice within the UDMR. Aside from one historical party (the Hungarian Smallholder's Party of Romania), these range from social democracy (the Social Democratic Platform–The New Left) via liberalism (although the Liberal Circle, concentrated mainly in Cluj, is itself rather heterogeneous) to Christian democracy (the Hungarian Christian Democratic Party of Romania being the UDMR's largest faction). In fact, only two platforms, the Transylvanian Hungarian Initiative, which verges on promotion of territorial separatism, and the Group for Reform of the so-called "young radicals," express what could be called a global ethnic ideology.[18] Nevertheless, the UDMR presents a united front politically as well as electorally, exhibiting a high degree of parliamentary voting discipline that extends to issues seemingly unrelated to ethnic interests.[19] Indeed, two of the parliamentary club's counselors expressed surprise that one could conceivably envisage a situation in which UDMR MPs would split along the party's internal ideological dividing lines.[20]

This reflects a logic of party composition that, consistent with Szocs's view, unites an underlying parallel civil society virtually in its entirety, including a wide array of organized interests such as the Federation of Hungarian Youth Organizations in Romania, the Gaudeamus Federation of Hungarian Students in Romania, and professional federations of physicians, pharmacists, engineers, and journalists. Also part of the UDMR are the Cultural Society of Hungarians in Transylvania, itself an umbrella organization, and the Bolyai Association (which advocates full restoration of the Hungarian-language school system and the re-opening of Cluj's Bolyai University, closed since 1959). The Foundation for the Defense of the Hungarian Language, established in August 1995, addresses much the same issues, as does the Association of Hungarian-Language Educators. The Transylvanian Museum Association and the Transylvanian Musical Association, the Transylvanian-Carpathian Association and the Lajos Kelemen Association (both devoted to environmental protection and the preservation of monuments), and Roman Catholic and Reformed Church associations do not exhaust the list. Altogether, the UDMR is comprised of twenty-one territorial branches and sixteen other associations.[21]

The direct inclusion of diverse civic, religious, cultural, and professional associations, however, holds little direct organizational significance, and the Coordinating Council, the body established to represent their interests within the party, seldom convenes.[22] Rather, the UDMR's institutional shape, like its political unity vis-à-vis the Romanian majority, has been molded by the national question, and by the steadily increasing influence of those party activists exclusively concerned with its articulation. A bellweather of their rise is Laszlo Tokes, the UDMR's first honorary chairman and a powerful symbol of Hungarians' struggle for cultural survival in Transylvania. At the outset, Tokes had been among the most moderate UDMR leaders, expressing the belief—at a time when some of his colleagues were already showing signs of desperation—that "sooner or later, co-operation [with the Romanians] will become unavoidable."[23] Over the next two years, however, he began using terms like "genocide," "holocaust," and "ethnic cleansing" to describe the Hungarians' predicament. By the Third Congress in January 1993, Tokes was a formidable candidate to replace the moderate leader Geza Domokos, an advocate of a policy of "small-steps," as Chairman.[24] He eventually yielded to the poet Bela Marko, but even Marko, certainly no moderate, proved to be more accommodating than was acceptable to Tokes's supporters. By the Fourth Congress in May 1995, Marko was challenged by Imre Borbely and another exponent of radicalism, Sandor Konya-Hamar.[25]

Although the bid failed and Marko was re-elected, the radicals' succeeded in getting the Congress to adopt a program calling for territorial autonomy. Their position was now stronger than ever, directly affecting the party's internal structure, rules, and procedures. For example, the Fourth Congress amended the UDMR's statutes to extend the interval between congresses from two years to four, a move that presumably would attenuate the leadership's accountability. However, it was agreed to hold an Extraordinary Congress in 1997 as a concession to the radicals, who threatened a walk-out that would have denied the Congress a quorum. Lacking confidence in Marko's ability to carry forward the autonomy program, the radicals thus gained an opportunity to attempt to unseat him again soon after the next scheduled national elections in late 1996.[26]

The same institutional dynamic has shaped lower-level decision-making bodies even more noticeably. The highest forum between party congresses, the Council of Representatives, was originally established with twenty-one of its 139 members elected by the Congress, the remainder being made up of the UDMR's MPs and appointees from the various political factions, territorial organizations, and other associations. A meeting of the Mediation Round Table, consisting of the leaders of the various political platforms and local organizations, would precede each bi-monthly Council session to set the agenda and reach a consensus on the submission of proposals. By 1995, however, the radicals had introduced a plan, compatible with the demand for territorial autonomy, that would provide for direct election of the Council by the UDMR's members, thereby transforming it into what they call a "mini-parliament."[27]

Viewing the UDMR's internal development as leading inexorably toward the creation of a state within a state, government politicians have reacted accordingly. Thus, as soon as it was established in early 1995, the UDMR's Council of Mayors and Counselors came under harsh attack by the Justice Minister, who threatened to have the UDMR disbanded as unconstitutional. Although other parties (including the PDSR) have similar bodies, the government portrayed the UDMR's as defying the law by promoting local autonomy based on ethnic criteria. While it is likely that the attack was at least partly a ploy to channel public opinion in support of the recent addition of the extremist PRM and PSM to the PDSR-PUNR coalition, the dispute was defused only after the UDMR added a provision to the new council's rules explicitly indicating that it would function "in accordance with Law 69/1991" on the status of local government.[28] The mix of likely motivations behind the government's behavior thus brought into sharp focus how the actions and alliances of each side have been endogenous to those of the other. Indeed, the episode's true significance lay in the extent to which the UDMR, in the course of five years of interaction with ethnic Romanian parties, could now be perceived as the institutional embryo of a separate political system.

Tactics, Goals, and Feedback Processes: The Anatomy of Radicalization

The policies of the UDMR, a Hungarian intellectual from Transylvania told Helsinki Watch in 1992, "are part of an interaction with, and response to, political developments in Romania." Were the Hungarians to "continue to feel frustrated," and perceive that "their needs and concerns are not taken seriously," they would "push more aggressively for their rights."[29] At the same time, however, changes in the UDMR's tactics correspond to changes in the goals it has declared in the name of securing collective rights, altering the status sought for those who claim them. This is clearly discernible in the evolution of the UDMR's demands: from establishment of an institutional mechanism to safeguard cultural provision, to changing the Magyar population's official classification to "partner nation" or "co-constituent element" within the Romanian state, to, finally, the adoption of a territorial component to the latter demand.

Each of these innovations, and the internal balance of political forces that has brought them about, broadly corresponds to the increments by which the UDMR's distance from effective political power has increased. This began almost immediately after the original FSN declaration renouncing Ceausescu's legacy. For, as soon as the FSN transformed itself into a political party in February 1990, its electoral ambitions and its roots in the old regime combined to produce an alliance with the cultural agenda of the newly-formed *Vatra romaneasca* [Romanian Cradle] and its political arm, the PUNR, whose social base is largely composed of Romanians who migrated to Transylvania under Gheorghiu-Dej and Ceausescu. Official discourse quickly became virtually indistinguishable from that of national communism, a reflection of this agenda's zero-sum conception of collective rights.[30] Following an outbreak of ethnic violence in Tirgu Mures in March 1990—widely believed to have been incited on both sides by former agents of Ceausescu's largely unreconstructed secret police, the Securitate—the government blamed not only the Hungarians, but Budapest itself.[31] Similarly, publications controlled by or supporting the FSN renamed Romanian political opponents, thereby explicitly promoting an ethno-national criterion of legitimate political participation. Human rights activist Doina Cornea became Doina Juhasz, Doina Juhasz-Kocsis, and even Doina Kornea Juhasz-Kocsis; Ion Ratiu, who ran against Iliescu in the 1990 presidential election, became Racz Janos.[32]

The UDMR's radicalization, however, is more a consequence than a cause of its political marginalization, for leaders such as Tokes defended the moderate line well after the FSN allied itself with Romanian nationalists. What drove them from this position? To be sure, ethnic Hungarians have faced a sustained pattern of provocation. Hungarian-language programs on state television were cut by more than half in early 1991 and moved to a channel that cannot be received in most of Transylvania, followed two years later by an order eliminating Hungarian-language news programming.[33] An official report on the Tirgu Mures disturbances issued in early 1991 virtually exonerated the Hungarians, but was never approved by the parliament and was apparently intended only to curry favor with the Council of Europe. Only Hungarians (and Magyarized Roma) were prosecuted, and many defendants received heavy sentences.[34] Meanwhile, another commission accused the Hungarians of Covasna and Harghita counties of murder and ethnic cleansing during and after the revolution, and its scurrilous report was republished in 1995 in the midst of negotiations over national minority provisions in a proposed basic treaty with Hungary.[35] Soon after his election in 1992, the mayor of Cluj, PUNR leader Gheorghe Funar, ordered the removal of all Hungarian-language signs erected after the revolution, and banned a Hungarian-language cable television station on the grounds that it could be used to send secret messages to Budapest. His administration erected monuments commemorating Romanian national figures that dwarf adjacent Hungarian symbols, and mass protests erupted in 1994 when he attempted to remove a statue of King Matyas from the main square to allow archeological excavations that would allegedly vindicate Romanians' historical claim to the city.[36]

Examples could easily be multiplied. However, as the progression of the UDMR's tactics and strategic goals suggests, the analytic utility of radicalization requires that its causes and consequences be confined to that which has explicitly and directly affected or sought to address the Hungarian minority's formal status and capacity to reproduce itself within the Romanian polity. This operationalization of the term thus focuses attention on the broad normative definitions underpinning both provocative state action and the UDMR's tactical and strategic choices and organizational form.

By this criterion, the first stage of radicalization followed the parliamentary debates on the country's new constitution. The draft's first article defined the Romanian state as "national, sovereign and independent, unitary and indivisible." Parliament thus opted to retain the term "unitary state," which featured both in the constitution of 1923 and 1965. Under Ceausescu, the term was interpreted to signify that national minorities did not really exist in Romania. Yet, although it is a staunch partisan of decentralization and devolution of power, the UDMR chose not to object to the "unitary" part of the definition. It did, however, object strongly to the term "national." Domokos and Zoltan Hosszu pointed out that no state that contains fourteen recognized national minorities should describe itself as a "national state," and that the term has largely disappeared from modern constitutions. Their suggested amendments, however, were voted down.[37]

Guarantees of equal rights and duties notwithstanding, the UDMR could not but conclude from other constitutional provisions that communal rather than individualist values formed the core of the state's ethos. The first section of Article 6 proclaims national minorities' "right to conservation, development, and expression of ethnic, cultural, linguistic, and religious identity," but the second section stipulates that these rights "must conform with the principle of equality and non-discrimination vis-à-vis other Romanian citizens." According to a commentary by the constitution's main architect, Antonie Iorgovan, they should never "degenerate into privileges."[38] Provisions declaring that "[t]he State foundation is laid on the unity of the Romanian people" (Article 4.1); that the national anthem is "Awake, Romanians" (Article

12.4); that Romanian is the country's sole official language (Article 13); as well as others others specifying that education "at all levels" be conducted in Romanian with the right to study in minority languages to be defined by future legislation (Article 32) and making the use of Romanian in court obligatory (Article 127), all contributed to the UDMR's opposition to the Constitution, although it made no recommendation to its electorate prior to the referendum that approved the basic document in December 1991.[39]

The UDMR's objections to the constitution's definition of Romania as a "national state" have never been withdrawn. As Marko put it in an interview with the weekly *22* in June 1995, "Our Constitution defines the state as a national state, consequently as the state of a single nation. Being of a different national identity, the Hungarian minority is not included in this definition."[40] For this reason, Marko said, the Fourth Congress had introduced in the UDMR's program the concept of "national autonomous community," to replace "national minority." In fact, however, the demand had first been raised at the Second Congress in May 1991, marking the first appearance of a division between moderates and radicals. In an attempt to maintain a united front, the UDMR encouraged some observers to believe that the differences were generational and/or linked to the communist past of the Domokos/Kiraly moderates, who were now allegedly being challenged by a younger generation led by Tokes and Szocs.[41] But subsequent developments demonstrated that the cleavage was not merely generational. Although formulated differently, the Second Congress demanded "partnership status" for the Hungarian minority, defining "Magyardom in Romania as a political subject in its own right," and consequently one that had to "be considered as a state-bearing factor and an equal partner of the majority of Romanian people."[42] This was the first victory of the emerging radicals, and it could be traced directly to the constitutional debates.

Since the adoption of the constitution, nothing contributed more to the Hungarian minority's growing feeling that its very survival as a separate ethnic entity was at stake than the education law passed by the Chamber of Deputies in 1994 and the Senate in 1995, and subsequently signed into law by President Iliescu. The UDMR, declared Iuliu Vida, the leader of its delegation in the lower house, considered the legislation to be "second in importance only to the Constitution."[43] Consistent with this evaluation, the law's enactment brought about the second decisive shift of power within the UDMR toward the radicals, and with it, the Hungarians' embrace of territorial autonomy as the only credible institutional framework for national partnership. This conclusion seemed to follow ineluctably from the operation of existing political institutions and the behavior of Romanian political forces, virtually all of which were arrayed against the Hungarians in a process that continued for almost a full year.

The UDMR objected to the draft bill's omission of the right to instruction in the mother tongue at all levels of public education, including vocational schools (a provision included in the communist-era law on education), and its failure to reinstate government financing of education in minority Church schools. It also objected to provisions requiring that all history, geography, and civic education courses be conducted solely in Romanian. Finally, the UDMR demanded that the right to instruction in the mother tongue at the university level be extended to all faculties.

Shortly before the debates on the draft bill began, the UDMR leadership contacted its allies in the CDR, whose Steering Committee agreed in a unanimous vote to support UDMR amendments in the Chamber of Deputies.[44] The leadership also contacted the PDSR and requested a meeting with Iliescu, during which Marko urged the president to intervene in a dispute whose outcome was likely to "fundamentally influence relations between the ethnic majority and an important segment of society."[45] The president seemed to oblige. He summoned the PDSR's deputies to the presidential palace and advised them to accommodate the UDMR as much as possible. And, indeed, the PDSR faction leader Dan Martian later proposed several amendments that evinced a more conciliatory posture, even if they did not meet all the UDMR demands.[46] However, in what seemed to be an implicit revolt against Iliescu himself, only some thirty deputies supported Martian's proposals. The president's courtship of the extreme nationalist parties (which had unambiguously rejected any concession to the Hungarians) proved to be his undoing. The internal opposition was led by Education Minister Liviu Maior, who had portrayed himself as politically independent but was later revealed to be a PUNR member.

For the UDMR, however, the real blow came from the CDR. Disregarding the decision of its Steering Committee, the bulk of the National Peasant Party Christian Democratic (PNTCD), the CDR's largest party, voted in favor of the draft bill's provisions. Of the other CDR parties, only the Liberal Party-'93 supported the UDMR consistently. The Party of Civic Alliance (PAC) and the Social Democratic Party of Romania (PSDR) abstained. As a result, the bill was passed with only minimal changes on June 23 by a vote of 206 to 39.[47]

The UDMR announced that if the law was not significantly altered by the Senate, it would consider civil disobedience. First, however, the Hungarians decided to submit to parliament their own bill for a separate educational system and began gathering the 250,000 signatures required by the constitution to exercise citizens' right of legislative initiative. By September 19, the UDMR had gathered nearly 492,000 signatures.[48] The Constitutional Court, however, took more than ten months to verify their authenticity, although it had taken only a few days to verify the 700,000 signatures gathered in support of presidential candidates before the 1992 elections. To the UDMR, this appeared to be a blatant case of foot-dragging aimed at creating a *fait accompli*.[49] Indeed, by the time the court completed its random verification process on July 27, 1995, the Senate had already finished its own debates on the education law.

The Senate bill was even less inclined to meet the UDMR's objections than the draft passed by the Chamber of Deputies. In view of the fact that the committee responsible for drafting it was headed by Gheorghe Dumitrascu, a member of the PDSR but a regular contributor to PRM weeklies, this was hardly surprising. Yet the draft, leaked to the press one week before the UDMR's Fourth Congress in an apparently calculated attempt by Romanian nationalists to provoke a reactive Hungarian extremism, was so obviously regressive that even Maior urged that the senators enact a version similar to that passed by the Chamber of Deputies, as did Prime Minister Nicolae Vacaroiu.[50] The Council for National Minorities, a body set up in 1993 which the UDMR was boycotting, made a similar appeal to the Senate and, swallowing its pride, so did the UDMR itself.[51] These recommendations were rejected, and only cosmetic changes were admitted. As a result, the UDMR walked out of the debate before the draft was put to a vote. On June 14, the Senate passed the bill by a vote of 94-2 with eight abstentions. The UDMR could now only hope that the versions adopted by the Senate and the Chamber of Deputies would be reconciled in favor of the latter. If not, Marko declared, the UDMR would appeal to the Constitutional Court.[52]

UDMR parliamentarians presented their arguments to the parliament's reconciliation committee, once more declaring their willingness to appeal to the Constitutional Court, and warning that "other forms of protest" were not to be ruled out. The UDMR executive chairman, Csaba Takacs, was more explicit, speaking of civil disobedience, by which, however, the UDMR meant "all legal and constitutional means" such as protest meetings, petitions, questions in parliament, and other similar action. But the committee refused to take their proposed amendments into consideration, and rejected those proposed by the Council for National Minorities. Declaring that the draft law was "a step backward" even when compared to the Ceausescu era, the UDMR decided, once again, to withdraw from the debates.[53]

On June 28, in a joint session boycotted by the UDMR deputies, the parliament voted on the bill article by article. In addition to the provisions passed by the Chamber of Deputies, the final version specified that Romanian-language schools must exist in all settlements in the country and at all levels of instruction.[54] Hungarian representatives were persuaded that this was aimed, as Marko put it, at "convincing Magyar children to study in a language other than the mother-tongue," and thus an indication of the authorities' intention to renew Romanianization, for many Transylvanian settlements have no ethnic Romanians whatsoever.[55] Similarly, Hungarian leaders viewed the law's requirement that university entrance examinations be administered only in Romanian as a further inducement to opt for Romanian schools, which in the medium-term would reinforce an already existing trend: whereas in the academic year 1991–92 Hungarians accounted for 4.5 percent of Romanian university students, their proportion had decreased in 1993–94 to 3.7 percent. Finally, Hungarian leaders, as well as the head of the Catholic Church in Romania (an ethnic Romanian), objected to the fact that the law precluded restitution of Church schools. The UDMR showed that 81.6 percent of such schools nationalized by the Communists, 1,300 in all, had been Magyar establishments.[56] In a declaration issued after the law was enacted, the UDMR called the law "more discriminatory, more anti-Magyar and anti-minority than the similar laws and regulations of the Ceausescu system."[57]

The majority of opposition deputies, whether members of the CDR or the PD-FSN, once again voted in favor of the law. The CDR stated that, though "imperfect," the education law's provisions on national minorities reflected "European standards."[58] Former allies, such as the PNTCD, now defended positions virtually indistinguishable from those of the PDSR and its more extremist allies. An article in the PNTCD monthly *Dreptatea* analyzed the UDMR legislative initiative held in limbo by the Constitutional Court in terms befitting the pro-presidential daily *Dimineata*.[59]

As expected, the Constitutional Court rejected the UDMR appeal. The unanimous decision held that the law contradicted neither the constitution nor the Universal Declaration on Human Rights or other international treaties.[60] Anticipating the decision, the UDMR requested a meeting with President Iliescu with the purpose of demanding that he refuse to promulgate the law.[61] The meeting was described by the UDMR as "very vehement," and Iliescu, according to a *communiqué* issued by the his office, accused the Hungarian minority leaders of promoting "separatism" and the "ghettoization" of Hungarian youth. He attacked their refusal to participate in the last phase of the debates on the law as "an insult to parliament," warned them about the legal consequences of civic disobedience, and said the fact that they had become isolated on the Romanian political scene should give them "food for thought." On July 24, Iliescu promulgated the law.[62]

Iliescu's comments appeared moderate in comparison with those of the PDSR's allies, however. Gheorghe Funar suggested that the Hungarian government set up a "Ministry of Absorption" to "facilitate the return of ethnic Magyars" who have been "a hotbed of instability and hate" during their "several centuries-long diaspora."[63] Ion Coja said the Hungarians were "genetically constructed" to stir up trouble and suggested that Romania "adopt the Baltic model" when dealing with its own minorities.[64] PRM leader Corneliu Vadim Tudor called the UDMR a "suicidal sect that defies the entire people [and] tramples under foot the laws of the state, engaging in physical and psychical terrorism," and declared that "only those who are stupid, ill-willed or traitors of their nation" would now defend "this Trojan horse...which should have been outlawed long ago." Like Funar, Tudor claimed that the education law was very liberal and that the UDMR was content with it, but merely wanted to embarrass Romania in international fora.[65]

Key elements of the nationalists' rhetoric, however, clearly resonate with sentiments shared by nearly all Romanian parties, particularly the suspicion of foreign manipulation. For example, Adrian Nastase, the executive chairman of the PDSR and chairman of the Chamber of Deputies, has claimed that "the UDMR's activities are ordered from abroad."[66] And, while the opposition does not go this far, it strongly disapproves of the UDMR's efforts to enlist international support. PAC chairman Nicolae Manolescu, once a close ally of the UDMR, called the UDMR's "unfavorable international propaganda" against the education law "not serious, [yet] at the same time...[t]he UDMR risks compromising itself."[67] Indeed, no UDMR appeal met with more hostility from the entire ethnic Romanian political spectrum than that addressed to the European Parliament, which passed a resolution condemning the education law two weeks before Iliescu signed it.[68] The PDSR denounced the "irresponsible role played by the UDMR" in the "shameful resolution," and presidential spokesman Traian Chebeleu demanded to know "how far the UDMR is prepared to go." Marko thanked the European Parliament and appealed to it again for support in the future.[69]

Meanwhile, the UDMR commenced a series of actions planned by a special commission set up by the Council of Representatives. Protest meetings were held in several towns in Transylvania, the largest of them involving some

10,000 demonstrators. In an attempt to counter hostile media depictions, a manifesto in Romanian explaining the Hungarian minority's opposition to the education law was distributed in the larger Romanian towns. The commission also encouraged Hungarian pupils and teachers to come to school wearing white armbands to mark their protest. A school boycott was considered, but the idea was ultimately dropped, pending a final decision after consulting parents.[70] The Cluj county prefect, Grigore Zanc, repeated official warnings against civil disobedience, which would be a "deliberate infringement on the law, leaving [him] no choice but to act for the purpose of ensuring legality."[71]

The UDMR's tactics reflected the exhaustion of all other means. The Hungarians had, in short, reached the dead-end of Romanian political institutions, unable to defend what both they and Romanian political forces understood to be interests of central importance. Indeed, this was precisely the message laconically delivered by the vice-chairman of the Senate's Education Committee, Emil Tocaci, referring to the UDMR's popular initiative to introduce a counter-proposal to the education law. The Hungarians' proposal, he remarked, should not worry its Romanian opponents. It would either be quashed by the parliament's Judicial Commission, which must approve all draft bills before they are considered, or it would reach the plenum, where it could be submitted in the form of amendments to the law already passed. But the parliament, Tocaci noted, would surely reject the amendments, just as it had rejected nearly every UDMR proposal when the law was first debated.[72]

Back to the Future: The Chimera of Autonomy

While the demand for "partner nation" status had been adopted at the Second Congress in 1991, changing the denomination of the Magyar community to "national autonomous community" was first raised by the radicals at the UDMR's Third Congress in early 1993. Several members of the UDMR parliamentary faction (who, in general, tended at the time to support the moderates), explained that they had had to put up a fierce struggle even to have references to "national minorities" included in the constitution. Doing away with it, they emphasized, entailed serious dangers, possibly serving only the interests of Romanian nationalists. Miklos Fazekas, a member of the Constitutional Court until 1995, warned that the adoption of any terminology other than "national minority" could trigger a constitutional crisis.[73] By 1995, however, the radicals were apparently ready for any sort of confrontation, and the moderates were now outnumbered. This did not make the Fourth

Congress a complete victory for the radicals, just as the 1993 congress had not been a complete victory for the moderates. In 1993, Tokes' bid to replace Domokos as UDMR chairman failed, although Marko, who did replace him, was certainly less inclined than Domokos to passively await a gradual democratization of political culture that would generate greater responsiveness to national minorities' demands. Similarly, in 1995, the radicals' bid for full control of the UDMR failed again. Nevertheless, each congress has marked a *programmatic* radicalization of the UDMR that has steadily delegitimated party moderates.

The 1993 congress took place in an atmosphere established by a UDMR declaration issued in Cluj of October 25, 1992.[74] The declaration reiterated the radicals' demand for equal partnership with the Romanian nation, adding, however, that equality could be institutionalized only by realizing what was termed "communitarian autonomy." This conception was said to derive from a long tradition of ethnic and religious autonomy in Transylvania. But the declaration never defined what communitarian autonomy would amount to in practice. It spoke of the need to achieve "self-administration" without explaining whether or not this implied territorial autonomy. Communitarian autonomy was inevitably what one analyst called a "murky" concept,[75] because it embodied an attempt to postpone confrontations between moderates and radicals within the UDMR itself, as well as moderates' fears of provoking a backlash among Romanians.

The latter consideration did not help the moderates, as the most extremist intentions were immediately imputed by the nationalist media. Yet the media were not alone, and the negative reaction of the Romanian ethnic majority cut across party lines. The UDMR's allies in the CDR made it clear that if communitarian autonomy implied territorial autonomy, their alliance would be endangered. The PUNR immediately called for the party's banning, and Iliescu rejected communitarian autonomy on several occasions, including speeches in parliament.[76] Domokos and his group tried to portray the Cluj declaration as merely an "offer of dialogue" with the ethnic majority, and by no means a step towards territorial autonomy. Tokes, however, was less assuring; he did not rule out territorial autonomy, stating only that "we do not think of secession, which, because of demographic and geographic reasons, would anyhow be impossible."[77] In fact, the Cluj declaration had been crafted by Tokes and his group while Domokos, unaware of the radicals' preparations, was recovering from a stroke. Domokos managed to render the radicals' text ambiguous in an effort to assuage the Romanian majority, but his maneuvering resulted in a vote of no-confidence by the UDMR presidium. And, while the vote was eventually repealed after Domokos pointed out that only a congress could discharge him, he preempted such a move by announcing that he would not seek re-election.[78]

The draft of the UDMR's 1993 program did indeed speak of territorial autonomy, confirming suspicions that despite Tokes's failure to ascend to the leadership, the radicals were emerging victorious. The moderates, led by Senator Gyorgy Frunda, once again emphasized the likely negative reaction of the Romanian majority and were able to salvage a compromise, with the formulation now speaking of "local and regional self-administration, personal and cultural autonomy." But, rendered in Hungarian (*belso onrendelkezens*), this terminology can also be translated as "self-government." And obviously the radicals had precisely this in mind. "Individual and cultural autonomy" was defined as "the preservation of our national identity, comprising culture in all its aspects, the use of the mother tongue, religion, public instruction, social organizations and the right to information." While, on one hand, this could be interpreted as merely an appeal to those individual rights already protected by the constitution, the radicals were already giving the concept another meaning altogether. For Imre Borbely it reflected the right of a Hungarian living in Bucharest, for example, to choose his representative to an ethnically defined parallel legislature. The democratization of the UDMR, according to Borbely, implied that all its political tendencies would be represented in such a legislature, which would have its own budget and decide on all matters pertaining to the Magyar community. This "would be the first step towards self-determination."[79]

A draft bill for a law on national minorities was worked out and submitted to parliament by the UDMR in November 1993.[80] Suffering again from conceptual ambiguity, the draft introduced four key concepts, each of them problematic: "autonomous community," "internal self-determination," "political entity," and "legal entity under public law." An "autonomous community" was defined as "that national minority that identifies itself as such and exercises its rights according to the principle of internal self-determination," yet "internal self-determination" is itself open to interpretations of territorial autonomy, whereas "legal entity under public law" closes the circle, aiming at a redefinition of the state that would introduce the concept of "partner-nation" via the back door. The Romanian Center for Human Rights-Helsinki Committee, by no means an adversary of the UDMR, produced a "critical study" arguing that the four concepts did not meet internationally accepted standards and dangerously played into the hands of Romanian extremists.[81] Small semantic differences notwithstanding, the Fourth Congress in 1995 introduced all of these concepts into the new UDMR program.

"National minority" was replaced by "national autonomous community," which strives to achieve personal, local and territorial autonomy.[82] Personal autonomy was defined in precisely the sense that Imre Borbely expressed it after the Third Congress: "the setting up of an independent Magyar institutional system" in the realm of "education, culture, information, and the preservation and protection of monuments." Personal autonomy is to be "exercised by the public bodies elected by persons belonging to the Magyar community of Romania." It is based on the principle of "self-determination,"[83] and is to be carried out through "electoral lists" that include all who have freely chosen to identify themselves as belonging to the community and through "general, secret and direct elections." The Council of Representatives is to be so elected, although the implementation of this decision has been postponed due to difficulties in conducting a census among the members of the "national autonomous community."

Local autonomy is no longer understood to be merely the "self-management" of local government provided for in existing Romanian legislation, as the moderates long sought to portray the demand. The UDMR program now speaks of "local administration entities with special status." The "special status" is "granted to those local administrative units where persons belonging to the national minorities live in significant proportion" and where the population "agrees to this status in a referendum."

To be sure, there are significant grounds for the Magyar population to feel frustrated and even persecuted as a result of policies on local government carried out by a centralized state that defines itself as national and unitary. The appointment by the Vacaroiu government of two ethnic Romanians as prefects in Harghita and Covasna Counties—one of them an avowed Vatra sympathizer—in 1993 revealed the degree of insensitivity to Hungarian feelings, all the more so since, under the previous government of Theodor Stolojan, a similar attempt to replace ethnic Hungarian prefects eventually led to a compromise whereby a Romanian and a Hungarian ethnic acted as joint prefects.[84]

The conduct of local government affairs was also a major cause of the UDMR's decision to boycott the Council of National Minorities six months after its establishment in March 1993. The timing of its establishment on the eve of deliberations on Romania's admission to the Council of Europe, the definition of its prerogatives, and its structure gave little ground for hope. Yet, as Gyorgy Tokay, then leader of the UDMR parliamentary club in the Chamber of Deputies and a prominent moderate put it, the UDMR decided in favor of "conditional participation."[85] One condition was enactment of a law on national minorities that had been promised in 1990, while the other concerned the pending education law. But participation was suspended due to the government's lack of political will to implement the council's recommendations even on more minor issues.[86] The body had drafted a law allowing for bilingual signs in localities where a national minority comprised 30 percent or more of the population. This was well above the 10 percent margin recommended by the UDMR, but Vacaroiu showed little enthusiasm, evidently wary of losing the nationalists' support.[87]

Against this background, the inclusion in the UDMR's new program of the clause on "local administration entities with special status" demonstrated yet again the radicals' symbiotic relationship with their Romanian counterparts, ensuring the UDMR's continuing isolation. Indeed, attempts by UDMR moderates to promote cooperation became costlier as the radicals gained greater control. At Tokes's and Borbely's instigation, Tokay and Frunda lost their positions as faction leaders in the two chambers in 1993 after they agreed to participate in a dialogue with the authorities organized by an American organization, the Project on Ethnic Relations.[88] Although Tokay was eventually re-elected, he was forced out again by Tokes not long before the Fourth Congress, accused of having instigated an attack on the bishop by Benedek Nagy, a UDMR deputy. In November 1994, the weekly *Tinerama* had reported that Tokes had been asked by the Securitate to report on fellow-students at the theological seminary he attended. Tokes flatly denied the accusation, and Nagy was expelled from the UDMR, but was then reinstated at the Fourth Congress at Tokes's own urging. As the bishop explained, the UDMR and the Magyar community were one, and no one could be expelled from the community.[89]

The Nagy incident showed how powerful the radicals, and their conception of the UDMR, had become. It is on the basis of this conception that the program adopted by the Fourth Congress finally included an explicit commitment to territorial autonomy. "Territorial autonomy," the program stipulated, "results from the association of local public administration entities, into a community of interests." In other words, local administration entities "with special status" could, if they so wished, consolidate control over larger blocks of territory, thereby confirming for most Romanians the grave threat posed by the Hungarians to the integrity of the Romanian state. It was the ultimate blow to the "national state," and at the same time one that had been invited by that very definition. To radicals like Imre Borbely, it was just another step toward Romania's transformation into a federation.[90] But the demographic considerations that, even for the radicals, appear to have ruled out territorial separatism are no less relevant with respect to ethnic federalization.

Postscript: How Much Change in the "Change to Change?"

The overthrow of communism in late 1989 signified not only a change of regime, but also a change in the political status of the national minorities. In the last decade of its existence, Nicolae Ceausescu's regime had pursued an exclusionary strategy toward the ethnic Hungarian minority based on a model according to which nation and demos must coincide.[91] The model (hardly new) practically encouraged the "exit" option for many members of the Hungarian minority, particularly its intellectual elites, who left for Hungary. In the context of the post-1989 transformation, however, this model was simply no longer available unless the country's new political elites were willing to risk Yugoslav-style international isolation. And this was obviously not the case.

Romanian political leaders' strategy toward the Hungarian national minority was consequently changed from an exclusionary to an inclusionary mode. However, inclusionary strategies can be of two types: national or civic. National inclusionary strategies are assimilationist and refuse any "special recognition of minority political or cultural rights."[92] As the foregoing analysis demonstrated, this was precisely the strategy pursued by the Iliescu regime from 1990 to 1996. Yet its success depends, among other things, on the "readiness of members of the minority to give up their identity, their language, and their culture and to accept the utility of the dominant nationality."[93] The very existence of the UDMR attests to the absence of such a readiness, while the "commitment of the majority to a relentless process of assimilation can lead to the frustration of the minority, to its radicalization, the split between moderates and radicals, and the turn to disloyal behavior by some of its members."[94] With the possible exception of the latter development, this accurately describes the evolution of the UDMR up to 1996.

Nothing illustrated this radicalization process more clearly than the initial negative reaction of the UDMR, triggered by fears of further assimilationist policies, to the Basic Treaty between Romania and Hungary signed by prime ministers Nicolae Vacaroiu and Gyula Horn in Timisoara in September 1996. The UDMR felt betrayed by the "mother country" because the Horn government had both excluded its representatives from the treaty negotiations and included minority rights provisions that, in adopting Council of Europe Recommendation 1201, were unacceptable to the UDMR given the Romanian side's insistence on interpreting Recommendation 1201 as ruling out territorial autonomy.

The signing of the treaty, very much driven by both states' aspiration to NATO membership, made evident the continuing importance of the international environment in shaping domestic developments in eastern Europe, including treatment of ethnic minorities.[95] Indeed, subsequent developments within the UDMR itself proved no exception to this influence. Its opposition to the treaty appeared to vindicate for many Romanians the extreme nationalists' portrayal of the party as a disloyal "fifth column," while its position was clearly viewed negatively by western organizations. Thus, in a rapid shift intended to restore its credibility, the UDMR nominated moderate Senator Gyorgy Frunda as its candidate in the November 3, 1996, presidential elections. While it was obvious from the outset that Frunda had no chance of winning, his campaign succeeded in convincing many ethnic Romanians that the UDMR could be sufficiently far-sighted to view the "national problem" as only one, and perhaps not the most important, issue facing Romania. While Frunda finished fourth (out of a field of sixteen) with 6 percent of the popular vote, many Romanians confessed that they would have cast their vote for him had he not been an ethnic Hungarian.[96]

In the parliamentary elections that took place concomitantly with the presidential vote, the UDMR's performance was poorer than in 1992. Its share of the popular vote fell from 7.5 percent to 6.6 percent in voting for the Chamber of Deputies (resulting in the loss of two of its 27 seats) and from 7.6 percent to 6.8 percent in voting for the Senate (which translated into a decline in seats from 12 to 11). This deterioration occurred despite slightly higher absolute numbers of votes in 1996 for both the UDMR's Chamber and Senate slates than in 1992. As in other post-communist countries, the increasing consolidation of Romania's party system meant that fewer votes were wasted on parties that failed to meet the electoral threshold, thereby increasing the "cost" in votes of parliamentary seats. At the same time, in protest against a party decision requiring candidates to reside in their districts, several UDMR deputies and senators ran as independents, thereby steering a significant share of potential votes away from the party lists.

Nevertheless, the decline in parliamentary representation was insignificant compared with the change prompted by the overall electoral outcome. This appeared to herald nothing short of a dramatic shift in Romania's strategy toward its Hungarian minority from national to civic inclusion, defined by a "major effort to accommodate minorities by crafting a series of political and civil arrangements that recognize minority rights."[97] The UDMR became part of the CDR-led coalition government, gaining two portfolios in the cabinet headed by Victor Ciorbea, one of which, the newly established Department for National Minorities, was taken up by Tokay. The creation of a ministry for national minorities had long figured prominently among the UDMR's demands, and, while the coalition agreement stopped short of such a step, the appointment of an ethnic Hungarian with full ministerial rank as head of the new department was an easily acceptable compromise. The change to civic inclusion was further reflected in the government's decisions in May 1997 to amend the controversial 1995 Education Law and the Law on Public Administration, thereby allowing increased use of multi-lingualism in public incriptions. Also of symbolic significance was the reopening in July 1997 of the Hungarian consulate in Cluj, which had been closed by Ceausescu in 1988.

Yet the two laws were amended by "government ordinance," that is, by decrees taking effect immediately but which are eventually abolished unless approved by the parliament. By late 1997, a pronounced shift in the direction of the ethnic Romanian political elite's strategy back to national inclusionary policies had become evident, despite further gains by ethnic Hungarian moderates, reflected most clearly at the UDMR's Fifth Congress in October 1997, which tacitly shelved demands for autonomy. The shift back was initiated and pursued by the UDMR's allies in the ruling coalition, the PNTCD.[98] In December 1997, the Chamber of Deputies amended the government's May decree, restoring the obligation to conduct history and geography courses in national minority schools in the Romanian language, and making practically impossible the establishment of Hungarian-language universities. The same shift prompted the Minister of Interior, Gavril Dejeu, a PNTCD member, to issue regulations effectively sabotaging the display of bilingual street signs and to describe the Hungarian flag atop Hungary's consulate in Cluj as a "provocation."

Two main factors have contributed to the gradual abandonment of civic inclusion. The first is, once again, linked to changes in the international environment, namely Romania's exclusion in June 1997 from the first wave of NATO expansion, and its failure the following month to win inclusion in "fast-track" accession negotiations with the European Union. Ethnic Romanian political leaders clearly saw the concessions made to the Hungarian minority as part of the price of western integration. Once that possibility was pushed into the nebulously distant future, the second factor, which might best be described in anthropological terms as the cultural inhibition of Romania's political elite, strongly reasserted itself. Indeed, just as the PNTCD had supported the PDSR's version of the education law in 1995, it continues to resent ethnic Hungarian demands, which it perceives as a threat to national and state integrity. More broadly, the return of political competition defined by the old polarity of ethnocultural difference versus national hegemony which Romania may now confront reveals much about the nature of its transition from communism, in which a key obstacle to democratic consolidation—the failure to embrace civic inclusion—has yet to be overcome.

Notes

1. See Agentia nationala de presa-Rompres, *Partide politice*, 1993 (Bucharest: Rompres, 1993), p. 147. Its Romanian name, Uniunea Democrata Maghiara din Romania, is commonly rendered in English either as above or as the Democratic Alliance of Hungarians in Romania.

2. See Michael Shafir, "Xenophobic Communism: The Case of Bulgaria and Romania," *The World Today*, vol. 45, no. 12, 1989, pp. 208-212; *idem., Romania: Politics, Economics and Society. Political Stagnation and Simulated Change* (London: Frances Pinter, 1985), pp. 158-165; Kenneth T. Jowitt, *Revolutionary Breakthroughs and National Development: The Case of Romania, 1944-1965* (Berkeley and Los Angeles: University of California Press, 1971), esp. pp. 281-282; Walker Connor, *The National Question in Marxist-Leninist Theory and Strategy* (Princeton: Princeton University Press, 1984), pp. 340-342; and Tom Gallagher, *Romania After Ceausescu: The Politics of Intolerance* (Edinburgh: Edinburgh University Press, 1995), pp. 50-58.

3. For general accounts of this period, see Michael Shafir, "The Revolution: An Initial Assessment," *Report on Eastern Europe*, vol. 1, no. 4, 1990, pp. 34-42; Nestor Ratesh, *Romania: The Entangled Revolution* (Washington: Praeger, 1991), pp. 19-31; Katherine Verdery and Gail Kligman, "Romania after Ceausescu: Post-Communist Communism?," in Ivo Banac, ed., *Eastern Europe in Revolution* (Ithaca: Cornell University Press, 1992), pp. 118-122; Matei Calinescu and Vladimir Tismaneanu, "The 1989 Revolution and Romania's Future," *Problems of Communism* (January-April 1991), pp. 42-59; Vladimir Tismaneanu, "The Quasi-Revolution and Its Discontents: Emerging Pluralism in Post-Ceausescu Romania," *East European Politics and Societies*, vol. 7, no. 2, 1993, pp. 309-348. On the Hungarians' role, see Judith Pataki, "Free Hungarians in a Free Romania: Dream or Reality?," *Report on Eastern Europe*, vol. 1, no. 8, 1990, pp. 18-26; and Gallagher, op. cit., p. 77.

4. *Radio Bucharest* and *Rompres* [in English], January 5, 1990.

5. See Appendices 2 and 4, in *Partide politice*, 1993, pp. 175-191.

6. See Appendix 5 in *ibid.*, p. 192.

7. On Fazekas's party, see *ARPress*, 28 July 1992 and *Dreptatea*, January 19, 1993. For Kiss's position on the UDMR, see, for example, the dispatch on his early September 1995 visit to Budapest in *Romania libera*, 5 September 1995; and *Curierul national*, May 22, 1995, and June 5, 1995.

8. For example, Czech and Slovak minorities, as well as the German minority centered around Sibiu in Transylvania, are each represented by a single deputy as a result of this provision, which was later also included in the Constitution.

9. Counties serve as both administrative units and electoral districts. For a detailed discussion of the proposals, see Michael Shafir, "Romania: Debating Electoral Change," *Transition*, vol. 1, no. 11, 1995, pp. 49-53.

10. See the interview with Chamber of Deputies chairman Adrian Nastase in the daily *Cronica*

romana, September 8, 1995; and the declarations of the PUNR executive secretary Valer Suian, *Radio Bucharest*, 16 August 1995. Victor Surdu, the leader of the small Democratic Agrarian Party (another adversary of the UDMR on national matters) has already predicted that the UDMR would not manage to be represented in parliament by more than one deputy if the law were changed along these lines. *Jurnalul national*, August 9, 1995.

11. See Appendix 3 in *Partide politice*, 1993; Aurelian Craiutu, "A Dilemma of Dual Identity: The Democratic Alliance of Hungarians in Romania," *East European Constitutional Review*, vol. 4, no. 2, 1995, pp. 43-49; and the leaflet "DAHR," undated, published by the UDMR.

12. See Romanian Institute for Human Rights, *Rights of the Persons Belonging to the National Minorities* (Bucharest: Monitorul oficial), 1993, Appendix I/1, p. 112. There are also large Hungarian concentrations in four other Transylvanian counties (Mures, 41.3 percent, Satu Mare, 35 percent, Bihor, 28.5 percent, and Salaj, 23.7 percent). Other counties with significant Hungarian minority concentrations are Cluj (19.8 percent), Arad (12.5 percent), and Maramures (10.2 percent). An additional seven counties have Hungarian populations ranging from 2.2 percent (Caras-Severin) to 9.8 percent (Brasov).

13. See Michael Shafir, "Agony and Death of an Opposition Alliance," *Transition*, vol. 1, no. 8, 1995, pp. 23-28.

14. See Edith Oltay, "The Hungarian Democratic Federation of Romania: Structure, Agenda, Alliances," *Report on Eastern Europe*, vol. 2, no. 29, pp. 29-35, and the DAHR leaflet cited above. The figure of 600,000, and an estimate that roughly 500,000 members regularly pay party dues, was given by two UDMR counselors, Anton Niculescu and Ana-Maria Biro, interviewed by the author in Bucharest in June 1995.

15. See Mircea Kivu, "O abordare empirica a relatiei dintre romani si maghiari" [An Empirical Approach to the relationship between Romanians and Hungarians], *Revista de cercetari sociale*, vol. 1, no. 4, 1994, pp. 3-21.

16. See *Adevarul*, July 18, 1995.

17. Cited in Oltay, "The Hungarian Democratic Federation of Romania."

18. These six platforms were officially recognized prior to the UDMR's Fourth Congress in May 1995. See *Monitorul U.D.M.R.*, no. 6, January 1995, p. 5.

19. Interview with UDMR chairman Bela Marko, Bucharest, June 1995. See also Varujan Vosganian, "Formatiunile politice constituite pe baze etnice," *Polis*, No. 2 (1994), pp. 171-190.

20. Interview with Nicolescu and Biro, June 1995.

21. Oltay, "The Hungarian Democratic Federation"; Aurelian Craiutu, "A Dilemma of Dual Identity"; and author's interview with Niculescu and Biro.

22. Niculescu and Biro interview; *Monitorul U.D.M.R.*, no. 6, 1995, pp. 6-8.

23. See Gallagher, *Romania After Ceausescu*, pp. 78-79.

24. On the Third Congress, see Michael Shafir, "The Congress of the Hungarian Democratic Federation of Romania: Postponed Confrontations," *Sfera politicii* (Bucharest), vol.1, no.3, 1993, pp. 11-12.

25. See Tom Gallagher, "Controversy in Cluj," *Transition*, vol. 1, no. 15, 1995, pp. 58-61.

26. Author's interviews with UDMR parliamentarians, Bucharest, June 1995. On the UDMR 1995 congress, see Tom Gallagher, "Controversy in Cluj," *Transition*, vol. 1, no. 15, 1995, pp. 58-61.

27. Interview with Niculescu and Biro.

28. See Michael Shafir, "Romania: Ruling Party Formalizes Relations with Extremists,"

Transition, vol. 1, no. 5, 1995, pp. 42-46. For the rules governing the functioning of the Council of Mayors and Councilors, see *Monitorul U.D.M.R.,* no. 7, 1995, pp. 7-8.

29. Helsinki Watch, *Struggling for Ethnic Identity: Ethnic Hungarians in Post-Ceausescu Romania* (New York: Helsinki Watch, 1993), p. 98.

30. Nor was the return to old patterns of discourse in 1990 limited to ethnic relations. The FSN's "main electoral base consisted of former party officials, peasants, and unskilled workers," inspiring a "campaign [that] made good use...of many ideas from Ceausescu's time." Verdery and Kligman, "Romania after Ceausescu: Post-Communist Communism?," p. 122.

31. See Vladimir Socor, "Forces of Old Resurface in Romania: The Ethnic Clashes in Tirgu Mures," *Report on Eastern Europe,* vol. 1, no. 15, pp. 36-42; Michael Shafir, "The Romanian Authorities' Reactions to the Violence in Tirgu Mures," *ibid.,* pp. 43-46; on the role of Securitate agents, see Cornel Ivanciuc's revelations in the weekly *22,* no. 27, July 5-11, 1995.

32. See *Viata capitalei,* June 26, 1990; *Azi,* July 22 and 25, 1990; and *Dimineata,* August 4, 1990 (for Cornea); and *Azi,* July 25, 1990 (for Ratiu). The first issue of the FSN daily, *Azi,* included an article by an FSN senator describing the Hungarians as hordes plaguing humanity. *Azi,* April 11, 1990. The same tone was echoed in publications supported by Iosif Constantin Dragan, an émigré sympathizer of the interwar fascist Iron Guard who amassed a fortune in Italy and was named honorary chairman of *Vatra.*

33. See Crisula Stefanescu, "Disputes over Control of Romanian Television," *Report on Eastern Europe,* vol. 2, no. 8, 1991, pp. 28-33; and Helsinki Watch, *Struggling for Ethnic Identity,* pp. 46-50. As a result of the protests, the directive was never implemented, but neither has it been officially rescinded.

34. Michael Shafir and Dan Ionescu, "The Minorities in 1991: Mutual Distrust, Social Problems, and Disillusion," *Report on Eastern Europe,* vol. 2, no. 50, pp. 24-28. Meanwhile, for a list of those arrested and sentenced (none of whom has a Romanian name) see Helsinki Watch, *Struggling for Ethnic Identity,* Appendix A, pp. 125-126.

35. Helsinki Watch, *Struggling for Ethnic Identity,* pp. 12-13; on the so-called Hargita-Covasna report's publication, see *Libertatea, Adevarul, and Evenimentul zilei,* August 23, 1995.

36. *22,* no. 16, April 24-30, 1992; Michael Shafir, "Transylvanian Shadows, Transylvanian Lights," *RFE/RL Research Report,* vol. 1, no. 26, 1992, pp. 28-33; idem., "Ethnic Tension Runs High in Romania," *RFE/RL Research Report,* vol. 3, no. 32, 1994, pp. 24-32.

37. See Michael Shafir, "Romania's New Institutions: The Draft Constitution," *Report on Eastern Europe,* vol. 2, no. 38, 1991, pp. 22-33.

38. Mihai Constantinescu et. al., *Constitutia Romaniei: Comentata si adnotata* (Bucharest: Monitorul Oficial, 1992), p. 23.

39. See Michael Shafir, "Romania: Constitution Approved in Referendum," *RFE/RL Research Report,* vol.1, no. 2, 1992, pp. 50-55.

40. *22,* no. 25, 21-27 June 1995.

41. See Oltay, "The Hungarian Democratic Federation of Romania." According to the prominent radical Imre Borbely, the first "great confrontation" of the two nascent tendencies had already occurred at the first Congress in 1990, and pitted those who had previously held functions in the PCR and the people promoted by then against those who had been "spontaneously elected" as delegates to the Congress. See the interview with him in *Cronica Romana,* May 12, 1995.

42. Romanian Magyar Szo, June 4, 1991, cited in Oltay, "The Hungarian Democratic Federation of Romania."

43. See *ARPress*, May 26, 1994; *Buletin informativ U.D.M.R*, no. 110, 1 June 1994; *Romania libera and Radio Bucharest*, June 1, 1994; and *Adevarul*, June 2, 1994.

44. *Buletin informativ U.D.M.R.*, no. 110, June 1, 1994.

45. *Ibid.*, no. 109, May 31, 1994.

46. See *Evenimentul zilei*, June 23 and 24, 1994; and *Romania libera*, July 1, 1994.

47. *Cotidianul*, June 24, 1994.

48. *Radio Bucharest*, July 10, 1994; *Rompres* [in English], July 12, 1994; *Buletin informativ U.D.M.R.*, no. 149, July 27, 1994; and *Evenimentul Zilei*, July 28, 1994; *Radio Bucharest*, September 19, 1994.

49. See the protest declaration released by the 4th congress of the UDMR on this matter in *Buletin informativ U.D.M.R.*, no. 352, May 30, 1995 and the statement in the Chamber of Deputies by UDMR representative Ferenc Asztalos in *ibid.*, no. 357, June 6, 1995. For the Constitutional Court's ruling see *Romania Libera* and *Curierul National*, August 16, 1995.

50. See *Evenimentul Zilei*, May 23, 1995, and the interview with Varujan Vosganian in *Expres Magazin*, No. 22, June 7-13, 1995.

51. *Buletin informativ U.D.M.R.*, no. 369, June 22, 1995, and the UDMR declaration of May 30, 1995, issued shortly after the beginning of the debates, in *ibid.*, no. 352, May 30, 1995; see also the interview with UDMR Senator Zoltan Hoszu in *Azi*, June 5, 1995.

52. *Buletin informativ U.D.M.R.*, no. 362, June 13, 1995; *Adevarul*, June 14, 1995; *Azi and Cotidianul*, June 15, 1995; *Buletin informativ U.D.M.R.*, no. 363, June 14, 1995; *Libertatea and Curierul National*, June 15, 1995.

53. *Buletin informativ U.D.M.R.*, no. 370, June 23, 1995; *Romania libera*, June 24, 1995; *Buletin informativ U.D.M.R.*, no. 373, June 28, 1995.

54. The text of the law was published in Adevarul, 11 July 1995 and Dimineata, 13 July 1995.

55. See the interview with Bela Marko in *Cronica Romana*, July 1, 1995; and *Curierul National*, August 17, 1995.

56. See the clarifications issued by the UDMR chairman's cabinet on the Federation's objections to the law in *Azi*, August 16, 1995; and *Curierul National*, August 17, 1995. For Archbishop Ioan Robu's denunciation of the law as "no better than the old communist one as regards relations with the Church," see Reuters, September 15, 1995.

57. *Buletin informativ U.D.M.R.*, no. 376, 3 July 1995.

58. *Curierul National*, July 22, 1995.

59. *Dreptatea*, no. 80, August 1995.

60. For the text of the decision, see *Romania Libera*, July 19, 1995. The only Hungarian-ethnic on the Constitutional Court had been recently replaced with a Romanian, eliciting further protest from the UDMR. See *Buletin informativ U.D.M.R.*, no. 360, June 9, 1995.

61. See *ibid.*, no. 380, July 7, 1995.

62. *Radio Bucharest*, July 24.

63. *Ziua*, July 25, 1995.

64. *Azi*, July 13, 1995 and *Adevarul*, July 12, 1995.

65. *Politica*, no. 175, July 8, and no. 176, July 15, 1995.

66. *Curierul National*, August 31, 1995.

67. *Curierul National*, July 26, 1995.

68. *Adevarul*, July 17 and 19, 1995; *Jurnalul National*, July 19, 1995. For the text of the resolution, see *Adevarul*, July 18, 1995.

69. See *Dimineata,* July 20, 1995; *Jurnalul National,* 21 July 1995; and *Curierul National,* July 26, 1995.

70. *Buletin informativ U.D.M.R.,* no. 379, July 6, 1995; Reuters, September 2, 1995; Ziua, August 4 and 26, 1995; *Romania Libera* and *Curierul National,* August 28, 1995; *Curierul National,* August 7, 1995. For the text of the UDMR manifesto, see *Adevarul,* August 4, 1995.

71. *Adevarul,* August 25, 1995.

72. See *Azi,* August 19, 1995.

73. See Shafir, "The Hungarian Democratic Federation of Romania: Postponed Confrontations."

74. See *Tineretul Liber,* October 27, 1992; *Romania Libera,* October 28, 1992; *Lumea Azi,* no. 45, November 5-11, 1992; Shafir, "The Hungarian Democratic Federation of Romania: Postponed Confrontations."

75. Craiutu, "The Dilemma of Dual Identity."

76. For details, see Shafir, "The Hungarian Democratic Federation of Romania: Postponed Confrontations."

77. *Radio Bucharest,* October 29, 1992; *Expres,* no. 44, November 3-9, 1992 (Domokos); *Flacara,* no. 44, November 4-10, 1992 (Tokes).

78. See the interviews with Domokos in *Dreptatea,* October 31, 1992, *Flacara,* no. 44, November 4-10, 1992, and *Brassoi Lapok,* December 23, 1992; and the interview with Tokes in *Romania Libera,* November 4, 1992. For the attempted dismissal of Domokos, see *Rompres* [in English], November 4 and 11, 1992, *Romania Libera* and *Adevarul,* November 11, 1992, and the interview with Tokes in *Romania Libera,* November 4, 1992. For Domokos's admission that the text of the Cluj declaration was ambiguous, *Radio Bucharest,* October 29, 1992.

79. See the interview with him in *Pesti Hirlap* (Budapest), January 27, 1993.

80. For the text of the draft, see Gabrial Andreescu, Valentin Stan, Renate Weber, *Study on the Conception of Democratic Alliance of Hungarians in Romania on the Rights of National Minorities: A Critical Analysis of the DAHR Documents* (Bucharest: The Center for Human Rights APADOR-CH, 1994), pp. 40-56. A law on the national minorities had been promised by the Council of the NSF in its early January 1990 declaration, but, as was the case with other promises, it was never carried out. This is what determined the UDMR to come out with its own legislative initiative. A draft worked out by the Council of National Minorities was submitted to the government, apparently accepted after alterations, but in the end never submitted to parliament. See *Cronica Romana,* May 24, 1995 and *Adevarul,* June 6, 1995. The Center for Human Rights-Helsinki Committee has worked out a third draft law on the national minorities. See *Legislatia in Tranzitie* (Bucharest: The Center for Human Rights-Helsinki Committee, 1995), pp. 103-112.

81. *Ibid.* For a response by the UDMR see Miklos Bakk, "Conceptia UDMR privind drepturile minoritatilor nationale," *Revista Romana de drepturile omului,* no. 6-7, 1994, pp. 86-103.

82. See *Buletin Informativ U.D.M.R.,* no. 353, May 31, 1995.

83. In *ibid.* the Romanian translation is rendered as "self-administration." This seems to be intentionally misleading, judging by the other specifications concerning "personal autonomy."

84. See Michael Shafir, "Minorities Council Raises Questions," *RFE/RL Research Report,* vol. 2, no. 24, 1993, pp. 35-40.

85. Author's interview with Tokay, May 1993.

86. Author's interview with Bela Marko, Bucharest, June 1995.

87. See Michael Shafir and Dan Ionescu, "Romania: A Crucially Uneventful Year," *RFE/RL*

Reasearch Report, vol. 3, no. 1, 1993, pp. 122-126.

88. *International Herald Tribune,* July 21, 1993.

89. See the interview with Tokes in *Expres,* no. 51-52, December 27, 1994-January 2, 1995; *Adevarul,* December 29, 1994, January 5, 1995; *Tineretul liber,* December 31, 1994; *Buletin informativ U.D.M.R.,* nos. 255 and 256, January 3-4 and 5-6, 1995; *Vocea Romaniei,* January 7, 1995; and Gallagher, "Controversy in Cluj."

90. See the interview with Borbely in *Transition,* vol.1, no. 19, 1995 (October 20, 1995), pp. 32-36.

91. The analytical framework applied here is adapted from that of Juan J. Linz and Alfred Stepan, *Problems of Democratic Transition and Consolidation: Southern Europe, South America, and Post-Communist Europe* (Baltimore and London: The Johns Hopkins University Press, 1996), pp. 428-432.

92. *Ibid.,* p. 429.

93. *Ibid.,* p. 430.

94. *Ibid.,* p. 431.

95. For a detailed discussion of pressures on both Hungary and Romania, see Michael Shafir, "A Possible Light at the End of the Tunnel," *Transitions,* vol. 2, no. 19, 1996, pp. 29-32.

96. See Michael Shafir, "Romania's Road to 'Normalcy,'" *Journal of Democracy,* vol. 8, no. 2 (April 1997), pp. 144-158. For a profile of Frunda, see Zsolt-Istvan Mato, "An Ethnic Hungarian in the Romanian Presidential Race," *Transition,* vol. 2, no. 26 (December 27, 1996), pp. 18-19.

97. Linz and Stepan, op. cit., p. 429.

98. For further details, see Michael Shafir, "Ciorbea si democratizarea: bilant intermediar," *Sfera Politicii,* vol. 6, no. 55 (December 1997) (in Romanian).

5

POST-IMPERIAL ETHNOCRACY
AND THE RUSSOPHONE MINORITIES
OF ESTONIA AND LATVIA

Neil J. Melvin

Introduction

With the disintegration of the Soviet state following the failed coup by
Communist hard-liners in August 1991, triumphant democratic forces in
Moscow and the international community quickly recognized *de jure* the independence of the Baltic republics of Estonia, Latvia, and Lithuania. However,
Russian support for the Baltic states was soon replaced by a growing hostility
toward Estonia and Latvia due to the discrimination faced by the Russian
and Russian-speaking populations at the hands of the titular nationalities.
The transformation of the settlers into a dominant political issue in Estonia
and Latvia, in relations between Latvia/Estonia and western Europe, and especially, in relations with the Russian Federation, is rooted in the Soviet annexation of the Baltic states in 1940 and the influx of Russians and Russified
settlers that followed. These developments created deep-seated resentment
among the titular populations, particularly among members of the cultural
elite. During and immediately after the independence struggle of the late
perestroika period, politics in the Baltic republics became heavily informed
by an ethnonationalist response to Russian colonialism, with tension in Latvia
and Estonia exacerbated by the growing political salience of the new Russian
diaspora, particularly those in the Baltic states, in Russia itself.[1]

The settler issue thus became central to nationalist movements that sought
to shape Baltic and Russian political identities. The issue developed simultaneously on three levels: between the indigenous and settler populations;

among the Russian-speakers themselves; and in bilateral relations with Russia. From late 1991, these nationalist movements increasingly focused their activities on the issue of citizenship for the settlers in the two Baltic states, which in turn powerfully shaped the Russian Federation's perceptions of its ethnic diaspora in, and its relationships with, the other former Soviet republics. Thus, to understand the dynamics of ethnic politics throughout Estonia and Latvia requires a careful unraveling of the manner in which the citizenship struggle, ethnicity, and political identity were bound together—indeed, to a degree unmatched in other Russian-speaking settler communities in the former Soviet Union.

Transitions from authoritarianism in eastern Europe have come to require three distinct projects: state-building, nation-building, and the development of relatively autonomous civil spheres.[2] Following independence, these projects failed to develop in tandem in the Baltics. Instead, nation-building emerged as the central process underlying state-building, while the development of civic institutions that could accommodate the Russified settlers remained stunted, particularly in Latvia. This was due in part to the form popular mobilization took in the late 1980s as the Soviet state's ability to exercise centralized control waned. With the weakening of the Communist Party, the bonds of culture, language, and family provided the foundations for collective action against Soviet rule. The cultural-linguistic basis for mobilization was further reinforced by perceptions of Russian expansion and gradual cultural assimilation of Baltic and Finno-Ugric peoples. As a result, protection of the Estonian and Latvian languages and cultures became one of the primary justifications for political activity in the Baltic states during *perestroika*.

In the post-independence period, the powerful ethnocultural national impulse that emerged during the latter years of Mikhail Gorbachev's tenure became the main political force in the two states, and raised three related questions: Who would gain citizenship? What were to be the conditions for obtaining it? And what would happen to those excluded from it? Both states adopted narrow definitions of citizenship that were derived from the citizenship laws that had operated in each country prior to Soviet annexation. Thus, automatic citizenship was granted only to citizens or residents of the states prior to annexation and their descendants. Those who did not qualify for citizenship under these terms were, at best, offered resident (alien) status. Residents were given voting rights in local elections in Estonia but not in Latvia.[3]

Estonia and Latvia share many common political features. Both are democracies featuring politically weak (and indirectly elected) presidents, unicameral legislatures elected by proportional representation, and still maturing state administrative apparatuses. In both states, party politics is marked by a high degree of fragmentation, weak parliamentary discipline, and high candidate turnover.[4] Estonia and Latvia also share cultural affinities owing to common historical predicaments and experiences with Russian and Soviet domination. The environments in which their political elites have made choices affecting the shape of ethnonational politics are also highly similar. Yet, although Estonia and Latvia adopted broadly similar citizenship policies, each republic has evolved in different directions and developed different approaches to the issue of the Russian-speakers. In Estonia, despite a greater social divide between the autochthonous population and the Russian-speakers, the latter have emerged as the most developed settler population in the former USSR, and Estonian officials have encouraged their cultural and political integration. In Latvia, on the other hand, a prolonged debate about naturalization kept inter-ethnic tensions high, and these tensions impeded the internal development of the settler community. At the same time, the Latvian authorities did little to help the Russian-speaking community in constructive ways. As a result, Latvia's Russian-speaking population remains disorganized, *lumpen,* and lacks influence in policy making.

This chapter compares the ethnic politics of the Russian-speaking minorities in both republics. First, it analyzes the political dynamics that lay behind the development of ethno-nationalism as the region's primary political force in the late 1980s and early 1990s. Second, it considers the legacy of this form of politics for the post-independence period, with particular attention devoted to understanding why Estonia has been more successful than Latvia in establishing relatively harmonious inter-ethnic relations.

Comparison of the two cases suggests that Estonia's relative success in integrating the Russian-speaking settlers stems from three mutually reinforcing factors: the adoption by the Estonian leadership of a pro-active strategy of fostering the development of political and cultural institutions among the Russified settlers; the early introduction of a naturalization regime which required the Russian-speakers to decide their relationship to the newly established Estonian state; and, finally, the use of inclusionary political measures to generate a "loyalist" constituency among the political elite of the Russian-speaking community.

The Prehistory of 1990s Nationalist Politics

The ethnonationalist drive amongst the titular populations of Estonia and Latvia that developed in the late 1980s can only be understood within the larger historical context of the Baltic peninsula's relations with Russia. Many

Balts have come to interpret this relationship through a nationalist prism that casts Russia as engaging in a steady process of assimilating Baltic and numerically small peoples in the region.[5] There is a long history of Russian settlement in the region stretching back over nine hundred years; Estonia and Livonia were brought under Russian control by Peter the Great and the region remained closely bound to the Russian Empire from this time until the first world war. However, it was only in the late nineteenth century that Russian ethnicity began to acquire political significance.

In the 1890s, the balance of social relations in the Baltic region began to change with the appearance of new demographic and economic forces. Rapid growth in the rural population, accompanied by industrialization, led to the migration of Estonian and Latvian peasants to urban areas, challenging the six-hundred-year hegemony of German-speakers.[6] Within a few decades, sizable Estonian and Latvian communities had emerged in most cities and towns. At the same time, increasing Russian migration to the Baltic cities as a result of economic development outflanked the Germans from the other side.

While these dramatic socio-economic changes were matched by growing ethnic and national awareness among Estonians and Latvians, in the period prior to the Bolshevik revolution most Baltic nationalists sided with the Russians to counter German dominance. The basis of the alliance was, however, always fragile and Russia's imperial leadership offered little support for Baltic nationalism. Under Alexander II and Nicholas II, imperial policy sought to exert greater control over the Baltic republics by policies designed to Russify the region.[7] The Imperial government aimed at complete Russian dominance within local institutions, particularly the educational system. Attempts were also made to settle Russian peasants on the land, even as Russians continued to stream to the rapidly growing Baltic cities. By 1913, the population of Riga was 39.8 percent Latvian, 20 percent Russian, 13.9 percent German, 9.5 percent Polish, 7 percent Jewish, and 6.9 percent Lithuanian.[8]

However, Baltic independence was not long in coming. The chaos that accompanied the 1917 Revolution allowed the Balts to replace German and Russian governing institutions with their own, while Bolshevik attempts to recapture the region ultimately proved unsuccessful. By the early 1920s, the Estonians and Latvians had established political control within their respective territories and had begun to build the foundations for independent and sovereign states whose status was formalized by the Treaty of Tartu in February 1920 and the Treaty of Riga in August 1920. Dictatorships in the mid-1930s interrupted democratic, parliamentary rule in both Estonia and Latvia. Both states resumed pluralist politics in the late 1930s; however, with the Ribbentrop-Molotov Pact of 1939, there was little opportunity to elaborate on their democratic experiment. Culturally, Russian influence continued in the interwar period. Many Russian refugees (White Russian officers, priests, aristocrats, Russian-speaking Jews, and much of the St. Petersburg intelligentsia) settled in the region, establishing Riga's Russian *émigré* community, the largest after Paris, as a center for Russian arts and letters.[9]

The End of Pre-War Independence

Soviet annexation of the Baltic states in 1940 and the Stalinist terror subsequently unleashed on the local population produced a strong anti-Russian reaction, although the local Russian communities also suffered heavily.[10] Indeed, Russians and Russian culture were key targets for Soviet repression. A combination of terror and an influx of Sovietized Russian-speakers ruthlessly broke up the Russian communities in Latvia and Estonia. By 1945, the pre-war Russian communities of the Baltic region had been all but destroyed by Soviet repression and Nazi wartime rule.

Prior to the Nazi occupation, the extermination of potential opponents of Soviet rule was accompanied by a policy to induce profound demographic change. Russian-speaking Soviet personnel were assigned to help establish political control and develop a core of reliable local administrators. However, the new Soviet order did not simply rely on Russian cadres to consolidate its position. As a result of the first World War and the Bolshevik Revolution, almost 200,000 Latvians ended up in the USSR, tens of thousands of whom were placed in strategic positions in the Baltic states by the Soviets in 1940. In Estonia, Soviet officials undertook mass deportations of ethnic Estonians in 1941 and 1949. Latvian peasants were also deported during this period. In this sense, the subjugation of the Baltic countries was far from being a new form of ethnic Russian imperialism.

After regaining control of the Baltic states following World War II,[11] the Soviet authorities returned to the demographic policies that they had begun to implement in 1940. New settlement began immediately with Red Army officers and soldiers demobilized in the region. Post-war economic reconstruction brought further migration, especially to the cities, where whole neighborhoods sprouted up to accommodate migrants. In the 1960s and

1970s, the economic development of the republics envisaged by *Gosplan* continued this trend, as large all-union, Moscow-directed industrial enterprises (often defense-related) were established in the Baltic republics with little regard for the availability of labor. Alongside the workers and technical intelligentsia who moved to the republics, military personnel were stationed in the area and often retired there. By the 1970s, the comparatively higher standard of living in Estonia and Latvia drew a further wave of migrants from other areas of the USSR.

In addition to providing the workforce necessary for the steady industrialization of the region and creating communities whose primary loyalty was to Moscow, the rising numbers of Russian-speakers acted as *kulturtrager* for the admixture of Soviet and Russian culture that formed the core of Soviet identity. The Russian language lay at the heart of this officially sanctioned culture. Soviet authorities pursued one-way bilingualism in the region—Estonians and Latvians were expected to know Russian as well as their native language, but migrants needed only Russian.[12] Gradually, indigenous culture and language were displaced from their previous positions of dominance. In Latvia, 227,783 non-Russians (about 18 percent of non-Russians) considered Russian to be their first language by 1989, while only 34,429 non-Latvians (fewer than 3 percent of non-Latvians) spoke Latvian as their primary language.

Although the majority of settlers identified themselves as ethnic Russians in Soviet censuses, the settler communities also contained significant numbers of non-ethnic Russians, including Ukrainians, Belarusians, and Jews. In fact, the identity of Baltic settlers was defined primarily by socio-economic and linguistic factors rather than ethnic ones. The core of the migrant population was drawn from those sectors of Soviet society most closely tied to the successes of the regime—industrial workers and members of the military and security apparatus. They were also largely rootless in an ethno-cultural sense; their settlement in the Baltic region was not merely Russian colonization in a new guise, but Sovietization using a Russian-speaking, de-ethnicized immigrant population.[13]

The most extreme case of Sovietisation in the USSR took place in Latvia, where the proportion of the republic's self-identified Latvian population fell to 52 percent by 1989. As early as the 1950s, a number of leading Latvian Communist Party officials expressed concern to Moscow about the number of migrants and were promptly removed from their positions by Khrushchev. The scale of migration to both republics can be seen in tables 1 and 2.

Table 1:
Population of Latvia by Ethnic Origin: 1935-1989 (thousands)

Ethnic Origin	1935	%	1959	%	1970	%	1979	%	1989	%
Latvian	1,467.0	77.0	1,279.9	62.0	1,341.8	56.8	1,344.1	53.7	1,387.8	52.0
Russian	168.3	8.8	5,564.0	26.6	704.6	29.8	821.5	32.8	905.5	34.0
Belorussian	26.7	1.4	61.6	2.9	94.7	4.0	111.5	4.5	119.7	4.5
Polish	48.6	2.6	59.8	2.9	63.0	2.7	62.7	2.5	60.4	2.3
Ukrainian	1.8	0.01	29.4	1.4	53.5	2.3	66.7	2.7	92.1	3.4
Lithuanian	22.8	1.2	32.4	1.5	40.6	1.7	37.8	1.5	34.6	1.3
Jewish	93.4	4.9	36.6	1.7	36.7	1.6	28.3	1.1	22.9	0.9
German	62.1	3.3	1.6	0.1	5.4	0.2	3.3	0.1	3.8	0.1
Estonian	6.9	0.4	4.6	0.2	4.3	0.2	3.7	0.1	3.3	0.1
Gypsy	3.8	0.2	4.3	0.2	—	—	6.1	0.2	7.0	0.3
Tatar	0.04	0.0	1.8	0.1	—	—	3.8	0.2	4.8	0.2
Other	3.9	0.2	7.1	0.4	19.3	0.8	13.3	0.6	24.7	0.9
Total	1,905.4		2,093.5		2,364.1		2,502.8		2,666.6	—

Source: Juris Dreifelds, "Immigration and Ethnicity in Latvia," *Journal of Soviet Nationalities*, vol. 1, no. 4 (Winter 1990-91), p. 48. *Note:* Shortly before annexation, the proportion of Latvians was even higher, reaching 83 percent in 1940. In Estonia, during the Soviet period there was a similar, though less large-scale in-migration.

Table 2:
Population of Estonia by Ethnic Origin: 1934-1989 (thousands)

Ethnic Origin	1934	%	1959	%	1970	%	1979	%	1989	%
Estonian	992	88.1	893	74.6	925	68.2	948	64.7	963	61.4
Russian	92	8.1	240	20.1	335	24.7	409	27.9	475	30.3
Ukrainian	—	—	16	1.3	28	2.1	36	2.5	48	3.1
Belorussian	—	—	11	0.9	19	1.4	23	1.6	28	1.8
Finnish	2	0.2	17	1.4	19	1.4	18	1.2	17	1.1
Jewish	4	0.4	5	0.4	5	0.4	5	0.3	5	0.3
German	16	1.5	2	0.1	8	0.7	4	0.3	3	0.2
Swedish	8	0.7	—	—	—	—	0.2	0.0	0.3	0.0
Latvian	5	0.5	3	0.2	—	—	4	0.2	3	0.2
Other	5	0.4	10	1.1	18	1.1	17	1.3	23	1.7
Total	1,126		1,197		1,356		1,464		1,565	—

Source: Estonian and Soviet Census Data. *Note:* Pre-1940 and post-1940 figures are not directly comparable due to border revisions undertaken in 1945, when territory that had been occupied by Estonia in 1920 was ceded to the Russian Federation. In 1945, the proportion of ethnic Estonians reached 97.5 percent, with only 23 000 non-Estonians living in the republic.

Many of the migrants to the Baltic republics occupied positions strategic to reproducing centralized Soviet control. The Russian-speaking settlers dominated the machine-building, energy, transport, construction, and manufacturing sectors of the economy. While Estonians and Latvians held important political positions, the presence of a Russian-speaking deputy usually ensured compliance with Moscow. Non-Balts were also over-represented in the republic-level Communist Party and in crucial areas of the local state administration. Moreover, the geographic concentration of the settlers reinforced their economic and political domination. In both Estonia and Latvia, rapid urbanization and the large-scale migration led to a two-way structural shift in the distribution of the population. Non-indigenous Russian-speakers were consolidated in the two capitals (Tallinn and Riga), where the share of the titular nationality fell dramatically—in Riga's case to less than half. At the same time, non-Balts predominated in industrial towns and districts. The smaller and less industrial the town, the higher the proportion of Estonians and Latvians was likely to be. By 1989, Latvians were minorities in the country's seven largest cities, constituting only 36.5 percent of the population in Riga. In Estonia, migration followed a similar pattern, with 80 percent of the non-Estonian population concentrated in the cities of the north (especially Tallinn), the northeast, and Paldisk, while only 8.5 percent lived in the countryside. However, unlike the integrated form of settlement that emerged in Latvia—districts and even blocks of flats often contain mixed populations of settlers and Latvians—in Estonia the migrants concentrated in Russian-speaking enclaves.

By the 1980s, Estonians and Latvians saw themselves as facing a demographic crisis. The age structure and rates of natural increase among the Russified settlers were such that even if migration stopped completely, the Latvian and Estonian populations would continue to dwindle relative to the non-indigenous populations. Yet, despite the growing threat to the indigenous population, relations with the migrants were not always tense. Latvia, in particular, featured relatively high rates of inter-marriage. In 1988, 19.7 percent of marriages in the republic involving Latvians were of mixed nationality, which was close to the rates in the predominately Slavic republics of Belorussia (20.1 percent) and Ukraine (20.9 percent), and compares to only 8.6 percent in Estonia and 4.3 percent in Uzbekistan.[14]

The historical prelude to Baltic independence is crucial for understanding contemporary ethnic politics in several respects. First, it reveals the resentment of Soviet and Russian rule after decades of oppression. As in other post-communist societies, this resentment would constitute a potentially renewable resource for political entrepreneurs seeking bases of electoral support. Second, the brief, and often turbulent, interwar period of Baltic independence meant that Estonia and Latvia lacked strong traditions of independent, democratic rule.

Third, by the 1980s, demographic trends and continued threats from the East had rendered these states' titular nationalities highly insecure about their prospects for ethnic survival. However, in contrast to titular nationalities elsewhere in the Soviet Union (e.g., Central Asia), the Balts could look back on long historical lineages and distinct cultures that were able to survive the Soviet period intact and robust.[15] Fourth, as is discussed below, the cultural ambiguity of Russian-speakers in the Baltics during the Soviet period meant that as the transitions to independence ensued, the ethnic and national status of Russian speakers would remain fluid. During this period, individual Russian speakers, influenced in part by collective political actors, would make important choices about their language use, civic allegiance, and cultural practices.[16] Significantly, then, the political dynamics of the transition from Soviet rule and the first decade of independence would have an important influence on the future self-understandings of Russian speakers in the Baltics.

Russian Speakers During the Independence Struggle

The struggle for independence that developed in the Baltic republics in the late 1980s exposed the precarious nature of the Russian-speaking population's identity. In response to the emergence of powerful national separatist movements (the Popular Fronts), the Russian-speakers began, for the first time, to question their position in the Baltics and their relationship to the Baltic peoples. Two main political tendencies emerged within the Russian-speaking population: one was based on a Soviet-Russian identity and loyalty to the Soviet state, and the other on a Baltic-Russian identity rooted in a territorially-based loyalty. The Soviet-Russian tendency was more noticeable and better organized than the Baltic-Russian movement because it was channeled to a significant degree through the existing structures of the Communist Party, the security apparatus, and the military. The Baltic-Russian tendency, on the other hand, was subsumed within the Popular Fronts and had little organization of its own. Opinion polls conducted at the time suggest, however, that there was more support among Russian-speakers for the Baltic-Russian tendency.[17]

Adherents of the Soviet-Russian tendency formed the basis of the anti-independence movement, and joined forces with groups in Moscow to create shadowy Soviet loyalist organizations—Interfronts (*Interdvizhenie*)—that were formed to craft popular appeals to the Russian-speaking populations.[18] In both republics, the Interfronts sought support from workers and administrators within all-union industrial plants and from the military and security apparatus, emphasizing economic entitlements in place of the Popular Fronts' stress on human rights. Although these organizations attracted a great deal of attention, they achieved only modest success in politically mobilizing Russian speakers, with the exception of a number of heavily Sovietized enclaves. In Latvia, Daugavpils emerged as an Interfront power base. In 1989, the city Soviet called for regional autonomy and in 1990 it adopted a resolution repudiating the Latvian Declaration of Independence of May 4, 1990. In Estonia, the Interfront drew support from the cities of the Northeast, particularly Narva, where similar demands for territorial autonomy were made. In both republics, pro-Soviet organizations were represented in parliament. In May 1990, radicals in Latvia's Supreme Soviet from the Latvian Communist Party and the Interfront formed the Equal Rights faction. In Estonia, the Inter-regional Council of People's Deputies, based on the Committee of the Defense of Soviet Power and Civil Rights in Estonia, was created the same month.

The Popular Fronts in both Latvia and Estonia deliberately fostered support among the non-indigenous population, in particular by seeking to co-opt representatives of the Russian-speaking intelligentsia. Special Russian cultural organizations were established and the Fronts in both Estonia and Latvia published Russian-language papers.[19] While representatives of the Russian-speaking communities in the independence movements always played a secondary role to Estonian and Latvian activists, support for the Popular Fronts among the settlers was by no means weak. From 1989 to 1991, the Russian-speaking populations demonstrated growing support for Baltic independence. A poll conducted in 1990, for example, indicated that 45 percent of non-Latvians favored independence. More revealingly, given that 74 percent of the deputies following the March 1990 parliamentary elections were ethnic Latvians, it is probable that far more Russian-speakers voted for Popular Front candidates than for Soviet loyalists.

In January 1991, Soviet troops quelled demonstrations in Riga, resulting in three deaths. On March 3, the Latvian Supreme Council called a non-binding consultative plebiscite on Latvian independence and democracy in order to pre-empt a referendum called by the USSR Supreme Soviet. Despite the efforts of the local Communist Party and the Interfront to organize a boycott, turnout was 87.6 percent; 73.7 percent voted for independence, with not a single district or city, including the highly Sovietized Daugavpils, opposed.[20] While a breakdown of voting by ethnic groups is not available, the magnitude of the pro-independence vote and its distribution indicates that sizable numbers of Russian-speakers voted for independence. Indeed, an opinion poll conducted just two days before the January 1991 Soviet crackdown in Riga indicated that two-thirds of Latvia's Russian-speakers supported the outlook of the Latvian Supreme Council, and support for the pro-Soviet organizations declined.[21]

A similar trend was evident in Estonia. Between April 1989 and June 1990, the share of non-Estonians supporting the idea of an independent Estonia increased more than five-fold (from 5 percent to 27 percent).[22] A poll conducted in December 1990 showed that the idea of an independent Estonia was supported by 28 percent of non-Estonians born in the republic and by 14 percent of those who had settled there.[23] In the 1990 elections for the Supreme Soviet, support for pro-Soviet organizations totaled only 28.2 percent. In the referendum on independence in the spring of 1991, 37–40 percent of non-Estonians supported the idea, while another poll published in September 1991 indicated that 55 percent of the Russian-speaking population had supported independence during the August putsch. The latter poll also indicated an even higher level of support for independence among the non-Estonians in the Northeast (Narva 77 percent, Sillamae 91 percent, and Kokhtla-Iarve 77 percent).

Research conducted by the sociologists Klara Hallik and Marika Kirch indicates the rapid and fundamental change in the way Russian-speakers in Estonia thought about the republic. In 1986, 72 percent of Estonians identified with the Estonian nation, 18 percent identified with the population of the Estonian Republic as a whole, and only 10 percent with all the people of the USSR. On the other hand, 78 percent of Russian-speakers in Estonia identified with the USSR as a whole, while only 14 percent of Russians felt close to Russia and only 8 percent identified with the Estonian Republic.[24] Yet by 1991, Russian-speakers in both Estonia and Latvia were the least pro-Soviet settlers in the USSR. Only 59 percent of Russian-speakers in Estonia and 52 percent of Russian-speakers in Latvia considered themselves to be citizens of the USSR, compared to 68 percent in Georgia, 77 percent in Kazakhstan, and 88 percent in Uzbekistan.[25]

Independence, Nationalism, and Citizenship

The defeat of the August 1991 coup by hard-liners in Moscow marked the triumph of the pro-independence forces in the Baltic republics. However, the Russian-speaking populations of the region were ill-prepared for independence and the dissolution of the USSR. While the forms of popular and elite mobilization used in the political struggles of the late 1980s and early 1990s had done much to affirm the ethnic and national identities of the Estonians and Latvians, the settler community faced a major crisis of identity. Russified settlers in the Baltic republics lacked well-developed indigenous social and political institutions capable of promoting new identities and were simultaneously confronted by powerful ethnonationalist movements. As a result, by the beginning of 1992 both Soviet-Russian and Baltic-Russian movements faced severe challenges.

Most of the the Baltic region's pro-Soviet organizations were banned after the August 1991 Moscow coup, while the end of the USSR meant that support from Moscow for these organizations largely ceased. Communist successor parties in both states collapsed. But the pro-Soviet organizations faced an even more serious ideological crisis as the Communist value system that had underpinned their political agenda was discredited. While a number of former Soviet politicians began to reorient themselves toward Russia and Russian nationalist organizations, many abandoned politics altogether, blaming the democratic forces now in charge in Moscow for the collapse of the USSR.

Like the pro-Soviet organizations, the Baltic-Russian tendency also faced an identity crisis. In the absence of independent civil structures and democratic institutions, nations and ethnic groups appeared as the only collective actors capable of representing anti-totalitarian and anti-imperial interests.[26] With the passing of the Soviet threat, the independence movements fragmented along ideological and personal cleavages. One of the few elements that united former allies was fear of the enemy within—the "fifth column" of Soviet-Russian influence. Russian-speaking activists within the Popular Fronts were quickly marginalized and support for Russian cultural organizations ceased as anti-Russian sentiments became the main substance of politics and the litmus test of loyalty to the new states. The transformation of the Baltic independence movements into largely ethnonationalist movements thus placed increasing pressure on the settlers, while the emergence of the Russian Federation as an independent state provided a surrogate entity that could claim the settlers' allegiance. In this climate, the issue of citizenship quickly emerged as the focal point for the political struggle to define the new nations in both Baltic republics. There were, however, important differences between the responses of the settler communities in Estonia and Latvia to these challenges. Initially, Estonia, more than Latvia, seemed to adopt a more confrontational approach to the Russian-speaking settlers by introducing a highly restrictive definition of citizenship and relegating the rest of the population to resident alien status or requiring that they undergo a rigorous process of naturalization.

In fact, the establishment of a clear process for determining the status of the settlers proved more significant than the substance of the original definition. In Latvia, by contrast, the immobility of domestic politics prevented the emergence of a process for defining the status and rights of the settlers until more than three years after independence. As will be demonstrated below, this variation in timing led to important differences between Estonia and Latvia in the political salience of the settlers issue and, consequently, in the quality of these states' transitions toward stable, democratic polities.

Latvia

After the 1991 coup attempt in Moscow the political composition of the Latvian parliament changed dramatically, with important consequences for the nature of the Latvian state. Until August 1991, political power in Latvia was distributed among three groups of deputies in the Supreme Soviet. The Popular Front of Latvia (PFL) comprised just under two-thirds of the deputies, and the Equal Rights group (*Ravnopravie*) made up about one-third of the deputies, many of whom were ethnic Russians and a majority of whom were pro-Soviet. The remaining deputies belonged to a small group of independents that generally voted with the PFL.

On August 24, 1991, the Supreme Council banned all organizations suspected of aiming to overthrow Latvia's government. The ban was particularly aimed at the Communist Party. The Equal Rights group lost more than half its strength because these deputies had supported the Communist leader Alfred Rubriks, who was accused of trying to seize power in the republic during the August coup. In October 1991, the Supreme Council dissolved the Soviet loyalist city councils of Daugavpils and Rezekne, along with the council in the Leningrad district of Riga. The arrest of Rubriks and the loss of 14 of the Equal Rights deputies gave the Latvian nationalist forces a majority in parliament. This majority allowed the nationalists great leeway in directing Latvia's political and social transition, particularly in defining the new Latvian state in exclusionary terms. On October 15, the parliament adopted the law on citizenship, based on the 1919 Latvian citizenship law, thereby denying citizenship to most non-Latvians. Similarly, with the demise the USSR, the May 5, 1989, language law, which required that Latvian become the sole official language, was fully implemented.

With the collapse of the USSR the Popular Front quickly disintegrated into a range of factions and independent deputies in which there was no place for the Baltic-Russian forces.[27] Thus, the local Russian community was unable to offer organized resistance to these measures. In an environment in which state institutions and ideological cohesion were weak, and with both pro-Soviet and pro-independence settler institutions ineffective, politics was reduced to the language of the "three D's"—de-occupation, de-Bolshevization, and decolonization. Extremist organizations such as the Citizens Congress (which had originally tried to usurp the role of the Supreme Council and government of Latvia) became particularly active with the support of a cluster of radical groups. More importantly, many leading Latvian politicians spoke openly about the need to "encourage" non-Latvians (especially Russians and Russian-speakers) to leave.[28]

In this environment, neither Latvia's executive nor its unicameral legislature (the 100-seat *Saeima*) developed a strategy to facilitate the creation of civil institutions within the non-Latvian community. On the contrary, Latvian elites rendered powerless those existing official institutions established to act as a bridge between Latvians and non-Latvians. For example, the Nationalities Department of the Council of Ministers was established in 1991 to assist organizations created by the Popular Front in 1988-89 to develop national cultures amongst non-Latvians and to foster support for the Front. The Department was meant to serve as a link to the Front and later the government, but was soon ignored by parliament. In 1992, it was transferred to the Ministry of Justice and downgraded. Not merely moderate Russian-speakers, but also those Latvians sympathetic to the problems of non-Latvians were largely driven out of mainstream Latvian politics, which since independence has been much influenced by several right-wing nationalist parties and other extremist groups. The only potential leader with the foresight or the political means to address ethnic problems directly, Janis Jurkans, was removed as Foreign Minister in November 1992 after claiming that the draft citizenship law was discriminatory. Although the development of a partly autonomous civil society among the non-Latvian population was not incumbent upon Latvia's state apparatus, important opportunities to assist this population with the articulatio, and aggregation of its interests, were missed.

As a result of the independence struggle in Latvia, the Russian and Russian-speaking population remained highly fragmented and leaderless.[29] In the years following independence, approximately 63 organizations claimed to represent the Russian-speakers. However, disfranchisement encouraged the Russian-speaking population to rely increasingly on the formerly anti-independence organizations, particularly Equal Rights.[30] Originally very close to the Latvian Communist Party, its leading figures were not Russians and therefore gained Latvian citizenship automatically.[31] Following the 1991 coup, when nine deputies left the faction and others were banned for their Communist affiliation, the organization attempted to distance itself from communist ideology, concentrating instead on the citizenship question and changing its name to the Socialist Party. In the 1993 elections, Equal Rights won seven seats in the Saeima. The party also gained seats in the local elections of 1994 and again in the parliamentary elections of 1995. Of all the parliamentary parties, only Equal Rights supported the "zero option" for citizenship—unconditional citizenship for all residents of Latvia at the time of independence.[32]

The more moderate Russian groups that emerged from the Baltic-Russian movement during *perestroika* fared little better than the pro-Soviet organizations after independence. In March 1989, the Latvian Popular Front, seeking to counter the influence of the Interfront through the promotion of Russian cultural organizations, created the Russian Cultural Association of Latvia (LORK), which immediately declared its solidarity with the Front and received assistance from the Latvian local council in Riga. Representatives of LORK, along with members of the Latvian intelligentsia, personally lobbied Gorbachev on behalf of Latvian independence. As the Front became more nationalistic, however, it withdrew support for LORK. After independence, LORK was abandoned and subsequently collapsed.

In 1988, elements of the Slavic cultural intelligentsia formed the Balto-Slavic Association for Cultural Development and Co-operation. Initially, it sought to occupy a position between the PFL and the Interfront, but it was closer to the latter. After the August 1991 putsch, its leadership accepted Latvian independence, although the organization subsequently embraced a strong form of Russian nationalism. Lacking financial support, however, the organization could do little, and, although new Russian cultural groups were established after independence, they were short of funds and could reach out to only a tiny percentage of the Russian-speaking population.

Drawing on the high number of military personnel in Latvia, several reactionary organizations emerged during the independence struggle.[33] On October 5, 1993, following the violent dissolution of the Congress of People's Deputies in Moscow, the Latvian government announced banned three organizations it termed "illegal and pro-Communist": the Union of Latvian Communists, the Union for the Defense of Veterans' Rights, and the Russian Citizens Association of Latvia. It charged that the leaders of these organizations —Igor Lopatin, Oleg Kapranov, and Viktor Alksnis—were planning a coup in Latvia with former members of the Soviet internal security service.[34]

Although ex-Soviet organizations shaped post-independence settler politics, some Russian-speaking elites attempted to form new, more moderate groups.

The Center for a Democratic Initiative (CDI), formed with the help of the nine defectors from Equal Rights, was established in late 1991 with the aim of organizing Russian-speakers on the basis of "liberal individualism, human rights, and support for universal citizenship." The CDI formed the core of the Russian Democratic List in the 1993 elections. However, as its leadership lacked Latvian citizenship, the list failed. The non-Latvian population consistently rated the Latvian politician Janis Jurkans one of its favorite politicians, and his party (Harmony for Latvia) received assistance from leading settler businesses.[35] However, Jurkans remained on the margins of Latvia's nationalist mainstream politics.

The settler community played a crucial economic role in the early 1990s. Forced out of state employment by the requirement of fluency in the Latvian language, many non-Latvians moved into the private sector and used former Soviet institutions, particularly the *Komsomol* (the former youth wing of the Communist Party), as the basis for new economic activity. By late 1993, non-Latvians controlled the majority of Latvian banks. The Russian-speaking business community built close ties to Russia, and Riga emerged as a major "off shore" center for capital from the Russian Federation. Although much of this money has been linked to criminal activity, some research has suggested that the close economic interests between Latvian and Russian-language businessmen may provide a basis for a degree of inter-ethnic reconciliation.[36]

Although Riga contained by far the largest concentration of settlers in Latvia, Daugavpils was also an area of settler political activity. Designated as a centre for the Soviet defense industry after World War II, Daugavpils emerged as a focus for Soviet resistance to the Latvian Popular Front. The local party-state *nomenklatura* became immensely powerful and promoted the region's thorough Sovietization.[37] This political network was then used in the late 1980s to build up a powerful base of support for the Interfront. In August 1991 the Daugavpils Soviet launched an initiative to mobilize towns like Narva and Tiraspol in Moldova in support of the coup.

With independence the Latvian authorities disbanded the Daugavpils Soviet and installed a new mayor, Valdis Lauskis, who sought to break the grip of Soviet loyalists by supporting various national-cultural organizations in the area. Alongside Jewish, Polish, and Ukrainian associations, he fostered the development of the Baltic-Slavic Society based on the area's Old Believer religious community. Here, as elsewhere, the Latvian state helped to develop an institutional infrastructure for the development of new, non-Soviet, primarily ethnic identities amongst the settlers, mainly for the purpose of dividing the non-Latvian population.[38]

Jurmalia constituted a second major regional center for settler activity. There, a Russian community developed in the final years of the *perestroika* period based on those in mixed marriages, long-term Latvian residents, and young Russian entrepreneurs. However, despite sizeable concentrations of settlers outside the capital, there was little cultural, political, or economic integration between either regional settler organizations or between groups in Riga.

The June 1993 elections revealed the cumulative problems facing the non-Latvian community.[39] With only citizens of Latvia eligible to vote, 34 percent of the population was disfranchised. Conversely, Latvia's electorate remained about 78 percent ethnic Latvian.[40] The elections signaled a popular shift to rightist forces comprising nationalist and radically pro-market politicians, with 75 percent of the vote going to center-right or far-right parties. Anatolii Gorbunovs, leader of Latvian Way, emerged as victor with 32 percent of the vote and formed a coalition with another center-right party, the Farmers Union (10.6 percent). Both parties aimed at a "gradual naturalization" of the non-Latvian population.[41]

Two parliamentary factions defending the interests of the non-Latvian population gained representation: Jurkan's Harmony for Latvia and Equal Rights. Equal Rights gained 5.77 percent of the popular vote, including one seat in a primarily Latvian area, Vidzeme, while receiving only 40 percent of the vote in Daugavpils. Jurkan's Harmony for Latvia gained 11.98 percent of the vote and 13 seats. The Russian List of Vorontsov and Gavrilov ran on a program of granting citizenship to all those resident in Latvia on May 4, 1990 (the date of independence), Russian language rights in regions of compact Russian settlement, and rapid privatization. Unable to find strong candidates fluent in Latvian, the Russian List gained only 1.16 percent of the popular vote, falling far short of the 4 percent electoral threshold.

With Latvian nationalist control of parliament consolidated, in November 1993 the *Saeima* chose from among the five draft laws the proposal on naturalization formulated by Latvia's Way. With nationalists expressing strong fears that rapid integration of the Russian-speakers would "overwhelm" the ethnic Latvian population, the rate of naturalization immediately emerged as a central issue.[42] After prolonged debate, the parliament passed a draft version of the law that would have imposed a very low annual quota. Under strong international pressure, President Ulmanis sent the bill back to the parliament. Under the terms of a revised bill enacted at the end of July 1994, 400,000 of Latvia's 700,000 resident aliens would be able to apply for naturalization, and the process should be completed by 2003.[43]

Although Latvia developed a legal basis for citizenship, the very slow naturalization process contributed to low levels of voting by Russian-speakers.

Little influence over electoral outcomes meant, in turn little meaningful influence over national politics. Because the overwhelming majority of the Russian-speaking population was unable to vote, the May 1994 local elections amounted to another victory for Latvian nationalist parties. This was most visible in Riga, where only 340,000 inhabitants out of a population of 800,000 were eligible to vote.[44] Although the introduction of the quota system did lead to the emergence of a new settler organization, the League of Non-Citizens, uniting some of the leaders of the Russian-speaking population, all such organizations remained weak in the absence of any capacity to compete for public office.

By the fall 1995 parliamentary elections, the political situation in Latvia remained inhospitable for the Russian-speaking population. A large majority of residents still lacked citizenship. The moderate nationalist Latvia's National Conservative Party (LNNK) gained only eight seats in the parliament, while the radical nationalist For Fatherland and Freedom (FFF) party captured 16 seats. The biggest surprise of the election was the capture of 14 seats by the far-right People's Movement for Latvia, led by German-born Joachim Siegrist. Siegrist was under a warrant for arrest in Germany for his alleged participation in anti-Roma violence.[45] The parties supportive of the settlers, the People's Harmony Party and the Socialist Party (the former Equal Rights party) received only six and five seats, respectively. However, as is common with Latvian political parties, the Socialist Party disintegrated, and its five MPs became independents.

Nationalist Latvian political forces, drawing on their secure place within the government's ruling coalition, continued to influence much of the country's policy-making concerning Russian-speakers. In 1996, the FFF continued to attempt to tighten the citizenship law. In the spring of 1998, it also blocked passage of an amendment aimed at liberalizing the law and secured passage of a new labor law that facilitated the firing of non-Latvian speakers.[46] In March and April 1998, a series of violent incidents by radical nationalist extremist groups caused serious damage to Latvia's relations with Russia, which imposed energy sanctions and threatened other economic measures.[47] The European Union expressed outrage; in June, 1997, it blocked Latvia from the first round of accession negotiations, partly due to Latvia's citizenship law and other policies relating to the treatment of Russian-speakers.[48]

Faced with the prospect of continuing international isolation, Prime Minister Guntars Krasts secured parliament's June 1998 passage of a liberalized citizenship law. The law abolished age brackets and the bizarre quota system that had slowed the pace of naturalization. The amended law also gave automatic citizenship to children of non-citizens born in Latvia. However, difficult history and language tests remained significant hurdles to Russian-speakers' naturalization.[49] In a very positive sign, the new law was ratified by a popular referendum in October, 1998. Moreover, the government had taken other steps to improve its international standing and stabilize policy-making regarding Russian-speakers. For example, in December, 1996, it established a Human Rights Bureau to monitor state policies and ensure compatibility with international standards (especially those set forth by the Council of Europe). However, the bureau reported to the *Saeima,* was given weak powers, and became marred in a financial scandal in June 1998.

Also in October, parliamentary elections resulted in the formation of another center-right government. The left-wing For Human Rights in a United Latvia, the pro-settler party, won 16 seats but remained without influence in parliament. Meanwhile, the governing coalition included the FFF-LNNK, which continued to wield its influence over the settler issue. For example, it compelled its partners, the two larger center-right parties, Prime Minister Andris Skele's People's Party and Latvia's Way, to pass a new law extending restrictions on the use of non-Latvian languages in public administration to the private sector. The more liberal parties passed the law over the objections of several international organizations, including the office of the OSCE High Commissioner on National Minorities. Latvia's new president, Vaira Vike Freiberga, vetoed the law in July 1999. However, given the position of the nationalist parties in the coalition, and the continuing salience of ethno-national politics amidst Latvia's highly disorganized partisan competition, it seems that Latvia will continue to be preoccupied with the settler issue.[50]

Estonia

Although the pattern of inter-ethnic relations in Estonia broadly followed developments in Latvia, important differences emerged between the two republics following independence. While Latvian elites continued to construct a narrowly ethnocratic state and society, key segments of Estonian society and many of its leading politicians came to accept that the Russian-speaking settlers should play an important role in the new order. The most important factors driving this development were international pressure, a greater willingness among Estonian politicians to compromise, and a more active non-Estonian community. In contrast to Latvia, the drive for cultural unity in Estonia declined in political salience. Instead, elites and masses became increasingly concerned with socioeconomic interests conceived in non-national terms.

The period of mono-ethnic state-building in Estonia lasted from August 1991 until the middle of 1993. During this time, Estonia became a member of the United Nations, the Organization for Security and Co-operation in Europe, and other international bodies, and the fundamental principles of the Estonian state were set forth in a series of basic laws. The Estonian Popular Front had originally proposed a zero-variant for citizenship based on residence in the republic on March 30, 1990, but was opposed by the nationalist Congress of Estonia. As in Latvia, Estonian nationalists grew more powerful following independence, introducing a citizenship law in November 1991 that reinstated the Citizenship Law of 1938 and thus granted citizenship (formally regardless of ethnicity) only to those who were citizens on June 16, 1941, and their descendants. Later amendments required that non-citizens pass difficult tests in the Estonian language and in civics. Until the end of the 1990s, the state allocated few resources to assist non-citizens in filing applications and passing these tests.

As a result of the new law, only one non-Estonian, an Estonianized Swede, gained a seat in the new unicameral parliament, the 101-seat *Riigikogu*, in the first post-independence elections in September 1992. Since most members of the non-Estonian population lacked citizenship, they were unable to vote or to stand as candidates. Ethnic Estonians comprised about 90 percent of the national electorate.[51] The Law on Aliens, which outlined the means by which individuals could become naturalized Estonian citizens, was passed by parliament on June 21, 1993, although it was subsequently revised following international pressure. The law had also precipitated a political and administrative crisis by requiring the reprocessing of the documents of all non-citizens. The new language law, taking into account the recommendations of international observers, entered into effect on February 10, 1993.[52]

A number of extreme nationalist organizations emerged in Estonia following independence, including the Decolonization Foundation, which was set up in early 1993 to promote the "peaceful" emigration of Russian-speaking settlers (particularly former KGB, security, and Soviet army officers) and thereby increase the percentage of Estonians from 63.5 percent to 80 percent. In contrast to Latvia, however, Estonia's Russian-speaking settler population developed as a far more integrated community and was able to withstand external pressures more effectively.

Indeed, despite facing fundamental questions about the Baltic, Slavic, Russian, or Russian-speaking nature of their identity, well-organized non-Estonian political, cultural, and economic associations emerged at an early stage and worked together to promote common interests. Although this owed much to the activity of leaders within the Russian-speaking community itself, independent Estonia's first prime minister, Edgar Savisaar, played a central role. The Savisaar government fell in January 1992, but during its tenure it promoted several items on the settlers' agenda—a relatively liberal citizenship regime for individuals currently living in Estonia, some form of regional autonomy for the Northeast, and a less strident position on the withdrawal of Russian troops. More importantly, Savisaar laid the foundations for the emergence of an indigenous non-Estonian political movement.

As in Latvia, the Russian-speaking community was traditionally organized around enterprises, the Communist Party, and the Soviet military, while Russian-speaking intellectuals were increasingly marginalized during the independence struggle by the growth of Estonian nationalism and Soviet loyalists' focus on industrial workers. However, in an attempt to draw the Russian-speaking intelligentsia back into the Estonian political system following their virtual exclusion immediately after independence, Savisaar encouraged the establishment of the Russian Democratic Movement to represent the settlers. Moreover, while the citizenship and naturalization debates pressured Russian-speaking leaders to clarify abstract ideals and to organize their social base, Savisaar greatly facilitated this process by enabling the establishment of an institutional forum, the Representative Assembly, in which non-Estonian civic and political structures could develop.

Originally, the Assembly, housed in the former Soviet Officers' Mess in Tallinn, was to function as an alternative parliament, although it subsequently became something more akin to a pressure group attempting to unify the various political, economic, and cultural organizations within the Russian-speaking community. These included the Russian Democratic Movement, the Narva Trade Union Center, the Russian Entrepreneurs Association, and the Union of Slavic Education and Charitable Societies in Estonia (which manages a Russian theatre in Tallinn, art and music schools, and a literary-cultural journal). The Russian Cultural Society of Estonia, although affiliated with the Representative Assembly, developed from the Baltic Russian tendency within the Popular Front, which, unlike in Latvia, was never entirely repudiated. Financial assistance from Russian-speaking businessmen was well-integrated with the new political and cultural organizations, and the Representative Assembly was funded in part by Rukon (Russian Auction Society), an umbrella organization for Russian businesses in Estonia which had representatives from the Assembly on its board of directors.

As in Latvia, the Estonian government and parliament also undertook a number of initiatives to foster the development of separate national and ethnic identities amongst the Russian-speakers. However, while there is little doubt that these initiatives were motivated by a strategy of *divide et impera*, in contrast to Latvia, they had the opposite effect and instead served to improve Latvian-Russian relations. Once again, the difference in outcomes can be attributed to the establishment of well-crafted institutions that embrace and co-ordinate the activities of non-Estonians. Three initiatives played particularly important roles: the creation of the Estonian Union of National Minorities (EUNM), the establishment of the President's roundtable, and a variety of policies designed to create a loyal Russian-speaking elite.

The EUNM emerged from national cultural societies established by the Popular Front in September 1988 to counter Soviet-Russian organizations. Following independence, it operated as a quango (quasi-non-governmental organization) headed by the parliament's only non-Estonian, the ethnic Swede Ants-Enno Lohmus. The EUNM aimed "to create national cultures as a way of destroying the communist mentality," and, although much of the work was directed against the Representative Assembly's social base (which Lohmus referred to as *homo sovieticus*), the Assembly's leaders supported the EUNM. This was due to Lohmus's role in enacting the November 1993 law on cultural autonomy, which allowed eligible minority groups to form councils with elected representatives at the municipal and national levels, and provided partial government funding for activities aimed at promoting cultural awareness.[53]

In July 1993, President Lennart Meri began a series of roundtable discussions on the problems of ethnic minorities with the leaders of the major minority groups. While these discussions were primarily consultative and non-binding in nature, they played a vitally important symbolic role by demonstrating official recognition of minority concerns. Moreover, the roundtable served as a means of channeling international pressure, which forced important legislative changes, most notably those concerning naturalization procedures.[54] As a result, language exams were made less difficult and the conditions for receiving citizenship were more clearly identified. Finally, in early 1998, the state provided additional resources to improve Latvian language teaching to assist non-Latvians with the citizenship test.[55] Throughout the 1990s, President Lennart Meri has played a key role in helping to stabilize partisan dynamics that might have heightened tensions surrounding the settler issue. The *Riigikogu* reelected Meri in September 1996.

At the same time, a clause in the Estonian Constitution that allows the President to grant citizenship for "special services" was used to co-opt leading members of the Russian-speaking elite, with editors of Russian-language papers, leaders of moderate political groups, and businessmen gaining automatic citizenship. The clause became an important tool for fostering a moderate Russian-speaking political and cultural leadership. Prior to the local elections in October 1993, the 15 candidates on the Representative Assembly list were granted citizenship so that they could stand. In contrast, the former pro-Soviet leaders of Narva and Sillamae were refused citizenship in response to their organization of the autonomy referendum in the Northeast.

While the Estonian Russian-speaking community was in general far better organized and more united than other Russian-speaking populations in the former Soviet republics, divisions nonetheless persisted. In particular, a split emerged between Russian nationalist groups (although with a lingering Soviet orientation) and the Westward-looking Representative Assembly leadership. In April 1993, the *Russkii Sobor* was established as a rival to the Representative Assembly, aiming to unite ethnic Russians to fight "for Russian cultural and national identity." It aimed to unite ethnic Russians to fight "for Russian cultural and national identity," and demanded unconditional citizenship for all residents and official recognition of Russian as a second state language. In the summer of 1993, the political wing of the organization was established as the Russian National Union. Both organizations attempted to develop links with radical nationalists in Russia, especially those in the former Supreme Soviet.

Estonia's most tense interethnic relations emerged in the Northeast, particularly in the town of Narva. There, both Russian-speaking and ethnic Latvian political entrepreneurs manipulated ethnic and national affiliations instrumentally in a situation fueled by economic and political conflicts. Indeed, the problems in Narva and the Northeast stemmed not from Russian separatism or a popular will to reunify with Russia, but from the processes of democratization and marketization initiated and supported mainly by Estonians but most directly affecting the region's non-Estonian elite. The struggle that developed between Tallinn and the cities of the Northeast in the course of 1992-93 was due to a complex mix of anti-market sentiment, pro-Soviet sympathy, center-periphery strains, and anxiety over blocked political mobility due to the suddenly dominant position of the Estonian language.

After World War II, Sovietized Russian-speaking migrants flooded into the Northeast. Before 1940, Estonians made up 79 percent of the region's population, but by 1989 this figure had fallen to 18.5 percent. The share of Russians in Narva rose from 30 percent before 1940 to 85 percent in 1989. Narva and the other towns in the Northeast became fortresses of Soviet control within Estonia; they were tightly integrated into centrally-directed all-union production and distribution networks (especially the military-industrial complex) and with little connection to the local economy. In this sense, Narva was similar to the heavily Sovietized enclaves of Daugavpils in Latvia and Tiraspol in Moldova. The Popular Front's challenge to Soviet control directly threatened the regional leadership's power base, which was built on political and economic control of Soviet company towns. In Narva and surrounding towns, unemployment was higher and wages lower than the rest of the country.[56] This challenge, then, existed regardless of how the citizenship question was to be resolved.

Indeed, opinion polling suggests that despite the claims of the local leadership, there was considerable support in Narva for an independent Estonia.[57] On February 2, 1990, the same day that Estonia's Supreme Soviet declared independence, a group of deputies (mainly representing Tallinn, Kokhla-Iarve, Sillamae, and Narva) created the Committee for the Defense of Soviet Power and Civil Rights in Estonia, and in May established the Interregional Soviet as a rival structure to the Supreme Soviet. However, a survey conducted in Narva at the time suggests that only 26 percent of the population opposed the decision of the Estonian Supreme Soviet and only 37 percent of the population recognized the Inter-regional Council as the "real expression of the will and interests of the non-Estonian population." Thirty-five percent opposed the proposition.[58] At the same time, while there was little support for the leadership of Narva, Soviet historical myths, especially regarding the annexation of the Baltic states, retained a powerful pull on the population.[59]

With support from Soviet elites, a number of organizations were founded in Narva, notably the Russian Citizens Rights Movement. Headed by Mayor Yurii Mishin, the Movement encouraged the local population to take Russian citizenship. In February 1993, the Russian Foreign Ministry dispatched a consular group to Narva in order to arrange Russian citizenship for those who wished to apply for it. At one stage the number of applications reached 1,500 per month, and by January 1995, there were estimated to be 20,000 Russian citizens in Narva.[60]

On July 16 and 17, 1993, the pro-Soviet leadership of the Northeast conducted the referendum on regional national-territorial autonomy that later resulted in its exclusion from presidential grants of citizenship. Despite reports of major irregularities, turnout was low (54 percent in Narva and 60 percent in Sillamae), and the local government of Kokhtla-Iarve (whose population was 70 percent non-Estonian) refused to hold the referendum altogether. In Narva, 97 percent of those who voted supported autonomy, while in Sillamae the figure was 98.6 percent. While the Estonian State Court ruled the referendum illegal, the ambiguity in interpreting Russian-speakers' support reflected the emergence of more moderate political forces in the area by mid-1993. In this climate, Yurii Mishin and other Soviet loyalists were gradually marginalized, and suffered a severe blow with Boris Yeltsin's assault on the Congress of People's Deputies in October 1993.

Estonia's municipal elections of October 1993 marked the final defeat of the old party-state *nomenklatura* in the Northeast. Unable to stand for election because they lacked citizenship, the former leadership lost power altogether. At the same time, the local elections marked a new stage in the development of inter-ethnic relations in Estonia. For the first time since independence significant numbers of non-Estonians were able to vote and stand as candidates. Two non-Estonian parties emerged to contest the elections: Our Choice (*Nash Vybor*) and Revel'. Our Choice was the political wing of the Representative Assembly, from whose leadership its candidates were mainly drawn. Its platform did not specifically address narrowly Russian-speaking issues, but concentrated instead on economic and social questions. Revel' represented the Russian patriotic bloc, in particular the *Russkii Sobor*, and thus was strongly tinged with Soviet revanchism.[61]

The municipal elections were a major success for the Russian and Russian-speaking blocs. In Tallinn, Our Choice received 17 mandates and Revel' 10. Lembit Annus, the former editor of the journal Estonian Communist and still a hard-liner, won 4,120 votes, second only to Arnold Ruutel, the former Estonian Communist Party leader. Mart Laar's ruling Isamaa party gained only 5 of the 64 city council seats. In Narva, on the other hand, while ethnic Russians captured three-fourths of the seats, a less confrontational council replaced the old Communist Party leadership.[62]

The success of the non-Estonian parties was primarily based on much higher turnout among Russian-speakers. In Narva and Sillamae, turnout was 67 percent, while in the predominantly Estonian south the figure was only 34 percent (Tartu). Equally important, the results suggested that socio-economic cleavages had begun to crosscut the ethnic division that had characterized Estonian society after 1992. This was reflected as well in the growing role of the Narva Independent Trade Union Center. The nationalist impetus within the Estonian parties and population was clearly diminishing; even economically disadvantaged ethnic Estonians voted for Revel' rather than Estonian nationalist parties.[63] In the northeast, however, economic and national questions remained closely intertwined. At the same time, while Narva continued to be plagued with the danger that socio-economic grievances might take an ethnic form, the Russian-speaking political parties received little support in the area because their candidates were invariably from Tallinn and were perceived as representing central interests.[64]

The integration of non-Estonians accelerated with the March 1995 parliamentary elections. As with the 1993 local elections, Russian-speaking politicians broke into moderate pro-Estonian and Russian nationalist camps.[65] In the run-up to the elections, three Russian parties emerged: the moderate United People's Party (Russian Assembly), the Russian Party headed by Sergei Kuznetsov, and the nationalist Russian People's Party.[66] Although the parties diverged on a wide range of issues, it became apparent to their leaderships shortly before the election that they risked splitting the Russian-speaking vote. As a result, a coalition called Our Home Is Estonia was forged on a moderate leftist platform that included demands for slower privatization, greater social guarantees, and closer ties to Russia.[67] With a potential constituency of 60,000-100,000 Russian-speaking citizens out of a total electorate of 790,000, Our Home Is Estonia won 5.9 percent of the popular vote and six seats in the 101-seat parliament, marking the first time Russian-speakers had gained state-wide representation since independence.[68] Yet, while this was an important advance for the Russian-speaking political elite, it was also clear that many settlers had voted for Estonian parties (notably the Centrist Party and the leftist Coalition Party). The elections thus reinforced the breakdown of ethnic polarization and the increasing salience of economic concerns that had become apparent in 1993.

Since gaining ostensible parliamentary representation in 1993, Russian-speakers have continued to face many, and often severe, difficulties in their cultural and political integration. The travails concerning citizenship and naturalization have already been mentioned. As well, Russian-speakers have often faced discrimination in the workplace, housing, and local and state administration due to various and often strict language requirements. Moreover, Russian-language primary and secondary schools will be completely phased out by 2007.[69] However, there has been some progress. For example, in 1998, the *Riigikogu*, over the objections of some Latvian nationalist parties, once again amended the citizenship law to grant automatic citizenship to the children of non-citizens who had been resident in Estonia for at least five years, a change in accordance with EU and OSCE norms.[70]

In the March 1999 parliamentary elections, center-right parties garnered sufficient support to establish a thin majority governing coalition led by previous Prime Minister Mart Laar. Laar's nationalist Pro Patria party tied for the largest number of seats in parliament, but has begun to soften its hard line on the settler issue. Prominent party members have even criticized past and present party stands on the integration of Russian-speakers. However, the party still pushed through parliament a law that requires government officials, including members of parliament, to be fluent in Estonian. Despite protests by Russian-speaking politicians and important international observers such as OSCE High Commmissioner Max van der Stoel, President Meri signed the law in February.[71] Our Home Is Estonia secured six seats, but does not participate in the ruling coalition. This and an array of other parties, organizations, and alliances representing Russian-speakers is now preparing to mobilize behind a unified banner for the October 1999 municipal elections.

Estonia and Latvia: Comparing Outcomes and Determinants of Ethnic Policy

The preceding discussion calls attention to the contrasting experiences of independence for the non-autochthonous populations of Latvia and Estonia. In the absence of a clear policy from Latvia's government and parliament, non-Latvians faced prolonged uncertainty about the possibility of naturalization. Moreover, while Latvia's authorities consistently pressured Soviet revanchist organizations, no alternative, more moderate means of interest articulation and representation were established or encouraged. As a result, few civic or political organizations helped to provide structure for the settler population, and there were very few points of contact with Latvian politics and society.

This approach had two main consequences. First, Latvia's state bureaucracy assumed an increasingly powerful role as the main arbiter of decisions influencing inter-ethnic relations. Since fluency in Latvian is required for civil service employment, non-Latvians were steadily purged, thus leaving them subject to authorities who were often unaware of the social problems they faced and who were often opposed to their presence in Latvia.[72] Second, the Russian-speaking population was forced to rely on organizations more inclined to confrontation such as Equal Rights to articulate their concerns.

While ethno-nationalism was no less a factor in post-independence Estonia than in Latvia, including similar bureaucratic insensitivity to the non-Estonian population, ethnic policy in Estonia achieved two distinctive successes. First, as a result of early official attempts to foster a Russian-speaking elite with citizenship and meaningful political institutions, vitally important links between ethnic Estonians and Russian-speakers were established. Official support also enabled Russian-speakers to develop their own political, cultural, and economic organizations. Such developments may well foster an identity among the Russian-speakers that is distinct from that in Russia or elsewhere within the Russian-speaking diaspora. Such an identity would be uniquely Estonian-Russian and would be reinforced as Russian-speakers campaign for their interests, and tensions are addressed within a framework of shared loyalty to the polity. Indeed, civic attachment to Estonia among Russian-speakers, manifest partly in a strong desire to gain residency status, has grown steadily, as over 325,000 of an estimated 400,000 settlers applied for residency by the deadline of July 12,1995.[73]

There are few, if any, significant differences between the pre-independence positions of the Russian-speaking settler populations in the two countries that can account for the different policy approaches adopted by Latvian and Estonian governments. Rather, the differences can be attributed to the Baltic populations themselves, particularly the degree of ethnic homogeneity and national unity at independence. In Latvia, there was both a higher proportion of settlers (48 percent by 1989) and far less social distance between Latvians and Russian-speakers. The latter is reflected in Latvia's much higher intermarriage rate prior to independence and a pattern of settlement characterized by wide dispersion of Russian-speakers among the indigenous population of Latvia's urban areas, in contrast to concentration in enclaves in Estonia. The "threat" of the Russian-speaking settlers thus became a more important means of promoting cohesion within the weakly united Latvian political community, which in turn prolonged the period of ethnonational mobilization well beyond independence.

Human Rights, Troop Withdrawal, and the Role of Russia

Domestic politics was the primary determinant of the Baltic states' majority-minority relations, but international pressure also played an important role. From late 1991, Russian politicians and political groups began to take an active interest in the settler communities in Latvia and Estonia.[74] Indeed, the issue of the Russified settler populations in Latvia and Estonia quickly became a central part of the broader debate about Russian national identity and Russia's role in the Commonwealth of Independent States. For this reason, the fate of the minorities was linked to debates about maintaining a Russian military presence in the Baltic region and, more generally, about the forms of influence that Russia could legitimately exert on its neighbors.

During the period of common struggle against the Soviet center, relations between Russian Democrats and the Popular Fronts in the Baltic republics were generally good. Boris Yeltsin strongly opposed the January 1991 Soviet crackdown in Latvia and Lithuania and quickly recognized Baltic independence following the August 1991 coup attempt. This atmosphere of goodwill was formalized (before full independence was achieved) in bilateral treaties signed by

Estonia and Latvia with Russia on January 12 and 13, 1991, respectively. However, while relations with Russia were generally friendly, even at this stage the issue of citizenship was emerging as an important source of tension.

In negotiations with Latvia, Russia initially demanded a guarantee of dual citizenship, which the Latvians firmly opposed. The treaty was due to be signed in September 1990, but representatives from Equal Rights, the Latvian Communist Party, the Soviet military, the Interfront, and the Council of War and Labor Veterans traveled to Moscow to lobby the Supreme Soviet against the treaty. As a result, ratification was delayed. When the Latvians conceded some ground on the Peace Treaty of 1920 and the status of Russian troops in Latvia, the Soviet crackdown in Latvia spurred Yeltsin, as president of the Russian Soviet Federal Socialist Republic (RSFSR), to sign the treaty. However, the Russian Supreme Soviet failed to ratify the agreement. The Committee of Latvia, the governing body of the Latvian Citizens' Movement, also opposed the agreement on the grounds that it allegedly granted citizenship to Soviet "occupiers." Negotiations with Estonia were not so protracted and, in contrast to the Latvian Russian Treaty, the Russian Supreme Soviet eventually ratified the agreement in December 1991. In Article Three of the treaty, both sides agreed to a "zero variant" on citizenship, whereby all persons living on the territory of the RSFSR or the Republic of Estonia at the time of signing "have the right to maintain or achieve citizenship in the RSFSR or the Republic of Estonia according to their expression of free will."[75]

Fear in Moscow of an anti-Russian bias in the treaties clearly played a role in delaying ratification. As ethnonationalism grew stronger in the Baltic states following independence, Russian nationalist and pro-Soviet forces used the issue to attack the Russian government. At the height of the Soviet-nationalist campaign against the Democratic movement, President Yeltsin on October 29, 1992, issued a decree linking the withdrawal of troops from the Baltic states with human rights guarantees for Russians.[76] On June 10, 1993, while addressing leaders of the armed forces, Yeltsin again linked human rights and troop withdrawal. Yeltsin stated explicitly that Russia could not withdraw without citizenship guarantees for the Russian settlers and expressed "profound concern over numerous infringements of the rights of the Russian-speaking population in the Baltic countries."[77]

The Baltic states' fears about Russia's intentions in the region were compounded in early 1993 by Yeltsin's appeal for a mandate from the United Nations to intervene in "trouble spots" in the former USSR. Speaking to a Russian military audience in Kaliningrad in March 1993, Andrei Kozyrev, the Russian foreign minister, spoke pointedly about the need to maintain troops in the Baltics.[78] In June 1993, Russian-Estonian relations deteriorated sharply following the introduction of the Law on Aliens. President Yeltsin and the Russian Foreign Ministry threatened economic, political, and "other" sanctions. Yeltsin appealed to the UN for measures against Estonia and warned that "Russia will take steps to defend its national interests in Estonia." He noted that "Russian cannot remain a disinterested observer if the Russian-speaking population should show a natural desire to defend itself against crude discrimination," while Kozyrev, striking a similar tone, accused the Estonians of "apartheid" and "ethnic cleansing."[79]

In the fall of 1993, relations between the Baltic states and Russia began to improve. Russia pledged in November to withdraw its troops by the end of August 1994 and Estonia made a major concession by amending the Law on Aliens to grant the right of residency to retired Soviet officers.[80] The Baltic governments reacted favorably to the troop withdrawal proposal, or at least accepted it with resignation. By the end of 1993, approximately 22,000 Russian troops remained in the region. However, during the electoral campaign for the December 1993 Russian parliamentary elections, the condition of the Russian diaspora, particularly in Estonia and Latvia, became an important issue nation-wide, and, following the success of nationalist and communist forces, the tone of Russian foreign policy became increasingly harsh. Speaking to a meeting of Russian ambassadors in Moscow in January 1994, Andrei Kozyrev claimed that Russia should not withdraw from those regions, which have been in the Russian sphere of influence "for centuries."[81]

Despite the bellicose statements made by leading Russian politicians, they accomplished little in developing concrete policies to "protect" Russian-speakers in Estonia and Latvia. On the contrary, through negotiation the Russian government secured important rights for ex-Soviet military personnel, while at the same time maintaining control over the more radical Russian groups that sought to exploit the issue. Indeed, the final withdrawal of Russian military units from Estonia and Latvia on August 31, 1994, signaled that the Russian government remained fundamentally committed to the existence of independent Baltic states. By 1999, both states had initialled border agreements with Russia. Moreover, Estonia and Russia formed an intergovernmental commission in March, 1998, to discuss and resolve various border issues. However, the Balts' ties to NATO and support for NATO's air strikes during the Kosovo conflict complicated bilateral relations, and Russia's December 1999 parliamentary elections caused further delays in the ratification of these border agreements.

Conclusion

This chapter has demonstrated that despite their many similarities, Estonia and Latvia differed substantially in their ethnic relations. While it is far too early to conclude that the Russian-speaking populations of the Baltic states have developed a new non-Soviet national identity, the basis for such a change is clearly in place, particularly in Estonia. The Baltic Russian-speaking settlers have emerged from the USSR as the most market-oriented and democratically inclined of the settler communities in the former Soviet Union. A majority in each community has consistently expressed support for the independence of the Baltic states, while any lingering affinity with Russia continues to wane.

These cases suggest that if civil society and a new national identity are to emerge quickly among Russian-speakers, it will be largely dependent on the actions of the Baltic governments and parliaments themselves. Following independence, the settler populations lacked their own institutions and their self-identity remained based on an ambiguous mixture of Soviet, Baltic, linguistic, and ethnic elements.[82] The distinctive identity of Russian-speakers who participated in the independence movements as non-indigenous loyalists and democrats was undermined as the Popular Fronts became increasingly nationalist, leaving them little other than Soviet values and institutions as avenues for political and social expression.

In Estonia, a series of harsh legislative measures mobilized Russian-speakers in protest. Out of this protest, coupled with assistance from Estonian politicians and state officials to create new, loyalist institutions within the minority community, there emerged a distinctive non-Estonian community. The ability of Estonian politicians to pursue inclusionary policies was, however, based on a pronounced social division between the Russian-speaking and indigenous populations. In Latvia, the lack of such a division and the far larger number of settlers reinforced the salience of ethnicity, and Latvian politicians more steadfastly identified loyalty to an independent Latvia with political exclusion of non-Latvians.[83]

This comparison is also relevant when considering the broader topic of the fluidity of national identity. The historical-cultural basis for a distinctively "Russian" presence is far more "authentic" in Latvia than in Estonia, yet, contrary to expectations, the Estonian Russian-speakers developed a stronger community and identity, one that might be characterized as territorial-political rather than ethno-cultural.[84] The Representative Assembly based its appeals for political inclusion largely on respect for basic human rights and on an attachment to Estonia, without any greater symbolic or mythical apparatus, as a people who simply live and work in the country.

At the same time, the degree of integration even in Estonia should not be over-emphasized. The majority of Russian-speakers remains unsure of their future place outside the activities of Russian-speaking organizations, while the process of integrating these populations into Estonian society is still at an early stage.[85] For this reason, the efforts of political groups in Russia to impede this process by challenging the Baltic states' sovereignty remain dangerous. Conversely, the willingness of both Estonia and Latvia to moderate the harshest elements of their legislation will be critical, and encouragement by European institutions will continue to play an important role.[86] In this regard, however, the cases examined here also demonstrate that the formal provision of citizenship and human rights regimes corresponding to international norms is not necessarily sufficient to ensure the protection of minorities.[87] Failure to integrate minorities politically can also establish dangerous tensions. Estonia's movement toward a genuinely pluralist democratic polity has entailed not only liberalizing citizenship, but actively and steadily drawing the leaders of the settler communities, including many former radicals, into the Estonian political process. In so doing, it has engendered a commitment, however incipient at present, to the inevitably collective enterprise of independence.

Notes

1. Neil Melvin, "Forging the New Russian Nation: Russian Foreign Policy and the Russian-speaking Communities of the Former USSR," *Royal Institute of International Affairs Discussion Paper No. 50* (London: 1994).

2. David Arter, "Estonia after the March 1995 Riigikogu Election: Still an Anti-Party System," *Journal of Communist Studies and Transition Politics*, vol. 11, no. 3 (September 1995). See also Juan J. Linz and Alfred Stepan, *Problems of Democratic Transition and Consolidation* (Baltimore: Johns Hopkins University Press, 1996), chapter 2.

3. This contrasts with Lithuania, where the so-called "zero-option" was employed: citizenship was offered to anyone resident in the republic prior to the introduction of the citizenship law. For details, see *The Citizenship and Alien Law Controversies in Estonia and Latvia* (Cambridge, MA: Strengthening Democratic Institutions Project, John F. Kennedy School of Government, Harvard University, April 1994).

4. For a full accounting, see Vello Pettai and Marcus Kreuzer, "Party Politics in the Baltic States: Social Bases and Institutional Context," *East European Politics and Societies*, vol. 13, no. 1 (Winter 1999), 148-189.

5. Estonians, in particular, see themselves as resisting a historic process of assimilation of Finno-Ugric peoples, such as the Mordvans, Urdmurts, and Komis, by the Russians.

6. The Baltic Germans dominated the region politically and economically following a

series of crusades by the Teutonic knights in the thirteenth and fourteenth centuries. With Russian conquest of the area, Peter the Great guaranteed German dominance in 1721. See Anatol Lieven, *The Baltic Revolution: Estonia, Latvia, Lithuania and the Path to Independence* (New Haven, CT: Yale University Press, 1993), pp. 42-53.

7. Edward C. Thaden, *Russification in the Baltic Provinces and Finland 1855-1914* (Princeton, NJ: Princeton University Press, 1981).

8. Stephen D. Corrsin, "The Changing Composition of the City of Riga, 1987-1913," *Journal of Baltic Studies*, vol. 13, no. 1 (1983), p. 87.

9. Lieven, *op. cit.*, pp. 38-53.

10. As a result of World War II and Stalinist repression, Estonia lost approximately 200,000 people (18 percent of its population).

11. It should be noted that sporadic guerilla resistance to Soviet rule persisted in Estonia until the mid-1950s.

12. Soviet language policy was based on the 1938 Communist Party and Council of People's Commissars decision "On Compulsory Study of the Russian Language in Schools of Non-Russian Republics and Regions."

13. In a survey conducted in Estonia in 1988, 78 percent of the Russians questioned identified themselves as members of the "Soviet nation," while only 15 percent identified themselves as belonging to another national group. The figures for Estonians were 10 percent and 73 percent, respectively. *Vikerkaar*, vol. 5 (1988), p. 76.

14. Robert J. Kaiser, *The Geography of Nationalism in Russia and the USSR* (Princeton, NJ: Princeton University Press, 1994), pp. 302-3.

15. See, e.g., David D. Laitin, *Identity in Formation: The Russian-Speaking Populations in the Near Abroad* (Ithaca: Cornell University Press, 1998).

16. Some of these choices are enumerated in David D. Laitin, "Language and Nationalism in the Post-Soviet Republics," *Post-Soviet Affairs*, vol. 12, no. 1 (1996): 4-24.

17. Rasma Karklins, *Ethnopolitics and Transition to Democracy: The Collapse of the USSR and Latvia* (Baltimore, MD: Johns Hopkins University Press, 1994), p. 82.

18. Toomas Hendrik Ilves, "Reaction: The Intermovement in Estonia," in Jan Arveds Trapans, ed., *Toward Independence: The Baltic Popular Movements* (Boulder, CO: Westview Press, 1991), pp. 71-83, and Karklins, *op. cit.*, p. 80.

19. Karklins, *op. cit.*, pp. 79-80.

20. For the results, see Appendix 2b "Results of the March 3, 1991 Referendum on Latvian Independence," *Nationalities Papers*, vol. xix, no. 1 (Spring 1991), pp. 109-10.

21. "Latvijas iedz votaju ekspresaptaujas rezultati," *Diena* (January 22, 1991), p. 3.

22. Data from the Estonian polling organization Mainor-EMOR.

23. Aleksei Semyenov, 'Mezhnatsional'nye faktory integratsii obshchestva Estonii', unpublished paper (1993).

24. Klara Hallik and Marika Kirch, "On Interethnic Relations in Estonia," *Estratto da "Annali" della Fondazionne Giangiacomo Feltrinelli* (1992), p. 158.

25. 'Khotyat li russkie bezhat?' *Moskovskie novosti* (January 27, 1991), pp. 12-13.

26. Hallik and Kirch, op. cit.

27. Dzintra Bungs, "The Shifting Political Landscape in Latvia," *RFE/RL Research Report*, vol. 2, no. 12 (March 19, 1993).

28. For example, Georgs Andrejevs, the Latvian Foreign Minister, called for the repatriation of "colonists." See "Biting the Biter: Georgs Andrejevs and Russia," *The Baltic*

Independent (March 12-18, 1993), p. 9.

29. On the diverse character of the Russian-speaking community, see Aadne Aasland, "The Russian Population in Latvia: An Integrated Minority?" *The Journal of Communist Studies and Transition Politics* 10, no. 2 (June 1994), pp. 233-60.

30. An earlier attempt had been made to transform the Interfront into a more effective organization stressing Russian rather than Soviet identity. Established in March 1991, the Russian Community of Latvia (*Russkaia obshchina Latvii—ROL*) was to operate under the control of the Soviet loyalist organizations and was initially led by leading members of the Interfront. Internal conflict soon arose, however, and the largely pro-independence rank-and-file removed the Soviet-loyalist leadership in September 1992. The contradictory principles of identity underlying this power struggle led to the ROL's rapid disintegration, leaving only a small Russian cultural organization. Author's interview with Vladimir Vladov, President of ROL (Riga, October 1993).

31. The triumvirate that formed the leadership consisted of two ethnic Latvians (Rubriks and Dimanis) and a Jew (Zdanok).

32. Equal Rights was close to the Committee on Human Rights and International Humanitarian Cooperation. The Committee campaigned extensively in the local Russian press in support of the "zero variant" for citizenship and in May 1993 held a press conference in the Moscow Ministry of Foreign Affairs. *Diena* (September 22, 1993), p. 8.

33. The main groups were: the Cossack Circle, closely linked to Soviet officers organizations; the Union of Latvian Communists, formed in early September 1992 from the core of the Communist Party of Latvia and the Interfront; the Union for the Defense of Veterans Rights, which succeeded the Council of USSR War, Work and Armed Forces Veterans (banned in August 1991); and the Association of Russians in Latvia.

34. *Diena* (September 24, 1993), p. 1, and (October 6, 1993), p. 1.

35. Interview with Janis Jurkans, Riga (October 1993).

36. Gundar King and J. Thad Barnowe, "Complementary and Conflicting Personal Values of Russophone Managers in Latvia," *Journal of Baltic Studies* XXV, no. 3 (Fall 1994), pp. 249-72. However, while the prospect of attaining a standard of living higher than elsewhere in the former Soviet Union suggested that Russian-speakers in Latvia would be prepared to endure many of the travails of the current situation, this amounted to tolerance, not commitment. Brian J. Boeck, "Legacy of a Shattered System: The Russian-speaking population in Latvia," *Demokratizatsiya*, vol. 1, no. 2 (1993), pp. 70-85. Moreover, traditional economic links with Russia such as joint manufacturing ventures were often rejected by the Latvian authorities for fear that such moves would presage loss of control of the national economy. See, for example, "Latvia Votes Down Russian Military Factory Deal," *The Baltic Independent* (June 4, 1993).

37. The city's population was 65 percent Russian, 12.5 percent Latvian, 12.5 percent Polish, 8 percent Ukrainian, and 3 percent Belorussian. Many ethnic Latvians, moreover, spoke Russian as their first language. "Language Is Key in Daugavpils," *The Baltic Independent* (June 2-8, 1995), p. 2.

38. For details of the pre-election period see Dzintra Bungs, "Twenty-Three Groups Vie for Seats in the Latvian Parliament," *RFE/RL Research Report*, vol. 2, no. 23 (June 4, 1993), pp. 44-9.

39. Eight parties entered Parliament: Latvian Way (36 seats), the Farmers Union (12 seats), Equal Rights (7 [8] seats), Fatherland and Freedom (6 seats), CDU (5 seats),

Democratic Party (5 seats), Harmony for Latvia (13 seats), and the Latvian National Independence Party (15 seats), making a total of 99. Rubriks was elected on the Equal Rights list but remained imprisoned.

40. Pettai and Kreuzer, op. cit., p. 151.

41. "Latvian Citizenship Bill Puts Critics on Offensive," *The Baltic Independent* (December 3-9, 1993), pp. 1 and 4.

42. Criticism from the Russian Federation and the suggestion that Latvian membership in the Council of Europe might be blocked if the bill was not changed concentrated parliamentary minds very quickly. "Ulmanis Blocks Disputed Citizenship Law," *The Baltic Independent* (July 1-7, 1994), p. 1.

43. "Latvia Passes New Citizenship Law," *The Baltic Independent* (July 29-August 4, 1994), p. 1. A law on the rights of non-citizens was passed in April 1995. See "New Law to Guarantee Non-Citizens' Rights," *The Baltic Independent* (April 21-27), 1995, p. 4. A variety of sources expressed dissatisfaction with this formula because it did not give "indigenous" Latvians and Livs who were born outside Latvia priority in their applications. Juris Bojårs, "The Citizenship Regulation of the Republic of Latvia," *Humanities and Social Sciences Latvia,* vol. 1, no. 6, (1995), pp. 4-28. On March 6, 1995, a new law was passed to permit the automatic naturalization of ethnic Latvians without citizenship.

44. "Local Councils Shaken Up in Latvia," *The Baltic Independent* (June 3-9, 1994), pp. 1 and 4, "Non-Citizens Plan Their Own Ballot," *The Baltic Independent* (March 11-17, 1994), p. 4 and "Protests against the Latvian Law on Citizenship," *Nationalities Papers,* vol. 23, no. 2 (June 1995), pp. 414-28.

45. In light of Siegrist's behavior, President Ulmanis blocked his party's inclusion in the diverse governing coalition formed in December 1995.

46. Economist Intelligence Unit, *Latvia (Country Profile)* (London: June 22, 1998), p. 11.

47. These incidents included a bombing near the Russian embassy in Riga, the break-up of a demonstration by mostly Russian-speaking pensioners, and the participation of a number of leading politicians in a march that featured Latvian veterans of the Waffen-SS. See Economist Intelligence Unit, *Latvia (Country Profile)* (London: June 22, 1998), pp. 10-12.

48. Moreover, because of its citizenship law, Latvia was in 1995 the last of the Baltic states to be admitted to the Council of Europe.

49. Economist Intelligence Unit, *Latvia (Country Profile)* (London: March 25, 1999), p. 13.

50. Currently, the Saeima contains *eight* parliamentary factions.

51. Pettai and Kreuzer, *op. cit.*

52. The original language law was passed on January 18, 1989. However, Estonia's republic-level administration lacked the authorization to implement it fully. See David D. Laitin, "National Revival and Competitive Assimilation in Estonia," *Post-Soviet Affairs,* vol. 12, no. 1, p. 31.

53. "Minority Law Revived Pre-War Legacy," *The Baltic Independent* (December 10-16, 1993).

54. Konrad Huber, "Averting Inter-Ethnic Conflict: An Analysis of the CSCE High Commissioner on National Minorities in Estonia, January-July 1993," *Occasional Paper Series of the Conflict Resolution Program of the Carter Center of Emory University* (1994). Laitin provides ground-level detail of the sluggish nature of naturalization procedures, administration of citizenship tests, etc. See Laitin, "National Revival and Competitive Assimilation in Estonia," *op. cit.*, pp. 25-39.

55. Economic Intelligence Unit, *Estonia (Country Profile)* (London: June 19, 1998), p. 17.

56. Economic Intelligence Unit, *Estonia (Country Profile)* (London: June 19, 1998), p. 16.

57. Interview with Sergei Gorokhov, a sociologist in Narva, October 1993.

58 An EMOR poll suggests that half the respondents in Narva were unhappy with the work of the local council there—much higher than in other areas of country. Fifty-four percent said the local council "should work in close cooperation and unity with the Estonian Government." "Second Referendum Called in Northeast Estonia," *The Baltic Independent* (July 5-9, 1993).

59. Sergei Gorokhov, "Spetsifika uchastiia neestonskoi chasti naseleniia respubliki v protsesse sotsial'no-politicheskoi aktivnosti," *Severnoe poberezh'e* (May 26, 1993), p. 4. The most powerful myths are that the Baltic states were not annexed but agreed to voluntary union with the USSR and that the Molotov-Ribbentrop Pact never existed.

60. An official at the Russian Embassy in Tallinn reported that by February 1995 there were 61,401 Russian citizens in Estonia. Since 1992, 48,491 Russian-speakers had been naturalized as Estonian citizens. *OMRI Daily Report* (February 7, 1995).

61. The party embraced Russian nationalists, such as Sergei Kuznetsov, as well as ethnic Estonian former communist elites such as Lembit Annus and Vladimir Kukk.

62. The distribution of seats was as follows: Democratic Labor Party (12), Narva Trade Union (12), and Narva Estonian Society (7).

63. Andrus Park, "Ethnicity and Independence: The Case of Estonia in Comparative Perspective," *Europe-Asia Studies,* vol. 46, no. 1 (1994), pp. 69-87.

64. "Northeastern Industrial Town Will Not Vote for Capitalists," *The Baltic Independent* (March 3-9, 1995), p. 3.

65. In 1994, a new Russian nationalist group was formed from a core of 12,000 retired Soviet officers: the Russian Community in Estonia. "Russian Vets Pose as Victims," *The Baltic Independent* (March 18-24, 1994), p. 3. Led by Yurii Kotenkov, the organization established close ties with the Congress of Russian Communities in Russia. "MP Views Russian Community Councils Statement," *FBIS-SOV-94-052* (March 17, 1994), p. 43.

66. "Russians Found Political Parties," *The Baltic Independent* (October 14-20, 1994), p. 1.

67. "Russian Parties in Estonia Form Pre-Election Coalition," *Baltic News* (January 17-31, 1995), p. 11.

68. "Russians Reach Parliament for the First Time in Estonia's Elections," *Baltic Observer* (March 9-15, 1995), p. 7.

69. This is in contrast to Latvia, which has continued Russian-language primary and secondary schools.

70. Economic Intelligence Unit, *Estonia (Country Profile)* (London: January 15, 1999), 12. The law took effect in June 1999.

71. Although enacted in December 1998, the law did not apply to the March 1999 elections.

72. Latvia's Department of Citizenship and Immigration was criticized by Helsinki Watch for "serious systematic abuses" in failing to uphold the December 1991 law on the registration of residents. "Watchdog Condemns Latvian 'Abuses,'" *The Baltic Independent* (November 5–11, 1993).

73. A series of surveys has found increasing support for Estonian statehood among the Russian-speaking population. Maley has found higher support among Russian-speakers in the Baltic states for their own governments than for the Russian government. William

Maley, "Does Russia Speak for Baltic Russians?" *The World Today* 51, no. 1 (January 1995), pp. 4-6. See also "Loyalty of Local Russians Has Increased," *The Baltic Independent* (July 15-21, 1994), p. 3, "Ethnic Tensions Evaluated," *The Baltic Independent* (July 1-7, 1994), p. 2, "Estonia's Russians Willing to Integrate, says Moscow report," *The Baltic Independent* (July 21-27, 1995), p. 6, and "Non-Citizens Eager for Residency in Estonia," *The Baltic Independent* (July 21-27, 1995), p. 3.

74. Neil Melvin, *Russians Beyond Russia: The Politics of National Identity* (London: Pinter, 1995), pp. 4-24.

75. Riina Kionka, "Russia Recognizes Estonia's Independence," *RFE/RL Report on the USSR*, vol. 3, no. 5 (February 1, 1991), pp. 14-16.

76. Stephen Foye, "Russian Politics Complicates Baltic Troop Withdrawal," *RFE/RL Research Report*, vol. 1, no. 46 (November 20, 1992), pp. 30-5.

77. "Yeltsin Officially Links Troops to Human Rights," *The Baltic Independent* (June 18-24, 1993), p. 3.

78. "Kremlin Defends Its Troops in Baltic," *The Baltic Independent* (March 19-25, 1993), p. 3.

79. *Ibid.*

80. "Estonia Grants Residence Rights to Ex-Soviet Officers," *The Baltic Independent* (November 26-December 2, 1993).

81. "Russians To Stay in Baltics, Says Kozyrev," *Financial Times* (January 19, 1994), p. 2.

82. In 1992, Estonian sociologists suggested that ethnic Russians saw themselves simultaneously as representatives of Estonian, Russian, Soviet, and "world" culture. See Aksel Kirch, Marika Kirch and Tarmo Tuisk, *The Non-Estonian Population Today and Tomorrow: A Sociological Overview* (Tallinn: December 1992). See also Marika Kirch and Aksel Kirch, "Ethnic Relations: Estonians and Non-Estonians," *Nationalities Papers*, vol. 23, no. 1 (March 1995), pp. 43-59.

83. In early 1996, the Fatherland and Freedom Party launched a drive to overturn the law on citizenship and naturalization introduced in 1994. In particular, they sought the introduction of quotas for naturalization by non-Latvians or Livs (a small group indigenous to Latvia). Significantly, the initiative was opposed by a variety of Latvian political parties, including Latvia's Way. "Latvia Votes on Non-Citizens," *The Baltic Independent* (January 18-24, 1996), pp. 1 and 5.

84. Juan Linz, "From Primordialism to Nationalism," in Edward Tiryakin and Ronald Rogowski, eds., *New Nationalities of the Developed West* (Boston: Allen & Unwin, 1985).

85. While tighter requirements for citizenship, introduced in January 1995, were aimed primarily at new arrivals to the country, this move was reinforced by the new, more conservative language law adopted in February 1995, which further restricted use of the Russian language. However, the Estonian authorities did display considerable flexibility in extending the period for non-citizens to register as residents beyond the deadline of June 12, 1995.

86. Konrad Huber, "Averting Inter-Ethnic Conflict: An Analysis of the CSCE High Commissioner on National Minorities in Estonia, January-July 1993," *Occasional Paper Series of the Conflict Resolution Program of the Carter Center of Emory University* (1994).

87. International organizations have generally given both countries a clean bill of health regarding formal legal rights. A United Nations mission to Latvia in October 1992 found that the laws did not infringe international norms and that there were no systematic vio-

lations of rights but that "it would be desirable if Latvia, for humanitarian reasons, would tend its nationality to the majority of its permanent residents who express a desire to be loyal citizens of Latvia." The report suggested that the problems were not legal but social. It was also noted that the Department of Citizenship and Immigration was involved in discrimination. See also the collection of reports including that from the CSCE "Human Rights in the Baltic States," *Finnish Helsinki Committee*, no. 6, (1993). However, in October 1995 a UN human rights committee criticized the citizenship regime adopted in Estonia. "UN raps citizen policy," *The Baltic Independent* (November 3-9, 1995), p. 3.

6

THE GREEK MINORITY IN ALBANIA: ETHNIC POLITICS IN A PRE-NATIONAL STATE

James Pettifer

Introduction

Bilateral relations between Greece and Albania have often been severely strained since the demise of communism in Albania, with breaks in diplomatic relations, violent border incidents involving military fatalities, and the expulsion of tens of thousands of Albanian migrant workers from Greece. At the heart of these growing tensions is the fate of the sizable ethnic Greek community in southern Albania. This chapter examines the historical basis of this national minority, its status and political behavior during the communist period, and the current factors contributing to ethnic tension in post-communist Albania. The dynamic interplay between Greek-Albanian bilateral relations, the sub-national divide among ethnic Albanians themselves, and domestic inter-ethnic politics, it will be argued, hold the key to determining the ethnic Greek minority's ability to pursue and achieve its interests, and thus to the development of a stable Albanian polity.

The emergence of ethnic tension, it should be noted, stands in sharp contrast to traditional western understandings of Albania. During the communist period, Albania was generally viewed from abroad as an ethnically homogeneous state (although its Balkan neighbors were well aware of the existence of the ethnic Greek minority within the country).[1] Even insofar as it was involved in international bodies under the isolationist communist regime established after 1944, this view was nonetheless maintained by an international community generally ignorant of most aspects of Albania's history and political development. As a small, relatively obscure country with neither a strong tradition of statehood nor a well-known and independent culture, the perception encouraged by Enver Hoxha's regime thus effectively structured foreign understandings. These assumed, in essence, a united country freed from the Turks by its hardy mountain people, who then emerged into nationhood as a homogeneous society with a strong national culture underpinned by shared traditions. Its political integration was further seen to be reflected in, and reinforced by, the struggle to free the country from Axis occupation during the Second World War and the Partisan struggle which brought Hoxha and the Communists to power.[2] And, while the outside world regarded the country as a grim, poverty-stricken gulag ruled by the world's most hard-line communist regime, a European analog of North Korea under Kim Il Sung, the prevailing view nonetheless presupposed that rigid political uniformity implied the absence of cultural and ethnic diversity.

Both images were misleading. First, while Albania did experience a growth of national consciousness in the late nineteenth century, it was quite slow in throwing off the Ottoman yoke, becoming in November 1912 the last Balkan state to declare its independence, which was formally recognized at the London Conference of Ambassadors in 1913. Achievement of national statehood had been impeded in large by the Ottoman authorities' strategy of dividing the Albanians among four imperial provinces and blocking the establishment of an Albanian-language educational system, with no common written alphabet until 1908. The result was a lingering heritage of cultural differences and political divisions, particularly between the two regionally-based sub-groups of the Albanian people, the Ghegs and the Tosks, whose relations were marked by only limited cooperation during the national renaissance and in opposing Ottoman rule.[3] In fact, until the 1930s, large areas of northern and central Albania had no relationship with the capital (Tirana) as a legitimate state center in the modern sense, and still lived according to the feudal code of *Kanun i Lek Dukagjinit,* the medieval body of lore and convention regulating the operation of the blood feud.[4]

The absence of cultural-territorial unity was again reflected politically within the anti-Axis resistance movement in 1943 and 1944, with bitter conflicts between communist and non-communist groups corresponding for the most part to the geographical divide between the distinct Albanian communities in the north and south of the country. In the south, the Tosks generally supported the left-wing National Liberation Movement organized and dominated by the Communists following the party's establishment, under the leadership of Enver Hoxha, in 1941. The northern Ghegs divided their support between the Balli Kombetar, comprised of right-wing pro-republican nationalists, and the royalist Legalitate Organization. The latter, supported by the northern Mati tribe, sought the restoration of fellow Mati Ahmet Zogu, who had established a monarchy in 1928 and ruled as King Zog I until fleeing the country when Italy invaded in April 1939.[5] Significantly, beneath the external uniformity imposed by the communist regime that Hoxha established in 1944 and led until his death in 1985, such regionally-centered patron-client relationships persisted, with the main difference being that the social base of the new regime shifted to the south. Kinship, tribal links, and the rigid friend-foe distinction central to the Kanun were retained as key elements of the system, accounting for many serious political and economic conflicts in the post-war years, including within the communist establishment itself.[6]

Second, in addition to the division among ethnic Albanians, there was, and remains, a substantial Greek minority, as well as a number of smaller groups of Vlachs, Roma (Gypsies), Jews, Armenians, Macedonians, Serbs, and Montenegrins. In political terms, the Greek minority is by far the most consequential group. But, while the Greek minority is culturally and politically more integrated within Albanian society, the other groups have some importance, if only to the extent that their persistence calls into question the universalist assumptions propagated by the communist regime, and, to a significant extent, by post-communist Albanian governments.

Demographics of Albania's Ethnic Minorities

Most members of the Greek minority live in the south of the country and in Tirana and are estimated to comprise 3 percent of a total population of about 3.4 million, although this is a highly contentious question.[7] Two thousand Serbs and Montenegrins live predominantly in the villages north of Shkodra, around Vraka, adjacent to Montenegro. The 15,000 "Macedonians," who speak a mixed dialect comprised of Bulgarian and Serbian elements, live either in the Peshkopia area in northeast Albania, or around Lake Ochrid in the southeast. The number of Albanian Roma is unknown, but may be as high as 75,000. Their settlement is scattered throughout the country, with all main towns having a Roma quarter, most of which are long-established and appear to date from early Ottoman times (if not before). The 80,000 Vlachs generally live in the southern mountains, with particularly large concentrations in the southeast around Korca and near Vlora, although the latter group has been seriously affected by industrialization and has become almost entirely assimilated into Albanian urban society. The Jewish community, comprised of about

800 people, lived mainly in Tirana but emigrated to Israel en bloc in 1991, although some families have since returned. The Armenian community, of similar size, exists in Tirana and Vlora, and is made up of well-qualified professionals, many of whom seem to have emigrated from Albania in the last two years, casting doubt on the general future of this group. There are also a number of individuals of direct Turkish descent. None of the communities of Soviet and Chinese citizens that existed temporarily in Albania under communism have remained, and there has been no evidence to date to suggest that they have had a lasting influence on patterns of ethnic minority settlement.[8]

The Politics of History: Placing the Greeks of Southern Albania

Census figures from the communist period do not provide accurate information about ethnic minorities in Albania, and controversy over the size of the Greek minority long predates communism. While historical memory and collective myths are always and everywhere of considerable importance in framing cultural identity and its political expression, in the case of Albania and its ethnic Greeks, ancient history is especially important in this respect. The ancient Illyrian tribes from which the modern Albanians claim descent occupied most of the territory of the present state of Albania, as well as adjoining parts of the Balkans, until the Roman conquest. Before, however, there had been ancient Greek colonization of the coast, beginning in the fifth century B.C., with the establishment of important ancient Greek settlements at Dyrrachium (modern Durres), Apollonia (near modern Fier), and Butrint (near Saranda). In addition to this colonization, in southern Albania, south of the river Shkumbini, there were large numbers of people known to the ancient geographer Strabo (writing in the first century A.D.) as Epirot. These people spoke and wrote mostly in Greek, although he recorded that some tribes, such as the Bylliones, were bilingual.

While most ethnic Greeks claim direct lineal descent from the ancient Epirot tribes, Albanian historians argue that all of these tribes were Illyrian in origin, even if they had begun to speak Greek as a result of coastal colonization. In contrast, Greek nationalists claim that most of Albania in the Tosk-dominated area south of the Shkumbi River is Vorio Epirus (or northern Epirus) and essentially Greek from ancient times, and that it should therefore ultimately be regarded as a part of Greece itself. Albanians claim that the minority as it currently exists is the result of population movements under the Ottoman empire, and that the great majority of the Greeks arrived in Albania as indentured laborers in the time of the Ottoman *beys*.[9]

In the modern period, as the struggle for Albanian independence developed under the disintegrating Ottoman empire, many parts of southern Albania were subject to violent inter-communal conflict, as Greek irredentists attempted to integrate parts of what is now southern Albania into a Greater Greece. Given its large Greek-speaking population, the city of Gjirokastra (in Greek, Agyrocastro), in the Vjoses (Aoos) River valley, only twenty miles from the Greek border, was a particularly active center of irredentist ambition. Outbreaks of ethnic violence in the area were particularly serious immediately after Albanian independence was declared and during the Second Balkan War, as some Albanian-speaking villages in Epirus fought on the side of the Turks against the Greek-speaking villages. In February 1914, a Pan-Epirote Association was founded in Gjirokastra, and the town and its vicinity were proclaimed a part of Greece. In May 1914, the Great Powers signed the Protocol of Corfu, which recognized the area as Greek, after which it was occupied by the Greek army from October 1914 until October 1915. Greece's administration under the Protocol was short-lived, however, and collapsed after the Italian invasion in 1915.[10]

Northern Epirus reverted to Albania under Italian protection, a state of affairs that was formally ratified in 1925 by the delineation of Albania's southern border under the Protocol of Florence, which Greece still has not officially recognized. Under King Zog, the Greek villages suffered considerable repression, including the forcible closure of Greek-language schools in 1933-1934 and the ordering of Greek Orthodox monasteries to accept the mentally disturbed as inmates. During the Second World War, the Greek minority supported the anti-Axis resistance, and when the Partisan campaign was started under communist leadership, a separate battalion of ethnic Greek Partisans (the "Thanas Ziko" battalion) was established.[11] During the national liberation struggle in the later stages of the war, the Albanian Communists were able to prevent contact between the Greek minority and the right-wing andartes of Napoleon Zervas (EDES) in southern Epirus, who sought to unite northern Epirus with Greece. In 1946, with Hoxha's regime already in place, Greece attempted to reincorporate northern Epirus into its territory at the Paris Peace Conference, but failed.[12]

Thus, southern Albania and its Greek-speaking population have represented a chronic point of contention—continuing to the present—in Albania's post-independence history, manifested mainly as a territorial dispute between Albania and Greece, but also as a normative struggle to define a distinct Albanian ethnicity and national heritage. And, as has been common throughout the Balkans in the twentieth century, central to these struggles are the ongoing historiographical debates that suffuse history, whether ancient or modern, with nationalist meaning. Indeed, as Albanian communism would clearly demonstrate, where nation- and state-building have been the order of the day for successive generations of political elites, the definition of minority status, crucial in reflecting and altering the balance of political power within multiethnic states, transcends the regime types according to which that power is exercised.

The Ethnic Greek Minority under Communism

An inquiry established in 1922 by the League of Nations to study the question of the Greek population in Albania concluded that there were about 25,000 Greek-speaking people in Albania. However, the area studied was confined to the southern border fringes, and there is good reason to believe that this estimate was very low.[13] At present, organizations in Greece pursuing issues concerning northern Epirus claim that the number is as high as 400,000 in Albania as a whole, although the figure used by Greek governments in public statements and documents is generally lower.

In contrast, Albanian governments use a much lower figure of 58,000, which rests on the unrevised definition of "minority" adopted during the communist period. Under this definition, minority status was limited to those who lived in 99 villages in the southern border areas, thereby excluding important concentrations of Greek settlement in Vlora (about 8,000 people in 1994) and in adjoining areas along the coast, ancestral Greek towns such as Himara, and ethnic Greeks living elsewhere throughout the country. Mixed villages outside this designated zone, even those with a clear majority of ethnic Greeks, were not considered minority areas and therefore were denied any Greek-language cultural or educational provisions. In addition, many Greeks were forceably removed from the minority zones to other parts of the country as a product of communist population policy, an important and constant element of which was to preempt ethnic sources of political dissent. Greek place-names were changed to Albanian names, while use of the Greek language, prohibited everywhere outside the minority zones, was prohibited for many official purposes within them as well.

Although some Greek-language education existed under communism, pupils were taught only Albanian history and culture, even in Greek-language classes at the primary level. In general, some secondary-level provisions for Greek-language education existed, but, again, only for towns and villages within the designated minority areas and with the additional proviso that there was a majority of Greek-speakers in each class in the school. Because school curricula in the Greek language in the designated minority areas were *de facto* identical with the standard Albanian-language curriculum, efforts to study many of the greatest works of ancient Greek literature were rendered impossible. Nor, with the exception of archaeology (which flourished during the communist period), was it possible to study other aspects of classical Hellenistic culture once opportunities for travel abroad to Moscow State University ended following Albania's 1961 break with the Soviet Union.

At the same time, even the formal obligation to provide Greek-language education was often evaded by the regime's continuous efforts to transfer ethnic Greeks to other parts of the country from villages containing a bare majority of Greek-speakers. Much of the knowledge that we have of this process necessarily relies on anecdotal evidence, as no official records of population displacement exist from the communist period and the number of people involved was quite small. Nevertheless, the process appears to have left considerable political and cultural traces in the remaining Greek-speaking areas, while the continuous threat of arbitrary administrative action by Tirana has sowed a heritage of distrust that underlies some of the contemporary problems affecting relations between post-communist governments and the Greek minority.

The repression of minority culture and education (with the exception of some independent cultural activity, such as folk dancing) was continuous with the policy pursued by the Royalist regime of King Zog, under which Greek-language education had been attacked and eventually virtually eliminated in the 1930s. However, this process was steadily intensified in the postwar years under communism, particularly with the onset in 1967 of the campaign by Albania's communist party, the Albanian Party of Labor (PPSH), to eradicate organized religion, a prime target of which was the Orthodox Church.[14] Many churches were damaged or destroyed during this period, and many Greek-language books were banned because of their religious themes or orientation. Yet, as with other communist states, particularly in the Balkans, where measures putatively geared towards the consolidation of political control intersected with the pursuit of national integration, it is often impossible to distinguish sharply between ideological and ethno-cultural bases of repression. This is all the more true in the case of Albania's anti-religion campaign because it was merely one element in the broader "Ideological and Cultural Revolution" whose main features, prior to its initiation in 1966, had already been outlined by Hoxha at the PSHH's Fourth Congress in 1961.[15]

While the inability to draw such a clear line makes it difficult to assess the full contemporary political implications of previous policies, their unambiguous impact on ethnic survival explains why the definition of "minority" remains highly controversial. If a minority member is defined as someone who speaks Greek at home and at work, actively practices Greek Orthodoxy, and lives in a Greek-speaking town or village, then the figure put forward by both communist and post-communist Albanian governments may have some coherence. But there are undoubtedly much larger numbers of people who are in general Hellenist in their descent, cultural identity, and beliefs. Generally, members of the Greek minority in Tirana and other cities appear to have been much more closely linked to the communist regime than were the rural majority of ethnic Greeks, who remained in the minority's heartland around Dervician and Gjirokastra. The latter have generally remained culturally conservative, anti-communist, and Orthodox. For some, a private adherence to the old ideal of unity with Greece must have remained alive, and, although there are no records of oppositional political activity during the communist period that would demonstrate this definitively, individual minority members were occasionally arrested and tried for "anti-state" offenses.[16]

Assessing the consequences of the old regime's repressive measures is further complicated by the difficulty of arriving at an exact view of the role and status of ethnic Greeks within the PSHH and the Democratic Front, the two main popular organizations officially sanctioned under communism. As with the rest of the population, most ethnic Greeks belonged to the Democratic Front, the umbrella organization, but the PSHH's membership records did not register ethnicity. It is likely that the number of ethnic Greeks in the party, along with the size of the Greek minority as a whole, was augmented by the wave of refugees fleeing Greece following the end of the Greek civil war in 1949. In the main, these were leftists, and some were active Communists who rose to important positions in the Albanian regime.[17] Their orientation was secular and anti-clerical, and they appear to have played little part in activities opposing the regime. At the same time, however, apart from a few prominent figures, it appears that many ethnic Greeks did not feel secure with their cultural identity as Greeks within the party, often adopting Albanian names and severing any remaining links with the Orthodox Church during the period in which it remained legal. Indeed, with no provision for higher education in Greek at Tirana University or travel abroad for such purposes after 1961, entrance to elite cadres for the nearly two-thirds of Albania's population born after the Second World War was restricted to those who affirmed, at least outwardly, an entirely Albanian cultural identity.

It is in the light of this legacy of state treatment of Greek-speakers in pre-communist and communist Albania that contemporary Greek demands must be understood. Moreover, this legacy serves to reinforce present-day Albanian government officials' understanding of how problems concerning the Greek minority should be managed. To be sure, the assertion of ethnic minority demands is partly a consequence of the opportunities for political entrepreneurship afforded by the fluid domestic context of post-communist politics. Most importantly, however, in the case of both the pre-communist and communist regimes, policies designed to impede the maintenance or growth of a distinct Greek ethnic identity within Albania were implemented within, and were powerfully shaped by, an environment of official irredentist claims by Greece. Following a brief rapprochement in the post-communist period, contemporary ethnic relations and official treatment of the Greek minority within Albania have been strongly conditioned by the sub-national division among the ethnic Albanian majority as well.

After the Fall: Positive Developments in Inter-Ethnic Relations

With the communist regime's collapse in the winter of 1990-1991 and its replacement by a democratically-elected National Unity government the following spring, independent ethnic minority organizations were quickly established. For example, the Vlachs formed the National Vlach Association, with offices in Tirana under the chairmanship of Thermistocles Cule, the Armenians organized the Armenians of Albania, and so on. The Greek minority formed the *Omonia* organization in February 1990. In all cases, these were originally loosely-organized human rights associations established with the aim of winning ethnic minority rights within a functioning multi-cultural civil society operating along western lines.[18] In general, they came into being as a result of popular movements imitating those seen across eastern Europe on Italian and Greek television broadcasts. Thus, there were no established leadership structures; instead, prominent individuals who had some knowledge of politics gained a more or less spontaneous following comprised of friends, neighbors, and acquaintances within the community. Conceived within a political context in which the one-party state was at least formally still in existence, even if its coercive powers had collapsed, their chief priority was the establishment of genuine cultural and political independence for their members.

In fact, most of the new leaders of the Greek minority in the south had at one time been part of the old political establishment, with the important consequence that the duration of *Omonia*'s initial organizational disarray was relatively short. As has been noted, some ethnic Greeks achieved considerable prominence in the postwar years under communism, particularly ex-Partisans from towns in the south such as Saranda, Himara, and Vlora who had fought alongside Hoxha against the Germans. And, as has been true throughout Albania, long-time Communists, whether at the local, regional, or national level, were able to metamorphose successfully and retain their positions within the political elite after the regime's collapse—often through a nationalist "switch in time" that has benefited elites in much of eastern Europe. At the same time, defense of Greek rights appears to have led in many cases to expulsion from the Party for promoting "nationalism" or "separatism," particularly in the late 1980s, while subsequent links with the opposition rendered the political past of these ethnic Greek leaders entirely unimportant. On the contrary, during the popular turmoil and street politics from 1989-1991, it appeared as though burgeoning political pluralism would usher in a new dawn both for minority identity and those political elites who sought to capitalize on it.

Given the centrality of Orthodoxy to Slavic and Greek ethnic identity, the restoration of religious rights played a large part in the activities of several groups. The ferocity with which the communist regime repressed religion, particularly in the years until Hoxha's death in 1985, meant that much of the country's religious infrastructure was decimated by the time the ban on religious observance, codified as Article 37 of the 1976 constitution, was rescinded in early spring 1989. For *Omonia*, the restitution of Church property lost during the forced appropriations of the late communist period became a clear priority. Thus, almost immediately after *Omonia*'s formation in 1990, a delegation of ethnic Greeks met the Albanian government to discuss religious issues.

Because the early leadership of *Omonia* was in large part comprised of former Communists, they were often well connected in Tirana and able to bring effective pressure to bear on the government. On the whole, their demands, as well as similar objectives on the part of other groups, were accomplished without much difficulty or official obstruction. Title to Church property was clearly delineated in the localities, with few of the competing ownership claims that have complicated the restitution process throughout eastern Europe. Under the chaotic conditions prevailing in Albania at the time, most local communities simply seized back their old church or mosque buildings from the state without official sanction.[19] In most cases, the buildings had been used for agricultural storage purposes, and villagers simply removed their contents and began to restore the buildings for religious use with makeshift altars and furnishings. For a time, there was a significant degree of inter-religious cooperation in these developments, as in 1989 and 1990 in the northern city of Shkodra, where Muslims, Catholics, and the region's few Orthodox Albanians combined forces to bring pressure on the local and national government to reopen religious buildings for worship.

In fact, most religious groups found that they were pressing at an open door with respect to the 1989-1991 Tirana governments. Despite the constitutional ban, relaxation of official repression of religion as such, not merely Orthodoxy, had begun in 1988-1989, exemplified by improved relations with the Catholic Church, which culminated in Mother Theresa's visit to Albania in February 1989. Reformist communist leaders such as Fatos Nano and Ramiz Alia, who led the PSHH's successor, the Socialist Party, after its decisive victory in the 1991 elections, were well aware of the gross human rights violations that had occurred during Hoxha's effort to make Albania an atheist state in the 1970s. They viewed generosity towards the various religious groups and churches as both a morally and politically desirable policy, one also likely to win approval from the international community. Indeed, foreign investment was being courted not only from the West, but also, increasingly, from Islamic countries, making a clear policy of religious tolerance essential.

This liberalizing trend with respect to religion was accompanied by an initial extension of formal national minority rights in political institutions. Faced with a multitude of pressing economic, social, and political problems, the last communist government in 1989 and the first National Unity governments in 1990 and 1991 had little difficulty in agreeing to such demands. In the south, Greek minority representation already existed, in a tenuous form, through many local decision-making bodies. Ethnic Greeks who were Communists, or who, if not, were prepared to work with the one-party system, were often involved in local administration in the southern minority areas and were thus able to assist with the projection of wider minority demands in Tirana. Indeed, Omonia's early success was greatly facilitated by the fact that already at this early stage, as in most later political debate, it acted as a united body with a clear and well-supported local and national leadership (who, given the geographical concentration of the minority, were often the same people). As a result, a generally agreed-upon agenda of human rights demands, in addition to those concerning religious exercise, quickly emerged. One of the most important demands, the right to travel, was immediately secured, thereby allowing ethnic Greeks, often after a fifty-year hiatus, to visit relatives in Greece.

Rising Tensions in Albania's Ethnic Relations

Despite *Omonia*'s early achievements in the immediate aftermath of communism's collapse in 1990 and 1991—a period culminating in the March 1992 election of the first completely non-communist government under Dr. Sali Berisha—problems for the Greek minority soon began to surface. While such basic human rights as freedom of religious worship, publication, and travel had quickly been secured, hopes on the Greek side for sustained progress in institutionalizing harmonious relations with the ethnic Albanian majority were not realized.

This reflected a change in atmosphere that was partly linked to the Albanian economy's growing dependence on income from migrant workers in Greece. Following the removal of border controls in December 1990, large numbers of poor Albanians fled to Greece as illegal migrant workers, contributing to increased tension between the two countries.[20] Within Albania, the economic status of many Greek communities quickly began to rise above that of ethnic Albanian communities, as minority members found work and residence rights in Greece easier to obtain. This disparity in treatment by Greece led to conflict, first, over ethnic Greeks' demands for greater Greek-language educational provision. While ethnic Greeks perceived a continuing absence of teachers and resources, as well as little interest at the national level in altering the communist-era definition of minority areas entitled to Greek-language schools, ethnic Albanians regarded Greeks as having access to financial aid from Greece and the Greek diaspora that were unavailable to them, as well as medical treatment and other benefits in the northern Greek town of Ioannina. In 1991, Greek shops were attacked in the coastal town of Saranda, home to a large minority population, and inter-ethnic relations throughout Albania worsened.

There was also a widespread view among ethnic Albanians that the Tirana government disproportionately favored the Greek minority in the process of land privatization. This perception was in turn nurtured by the underlying division within the ethnic Albanian majority. Berisha's newly elected anti-communist government, dominated by northern Ghegs, was viewed as attempting to buy off ethnic Greek radicalism while providing few benefits to ethnic Albanians in the Tosk-dominated (and historically far more pro-communist) south. In fact, the Greek minority was indeed regarded by the Berisha government as being highly susceptible to extremist Orthodox revivalist propaganda broadcast from expanding irredentist organizations based in northern Greece. However, while religious differences among Albanians, who adhere to Catholicism, Eastern Orthodoxy, and Sunni and Bektashi Islam, have historically played little role in shaping domestic political conflict, Tirana's suspicion embraced Orthodox Albanians as well, as they, too, have often been influenced by anti-government propaganda from northern Greek bishops. With very few Orthodox Albanians whatsoever in the north, the Berisha government, comprised almost entirely of Sunni Muslims, demonstrated its lack of sympathy for either Orthodoxy in general or the Greek minority—all of whose members are Orthodox—by proposing in 1994 a requirement that all heads of religious groups be Albanian born. While the constitutional draft containing this provision was voted down in a referendum in November 1994, an important reason for its rejection was that the Albanian Orthodox Church had invited Archbishop (Eparch) Anastasios Giannulatos, a Greek citizen, to lead it temporarily in its effort to rebuild.[21]

Thus, what many southern Tosks perceived as an alliance between the Greek minority and the Gheg north could be (and for many Orthodox Tosks evidently was) interpreted as Gheg power exercised with a view to asserting northern interests over those of the south as a whole. With respect to the Greek minority's demands for recognition of cultural difference, this meant that ethnic Albanians' deep-seated suspicion of irredentism, which could be expected under any government, was exacerbated by the sectionally-based Gheg hegemony—justified partly in terms of hostility toward residual Communist influence—extended throughout its region of settlement.

The most visible focus of the Berisha government's fear of Greek irredentism was the Northern Epirus Liberation Front (MAVI), which claimed responsibility for the car bombing of Albania's ambassador to Greece in 1991 and was accused in 1994 and 1995 of orchestrating attacks on Albanian border posts and military personnel.[22] However, the MAVI threat could be magnified only after relations between ethnic Albanians and Greeks had already deteriorated following the attempt by the Socialist-led government to prevent *Omonia*'s participation in the 1992 elections on the grounds that it represented exclusively ethnic interests and was therefore illegal. Following strong protests by the Conference on Security and Cooperation in Europe, the Council of Europe, the United States, and other powerful international actors, this decision was reversed. However, while *Omonia* ultimately did participate, under the name of the Party of Human Rights, and won seven seats in the 140-seat Assembly, the episode was extremely damaging to inter-ethnic relations. The government's attempt to restrict the ethnic Greek presence in parliament undoubtedly contributed to the growing radicalization of ethnic minority politicians in 1992 and 1993, as many ethnic Greeks came to believe that avenues for the legitimate expression and realization of their long-term interests within the emerging new political order would remain substantially blocked.

This belief was reinforced by the Greek minority's demographically determined weakness within the national electoral sphere. Under the mixed electoral system introduced by Vilson Ahmeti's interim government prior to the 1992 elections, 100 seats are allocated on a majority basis in single-member districts, with the remaining forty seats divided proportionally among parties receiving at least 4 percent of the popular vote.[23] The concentration of ethnic Greeks in and around centers of Hellenism such as Saranda and Gjirokastra could guarantee their election there, but nowhere else in the country is success for an *Omonia*-based candidate possible. While it has been possible for the overwhelmingly ethnic Greek villages along the Aoos River valley stretching toward the Greek-Albanian border to secure majorities on municipal councils, the same electoral calculus generally applies at the local level. Faced with their inability to secure significant representation in national bodies, disagreement began to arise within *Omonia*, and among the Greek population generally, as to the surest means toward amassing the political power necessary to secure their demands, particularly expansion of Greek-language education to areas outside the old Communist-designated minority zones. This debate over means rapidly developed into a debate over ends.

As the internal debate that accompanied *Omonia*'s evolution from a human rights association into a political party became marked by the formal emergence of moderate and radical wings, the absence of either Albanian or Greek government support for their agenda quickly put party moderates at a serious disadvantage. The moderate wing has campaigned for ethnic Greek interests within a modified framework of the current Albanian state, while *Omonia*'s radical wing calls for border revisions and *enosis* (union with Greece). An important turning point came in April 1992, when *Omonia*'s chairman, the moderate Sotir Qiriazati, wrote an open letter to the Greek Prime Minister, Constantine Mitsotakis, calling for an autonomous region to be established in southern Albania and requesting substantial Greek government support for the region's social and economic development. These proposals were rejected not only by the Albanian side, which unanimously views ethnic territorial autonomy as tantamount to eventual secession, but also by Athens. This failure resulted in a transfer of the political initiative within *Omonia* to the radicals, who, entirely unbeholden to Albanian government support, argued that only a strategy guided by *enosis* would secure the necessary commitment from Athens.

The moderates' view of the Greek minority's position within the Albanian polity has been weakened further by the highly constitutive role of religion in ethnic Greek identity. Indeed, disputes between *Omonia*'s moderate and radical wings have been subsumed in the complex history of the auto-cephalous Albanian Orthodox Church, with religious leaders playing a central part in defining alternative conceptions of the ethnic group's political status.[24] The radicals were supported by the influential Orthodox bishop of Konitsa in Greece, Metropolitan Sevastianos, whose diocese includes parts of southern Albania, while Archbishop Giannulatos is a leading moderate who has attempted to mitigate irredentist claims. However, while the lack of trained clerics led Albanian Orthodox authorities in 1990 to invite the Patriarchate of Constantinople (Istanbul), with Albanian government approval, to appoint ethnic Greeks to senior positions in the Church, many Albanians view this as part of a Greek effort to gain lasting control over Albanian Orthodoxy. Thus, given that the Albanian Church's establishment in 1929 and independence (recognized in 1937) represented a key element of state-building in interwar Albania, and that Orthodoxy alone underpins the Greek conception of southern Albania as northern Epirus, Archbishop Giannu-latos's mere presence in his religious role has served to undermine the credibility of his political position.

Against this background, it is not surprising that the first substantial open conflict in the Gjirokastra region, in the spring of 1993, occurred after the expulsion of an ethnic Greek Orthodox priest, Archimandrite Chrysostomos Maidonis, for allegedly taking part in subversive, anti-Albanian activities. He was accused by Tirana of abusing his ministry by preaching separatism and *enosis* among the Greek minority. In widespread unrest in the Greek villages, local leaders were arrested and there were well-attested accounts of human rights violations in the area, including the sentencing of the mayor of Dervician, a minority village, to six months in prison for raising the Greek flag on Greece's national day.[25] This was followed by a noticeable expansion of surveillance of the minority by the reformed secret police in the minority areas, as well as a revival of the population movement controls that originated under the communist regime. The Greek government's response was swift: stepped up deportation of Albanians working illegally in Greece and cancellation of three official visits to Tirana after pro-Maidonis demonstrations outside the Albanian embassy in Athens led the Berisha government to recall its ambassador.[26] Thus, the increase in the level of Albanian repression, and the Greek government's reaction to it, demonstrated how porous boundaries between politically salient organizations and actors at the sub-governmental level in the "home state" and the "kin state" can shape official behavior in ways dangerous for inter-ethnic, and inter-state, peace.[27]

Bilateral Politics, Emigration, and Domestic Ethnic Relations

Since the end of communism, there has been a considerable increase in Albanian-Greek trade relations, with the very large illegal migrant work-force in Greece representing a major factor in bilateral ties.[28] Greece is the second largest source of foreign investment in Albania, after Italy. Road links with Greece have expanded rapidly, particularly with the improvement in the Ioannina/Kakavia border route and the rebuilt road connection to the south-eastern frontier post at Kapstica. These link the Korca region with the northern Greece region around Kastoria and offer good road connections to the economic center of Thessaloniki.[29]

This represents a major change over the past decade. There was virtually no trade at all between the two countries until 1976, when an economic agreement between Tirana and the Karamanlis government was signed. Even then, a formal state of war, dating back to the Italian invasion of Greece from occupied Albania in 1940, remained in effect until 1981. In the years between 1976 and 1989, electricity imports from Albania were integrated into the Greek national power grid, and a number of smaller-scale bilateral relation-ships developed. Recently, plans have been proposed for a new major hydro-electric scheme on the Aoos River.

In the period since the end of communism, these economic ties have been augmented by a new and central relationship: the very large sums of money remitted back to Albania by the migrant workers. While accurate official data are not available, independent analyses have estimated that as much as one-third of Albania's total hard currency earnings emanate from this source, with as many as 100,000 workers active in the Greek economy at any one time. This amounts to 400 million U.S. dollars per year and con-tributed significantly to the stability of the Albanian lek for much of the post-communist period. (Smaller sums are remitted from Italy, Germany, and Switzerland, as well as from other countries with a sizable Albanian diaspora community.)

The Greek remittances have given Greece a great deal of leverage over the Albanian economy, as was demonstrated following the expulsion of Maidonis in 1993 and again in the autumn of 1994 with another mass expulsion of Albanian migrant workers by Greece after five *Omonia* activists were charged with espionage and arms possession in connection with a MAVI raid on an

Albanian army barracks in which two Albanian soldiers died.[30] At the same time, the pattern of migration in search of employment has extended this leverage over Albanian governmental policy to the Greek minority to a much greater extent than its relative size would indicate, significantly affecting Albanian domestic politics. The centrality of emigration and employment policy at the meeting between Greek Foreign Minister Karolos Papoulias and his Albanian counterpart in March 1995, for example, is a clear indication of how Greek diplomacy has focused on balancing both visas and economic aid against issues affecting the Greek minority.

At the same time, however, emigration patterns into Greece have proven to be a source of disruption and increased ethnic tension for many of Albania's Greek communities. With the demise of authoritarian rule and the advent of freedom of movement, a substantial number of ethnic Greeks, too, immediately began to work in Greece as part of the estimated 100,000 Albanian nationals in the current Greek labor force. Greek Prime Minister Constantine Mitsotakis appealed to the northern Epirus villagers in 1991 to remain in Albania in order to preserve the area's "Hellenism," but this had little effect. As a result, some villages have suffered from severe depopulation, with quite serious consequences for the social structure of many localities, particularly those on the coastal fringe between Saranda and Himara, where an absence of able-bodied young men has caused additional work burdens to fall on women and the elderly.[31]

These developments became politically salient to the extent that they structured controversy surrounding the land privatization process around the ethnic cleavage. While accurate statistics are unavailable, visual inspection confirms that large areas of fertile privatized land in and around ethnic Greek villages lie derelict and uncultivated due to ethnic Greek migration, whereas neighboring ethnic Albanian villages, whose inhabitants find it difficult to obtain visas to work in Greece, are clearly land-hungry. Indeed, in addition to the belief that ethnic Greeks benefited from a political alliance with the Gheg-dominated government, the higher birthrate within the Albanian villages, particularly those that are predominantly Muslim, has exacerbated the communal relative deprivation that fuels perceptions among ethnic Albanians in the south. Thus, inter-ethnic relations have been affected not merely by political developments at the national level, but also by the local-level politics of resource scarcity. While decisions made in Tirana regarding the treatment of Albania's Greek minority have clearly shaped these relations, the politicization of ethnicity must also be viewed in terms of the operation of economic forces and social change driven by the opening of an often unruly border.

Conclusion: The Uncertain Political Future of the Greek Minority

Since the demise of one-party rule, the Greek minority has thus far been the only ethnic minority in Albania to pursue independent political participation. In all other cases, minorities are either very small and have confined their activities to cultural and human rights campaigns, or have failed to overcome internal obstacles to collective action (particularly the Roma and, to a lesser extent, the Vlachs). Others, such as the Jews, have left the country altogether, while, given their economic acumen, external links, and cultural cohesiveness, the ethnic Greeks' position corresponds in many ways to that of the Jews in Hapsburg (or Armenians in Ottoman) society, attracting similar political distrust. Unlike these groups, however, the acute climate of anti-Greek feeling in Albanian politics and society produced by the Greek minority's assertiveness is linked to deep-rooted problems in bilateral relations and national disunity among the Albanian majority.

Although there are no significant explicitly racist or chauvinist political parties in Albania, there are many individual politicians who adhere to very strong anti-Greek views, which in turn affects the orientation of virtually all ethnic Albanian political parties.[32] In fact, problems concerning the minority have been manipulated by the widespread use of xenophobic stereotypes on both sides of the border. Even quality newspapers in Greece often discuss Albania as though it were a protectorate, while many well-educated Albanians appear tacitly to believe that their country will become one if Greek minority demands are met. Yet, again, it is important to bear in mind that such anti-minority prejudices are manipulable in the post-communist period and serve to politicize religious, cultural, and economic cleavages along ethnic lines precisely because they are entrenched in the irredentism of the post-independence and inter-war periods and the national division among Albanians reinforced during the wartime resistance.

These factors have combined not only to make *Omonia*'s inclusion in any governing coalition in Tirana in the near future unlikely, but also call into question whether *Omonia* will continue to participate in the electoral process at all. Greek minority politics and political views have been radicalized to such an extent that a significant proportion of ethnic Greeks view their future as lying outside the confines of the existing Albanian state. This would amount to a revision of borders and, given the regional environment in the southern Balkans, a strong likelihood of armed conflict. Indeed, the more general future of the Greek minority may become increasingly linked with the wider Balkan crisis, in particular aspirations within the Albanian-dominated Kosovo region of Serbia for union with Albania. In such a scenario, the demands of Kosovar Albanians for autonomy or independence may well reinforce those of the Greek minority in Albania. While neither Greek leaders within Albania nor their protagonists in Greece have ever called for reconsidering the Greek minority's position as part of a wider Balkan settlement involving Kosovo, the Berisha government's repression should be understood in part as a reaction to Greek minority demands for an autonomy arrangement similar to that enjoyed by Kosovar Albanians prior to Serbian president Slobodan Milošević's own crackdown on the province.[33]

In these circumstances, it is likely that government pressure to restrict Greek aspirations will continue, even if some of the more extreme methods of surveillance and control adopted by the Berisha government were defeated by internal opposition or modified by international pressure. This is true despite developments since late 1996, when serious strains linked to the growth of high interest "pyramid" investment schemes began to appear in the Albanian financial system. By December, a financial collapse, beginning in Vlora and Tirana, but soon affecting the entire country, had become imminent. After a period of chaotic street protest, anarchy overtook many southern cities. The Berisha government's attempts to restore order failed, and an armed population took control of most towns.[34] The Greek minority played a significant role in these events, with some of the strongest oppositional activity focused in the most densely Greek-populated areas.[35] Although allegations of Greek involvement in the leadership of the uprising were made by the Berisha government, there was no evidence of ethnic conflict between Greeks and Albanians in the popular struggle leading to early elections and the return of the Socialist government in June 1997. On the contrary, while many of Berisha's right-wing supporters (particularly ex-emigres) had their property ransacked, most ethnic Greeks were left alone.[36]

Nevertheless, there may be some truth to the view held by many Berisha supporters, including Kosovar Albanians, that the victory of the Socialist Party—with its predominantly southern support base—was a victory for Greece and Greek regional influence. During the transition period between the Berisha government's resignation and the election of the Socialist government, the emigration question reemerged to dominate the bilateral agenda, with the Greek government promising to make available to Albanians an extensive work permit scheme that would legalize tens of thousands of guest workers. However, although relations between the two Socialist governments appear amicable, there has been significant parliamentary and public opposition to the proposals in Greece, and it is doubtful that real progress will be made on other traditionally divisive issues.[37] Revealingly, an agreement on improving Eparch Athanasios Giannulatos's status and position, concluded during Greek Foreign Minister Papoulias's visit to Tirana in 1995, has done virtually nothing to diminish controversies concerning the appointment and influence of Orthodox Church personnel.[38]

At the same time, it seems unlikely that the Greek minority in Albania will be able to insulate itself from the wider fate of the country, which is bound to be uncertain and fraught with social and economic tensions for the forseeable future. Even prior to the outbreak of widespread civil unrest following the collapse of the investment schemes in early 1997, the attack on the United States Embassy in Tirana by over one thousand youths in March 1995 provided a strong indication of the very high social tension within Albania caused by mass employment and inflation. Such factors may very well aggravate national security concerns whose resolution awaits a wider Balkan settlement. For, while the removal of Sali Berisha's highly confrontational and polarizing government may benefit bilateral relations and contribute to regional stability, particularly in terms of economic cooperation, the more fundamental and historically ingrained cultural, religious and social divisions that have shaped Albania's polity and political regimes will remain.

Notes

1. See Enver Hoxha, *Two Friendly Peoples* (Tirana: 8 Nentori, 1985) for a general view of how the Albanian communists viewed the Greek minority issue after 1944 and under communism. It is clear that Hoxha had little information on the early stages of the Greek Civil War and its effects on the Greek minority in Albania.

2. See Institute of Marxist-Leninist Studies, *History of the Party of Labour of Albania*, 2nd ed. (Tirana: 8 Nentori, 1982) for the official communist view of Albanian history. See also Stefanaq Pollo and Arben Puto, *The History of Albania*, trans. Carole Wiseman and Ginnie Hole (London: Routledge & Kegan Paul, 1981).

3. See Stavro Skendi, *The Albanian National Awakening, 1878-1912* (Princeton: Princeton University Press, 1967). See also Miranda Vickers, *The Albanians: A Modern History* (London: I.B.Tauris, 1995), pp. 32-53.

4. See Vickers, *op. cit.*, Chapter 5.

5. The history of Albania during the Second World War has been highly controversial, with most of the protagonists in the argument British ex-Special Operations executive officers involved in the anti-Axis campaign. The best general account is to be found in Sir Reginald Hibbert, *Albania's National Liberation: The Bitter Victory* (London: Pinter, 1991). For a contrary view, see Sir Julian Amery, *Sons of the Eagle* (London: Macmillan, 1948). A good account of an important part of the military campaign is to be found in Brigadier T. Davies, *Illyrian Venture* (London: The Bodley Head, 1952).

6. For an analysis of how elements of clan-based social organization and its core principles of unbending loyalty and honor have influenced Albania's post-communist political culture, see

Fabian Schmidt, "An Old System Blends into the Present," *Transition,* vol. 2, no. 18 (September 6, 1996), pp. 50-53.

7. The figure of 3 percent is taken from estimates by the U.S. Central Intelligence Agency, *CIA World Factbook,* 1994.

8. Miranda Vickers and James Pettifer, *Albania: From Anarchy to a Balkan Identity* (London: C. Hurst, 1997), Chapter 10.

9. For a clear and accessible account of ancient history in the area that is now Albania, see Frank Walbank, "Albania in Antiquity," in James Pettifer, ed., *Blue Guide: Albania* (New York: Norton, 1996), pp. 15-22.

10. For the best account of the destruction caused in Epirus and southern Albania by inter-communal violence during this period, as well as the main diplomatic intrigues which affected this region, see Rene Puaux, *The Sorrows of Epirus* (Chicago: Argonaut reprint, 1963).

11. See Hoxha, op. cit., pp. 15 ff.

12. There has been very little study of the Northern Epirus issue in this period. For an interesting but highly pro-Greek view, see Pyrrus Ruches, *Albania's Captives* (Chicago: Argo Press, 1964).

13. See *Albania* (London: Naval Intelligence Handbook, 1945), pp. 178 ff.

14. For a valuable collection of documents, see Basil Kondis and Eleftheria Manda, eds., *The Greek Minority in Albania - A Documentary Record (1921-1993)* (Thessaloniki: Institute of Balkan Studies, 1994). For important background, see also Basil Kondis, *Greece and Albania, 1908-1914* (Thessaloniki: Institute of Balkan Studies, 1976).

15. The best account of this period can be found in Peter R. Prifti, *Socialist Albania Since 1944* (Cambridge: MIT Press, 1978).

16. See *Albania: Political Imprisonment and the Law* (London: Amnesty International, 1984).

17. Some important Albanian communist leaders were wholly or partly Greek, like long-serving Politburo member Spiro Koleka, who came from the predominently ethnic Greek town of Himara.

18. See Vickers and Pettifer, *op. cit.,* Chapter 10.

19. See my report in *The Independent* (London), February 6, 1991. The best account in English of the outlook of the northern Greek bishops on the persecution of the Orthodox Church under communism is to be found in Metropolitan Sevastianos of Dryinoupolis, *Northern Epirus Crucified* (Athens, 1986).

20. See Vickers and Pettifer, *op.cit.,* Chapter 10.

21. See Fabian Schmidt, "Between Political Strife and a Developing Economy," *Transition* (1994 in Review: Part 1), p. 8.

22. It is not clear to what extent MAVI was a significant political and paramilitary formation rather than merely a fanatical splinter group. At the time, the Albanian government claimed that Greek army and secret police personnel were involved in the attacks. The name is adopted from the wartime Northern Epirot organization which fought as a separate resistance group against the Axis in 1943. It was destroyed in vicious fighting with the German occupiers and the Albanian nationalist forces of the Balli Kombetar, and it played no part in the final liberation of the country.

23. See Fabian Schmidt, "The Opposition's Changing Face," *Transition,* vol. 1, no. 11 (June 30, 1995), p. 50.

24. For a comprehensive overview of church history from a Greek perspective, see Apostolis Glavina, *The Albanian Autocephalous Orthodox Church* (Thessaloniki: Zita, 1992). See also Sevastianos, *op. cit.*

25. See Vickers and Pettifer, *op. cit.*, Chapter 10.

26. Marianne Sullivan, "Mending Relations with Greece," *Transition*, vol. 1, no. 15 (August 25, 1995), pp. 11-16.

27. Focusing on the role of such organizations as the Orthodox Church thus represents an important qualification and extension of Rogers Brubaker's very useful "triadic" framework for analyzing ethno-politics in eastern Europe, where twentieth-century border movements have left national minorities in "home states" adjacent to their ethnic "kin states." See Rogers Brubaker, "Home States, Kin States, and Ethnic Minorities in the New Europe," *Daedelus* (1995).

28. See Economist Intelligence Unit, *Albania Country Reports* (London: EIU, 1992-1997).

29. See generally *Blue Guide to Albania, op. cit.*

30. *Balkan News* (Athens), November 1994. A great deal of other material related to the "*Omonia* five" appeared in the Greek press at the time. The Greek police later began their own investigation of MAVI, arresting three Greek citizens and four Greek Albanians following another thwarted border raid in the spring of 1995. Confirming Albania's earlier accusations, the police said MAVI was likely headed by Anastasios Giorgos, a former Greek army officer, while the Greek press suggested that the Greek secret service may indeed have been either involved with the organization or had overlooked its activities. At the same time, a former Greek government minister, Theodoros Pangalos, admitted that the *Omonia* five had "very probably been linked" to MAVI. See Sullivan, *op. cit.*, p. 16.

31. See Vickers and Pettifer, *op.cit.*, Chapter 10.

32. Rightist forces such as the group led by Tomas Dosti within Berisha's Democratic Party, for example, played a prominent role in shaping the government's repressive anti-Greek measures from 1994 to 1996.

33. These themes have frequently been aired in Albanian public debate, particularly in such newspapers as *Rilindja*, in which the Kosovar influence is apparent.

34. See Fabian Schmidt, "Pyramid Schemes Leave Albania on Shaky Ground," *Transition*, vol. 3, no. 3 (March 7, 1997), pp. 8-10.

35. See reports by Antony Loyd and James Pettifer in *The Times* (London), March 7-21, 1997. The Greek minority in Saranda scored the first military success for the opposition by capturing a government tank on March 6.

36. For a more detailed examination of the role of the Greek minority in the uprising, see James Pettifer, "The Greek Minority in the Albanian Rising," *Anglo-Hellenic Review*, no. 16 (Autumn 1997), p. 7 ff.

37. Indeed, a new problem has emerged, as it is widely believed in Tirana that a large sum of aid money was stolen by the Berisha government or people close to it and placed in Greek banks. However, given restrictive Greek banking legislation, recovery will likely prove difficult for Fatos Nano's Socialist government even if criminal activity can be demonstrated.

38. For example, conflict over Greek control of the Orthodox Church arose in 1996 in Elbasan.

7

THE ROMA OF CENTRAL
AND EASTERN EUROPE:
CONSTRUCTING A STATELESS NATION

Erin Jenne

The Romani population of eastern Europe is difficult to characterize.[1] Does it comprise a single trans-national minority, many different national minorities, or simply a multitude of atomized communities? Even the number of Roma in eastern Europe is a matter of considerable uncertainty. Most estimates fall somewhere between 4.5 and 5.5 million, with the highest concentrations in Romania, Bulgaria, Hungary, the Slovak Republic, Yugoslavia (Serbia-Montenegro), and the Czech Republic.[2] Yet, notwithstanding a past in the formerly communist countries that was distinguished primarily by their virtual invisibility, the Roma have been establishing a more stable collective identity and, with it, a stronger political voice in the post-communist period.

This can be traced to several factors. A vitally important precondition of all ethnic activism is the array of civic freedoms that allow ethnic identity to be expressed through the establishment of independent associations and political parties. The fall of communism produced a wide array of such organizations, which regularly demand that governments recognize various group rights. Movements for Romani rights are no exception to this more general phenomenon. However, three other factors have galvanized Romani self-organization. First, the severe socio-economic dislocation throughout the region since 1989 has fueled ethnic scapegoating among majority populations against persons of Romani origin. Because such external stresses operate on the basis of ascriptive distinctions, they have underpinned a growing subjective awareness of the salience of these distinctions. As Immanuel Wallerstein has put it, "Membership in an ethnic group is a matter of social definition, an interplay of the self-definition of members and the definition of other groups."[3]

This condition alone, however, cannot fully account for sustained political mobilization, as Romani leaders initially met with little success in defending Romani interests against governments that are often tacitly, and sometimes openly, hostile to their demands. A second, and decisive, factor has been heightened external pressure on the political units in which ethnic minority demands are made, with the West's attention to problems faced by central and eastern Europe's Roma particularly visible. Motivated largely by an interest in stemming the post-1989 exodus of eastern European Roma to Germany and France and, more recently, of Czech and Slovak Roma to Great Britain and Canada, the European Union (EU), the Council of Europe, and the Organization for Security and Cooperation in Europe (OSCE) have maintained initiatives to investigate and monitor the status of Roma throughout the region.[4] Similarly, the expansion of international human rights organizations into the region since 1989—Helsinki Watch, Romani Crisis, and the European Roma Rights Center (EERC) being the most prominent—has contributed to maintaining western interest in Romani issues. As a result, Romani elites have become increasingly aware of outside support to which they can appeal for assistance in relations with their home governments, thereby facilitating collective action.

A third, and related, factor is that heightened international scrutiny comes at a time when most countries in the region are bound by association agreements with, and are actively lobbying for entrance to, the European Union. By making membership in European organizations contingent upon protection of minority rights, west European countries have signaled post-communist governments that they will be held accountable for the status of Roma in their societies, thereby creating a strong incentive to accommodate the interests of Romani communities and bestow political legitimacy on their leaders. In sum, the influence of outside lobbying organizations and supra-national institutions on both post-communist governments and Romani leaders has served to heighten organizational capacity on the basis of Romani identity, enabling Romani elites to press more effectively for group demands that follow from its acknowledgment.

Nevertheless, the Roma face high barriers to ethnic organization and mobilization that follow from a position within their host states that differs from that of other minorities examined in this volume in two important respects. First, the Roma of central and eastern Europe constitute an ethnoclass whose members, with very few exceptions, occupy the lowest social and economic strata in large part as a result of their ethnic identity.[5] The reproduction of extremely low socio-economic status over time has not only aggravated their own isolation and the hostility of majority populations, but has prevented the accumulation of cultural and material resources required to organize and mobilize more effectively.[6] Second, unlike ethnic Hungarians, Greeks, Russians, or Turks, the Romani minority has no external homeland on which it can rely for virtual representation of its interests vis-à-vis its host states. While the recent intervention of international organizations mitigates this to some extent, the Roma are nonetheless far more dependent than the region's other minorities on historical fluctuations in these organizations' influence and the norms embedded in them, which in turn has underscored the achievement of nationhood as a strategic imperative.[7] This chapter focuses on the role of both these distinguishing factors in shaping the goals and effectiveness of Romani political participation in central and eastern Europe.

A Socio-Political Profile of a European Underclass

Compared to eastern Europe's majority populations, the Roma are disadvantaged on almost every level. Due in large part to poor health care and malnutrition, Romani life expectancy is roughly ten years shorter than country averages, while poor pre-natal and nursing care have resulted in high infant mortality rates and low birth weight among Romani children. In the 1980s, infant mortality for Roma in Czechoslovakia was twice the national average, with 40 to 50 deaths per 1,000 births.[8] In Hungary, Romani newborns are on average two pounds lighter than non-Roma babies.[9] For many Roma, poor health care is the result of a migratory lifestyle, which often leads to residence in countries in which they lack citizenship and thus access to national health insurance. In addition, many Roma live in poor, peripheral regions where delivery of social services is inadequate. The birthrate of Roma across eastern Europe is also significantly higher than that of majority populations, with the rate among Hungarian Roma, for example, double that of Hungary as a whole at a time when the country's population is shrinking. Two-thirds of Romania's Roma are married by the age of 17, with an average of 4.75 children per family—more than twice the national average.[10]

These factors have combined to produce a demographic structure radically different from that of eastern Europe's aging population. More than half of Slovakia's Romani population, for example, is under 15 years of age, and the Romani population is expected to double within the next 17 years.[11] As elsewhere, the majority population widely views this trend as threatening a future in which it will be overwhelmed. In the 1970s, such fears led the Czechoslovak government actively to support sterilization and abortions for Romani women, with such practices continuing, through bribes or coercion, until the spring of 1991. In the post-communist period, opportunistic politicians have also learned to play upon these fears to attract votes. In reference to his country's Roma, for example, Prime Minister Vladimir Mečiar of Slovakia said that it would be necessary to reduce the "(e)xtended reproduction of the socially unadaptable and mentally backward population by decreasing family allowances."[12]

Educational deficiency is one of the most significant problems faced by Romani communities. Widespread illiteracy has effectively barred many Roma from access to professional employment, while seriously impeding their ability to compete for most skilled and semi-skilled jobs. In Romania, the illiteracy rate among Roma is 20-25 percent higher than the national average, only 4 percent of the country's Roma graduate from high school, and 58 percent of Romani men and 84 percent of Romani women have no professional training whatsoever.[13] In Slovakia, 38 percent of non-Roma are enrolled in secondary schools, compared to 2.8 percent of Roma.[14] Very few Roma in eastern Europe earn the equivalent of a high school diploma, while only a tiny percentage of Roma attain some form of higher education.

These deficiencies are attributable to two main causes. First, many Romani parents, fearful of cultural assimilation and deeply distrustful of majority institutions, are unwilling to place their children in *gadje* (white) schools, while Romani communities generally lack any educational provisions of their own.[15] Second, Romani children are generally unfamiliar with the language of instruction by the time they enter school, having been raised speaking Romani. Teachers commonly misinterpret their poor performance as being due to laziness or lack of ability. As a result, a disproportionate number of Roma throughout the region are placed at an early age in schools for the mentally disabled, often as a virtually routine matter of course. Although such classes are designed to prepare students for integration into regular schools, most Romani pupils never complete these courses. In Slovakia, for example, Romani children are 28 times more likely than non-Romani children to be sent to schools for retarded children, and they are 30 times more likely to drop out.[16]

Relative unemployment figures paint a similarly grim picture. For example, despite the constitutionally embedded "right" to a job, unemployment among the Roma under Czechoslovakia's communist regime never dropped below 25 percent. In the Czech Republic, the Roma unemployment rate is now over 30 percent, and in some places has reached 90 percent, compared to 4-5 percent for the country as a whole.[17] In Hungary, Roma unemployment is currently between 60 and 70 percent. Unemployment in the Romani community in Bulgaria has reached as high as 80-90 percent, compared to the national average of 16 percent.[18] Aside from educational deprivation, exceptionally high unemployment among Roma throughout eastern Europe has been caused by severe discrimination in the labor market. Employers, for example, regularly run advertisements of job openings in local newspapers stating that "gypsies need not apply." While these have sometimes been modified to read "Roma (or 'Rroma') need not apply," employers justify openly discriminatory hiring practices by claiming that Romani employees are lazy or dishonest. There are typically few, if any, laws prohibiting ethnic discrimination in the workplace, and constitutional guarantees of civil equality frequently go unenforced.

Denied access to the workforce, or unwilling to accept the predominantly menial jobs that are available to them, many east European Roma have returned to more traditional Romani livelihoods, working as traveling fairground proprietors, horse-dealers, smiths, and musicians, while some have become still more marginalized as beggars. Others engage in a variety of illegal or semi-legal activities, frequently serving as "migrant middlemen."[19] Indeed, although some Roma have prospered financially, many more are destitute, with widespread poverty an important factor in the disproportionate level of criminality among the Roma throughout the region. This discrepancy has grown wider since the collapse of communism. The reported increase in crimes committed by Roma in Bulgaria since 1989, for example, is 70-90 percent, compared to a 20 percent increase among the population as a whole.[20] These statistics have often been used quite explicitly to reinforce stereotypes of the Roma as parasitic and dangerous, resulting in further marginalization and impoverishment. Bulgarian newspapers divide crime reports into two columns: those committed by Roma and those by non-Roma.

In addition to disadvantages in health, education, and employment, the Roma also face increasing racial violence, while lacking adequate legal and police protection. According to the Czech Movement for Civic Solidarity and Tolerance (HOST), there were 209 documented racially motivated attacks from 1989 to 1993 in the Czech Republic and more than 700 from 1994 to 1997. According to the ERRC, neo-Nazi skinheads have killed at least nine Roma in the Czech Republic since 1989. When suspects are charged and convicted, they commonly serve extremely light sentences. In several countries, members of the majority population have attacked entire Romani settlements in retribution for a crime allegedly committed by a Rom, while in some cases law enforcement officials themselves have justified their own violations of civil rights in terms of crime prevention.[21] There has been little public outcry in the wake of such episodes. On the contrary, a public opinion survey conducted in Czechoslovakia in February 1992 found that more than half of those polled either approved of the skinheads' activities or did not condemn them. Skinheads received tacit support from the majority population, the survey found, because "when they appear, the gypsies vanish."[22]

The Roma face other legal problems as well. In a case that attracted the attention of numerous outside organizations, including the Council of Europe and the United Nations High Commissioner for Refugees (UNHCR), the Czech parliament passed a new citizenship law in 1992 prior to the disolution of Czechoslovakia that rendered stateless many "Slovak" Roma who had spent their entire lives in the Czech Republic. Non-governmental organizations argued that the law was specifically designed to disenfranchise Roma residing on Czech territory by requiring that applicants for Czech citizenship prove residence for at least two years in the Czech Republic and possess a clean criminal record for the previous five years. Many legal experts argued that the latter requirement violated the principle of non-retroactivity and was inconsistent with international practice concerning permanent residents on the territory of successor states.[23]

In response to international pressure, the Czech government finally amended the citizenship law in April 1996, granting the Ministry of the Interior discretionary power to waive the requirement of a clean criminal record. In the wake of continued criticism of the remaining requirements (many Roma could not prove permanent residence, nor could many afford the application fee) and highly publicized exoduses of Czech and Slovak Roma to Great Britain and Canada in the fall of 1997, the Czech government announced that the only requirement for obtaining citizenship would be proof of residence prior to the January 1, 1993, split of Czechoslovakia.[24] Since these amendments were enacted, many applicants originally turned down for citizenship received it. However, as HOST points out, they do not alter the fact that the requirement of a clean criminal record remains in the law and that, because many Roma never held legal residence in the Czech Republic prior to the country's independence, they cannot meet the requirement of proving residence.

Obtaining official documentation is, moreover, a problem for Roma everywhere, with Romani leaders claiming that Romani applicants are often turned down flat on the basis of their ethnic identity. In Ukraine, as in other countries, many Roma live without documentation.[25] Roma are thus often unable to travel legally, send their children to school, or receive many other social, cultural, and economic benefits that follow from citizenship or legal residence. The uncertain legal status of many Roma in eastern Europe thus renders their economic and social position even more precarious, while leaving them vulnerable to formally neutral government policies directed against unofficial residents.

In sum, the problems faced by eastern Europe's Romani population are multi-faceted and, like other underclasses, interconnected in chain-like fashion. It is impossible to understand the problem of high criminality without also taking into account widespread poverty, which in turn is driven by high unemployment caused by poor education and discrimination in the labor market. Non-governmental organizations and social workers have consistently concluded that the current status of this minority, while gaining political salience only in the post-communist period, is the product of a centuries-long history of social decisions made on the basis of ethnic markers, resulting in what Donald Horowitz has termed a "deeply divided society."[26]

The Origins of Romani Marginalization and National Awakening

The Roma are believed to have left their original homeland in northern India in the 10th century, reaching Europe via Asia Minor and the Balkans around 1250 AD[27] Evidence suggests that the Roma were present in Romania's medieval provinces of Wallachia and Moldavia by the end of the 11th century. By the close of the 14th century, large groups of Roma had settled in the Danubian region, where they were generally incorporated into the region's various social and political orders. At first, these Roma found work as metalsmiths and craftsmen, but in the 13th and 14th centuries, many Roma in Romania and in the Balkans were enslaved for a variety of reasons, perhaps the most important of which was the labor shortage caused by the demand for men to fight in the Crusades. By the late 15th century, as regional rulers brought back thousands of Roma from military conquests in northern Bulgaria, slavery in Romania had become institutionalized, while the establishment of urban guilds under Ottoman rule solidified Romani craft specialization. The slave trade was regulated, Romani slaves were categorized by owner and craft, and legal restrictions were placed on their movement. Although slavery in Romania was outlawed in the middle of the 19th century, full emancipation of Roma did not occur until after the First World War.

Meanwhile, Roma who had settled in the areas of Hungary and Czechoslovakia faced varying degrees of persecution. In the 18th century, the most extreme forms of persecution within the Habsburg Empire ceased as Maria

Theresa and her son, Joseph II, attempted to assimilate the Roma into the peasantry. Housing was built in order to settle "wandering" Roma, and they were pressured to enter mainstream occupations, such as road construction and agriculture. They were also prohibited from travelling, speaking Romani, and wearing traditional dress. In 1780, over 8,000 Romani children were taken from their families for "re-education" as wards of the state. Another 9,463 children were placed in foster homes. Within a few years, however, nearly all of the children had run away from their foster families and schools.

While Roma who made their way to northern and western Europe were often charged with spying for the Turks or plotting against the Christian establishment, their lifestyle differed significantly from that of Roma in eastern Europe. Due to the persistence of a feudal economy and chronic labor shortages, east European rulers required a large, coerced labor force. Roma in eastern Europe were therefore often forcibly settled. The spread of capitalism and industrialization in western Europe, on the other hand, was able to accommodate a variety of marginal groups and encouraged personal mobility, thereby sustaining Roma nomadism. Moreover, from the beginning of the 15th century, nomadism served as a way to evade repressive policies adopted by western rulers as a means of eliminating vagrancy.[28]

At the close of the First World War, international politics became infused with a new sense of morality based on "universal" individual and group rights. The multi-national Habsburg Empire collapsed and new states, based on Wilsonian principles of national self-determination, were established in its place, while a steady accumulation of protocols and treaties sought to protect the rights of large minority groups left outside the borders of their "national" states by the redrawing of international frontiers. The recognition of minority rights was also included in the constitutions of several new east European states. Czechoslovakia's 1920 constitution, for example, named the Roma as a national minority, whose cultural and linguistic rights were protected by law.

Spurred by the new language of group rights and the establishment of the League of Nations, Romani organizations began to flourish in the 1920s and 1930s throughout eastern Europe. The Pan-Russian Romani Union coordinated some thirty Romani-managed artisan cooperatives in Moscow alone until Joseph Stalin banned Romani activism in 1929. In Romania, the Association of Roma was founded at Clabor in 1926 and published a journal called *Romani Family* from 1930 to 1934. Another organization, more nationalist in orientation, produced two widely-circulated publications, *Romani Voice* and *Rom,* remaining active until 1933. In October of that year, the

General Association of Romania organized and held an international conference in Budapest under the heading "United Gypsies of Europe." The conference proposed establishing a Romani library, hospital, and university, and to create an umbrella organization for Romani representatives throughout Europe with the aim of strengthening ethnic solidarity and redressing social inequality between the Roma and majority populations. The Romani deputies also adopted a Romani national flag.[29]

In this sense, the first organized expressions of Romani nationalism drew upon models of national development of other groups. More specifically, by linking a long-recognized identity based upon shared ethnic traits to claims for political association and self-determination, "nineteenth-century nationalism, centered on the idea of a nation-state, presented to Gypsies above all the example of Zionism."[30] And, as with the Zionists, Romani leaders recognized the need to gain the support of national governments, and ultimately the international community, in order to achieve their goals. To this end, some Roma capitalized on the popularity of the image of Romani "royalty" in the *gadje* imagination, proclaiming themselves kings, barons, and so forth, thus staking a claim to represent the broader Romani community making deals with government bodies in exchange for recognition as the highest Romani authorities within a particular state.[31] Although some of these royals were motivated by individual enrichment, others were genuinely interested in furthering the interests of their community through negotiations with national governments and the League of Nations.

A prominent example of this type of leadership was the royal line established in Poland in the 1920s by the Kweik family, descendants of slaves emancipated in Romania in the 19th century, and recognized by the government and local police. Michael Kweik II, coronated in 1930, announced his goal of creating a Romani state in India, close to the presumed homeland of the original Roma nomads.[32] The plan never came close to fruition, however, as Kweik was soon deposed by competitors. Later, Janusz Kweik, who won recognition from the Archbishop of Warsaw as king of the Polish Roma, announced that he would petition Mussolini to provide land in Abyssinia for the Romani people. He also expressed the hope that the Roma would acquire representation in the League of Nations. This agenda was, once again, clearly inspired by the Zionist example. However, support for these national programs never took root, as fascist governments began recommending the elimination rather than the deportation of the Romani population. During the war years, approximately 500,000 Roma were exterminated in concentration camps across Europe.

The Post-War Quiescence of Romani Nationalism in Eastern Europe

Following the Second World War, the experiences of Roma in eastern and western Europe diverged sharply. To be sure, Romani political activity was hardly welcomed by west European countries and many Roma were reluctant even to declare their ethnicity. Much of the pre-war anti-Roma legislation remained in effect in Germany until the early 1950s; indeed, until 1947, Roma still faced incarceration in labor camps if they emerged from hiding without German identification papers.[33] International organizations, meanwhile, failed to lobby on the Roma's behalf as they had for the remnants of European Jewry that had survived the Holocaust. Nevertheless, several Romani organizations were founded in western Europe. In France, the National Romani Organization and the World Romani Community were established by a Romanian Rom, Ionel Rotaru, who lobbied for an autonomous territory for the Romani community in France and for a Romani homeland in Somalia. In 1972, twenty-three international organizations in twenty-two countries were linked through the International Gypsy Community, which followed the first World Romani Congress in 1971. This committee eventually became known as the International Romani Union (IRU) and acquired non-governmental consultative status within the United Nations in 1979.[34] In 1986, the IRU established formal relations with UNICEF and currently has a pending application with UNESCO and the World Health Organization. The IRU actively lobbies for standardization of the Romani language, cultural preservation, increased media attention, and war crimes reparations.[35]

In eastern Europe, however, the Romani communities were ravaged by communist regimes that generally forbade unsanctioned expression of ethnic identity. In the first few years after World War II, when Communism's anti-fascist prestige was at its height, many Roma joined the region's communist parties and took positions as local and district-level officials. Shortly thereafter, however, communist regimes across the region undertook large-scale attempts to assimilate the Roma into majority cultures, as their continued existence as a distinct ethnic group was viewed as a barrier to the establishment of integrated socialist societies.[36] Unlike other national minorities in east Europe, Romani culture contrasted too sharply with that of ethnic majorities and was branded as anti-modern and uncivilized. Thus, eastern European governments maintained that the Roma needed first to adopt a more settled, culturally "advanced" life-style before they could be granted the rights that had been accorded to other, better integrated minority ethnic groups.[37] Assimilationist pressures forced Roma to leave their traditional occupations and migrate to cities, where they became manual laborers, or to join the new agricultural collectives in the countryside. The Romani intellegentsia, while small in the interwar period, suffered further setbacks. The number of Romanian Roma in the professions, for example, declined in the period between 1956 and 1966.[38] Although the number of Romani children in primary education increased under communism, classroom performance was poor and dropout rates were high, with very few students gaining higher education.

The Communists' efforts to absorb Roma into the mainstream workforce were partly successful. In Czechoslovakia, around 66 percent of Romani males and 41 percent of females of working age had jobs in 1970, with employment rising to 75 percent for both men and women by 1981.[39] However, while Czechoslovakia's socialist regime tied the Roma to permanent addresses and permanent jobs, it also effectively consigned them to the most menial, undesirable positions in the formal economy's secondary labor force.[40] Meanwhile, the Roma were faced with deeply ingrained anti-Romani prejudice in the more rural societies of Romania and Hungary. Roma in these countries were consequently forced to live on the outskirts of villages, where they similarly languished at the bottom of local economies.[41]

In some cases, Roma were forcibly resettled as part of broader assimilationist policies. The Czechoslovak government, in particular, undertook a large-scale project of resettling the Roma by moving them out of their makeshift encampments and into towns, thereby dispersing them throughout the majority population. The consequence was invariably a dramatic improvement in amenities, but this was accompanied by profound isolation within communities that viewed the new inhabitants with suspicion and often hostility. Indeed, while the central government forced Roma to leave the shantytowns, local officials were often unwilling to integrate them into existing housing developments. Even so, ethnic relations worsened as the majority population grew increasingly resentful of the perceived privileges accorded to the Roma in housing and social assistance, thus compounding the effects of resettlement's weakening of traditional Romani social structures.[42]

The Perils of Post-Communism

The collapse of eastern Europe's communist regimes put the Roma in an extremely precarious position. The minority could no longer count on guaranteed social assistance—upon which a large proportion of the Romani population had grown to depend—and simultaneously faced the prospect of working in an increasingly privatized economy, in which employers could freely discriminate against them.[43] For example, one businessman in the Czech Republic paid his Romani workers half the salary paid to other employees for the same amount and type of work, continuing this practice until the town's Roma finally boycotted his job offers.[44] Moreover, economic, social, and political reforms have traumatized post-communist societies, giving birth to numerous extremist groups who exercise their new-found civic freedoms by openly persecuting persons of Romani origin. Law enforcement officials typically view the Roma as a criminal element and are frequently indifferent to protecting them against such violence. Indeed, according to a recent government report on the Roma in the Czech Republic, roughly 62 percent of police officers feel that racially motivated crimes are provoked by Roma themselves and their "bad reputation."[45]

The social marginalization evident in the history of relations between eastern Europe's Roma and non-Roma populations is clearly reflected in the nature of Romani political participation during the post-communist period. The Roma are extremely isolated politically, significantly underrepresented in national voting statistics, and difficult to mobilize at the grass roots. While there are important exceptions to widespread political apathy, several factors underlie the general pattern. First, while Romani political parties and associations, largely fueled by euphoric expressions of new civic freedoms, were established throughout the region immediately following the collapse of communism, efforts to sustain these parties have failed. In a few cases, Roma were actually elected to parliament, but continued representation at the national level was effectively foreclosed after the broad revolutionary movements on which these groups depended for a share of power crystallized into party systems.[46] At the same time, while individual Roma have appeared on the candidate lists of ethnic majority parties (typically those on the Left), none of these parties has actively championed Romani issues, given majority populations' hostility toward the Roma and to programs designed to assist them. A public opinion poll conducted in Czechoslovakia in 1993, for example, indicated that 67 percent of Czechs believed that minority rights should be restricted in the interests of the majority.[47] These developments have resulted in deep voter apathy, as the Roma perceive that no major political party represents their interests.

The lack of resources within the Romani community is a second impediment to political participation. An important implication of the poor educational attainment relative to majority populations noted earlier is that there are few Romani leaders who can both mobilize the Roma at the grass-roots level and serve as skilled mediators between the two communities.[48] Economic, cultural, and social marginalization as a result of centuries of persecution has led to a lack of political sophistication characterized by an inability to define and effectively pursue common interests.[49] Czech Romani leader Ondřej Giňa, for example, notes the corrosive effect of communist assimilation projects on the Roma's organizational capacity:

> The Roma have very strong family links [that affect] the whole community. For example, in Rokycany [a town in the Czech Republic] the Romani population is divided into...eight families. The Romani community used to be very well-organized; there used to be a council that would solve all the problems within the community. So the community was totally independent [from the majoritarian population] and it had its own rules. Nobody dared to break these rules because he would be excommunicated or...other Roma would ignore him and no one would ever help him. That's how it used to work. All these structures were broken under communism...and right now there is...chaos.[50]

This "chaos" is often manifested in clan-based clientilism, with government benefits intended for the entire Romani community routinely captured by individuals who then limit their dispersion to his or her own family. Alexander Slafkovský, Municipal Councillor of Lipovský Mikuláš in Slovakia, described his town's experience in attempting to form an advisory panel to the town council on Romani issues:

> It was difficult to get the Roma to come to the city hall and take up positions on the Housing and Social Committee. It required four attempts. Feuds between families broke out because each thought the others intended to take advantage of the body. We then asked the committee [comprised entirely of Roma] to identify those people who were the most needy. We had big problems with patrimonialism...usury is [also] significant in each family, impoverishing some and enriching others...They understand that they need political representation, but there is too much infighting among them.[51]

Such in-fighting has been noted everywhere, from disputes between Romani representatives who sit on governmental advisory bodies in eastern Europe to the bitter conflict among American Roma over the qualifications of the Rom appointed by President Ronald Reagan in 1987 to sit on the U.S. Holocaust Memorial Council. Government officials often point to such episodes in support of claims that the Roma are incapable of self-representation. Mirga and Gheorghe point out, however, that it is precisely "(t)he state legitimization of some leaders rather than others [that] fosters dissent and internal conflict."[52] Indeed, in their haste to mediate worsening inter-ethnic relations, governments have often assigned self-proclaimed Romani leaders to advisory positions without adequate regard to their legitimacy within Romani communities.[53] As several scholars have noted, the problem stems partly from treating the Romani population as a homogeneous group. In most countries, successive waves of migration have resulted in a "Romani" population that consists of many different communities differentiated by custom and belief. Thus, what governments and majority populations see as a "naturally" contentious ethnic minority is, in fact, a profoundly heterogeneous population faced with the problems of being forced to agree upon common understandings and goals.[54]

Finally, and perhaps most importantly, political apathy among the Roma can be viewed as the outcome of historical mistrust and fear toward the *gadje* and their institutions. Given the experience of persecution and slavery during the Middle Ages, genocide during the Second World War, and the destruction of Romani society and culture by the assimilationist policies that followed, the open expression of Romani identity is still perceived as risky, particularly given the significant increase in hate crimes during the post-communist period. As Fonseca notes, "(t)he passionately held view of most Gypsies is still that *gadje* are dangerous, not to be trusted, and, in the interest of survival of the group, they are to be avoided except for dealings in business."[55] Largely for reasons of self-preservation, then, Romani communities have become profoundly insular, with the fear of assimilation and loss of Romani identity that underlies Romani parents' ambivalence about the region's education systems extending across the full range of *gadje* political institutions.

Post-Communist Romani Activism: Toward "Internationalist" Nationalism?

Notwithstanding the deep-seated pathologies influencing Romani political participation, the post-1989 period has also been one of re-emerging activism, with more than 300 new Romani groups established throughout eastern Europe.[56] Although some of these organizations lie dormant for lack of resources or poor management, many others actively assist Romani communities, pursuing goals that range from monitoring human rights violations to raising Romani civic consciousness. Nevertheless, while these include some locally-based non-governmental organizations, the most durable and successful initiatives have been those supported by the Council of Europe, the Organization for Security and Cooperation in Europe, and the European Union. The latter organizations have also become active in administering conferences on Romani issues. While some Romani activists rightly point out that such events rarely have a direct impact on government policies, they have nonetheless provided important fora in which Roma activists formulate programs and tactics, establish wider political networks, and raise their visibility to government representatives, the general public, and within the Romani community itself. Most Romani activists, in fact, acknowledge the important role played by outside actors given the absence of a state and the lack of political resources and poor representational linkages within the Romani community.[57]

While contemporary western interest in eastern European Roma can be attributed to growing recognition and codification of universal human rights standards, it seems to be no less evidently due to the impact of post-1989 east-west migration. Of course, such population movements occurred throughout the communist period, as anti-Roma policies and poor economic conditions in eastern Europe fueled successive waves of Romani migration to western Europe. In the 1960s, Germany, Austria, Italy, France and the Netherlands faced particularly large inflows of Roma, primarily from Yugoslavia. In the 1980s, a significant number of Romanian Roma began to migrate westward. During this time, the European Community and the Council of Europe began to establish educational programs adapted to the itinerant lifestyle of many Romani pupils.

It was not until the 1990s, however, that eastern European Roma began to attract substantial attention in the West, with press reports widely publicizing that they comprised a disproportionate share of the migratory wave of spurred by the collapse of communism.[58] Starting in 1990, the number of Romani asylum seekers in west European countries (particularly Germany, Austria, and Italy) increased sharply. For example, Germany received 140,000 Romanian nationals from 1989 to 1992, with 21,000 identified as Romani.[59] In 1992, Germany received around 100,000 asylum applications from Romanians, 50 to 60 percent of whom were thought to be Romani. As the total number of Roma who have emigrated to the West since 1960 is estimated to be 250,000, these figures suggest that the most recent wave of Romani migration is by far the most significant.[60] In the face of this dramatic increase, some western governments adopted measures to stem the flow of migration. For example, Germany signed a re-admission agreement with Romania on September 24, 1992, allowing German officials to repatriate asylum-seekers, and has since designated those states on its eastern border as "safe countries" to which asylum seekers can be returned if these countries served as transit points.[61]

In addition to tightening immigration policies, western countries also pressured international bodies to adopt resolutions calling on member states to assist their Romani populations. For example, the final document of the Conference on Security and Cooperation in Europe's (CSCE) first Human Dimension Seminar on Roma in Copenhagen in June 1990 urged participating states to acknowledge problems specific to the Romani population.

This initial international recognition of the unique position of the Roma was echoed at a meeting of the CSCE expert group on national minorities in Geneva in July 1991. Subsequently, the United Nations Commission on Human Rights adopted a resolution calling for the protection of east European Roma, and the CSCE and the Council of Europe jointly organized a Human Dimension Seminar on Roma in the CSCE region.[62] In 1993, the Council of Europe adopted Recommendation 1203, assigning its Committee of Ministers to urge member states to improve the status of their countries' Roma populations through cooperation with Romani organizations as well as with the Council of Europe. In November 1994, the Council of Europe adopted the Framework Convention for the Protection of National Minorities, under which contracting states committed themselves to protect the rights of their national minorities.[63] Other international bodies have followed suit, commissioning studies and sponsoring meetings on the special problems facing Romani communities. Due in large part to this international pressure, the new east European regimes have adopted laws, often executing provisions embedded in their constitutions, that enact broad guarantees ranging from assured political representation to the protection of cultural and linguistic rights.

A clear example of the impact that outside actors have had on relations between Roma and their governments is the case of the Czech citizenship law discussed above. Suspecting that the law violated human rights, both the UNHCR and the Council of Europe sent commissions of experts into the Czech Republic to study the status of the Romani community. Largely in response to the recommendations of these international bodies, the Czech government introduced administrative changes to the law designed to resolve the problem of statelessness, and, in the aftermath of widely-publicized exoduses of Czech and Slovak Romani refugees to Great Britain and Canada, formally approved a critical report (rejected by the same government a month earlier) on the status of Roma in the Czech Republic.[64] In addition, the government created a standing interdepartmental Roma Commission, with twelve ministries assigned to formulate policies to address problems faced by Roma in political representation, housing, social welfare benefits, and education.

Romani leaders, in turn, have become well aware of the increased leverage that international interest has given them in relations with their national governments, leading them to look outside their host states for solutions to the Romani community's problems. The prospect of continued emigration and application for asylum in western countries, while not necessarily amenable to the influence of political leadership, has maintained pressure on post-communist governments. A second tactic has been to self-consciously adopt the rhetoric of universal rights to secure minority protection in their home countries. Indeed, observers have noted that the language of international organizations is now regularly invoked by many Roma in their interactions with government officials, underpinning growing confidence in Romani identity. Slafkovský, remarking on developments at the municipal level, recognizes this connection clearly: "Governments, organizations and human rights documents are restarting the Roma nation. [The Roma] know they have rights. They go to the housing department or the mayor's office, and sit in the hall with their kids and wait... 'I am a human being,' they say when they come asking for help."[65]

The disadvantages of lacking a state that can lobby governments on behalf of its co-ethnics have long been apparent to Romani activists and observers.[66] Thus, the nexus of identity, rights, and "national" status identified by Slafkovský suggests a third tactic available to the Roma to increase their leverage in negotiations with home-state governments. At the same time, however, the reassertion of Romani nationhood directly implicates the nature of Romani identity. If the Roma in fact constitute a nation rather than merely an "ethnic group," how is it to be bounded? Put another way, what *kind* of "nation" would the Roma constitute? Should it be a non-territorial nation encompassing all Roma divided along state, regional, and municipal lines, an "Indian" diaspora nation harkening back to its pre-nomadic roots, or a "European" nation aiming to establish a territorial state?

In making such decisions, Romani activists often appear less concerned with "authenticity" regarding the actual nature of their present identity than they are with constructing an identity that is the most useful in formulating and advancing collective interests. For example, the construction of an Indian identity would be to court the assistance of India in lobbying on behalf of the European Roma. In fact, India has already provided financial and political support to Roma in their efforts to obtain political representation in international organs. In his evaluation of the advantages and disadvantages of constructing and openly adopting an Indian identity, Ian Hancock states: "(t)he arguments for stressing the 'Indian connection' seem clear. In these times, when Europe is divided into nation-states, being identified with an actual homeland brings legitimacy and a measure of security."[67] In contrast, Ondřej Giňa, reflecting a view more widely supported among east European Roma, favors embracing a trans-national European identity:

[The Roma] should create a certain strategy within the European Union and focus on the ten-million-population [sic] of the Roma and try to integrate them into European civilization. Our big problem is that we don't have our own land, our own country with an embassy that we could address in case of a problem. We are a diaspora living somewhere in the air.[68]

While this strategy necessarily entails accepting the pitfalls of statelessness, it is clearly motivated by a sober political realism. During the interwar period, the Roma looked to European Jews and Zionism as offering the most promising source on which to model their own political strategy. However, while permanent membership in international organizations remains a central goal of contemporary Romani leaders, the problems resulting from that particular national project have long since contributed to an international consensus that relations between stateless minorities and their home governments should be resolved within existing state boundaries.[69] Aware of the low likelihood of rallying international support around the foundation of a national homeland for the Roma in the present era, contemporary activists have thus borrowed tactics from other minorities who have sought to achieve goals—civil equality, political influence, and expanded economic opportunity—defined by these limits. African-Americans serve as a particularly useful example, because, like many Roma, they are descended from slaves, constituted an ethnoclass disadvantaged in housing, education, and employment following emancipation, and have no lobby state of co-ethnics.

Despite differences between the two groups (most importantly, the absence in the case of Romani citizens of de jure social segregation and political disenfranchisement), Romani activists have sought to emulate the tactics of passive-resistance used by black civil rights activists in the 1950s and 1960s. At a meeting between veteran African-American activists and Romani leaders in Szentendre, Hungary, in December 1995, one Czech Romani participant described a sit-in at a restaurant organized to protest the wide-spread practice of excluding Roma from public amenities. The Rom drew parallels with the 1960 Woolworth lunch counter sit-in in Greensboro, North Carolina, in which four African-American activists asked for service in a "whites-only" establishment.[70] Ondřej Giňa also affirmed the importance of the civil rights movement in contemporary Romani politics: "We have been watching the blacks closely and trying to use some of their experiences," adding that he had met some African-American activists in Budapest in 1994, who had suggested sending groups of Romani children to the United States to teach them methods of political organization.[71] At the close of the Szentendre meeting, Romani and African-American activists proposed further joint meetings, including a summer institute in eastern Europe involving activists and attorneys from both groups as well as visits of delegations of Roma to the United States to learn from various activists concerning their political tactics.[72]

Conclusion

In this chapter, I have attempted to trace the roots of an extremely young political movement and explore the choices that confront it. Although a distinctively modern Romani nationalism originated in the interwar period, it was short-lived, while the expression of Romani identity was widely prohibited by the post-war communist regimes, with Romani culture and social structures largely undermined. Indeed, Romani activism has been closely tied to follow major shifts of international power and domestic regime change in the region, during which political opportunity structures have been altered to accommodate a broader or narrower range of social actors. Thus, the peak of Romani activism in the twentieth century was reached in the aftermath of World War I, when the Roma were widely recognized as national minorities, and has resurfaced after the collapse of communist regimes in 1989-1991, with internal democratization and international integration constituting the two driving factors. During both periods, the exposure of formerly repressive states to the influence of international organs committed to promoting democracy and minority rights increased dramatically. Conversely, the consolidation of communist control over the east European countries during the post-war period effectively closed off these states' policies toward the Roma from international observation.

Particularly given the exceptionally fluid environments that prevail within post-communist systems as they undergo simultaneous political, economic, and social transition, we can safely conclude that international organizations will play a crucial, if not predominant, role in determining the prospects of the current resurgence of Romani political activism in the region. At the same time, aware of the need to secure greater political recognition and influence, Romani activists are intently engaged in an attempt to construct a Romani "nation" that either attaches itself symbolically to a lobby state (India) or that transcends the state as a non-territorial nation with permanent representation in international organs such as the European Union, the Council of Europe, and the United Nations. Whatever form it ultimately assumes, nation-building may be understood as a hedge strategy simultaneously enabled by heightened international scrutiny and promising to strengthen the Roma's position vis-à-vis traditionally hostile host states by ensuring that it is maintained. Yet, with contemporary east European Romani politics possessing very little historical grounding, impeded by geographical dispersion, and beset by the pathologies of subaltern status, negotiating the still-evolving agendas of Romani identity will be a profound challenge for even the most capable leadership.

Notes

1. Throughout this chapter, I use "Rom" and "Roma" to refer to persons of Romani origin. The term "gypsy," while still widely used, is a malapropism and has its roots in the historic European belief that the Roma originated in Egypt.

2. This can be compared with a Europe-wide estimate of 7 to 8.5 million, including Russia. See Commission of the European Communities, "School Provision for Gypsy and Traveller Children," COM (96) 495 final (Luxembourg: Office for Official Publications of the European Communities, 1997), pp. 8-10. On the difficulties of obtaining accurate population statistics due to their inflation by Romani leaders, underestimation by governments, and reluctance by many Roma to identify themselves as such, see Jeremy Druker, "Present but Unaccounted For," *Transitions,* vol. 4, No. 4 (September 1997), p. 22.

3. Quoted in Donald M. Horowitz, "Ethnic Identity," in Nathan Glazer and Daniel P. Moynihan, eds., *Ethnicity: Theory and Experience* (Cambridge: Harvard University Press, 1975), p. 113.

4. While the emigration of Czech and Slovak Roma to Great Britain and Canada involved a relatively small number of Roma and constituted discrete episodes, its significance was heightened by broad coverage in western media, putting pressure on the Czech government, in particular, to persuade Roma to remain. See, for example, "Outcasts of Europe," *Time,* November 3, 1997, pp. 32-35.

5. Ted Robert Gurr, *Minorities at Risk: A Global View of Ethnopolitical Conflicts* (Washington, D.C.: United States Institute of Peace Press), Ch. 1.

6. On the importance of such resources in determining a group's ability to successfully pursue collective goods, see Charles Tilly, *From Mobilization to Revolution* (New York: McGraw-Hill, 1978).

7. Indeed, Romani communities are still subject to the discretion of their governments, as international documents still allow signing governments to define their national minorities.

8. Josef Kalvoda, "The Gypsies of Czechoslovakia," in David Crowe and John Kolsti (eds.), *The Gypsies of Eastern Europe* (Armonk, N.Y. and London: M. E. Sharpe, 1991), p. 107.

9. Mark Braham, *The Untouchables: A Survey of the Roma People of Central and Eastern Europe,* report to the Office of the United Nations High Commissioner for Refugees, 1993; Isabel Fonseca, *Bury Me Standing: The Gypsies and Their Journey* (London: Vintage, 1996), pp. 14-15.

10. *Minorities at Risk Project* (Center for International Development and Conflict Management, University of Maryland, 1995), *http://www.bsos.umd.edu/cidcm/mar/tableee.htm.*

11. *Ibid.*; Fonseca, *op. cit.,* p. 14.

12. Sharon Fisher, *OMRI Daily Digest,* September, 7, 1993.

13. *Minorities at Risk Project, op. cit.*

14. Anna Koptova and Miroslav Lacko, *Human and Civil Rights of Roma in Slovakia and the Czech Republic,* 1993, cited in *Transitions,* vol. 4, no. 4 (September 1997), p. 38.

15. Andrzej Mirga and Nicolae Gheorghe, *The Roma in the Twenty-First Century: A Policy Paper,* (Princeton, N.J.: Project on Ethnic Relations, May 1997).

16. Koptova and Lacko, *op. cit.*

17. *The Media and the Roma in Contemporary Europe: Facts and Fictions* (Princeton, N.J.: Project on Ethnic Relations, September 1996), p. 9.

18. *Minorities at Risk Project, op. cit.*

19. Fonseca, *op. cit.,* pp. 97-98.

20. These crimes generally consist of petty theft. *Minorities at Risk Project, op. cit.*

21. The highest number of reported Roma deaths at the hands of police are in Romania and Bulgaria. See Dimitrina Petrova, "'Get Out, You Stinking Gypsy," *Transitions*, vol. 4, no. 4 (September 1997), p. 17.

22. *Minorities at Risk Project, op. cit.*

23. In 1969, Czechoslovakia officially became a federation with two "citizenships" (called "nationalities") established under the umbrella of federal citizenship but unrecognized internationally. The new Czech citizenship law deemed "Slovaks" under the 1969 law aliens as of Jan. 1, 1993, with eligibility to become Czech citizens. See *Report of the Experts of the Council of Europe on the Citizenship Laws of the Czech Republic and Slovakia and Their Implementation and Replies of the Governments of the Czech Republic and Slovakia* (Strasbourg: Council of Europe), November 13, 1995, *and The Czech and Slovak Citizenship Laws and the Problem of Statelessness* (Prague: Office of the United Nations High Commissioner for Refugees, February 1996).

24. Interview with Václav Hených, Director of the Second Section of General Administration and Legislation, Interior Ministry, Czech Republic, December 3, 1997.

25. Petrova, *op. cit.*, p.21.

26. Donald L. Horowitz, *Ethnic Groups in Conflict* (Berkeley, Los Angeles, London: University of California Press, 1985), pp. 7-8.

27. This historical overview draws substantially on David Crowe and John Kolsti (eds), *The Gypsies of Eastern Europe* (Armonk, N.Y., M. E. Sharpe, 1991).

28. Mirga and Gheorghe, *op. cit.*, 9. Almost every consolidating nation-state in western Europe had adopted anti-Roma legislation between the years of 1471 and 1637. Road signs were erected in many countries warning Roma that they would be expelled or even hanged if found there. England favored hanging and expulsion, while France under Louis XIV branded and shaved the heads of Roma. In the Czech lands, Bohemia severed the right ear of Romani women, while Moravia severed the left. Fonseca, *op. cit.*, pp. 229-30.

29. See Ian Hancock, "Romani Nationalism," in Crowe and Kolsti, *op. cit.*, pp. 140-41.

30. Thomas A. Acton, *Gypsy Politics and Social Change* (London, Boston: Routledge and K. Paul, 1974), pp. 233-34, cited in Hancock, *op. cit.*, 141-42.

31. Many observers note that there is no such tradition within the Romani community itself, and that self-proclaimed royalty do not enjoy legitimacy among the Roma. See, for example, Rudko Kawczynski, "The Politics of Romani Politics," *Transitions*, vol. 4, no. 4 (September 1997), p. 27; Fonseca, *op. cit.*, pp. 287-91.

32. Hancock, *op. cit.*, pp. 142-43.

33. *Ibid.*, p. 143.

34. Although founded by Roma, some Romani activists have criticized the IRU as lacking a proper organizational structure and thus lending itself to capture by "representatives (who) are often found by chance, just because they happen to be there." Kawczynski, *op. cit.*, p. 28.

35. Hancock, *op. cit.*, pp. 145-49.

36. This contrasts with the official recognition of ethnic identity in the communist federations of Yugoslavia, Czechoslovakia, and the U.S.S.R. In these cases, central governments constitutionalized the existence of particular "nations" in the context of territorial frameworks that gave them considerable de jure power. Such guarantees meant little in practice, however, since these "federations" were remained subject to single-party rule. For the most exhaustive treatment, see Walker Connor, *The National Question in Marxist-Leninist Theory and Strategy* (Princeton: Princeton University Press, 1984).

37. Although policies toward the Roma throughout the region were largely uniform, there

were important variations. The Hungarian government, for example, provided the Roma some cultural autonomy and formal political representation. These policies were intended to serve as models for neighboring states with large Hungarian minorities. However, the Romani minority was denied the same level of minority status as other national minorities in Hungary. See David Crowe's Conclusion, in Crowe and Kolsti, *op. cit.*, p. 155.

38. David Crowe, "The Gypsy Historical Experience in Romania," in Crowe and Kolsti, *op. cit.*, p. 72.

39. See Josef Kalvoda, "The Gypsies of Czechoslovakia," in Crowe and Kolsti, *op. cit.*, p. 106.

40. Tomáš Sirovátka, "Labour Market Exclusions of Handicapped Groups in Full Employment Society with Emphasis on Gypsy Community: The Case of the Czech Republic," paper presented at the ESA Third European Conference 20th Century Europe: Inclusions/Exclusions, August 27-30, 1997.

41. David Crowe, "The Gypsies in Hungary," p. 121, and "The Gypsy Historical Experience in Romania," pp. 72-74, in Crowe and Kolsti, *op. cit.*

42. Kalvoda, *op. cit.*, pp. 97-101.

43. In his detailed analysis of Roma labor strategies in the Czech workforce, Sirovátka argues that chronic unemployment within the Romani community is due more to employers' responses to institutional incentives than to cultural factors. After the fall of communism, employers responded to new economic uncertainties by laying off sectors of their workforces and increasingly relying on a secondary or "shadow" low-wage labor force, often using ethnic markers to reduce information costs concerning the likely productivity of prospective employees. Because the Roma were tied to unskilled positions under communist regimes and had few competitive advantages in the labor force, they were an obvious group to consign to the secondary market. Moreover, the consensus among government actors and employers concerning the need for this market and that employment offices should primarily serve employers' interests reproduces ethnic stratification. In economic terms, this generates a moral hazard insofar as it is often more rational for Roma to refuse employment altogether, as anticipated wages fail to exceed welfare benefits. Sirovátka, *op. cit.*

44. *Ibid.*, p. 10.

45. Rene Jakl, "Police Struggling With Own Racial Prejudices," *Prague Post*, March 4-10, 1997.

46. Interview with Ondřej Giňa, Minority Representative on the National Council for Minorities, Czech Republic, November 24, 1997; Interview with Karel Holomek, Minority Representative on the National Council for Minorities, Czech Republic, and Co-founder of the Romani Civic Initiative, the single Romani political party in post-1989 Czechoslovakia, March 9, 1998.

47. *Minorities at Risk Project, op. cit.*

48. The dearth of skilled Romani political leaders has been noted by many activists. Ondřej Giňa cites it as one of the most urgent problems faced by the Romani community. Mirga and Gheorghe note that while many older elites command authority among the Roma, they often have little training to assist them in negotiating the increasingly complex political landscape. In contrast, while the younger generation of better-educated Romani elites possesses these skills, they lack traditional legitimacy among the Romani population. Mirga and Gheorghe, *op. cit.*, p. 13.

49. This phenomenon is aptly described by a Council of Europe report: "... all major institutions in a society are governed by certain habits, rules and regulations, whether formal or informal, that are rooted in the dominant culture of that society. The more people are familiar with these rules and regulations, the easier it will be for them to gain access to those institu-

tions." *Community and Ethnic Relations in Europe*, final report of the Community Relations Project of the Council of Europe, MG-CR (91) 1 final E (Strasbourg: Council of Europe)

50. Giňa Interview, *op. cit.*

51. Interview with Alexander Slafkovský, October 23, 1997.

52. Mirga and Gheorghe, *op. cit.*, p. 13.

53. Giňa interview, *op. cit.* Mirga and Gheorghe, however, go much further, questioning whether negotiations between governments and Roma appointed to advisory positions can conceivably represent negotiations between the Roma and non-Roma communities at all, for a democratic leadership "legitimized by the constituency of a formal organization," they argue, is a notion that has not yet taken root in Romani communities. Mirga and Gheorghe, *op. cit.*, p. 13.

54. Similarly, the widely-noted patrimonialism and clan-like nature of Romani communities can be understood as the result of the break-down of self-policing mechanisms in a context of close proximity with Romani communities governed by different social norms. Thus, social and economic transactions have largely been confined to the family level where rules are known and enforceable. In contrast, transactions between families or communities are perceived as being open to mutual defection. See Edward C. Banfield, *The Moral Basis of a Backward Society* (Chicago: The Free Press, 1958), Mancur Olson, *The Logic of Collective Action* (Cambridge: Harvard University Press, 1965), and Diego Gambetta, *The Sicilian Mafia: The Business of Private Protection* (Cambridge: Harvard University Press, 1993). The logic underlying this phenomenon can be extrapolated to behavioral differences in inter-ethnic as opposed to intra-ethnic interactions. See James D. Fearon, "Ethnic War as a Commitment Problem" (unpublished manuscript, 1993) and Barry Weingast, "Constructing Trust: The Political and Economic Roots of Ethnic and Regional Conflict" (unpublished manuscript, 1996).

55. Fonseca, *op. cit.*, p. 12.

56. Kawczynski, *op. cit.*, p. 28.

57. See above.

58. European Committee on Migration (CDMG), *The Situation of Gypsies (Roma and Sinti) in Europe*, Strasbourg, August 1, 1995, cdmg 11.95e, p. 11.

59. Alain Reyniers, *Gypsy Populations and Their Movements Within Central and Eastern Europe and Towards Some OECD Countries*, OECD (International Migration and Labour Market Policies, Occasional Papers, No. 1), 1995, as cited by European Committee on Migration, *op. cit.*, p. 18.

60. *Ibid.*

61. *Ibid.*, pp. 18-19.

62. *Ibid.*, pp. 6-7.

63. *Ibid.*, p. 15.

64. Although the Czech government claimed that it initially rejected the report because "the research was too basic," alterations amounted to "less than 1 percent" of its original content, while a deputy minister confirmed that there had been "political pressure" to adopt following the Roma exodus to Great Britain and Canada, which resulted in the latter re-imposing visa requirements on Czech citizens. Michele Legge, "Cabinet Approves Romany Report," *Prague Post*, November 5-11, 1997, A3.

65. Slafkovský interview, *op. cit.*

66. See, for example, Mirga and Gheorghe, *op. cit.*, p. 15, and Hancock, "The Struggle for Control of Identity," *Transitions*, vol. 4, no. 4, (September 1997) p. 44.

67. Ian Hancock, "The Struggle for the Control of Identity," *Transitions,* vol. 4, no. 4 (September 1997), p. 44.

68. Giňa interview, *op. cit.*

69. See Rodolfo Stavenhagen, *Ethnic Conflicts and the Nation-State* (Houndmills, Basingstoke, Hampshire: Macmillan, 1996).

70. East-West Program of the American Friends Service Committee, *Out of the Margins: A Report on a Roma/African-American Exchange,* Szentendre, Hungary, December 6-9, 1995.

71. Giňa interview, *op. cit.*

72. East-West Program of the American Friends Service Committee, *Out of the Margins: A Report on a Roma/African-American Exchange,* Szentendre, Hungary, December 6-9, 1995, p. 21.

8

ETHNIC WAR AND DISEMPOWERMENT: THE SERB MINORITY IN CROATIA

Nenad Zakošek

The conflict that erupted at the beginning of the 1990s between Serbs and Croats within the former Yugoslavia gave rise to one of the most violent and vexing political problems in contemporary Europe, with the international dimension of the conflict and the consolidation of independent ethnically-defined states decisively shaping domestic policy towards the Serb minority within the Republic of Croatia. Indeed, any examination of Serb political participation and representation in contemporary Croatia must necessarily take this wider context—particularly the related Serb-Moslem-Croat conflict in Bosnia—as its focal point. After more than five years of violence and war between Serbs and Croats, 1995 marked a turning-point in the conflict's dynamics: the Croatian military victory over the rebel Serb army in Croatia itself and the termination of the war between Serbs and the Muslim-Croat alliance in Bosnia as a result of the Dayton peace agreements created a new equilibrium which will probably become the basis for a final resolution. The future status and political position of the Serb minority in Croatia will essentially be determined, therefore, by the consequences of the balance of power—both in Croatia and in the former Yugoslavia as a whole—memorialized in the peace accords.

Thus, in order to assess the contemporary political status and representation of Serbs in Croatia, it is necessary to examine the origins, dynamics, and probable consequences of the Serb-Croat conflict. My analysis focuses on five areas: the demographic preconditions and historical background to the conflict; the genesis and dynamics of full-scale inter-ethnic war; the changing constitutional and legal framework for Serb minority status and representation; the nature and forms of Serb political organization; and the prospects for normalization and inclusion of Serbs into Croatian political life.

Demographic and Historical Background

The status of the Serbs in Croatia has been shaped by the demographic characteristics of the Serb ethnic community and the historical conditions under which its political subjectivity has developed. Serbs have constituted an autochthonous ethnic group in the territory of the current Republic of Croatia since the late Middle Ages and early modern age, having settled in several migratory waves caused by the Ottoman wars and territorial conquests.[1] The development and preservation of a distinct ethnic identity, despite cultural and linguistic similarities with Croats, was mainly due to the continued existence of the Serb Orthodox Church, which enjoyed a high degree of autonomy and organization under the Habsburg and Ottoman empires.[2]

According to available census data from the Habsburg empire and calculations based on language and religion (necessitated by the fact that ethnicity was not directly registered by these censuses), Serbs comprised a very strong minority in the Croatian provinces belonging to Austria by the mid-19th century. In 1840 the proportion of Serbs in the civil and military parts of Croatia and Slavonia (both historical provinces of present-day Croatia) was as high as 31.4 percent, and in Dalmatia reached 19 percent.[3] Over the past century, however, and especially in the second half of the twentieth century, the demographic development of ethnic Serbs in Croatia was characterized by stagnation and even decline (both in absolute and relative terms). According to the official census data (which are not wholly comparable due to territorial changes), the number of Serbs in Croatia in 1931 was 633,000 (18.4 percent of the total population), in 1948 it was 544,000 (14.4 percent), in 1953, 588,000 (14.9 percent), in 1961, 625,000 (15.0 percent), in 1971, 627,000 (14.2 percent), in 1981, 532,000 (11.5 percent), and in 1991, 581,000 (12.2 percent).[4]

These trends reflect several phenomena: a steady decline in natural population growth among ethnic Serbs; continuous migration among the Serb population, a considerable part of whom have traditionally inhabited less developed rural areas, to Serbia or abroad (mostly to western Europe); and increasing ethnic fluidity as a growing number of children from mixed marriages preferred Yugoslav national identity rather than Serb or Croatian. In the 1961 census only 0.4 percent of the Croatian population identified itself as Yugoslav and by 1971 the share of Yugoslavs stood at 1.9, then rising sharply to 8.2 percent by 1981. It was only in the 1991 census, after the crisis of the Yugoslav state already reached its final stage, that the proportion of Yugoslavs decreased to 2.2 percent.[5]

Ethnic Serb settlement in Croatia is concentrated in three areas. According to the 1991 census data, approximately one-half of Serbs lived in underdeveloped rural areas adjacent to Bosnia (the Dalmatian hinterland, Gorski kotar, Lika, Kordun, and Banovina) and in rural but wealthier western Slavonia (most of these territories were part of the economically and socially backward "military border" under the Habsburg Empire); one-sixth lived in the developed rural area of eastern Slavonia, adjacent to Serbia; and one-third resided in urban centers of continental or maritime Croatia (Zagreb, Split, Rijeka, Pula, etc.). It is due to this differentiated character of Serb settlement that the Serb ethnic community in Croatia was already able in the 19th century to establish its urban elites, including commercial and entrepreneurial classes, intelligentsia, and modern cultural and political organizations, while its majority still lived in underdeveloped traditional peasant communities.

Along with its demographic development and differentiated socio-economic bases, the political articulation of the Serb ethnic community in Croatia was decisively shaped by specific historical conditions. The processes of national integration of Croats and Serbs in Croatia within the framework of the Habsburg Empire occurred simultaneously, giving rise to concurrent and competing national ideologies and policies in the late 18th and early 19th centuries.[6] On one hand, ethnic and linguistic proximity contributed to solidarity against external pressures and threats posed by non-Slavic rulers and neighbors (Austrian Germans, Hungarians, and Italians) and thus provided the basis for the emergence first of "Illyrism" and then Yugoslavism as an ideology of Southern Slav unity and cooperation. The Yugoslav ideology, in particular, provided a possible common ground for combining parallel nation-building processes. On the other hand, however, within the same setting Serb and Croatian expansive nationalisms emerged by the mid-19th century, proclaiming mutually exclusive nation-state projects and defining persistently conflictual issues including historical, cultural, and political primacy, as well as claims to population and territory encompassing a large part of Croatia and all of Bosnia-Herzegovina.

Alongside their national orientation, another, more pragmatic dilemma shaped the political action of the emergent Serb parties in Croatia: the choice between collaboration with a dominant foreign power (Austria or Hungary) against the Croatian national movement in exchange for political benefits and privileges, and cooperation with Croatian parties in a common struggle for independence. (Of course, the Croatian national movement faced the same dilemma in reverse: whether to seek Serb support and attempt to integrate Serb political demands into the Croatian national program or to define the "Serb question" in Croatia as an obstacle to independence). The first two decades of the 20th century were characterized by Croatian-Serb accord: after 1905 the so-called Croatian-Serb coalition was the political option chosen by the major Serb and Croat parties in Croatia and remained the dominant tendency until the breakup of the Habsburg Empire.[7]

The historical burden of Serb-Croat relations in the common Yugoslav state, established in 1918, set in motion a distinctive set of political dynamics, which decisively shaped the political imagination of both Serbs and Croats and influenced their strategies of action as the crisis of the state deepened at the end of the 1980s.[8] This burden can be broken down into three particularly weighty components.

First, Yugoslavia was initially established as a Serb-dominated state in which Croatia ceased to exist as a political (and even administrative) entity. This resulted in a strong Croatian national movement and a concomitant deepening of the Serb-Croatian cleavage. However, the royal dictatorship established after 1929 was opposed by a united front of Croatian and allied Serb parties. Thus, the two decades of the first Yugoslav state were characterized not only by Serb-Croatian confrontation, but also by the experience of cooperation in opposition. Besides, in 1939, two years before the state's collapse, the regime in Belgrade accepted an agreement with the Croatian opposition according to which the centralized monarchy would be transformed into a more decentralized system, with "Banovina Hrvatska" to become a *de facto* federal unit.[9] This solution included a new territorial organization of Yugoslavia which implied the division of Bosnia-Herzegovina between Croatia and Serbia, a "model" that has a significant impact on some current Croatian and Serb politicians.

A second decisive episode was the fascist Ustaša regime of the so-called "Independent State of Croatia," installed by German and Italian invaders on the territory of Croatia and Bosnia-Herzegovina, which conducted a genocidal policy against Serbs during World War II. Serb nationalist armed units, *četniks*, responded with counter-terror. However, like the inter-War-period, World War II also produced an experience of Croatian-Serb unity, this time in the form of an anti-fascist struggle based within the communist-led partisan movement. The partisan movement was particularly strong in Croatia, and developed and institutionalized the idea of the Croatian republic as the common state of Croats and Serbs, within the framework of a federalized Yugoslavia.[10]

Finally, the Yugoslav federation established after World War II was based on communist dictatorship.[11] The system was thus once again strongly centralized, with functioning institutions of a genuine federation emerging only in the 1960s. However, the repressive character of the regime continued to impede political articulation of diverse interests in Croatia and the other constituent republics of the federation. The result was a negative conflict dynamic as controversies between federal republics and their constituent ethnic communities were postponed, especially following the early 1970s. Indeed, this postponement was directly linked to the regime's withdrawal of liberal and democratic reforms which might lead to their peaceful resolution, thereby increasing the probability of the state's violent collapse.

Genesis and Dynamics of Conflict

Despite the official communist Yugoslav ideology of "brotherhood and unity," strong Serb and Croatian nationalisms emerged in the mid-1960s, among both communist political elites and the anti-communist opposition.[12] This resulted in a struggle over the distribution of power between the federal government and the republics: Serb political elites demanded stronger centralization with Serb domination, while Croatian and other non-Serb political elites fought for decentralization and a de facto confederal reorganization of power.

Given the World War II experience, the Socialist Republic of Croatia had established particularly strong guarantees of political equality and power-sharing, from the constitutional definition of the Croatian republic to the more informal practice of ethnic balancing of leading party and government positions between Croats and Serbs. In many respects, especially regarding key political decisions, this gave Serb political elites in Croatia a considerable and highly disproportionate share of power. This state of affairs was strongly resented by Croatian nationalists and widely criticized as limiting Croatian autonomy. During the period of liberalization and decentralization of the Yugoslav communist regime in the late sixties, a mass nationalist movement with an independent Croatian political leadership emerged, but was harshly repressed in 1971-1972.[13] The repression affected not only Croatian nationalist tendencies, however, but was carried out against similar political currents in other republics as well. Nevertheless, the attempt to maintain an unstable communist status quo by means of coercion in the republics proved unsuccessful. On the contrary, it quite likely caused, or at least hastened, those disintegration processes that emerged shortly after the death of the charismatic Yugoslav communist leader Josip Broz Tito in 1980.

The final collapse of the Yugoslav state was brought about by the fatal political conjuncture which developed in Serbia in the mid-1980s: a disoriented population, stirred by nationalist ideas proclaimed by a significant segment of the intelligentsia, was "captured" and mobilized into a mass movement by a nationalist-authoritarian faction within the ruling communist party, led by Slobodan Miloševic.[14] The objective of the new Serbian nationalist coalition was to upset the ideological and political status quo: its political program included subjugating two Serbian Autonomous Provinces (Vojvodina and Kosovo) which had enjoyed generous rights of self-government; installing a dependent puppet leadership in Montenegro; and finally establishing Serb control over the Yugoslav federal party and state institutions with the support of the Serb-dominated and ideologically rigid officer corps of the Federal Army. The first two objectives were achieved after two years of mass mobilization and political pressure. However, the attempt to attain the third and most important goal, the recentralization of Yugoslavia under Serb control, ultimately destroyed Yugoslavia and led to the outbreak of war.

The strategy of the Serbian leadership included the mobilization of Serbs in Bosnia and Croatia. Under the patronage of Serbia, extremist Serb nationalists began organizing in Croatia in 1989, focusing initially on the Knin region (with a 90 percent Serb majority), and from there gradually expanded their activities to the neighboring regions of Lika, Kordun, and Banovina. At the beginning of 1990 the federal structures of the League of Communists of Yugoslavia (the ruling communist party) collapsed: Croatian and Slovenian Communists withdrew from the federal party congress and central party organs and turned to instituting free parliamentary elections as the most effective protection against the pressure of Miloševic's regime and Serb nationalism.[15]

Within only a few months (essentially from January to April 1990), new pluralist conditions gave rise to an exclusionary Croatian nationalism triggered off by the threat of the Serb national movement's professed expansionist aims.[16] As a result of a broad and intensive mass mobilization, the populist Croatian Democratic Community (*Hrvatska demokratska zajednica—HDZ*) swept the election and gained an overwhelming parliamentary majority. The Croatian Communists conceded defeat and peacefully handed over power to the new HDZ government.

The dramatic pace of political change took most Serbs in Croatia by surprise. The new Serb nationalist party in Croatia, the Serbian Democratic Party (*Srpska demokratska stranka—SDS*), was established in the spring of

1990, but it was able to nominate candidates only in those few electoral districts where Serbs formed an overwhelming majority and imported Serb nationalism had been successfully rooted. SDS candidates won only five of the 352 seats in the three chambers of the *Sabor*, the Croatian parliament. It was thus evident that the SDS could not claim to represent a majority of Serbs in Croatia, yet their overwhelming rejection of ethnic nationalism would leave them, paradoxically, with no representation whatsoever.

According to pre-election survey data, a considerable number of Croatian Serbs rejected regime change and free elections: only 18 percent of Serbs supported the introduction of multi-party democracy without reservation · (compared to 68 percent of Croats).[17] Agitated by the deepening conflict within the leadership of the Yugoslav federation and threatened by nationalist political rhetoric during the electoral campaign, most Serbs in Croatia supported the political bloc of the old regime, the (reformed) Communists and their allies. This left bloc was able to win about 34 percent of the popular vote (measured by the first ballot for the lower chamber of the *Sabor*). Due to the majority electoral system, it received about 29 percent of seats in all three parliamentary chambers. Survey data indicate that approximately 35–45 percent of the left's votes came from either Serb or "Yugoslav" voters.[18] Even stronger evidence of the electoral preferences of Serb voters is the fact that most mandates for the left bloc were won in areas with a majority or at least a high proportion of Serbs, namely Serb-populated districts along the Bosnian border and Western and Eastern Slavonia. Out of 101 left-bloc MPs, 32 were Serbs. Together with the five SDS Serb deputies they comprised 10.5 percent of all members of parliament, or slightly less than the Serb share of the population of Croatia, according to the 1991 census.[19] The voting behavior of a large majority of Serb voters in Croatia demonstrates that they regarded the left bloc, and especially the reformed Communists, as their political representatives.

However, the expectations of Serb voters vis-à-vis left bloc representatives were frustrated after the outbreak of violent conflict in Croatia, which was initiated by Serb extremists but also nurtured by the rigid policies of the HDZ government. The left-bloc representatives were torn between loyalty to the Croatian state and acting as advocates of Serb protection and protest against the discriminatory measures of the new regime. The result of this dilemma was rapid dissolution of the left bloc itself. While the majority of reformed Communists and other left-bloc deputies supported the establishment of an independent Croatian state and its protection against threats from the federal army and the Serbian regime, most of the Serb representatives adhered to the idea of preserving the Yugoslav federation, thus aligning themselves with the goals of the Serbian regime. Twenty-one Serb representatives elected as left-bloc candidates withdrew from parliament (they never formally resigned but simply stopped attending parliamentary sessions), thus following the five SDS deputies who left the *Sabor* almost immediately after it was inaugurated at the end of May 1990. Only 11 Serb representatives remained at the outset of the crucial period of the deepening Serb-Croatian conflict, and of these one was killed at the start of the war and two officially resigned.[20] The *Sabor* thus remained without legitimate representatives of the Serb ethnic community, a fact which was both caused by and exacerbated the crisis of 1990-1991.

The first violent insurrection began in August 1990 in the Knin region, where Serb extremists captured police arms depots and erected barricades to cut road and railway communications.[21] These actions gradually spread to other rural Serb-populated regions and were accompanied by simultaneous political action: in areas with a Serb majority, the SDS—before turning to organizing violent actions—took over local governments and municipal assemblies previously controlled by reformed Communists. The Croatian government was thus under pressure on two fronts: from the Serbian regime and federal army command at the level of the Yugoslav federation, and from the rebellious Serb extremists in Croatia. It attempted to settle the conflict through parallel negotiations with the leadership of Serbia and with SDS leaders in Croatia. However, the outcomes of these two-track negotiations were interconnected. Thus, the failure of negotiations over federal reform led ineluctably to the breakdown of talks with SDS leaders. In June 1991, the *Sabor* declared Croatian independence (as did Slovenia), bringing on the collapse of federal institutions (the federal parliament and presidency) and the Yugoslav Federal Army's open involvement in the war against Croatia following a period during which it had only indirectly supported the Serb rebels.[22]

As Croatia declared independence, the SDS-controlled municipalities with dominant Serb populations proclaimed their secession from Croatia. Sporadic and localized armed incidents turned into the full-scale war that lasted from September 1991 until January 1992, when a cease-fire agreement was signed in Sarajevo.[23] The war resulted in the occupation of approximately one-third of Croatian territory: precisely those areas with a Serb majority (areas along the Bosnian border in the Dalmatian hinterland, Lika, Kordun, and Banovina) or with a strong Serb presence but a non-Serb majority (parts of western Slavonia and areas along the Serbian border in eastern Slavonia). The SDS proclaimed the establishment of the "Republic of Serb Krajina" in the occupied territories and set up independent authorities (president, government, parliament).

The cease-fire agreement provided for the engagement of the United Nations Protection Force (UNPROFOR) in the Serb-occupied areas, consisting of about 10,000 soldiers, with the task of establishing effective control over UN Protected Areas (UNPAs). However, despite UNPROFOR's presence, the Serb extremists were not disarmed, the SDS was able to strengthen its authority, and ethnic cleansing of non-Serbs continued. It is estimated that about 175,000 Croats and 50,000 members of other non-Serb minorities were banished from the occupied areas and that less than 10 percent of the prewar Croat population remained on Serb-controlled territory.[24] The cease-fire remained unstable, punctuated by artillery duels and minor clashes, until in May 1994 a second cease-fire agreement was signed, which included an effective disengagement of the troops and removal of heavy artillery from combat zones.

As this unsteady armistice was established in Croatia, Bosnian Serbs launched a war in Bosnia-Herzegovina in April 1992, following a referendum in which a majority of the republic's citizens (about 65 percent) supported establishment of an independent state of Bosnia-Herzegovina. The outbreak of war in Bosnia-Herzegovina had a decisive influence on Serb-Croatian relations in Croatia, with all hope of a final political settlement resting on the military fortunes of the respective sides. This interconnection was demonstrated most clearly by the events of 1995, which opened the door for the end of hostilities in both Croatia and Bosnia-Herzegovina.

The continuation of the status quo in relations with the rebel Serbs was extremely unfavorable from the standpoint of the Croatian authorities. The HDZ government had become very disillusioned with UNPROFOR due to its ineffectiveness and inablity to fulfill its mandate to demilitarize the occupied zones, establish law and order, halt ethnic cleansing, and oversee the safe return of Croatian refugees to cities and villages under Serb control. At the same time the "Krajina" Serbs were preparing for unification with their Bosnian counterparts and thus threatening to complete their secession from Croatia. Although some progress was made through negotiations between the Croatian authorities and representatives of the "Krajina" Serbs in late 1994 and early 1995, especially agreements concerning economic cooperation and the opening of an important highway in western Slavonia, no settlement on peaceful reintegration of the occupied territories could be reached. A very comprehensive and generous proposal by international mediators (the so-called contact or Z-4 group) in January 1995, which involved a degree of political autonomy for the Serb-controlled areas going far beyond Croatian constitutional law, was accepted as a basis for further negotiations by the Croatian side but was rejected by the

"Krajina" Serb representatives.[25] In these circumstances the political balance within the Croatian leadership shifted towards a military solution.

The decisive turning point came with the military operations undertaken by the Croatian army in May and August 1995, which returned the main part of the territories held by Serb rebels (the UNPA sectors west, north, and south) to Croatian government control. Both operations accomplished their goals very quickly–the May action in western Slavonia lasted only 48 hours, while the August action in "Krajina" took about five days.[26] The territory of eastern Slavonia (UNPA sector east), which comprises about 5 percent of Croatia's territory, remained under Serb occupation. In the aftermath of these operations a mass exodus of the local Serb population, at the very least welcomed by the Croatian government, was organized by their authorities: estimates range between 150,000 and 200,000 refugees for both regions (Western Slavonia and the "Krajina").[27] No more than 12,000, mostly elderly, Serbs remained in these areas.[28]

Closely linked with these developments was a change in the military position of the warring sides in Bosnia during 1995. This change was effected by the Croatian army's intervention on the side of Bosnian Croats early in the year, but the decisive turn followed massive NATO air strikes against Bosnian Serbs in August and September, followed immediately by a common military offensive by Muslim and Croatian forces in western Bosnia. The Serb forces were forced to retreat from some 20 percent of Bosnian territory and were in fact threatened with total military defeat. The new strategic balance in Bosnia was the foundation on which the Dayton peace agreements were negotiated in November and signed in Paris in December 1995. Although some Serb territorial gains in Bosnia were accepted and their "political entity," *Republika Srpska*, was recognized by the Dayton accords, Bosnia-Herzegovina was formally preserved as a united state and a complete Serbian secession was thwarted.

Within the framework of the Dayton agreement the last open source of conflict in Serb-Croatian relations was also resolved: the question of eastern Slavonia and its integration into Croatia. The agreement on eastern Slavonia included the following provisions: establishment of a UN Transitional Administration in the region of eastern Slavonia (UNTAES) for a period of 12 months (which can be prolonged for another 12 months); complete demilitarization implemented by an international military force; return of refugees and displaced persons combined with the right of immigrants to the region from other parts of Croatia (including Serb refugees from other former occupied territories of Croatia) to remain; establishment of ethnically-mixed temporary police forces; restoration of previous property rights and assistance in the reconstruction of damaged property; control of Croatian borders by an international force; and organization of local elections before the end of the transitional period, including the right of the Serbian community to a Council of Municipalities (as a kind of regional representation).[29] While the beginning of the agreement's implementation suggested that it might serve as an adequate instrument of peaceful reintegration of eastern Slavonia into the Croatian state, it soon became apparent that this is unlikely to be achieved within the established time frame.

Whatever diplomatic and political setbacks may occur, the events of 1995 clearly set the stage for the final resolution of the post-Yugoslav Serb-Croatian conflict. Indeed, the overall situation looked much different than it did immediately following Croatia's independence. While Croatia as a whole suffered serious human losses and material damage, its territorial integrity was restored and was no longer seriously threatened. These gains were clearly zero-sum, however, produced by corresponding dramatic changes in the position of the Serb minority. The power of its secessionist rebellion was broken and the total number of Serbs in Croatia was reduced by nearly two-thirds. Both facts have had a significant impact on official provisions shaping the conditions for Serb political representation in Croatia.

Constitutional and Legal Framework

The development of constitutional and legal instruments defining the rights of the Serb minority in Croatia has followed the general dynamics of the Serb-Croatian conflict. Thus, it is likely that many of the provisions established in the early stages of the conflict will ultimately become obsolete and will not be implemented at all, while new and far less generous measures will be adopted. While the constitutional and legal institutions regarding minority rights are still in a state of transition, a short overview of legal developments in this area during the last six years is sufficient to support this view.

The essential acts defining Serb minority political status in Croatia include the new constitution adopted in December 1990;[30] the Charter on the Rights of Serbs and other Nationalities in the Republic of Croatia adopted in June 1991 concurrent with the Croatian Declaration of Independence;[31] the Constitutional Law of Human Rights and Freedoms and the Rights of National and Ethnic Communities and Minorities in the Republic of Croatia enacted in December 1991, along with amendments passed in September 1995 suspending implementation of some of its provisions;[32] and the Electoral

Law approved in April 1992 (together with its interpretation by the Constitutional Court), along with amendments enacted in September 1995.[33]

The constitution does not explicitly regulate the rights of the Serb minority, but it does include provisions that affect the symbolic and substantive status of Serbs. At the very beginning of the constitutional debate it became evident that the new government's proposals concerning the definition of the state, its official language, and state symbols (all of which were finally adopted with only minor modifications) held great political importance and that the majority of Serbs in Croatia strongly opposed them. The primary cause of the conflict was the new definition of the Croatian state, with Serbs alleging that they were being "thrown out of the Croatian constitution," a judgment that continues to be professed by many Serb politicians and intellectuals. While this characterization seems somewhat exaggerated in light of the changes that actually took place, it certainly reflects the high level of sensitivity vis-à-vis the constitution's obvious diminution of the Serb minority's collective status.

The 1974 socialist constitution contained the following definition of the Croatian state (in Article 1): "The Socialist Republic of Croatia is the national state of the Croatian nation, the state of the Serb nation in Croatia and the state of national minorities that live here."[34] In contrast, the 1990 constitution includes in its preamble's section on "Historical foundations" the following formulation: "... the Republic of Croatia is hereby established as the national state of Croatian nation and a state of members of other nations and minorities who are citizens: Serbs, Moslems, Slovenes, Czechs, Slovaks, Italians, Hungarians, Jews and others, who are guaranteed equality with citizens of Croatian nationality...." In Article 1 the Croatian state is then defined as follows: "The Republic of Croatia is a unitary and indivisible democratic and social state. The power of the Republic of Croatia derives from the people and belongs to the people as a community of free and equal citizens."[35] The new formulation thus abandoned treatment of the Croatian and Serb nations as equals, a principle enshrined in every constitutional text since World War II, and reduced Serbs to the status of all other ethnic minorities.

The practical impact of this symbolic change is clearest in the new formulation concerning official use of language. According to Article 12, "The Croatian language and the Latin script shall be in official use in the Republic of Croatia." Thus, the state dissociated itself from the Serb language and Cyrillic script, classifying them as the progeny of a minority culture and thereby providing the normative basis for limiting their official use to particular regions. Even the change of basic state symbols, including the coat-of-arms and flag, was a source of conflict. While a majority of Serbs in Croatia were emotionally attached to the red star (symbolizing common anti-fascist struggle), for most Croats it symbolized communist dictatorship. On the other hand, the new symbols were portrayed as being too similar to those used by the Ustaša fascist state during World War II. While questions concerning the symbolic status of Serbs in the Croatian Constitution were and still are highly disputed, a few general constitutional stipulations about minority rights attracted far less attention. Nevertheless, these protective provisions are not insignificant. Thus, there is a guarantee of cultural autonomy and free expression of nationality (Article 15), and prohibition of national hatred and intolerance (Article 39). An important protective institution is also entailed in the stipulation (in Article 83) that laws regulating national rights of minorities shall be passed by a two-thirds majority vote of all representatives in the *Sabor*.

The Charter on the Rights of Serbs and other Nationalities in the Republic of Croatia, adopted in June 1991 along with the Declaration of Independence, has no legal implications. It was meant rather as a political act demonstrating that special minority rights would be acknowledged. These rights include cultural autonomy and collective self-preservation, proportional representation in local self-government bodies, international protection of minority rights, and the right to have an organization represent the Serb national community as a whole, in domestic as well as international relations.

The Constitutional Law of Human Rights and Freedoms and the Rights of National and Ethnic Communities and Minorities in the Republic of Croatia adopted in December 1991, in contrast, was by far the most important constitutional instrument intended to ensure Serb minority rights. It was drafted under pressure from, and with the assistance of, international mediators, and its enactment was more or less defined as a precondition for international recognition of Croatia. At the time it was adopted, its purpose was also to serve as the foundation for political reconciliation with the rebellious leaders of the Serb minority in Croatia involved in the war against the Croatian government. The paradox of the law is that its main stipulations have never been implemented. After the events of May and August 1995, it has become highly unlikely that the law's guarantees will ever be realized in the future.

The Constitutional Law included a wide range of special provisions for Serb minority rights which amounted to an assurance of extensive political autonomy. The law's most important stipulations were the right to self-organization and relations with the "mother-state"; the right to institutionalize cultural autonomy, including free use of language and alphabet, with the Serb language and Cyrillic alphabet in official use in municipalities with a Serb majority, free use of national symbols, establishment of state-funded educational institutions, and state subsidies for information and publishing activities; the right to proportional representation in the *Sabor*, government cabinet, supreme judicial bodies, and local self-government; the establishment of an inter-ethnic relations office as a special agency of the Croatian government responsible for fulfilling provisions of the Constitutional Law and securing proportional representation at all levels of state administration; the right to protection of human rights and freedoms by the Court for Human Rights, whose final establishment was dependent on agreement between all states of the former Yugoslavia;[36] and finally, and most importantly, the designation of Knin and Glina as special status districts which would establish an autonomous legislative assembly authorized to pass bylaws, an executive council and other agencies, and municipal and district courts. These institutions, as well as the police force, would be based on proportional representation of Serbs, Croats, and other ethnic communities inhabiting these districts.

After the military defeat of the Serb secessionists in August 1995, however, the *Sabor* reacted very quickly by enacting in September what it termed "temporary non-implementation" of the Constitutional Law's main provisions. The right to proportional representation in the Croatian parliament, government, and supreme judicial bodies, all provisions concerning the establishment of special status districts, and the establishment of the Court for Human Rights were rescinded. The rationale for this decision was found in the fact that the Constitutional Law's mandate of special institutions for the Serb minority was framed in terms of the entirely formalistic general condition that they were reserved for minorities which make up more than 8 percent of the Croatian population, while the provisions concerning special status districts were intended for areas where an ethnic minority comprises more than 50 percent of the population (both of which, according to the 1991 census, applied only to Serbs).

Given the Serb exodus following the 1995 Croatian military actions, probably neither of these conditions could be fulfilled by the Serb minority. New census was scheduled by the decision postponing the implementation of the Constitutional Law's key measures, in order to establish the exact number of Serbs in Croatia. However, the planned census has not been organized yet.

All estimates indicate that not only had the proportion of Serbs in Croatia fallen below 8 percent, but there were no more areas with a local Serb majority (except for eastern Slavonia, the region which had to be fully integrated into the constitutional and legal system of Croatia). "Temporary non-implementation" of much of the Constitutional Law will therefore most likely become permanent, which means that important political institutions protecting Serb minority rights in Croatia will ultimately be abandoned.

The guarantees of proportional representation of Serbs adopted in the Constitutional Law were also incorporated into the Electoral Law for the Croatian *Sabor*, enacted in April 1992. The law established a mixed electoral system combining pure plurality vote (in 60 single-member districts) and proportional allocation in one at-large district, with a 3 percent electoral threshold. Article 10 of the law once again stipulated that minorities making up more than 8 percent of the Croatian population would be entitled to proportional representation in the *Sabor*. Article 26 stipulated that if adequate proportionality was not reached through a regular electoral outcome, the number of representatives would increase by ethnic minority representatives selected from party lists, following the rule that "the members of a certain community or a minority ... shall be considered as elected representatives in the order corresponding to the proportional success of each individual list in the elections." If proportionality could not be attained through this procedure, by-elections would be held. However, other provisions of the law virtually ensured that ethnic proportionality would apply only to the *Sabor*'s main legislative chamber, the House of Representatives. The law provided for proportional elections to the House of Counties in three-member districts, a magnitude which in fact guarantees a very low degree of proportionality.

Along with the legal changes "temporarily" abandoning certain provisions of the Constitutional Law, the Serb minority's proportional representation in the Croatian parliament was also weakened in September 1995. Instead of 13 parliamentary mandates (calculated on the total of 120 seats in the House of Representatives), the Electoral Law was amended to guarantee only three Serb mandates.[37] The election procedure for these seats has also been changed, with members of the Serb ethnic community casting a second vote in one special at-large electoral district. While ethnic Serbs may cast their first vote for any party list (including that of a Serb party), the electoral threshold makes it is unlikely that this will increase the number of Serb representatives in the parliament.

Thus, the elaborate constitutional and statutory framework for Serb political representation that was established at the outset of Croatian independence has been dramatically pared, once again reflecting the equally dramatic zero-sum gains made by Croat nationalists in 1995. In fact, even those provisions designed to protect cultural and national rights that were not subject to "temporary non-implementation" appear to have been profoundly weakened in practice. The governmental inter-ethnic relations office has been established, with its activities focused on human rights issues, but it has proven largely ineffective. There have been scattered attempts to incorporate an adequate proportion of Serbs into judicial institutions and local self-government bodies, but this goal has hardly been completed (indeed, no official data concerning Serb participation are available). Finally, state financing of some information and cultural activities of Serb organizations has been provided, but no special educational programs and schools for the Serb minority have yet been established (except for the first such attempts in eastern Slavonia UNTAES).

The Nature and Forms of Serb Political Representation

The escalation of violent Serb-Croat conflict confronted moderate Serbs in areas of Croatia outside the control of Serb extremists with a very difficult situation. In less than a year they were deprived of any articulate political organization to represent their interests. The former left-bloc parties comprising reformed Communists in the Social Democratic Party (*Socijaldemokratska partija—SDP*) and the Socialist Party (*Socijalisticka stranka Hrvatske—SSH*), refused to assume the role of advocates of the Serb minority in the *Sabor*, while most Serb deputies quit. As a result, Serb voters turned away from the left-bloc parties. Meanwhile, the only ethnic Serb party in Croatia—the SDS—organized violent insurrection and practically ceased to exist in the non-occupied part of Croatia by the autumn of 1991 (in 1994 it was formally declared unconstitutional by the Constitutional Court). While the SDS developed into the dominant political force in "Krajina," other parties emerged there as well, mostly as analogs of parties in Serbia. However, as with the SDS itself, the military defeat of the Serb rebel forces in western Slavonia and "Krajina" practically destroyed these parties' political significance in Croatia.

The fact that practically no channels for political articulation of Serb interests in the non-occupied part of Croatia existed under conditions of violent Serb-Croatian conflict was even more consequential because Serbs in these areas faced serious violations of their human rights.[38] Although terrorist murders of ethnic Serb civilians inside and outside the war zones, which reasonable estimates put at several dozen, have been documented (even by the police or other official organs), no one has been sentenced or even prosecuted. Similarly, Serb houses and other property have been bombed, with this activity reaching its peak during the war in 1991 and in 1992. Since 1991 more than 6000 Serb-owned houses have been destroyed. The state itself has also been directly complicit in human rights violations, most notably by forcibly evicting Serb tenants from former Federal Army apartments now administered by the Croatian Ministry of Defense. While the evictions include illegal private seizures, state authorities have also acted on the basis of administrative decisions that leave tenants without legal recourse. It is estimated that between 5,000 and 7,000 evictions have occurred since 1991. Finally, some Serbs resident in Croatia were denied citizenship or received it only after a long and humiliating procedure, with about 7,500 such cases remaining unresolved. Those without citizenship have faced social deprivation of various kinds (loss of employment, social security benefits, pensions, etc.), while roughly 6,000 Serbs have been dismissed from their workplace despite holding Croatian citizenship.

The most profound human rights violations occurred in UNPA sectors North and South after the August 1995 military action. Reports of the Croatian Helsinki Committee for Human Rights, which refer to the observations of numerous witnesses and international observers, mention "several hundreds" of uninvestigated murders, widespread plundering, and the deliberate destruction of about 14,000 houses and other buildings outside the field of combat.[39] Growing international criticism, including UN Security Council resolutions, put pressure on Croatian authorities to engage more seriously in prosecution of these criminal acts. According to statements by the Croatian ministers of justice and foreign affairs, investigations have been initiated in 1,005 criminal cases, of which 25 are murder cases.[40]

The grave human rights situation and lack of political representation caused a significant wave of Serb emigration from non-occupied Croatia. According to the estimates made by officials from the Governmental Office for Refugees, approximately 280,000 to 300,000 of the 580,000 Serbs living in Croatia in 1991 inhabited the former UNPA sectors.[41] It is estimated that about 100,000 to 110,000 Serbs have left the non-occupied part of Croatia, moving to the occupied areas, Serbia, or other countries. This is significantly fewer than is claimed by Serb leaders, who give figures ranging from 110,000 to 200,000. The government figure is roughly consistent with that which can be inferred from the number of Serbs (174,611) registered on voter lists in 1995, although the actual number may be significantly lower if turnout (55,013), admittedly a crude indicator, is taken into consideration.[42]

Despite the rapid breakdown of the old channels of Serb political representation, these overall conditions seriously impeded the development of new Serb political and other organizations since 1991. The first organization to emerge was the Serb People's Party (Srpska narodna stranka—SNS), established in Zagreb on May 18, 1991. Until late 1994 the SNS was the only Serb political party in non-occupied Croatia. Its founder and president Milan

Dukić was a former SDS member and the elected head of the executive council of the municipality of Donji Lapac. After criticizing the SDS and Miloševic's extremist politics, he was forced to flee from his home to Zagreb. The SNS's ambition was to become the sole political party representing the Serb minority in Croatia. This was not to be. Despite the fact that the SNS and its state list participated as the only Serb party in the proportional part of the 1992 elections (there were no Serb candidates in the single-member districts with plurality voting), it received only 28,620 votes, or 1.06 percent of total votes cast.[43] According to the findings of an electoral survey conducted by the Zagreb Faculty of Political Science, the distribution of Serb votes was very heterogeneous. The votes were more or less equally shared among the SNS, several left parties (SDP, SSH, and the Social Democratic Union [*Socijalnodemokratska unija—SDU*]), the liberals, and even the ruling HDZ, despite its Croatian nationalist orientation. Serbs also appeared as candidates on different party lists, particularly those of the leftist parties.

This result would not have entitled SNS to send any representatives to the first chamber of the *Sabor*, since it failed to pass the 3 percent electoral threshold. However, immediately after the elections in August 1992, the Constitutional Court ruled that the threshold should not be applied to the SNS as an ethnic Serb party and that it should (in accordance with the Electoral Law) participate in the distribution of the additional 13 parliamentary seats necessary to secure proportional representation of the Serb ethnic community in the House of Representatives. Since ten seats were distributed among candidates from the two party lists which received more votes—the Croatian People's Party (HNS), a middle-sized party belonging to the political center (two seats), and the SDP (eight seats)—the SNS received only the three remaining seats. Thus Milan Dukić, Veselin Pejnović and Dragan Hinić from the SNS list became representatives in the *Sabor*. The SNS strongly criticised this procedure, questioning the legitimacy of Serb representatives selected from other party lists and demanding that political representation of Serbs in Croatia be reserved only for "genuine" Serb parties.[44] At the same time, however, Dukic was elected to serve as one of the three vice-presidents of the *Sabor* in the 1992-95 legislative period.

The February 1993 elections confirmed the inability of the SNS to organize its candidates throughout Croatia and attract even a majority of Serb voters. The elections were organized in 21 county electoral districts for the second parliamentary chamber, the House of Counties. The SNS ran candidates in only four counties (Zagreb, Osječko-baranjska, Požeško-slavonska, and Primorsko-goranska) and received only 14,239 votes (about 0.6 percent), more than half of which came from Zagreb. In the four respective counties, the SNS's share of the total vote ranged from 1.5 percent to 2.3 percent.[45] In parallel local elections for county, city, and municipality assemblies, the SNS participated only marginally and did not win any seats. Proportional representation of Serbs at the local level (also provided for by the Constitutional Law) was secured through independent candidates or from other party lists, including small leftist parties such as the SDU, which placed five Serb representatives in the city assembly of Karlovac.

In the October 1995 elections, two SNS candidates managed to enter the *Sabor* according to the new electoral procedure for Serb minority representatives. SNS leaders Milan Dukić and Veselin Pejnović even managed to win the first and second highest number of votes—30,382 and 24,857 votes or 27.0 percent and 22.1 percent, respectively (Election Results 1995). The three SNS candidates won 68,060 votes altogether (one should bear in mind that Serb voters could select up to three candidates on their ballot). Thus, the SNS remains the strongest Serb party in the new *Sabor*. Nevertheless, the party represents only one segment of Serbs in Croatia, namely those living in Zagreb and a few other urban centers. Its activities are predominantly focused on Zagreb and central state institutions, while its political presence and organizational network in the countryside remains negligible.

The other explicitly political organization of Serbs in Croatia is the Serb Democratic Forum (*Srpski demokratski forum—SDF*), founded in Zagreb on July 13, 1992 by a group of Serb intellectuals led by Dr. Milorad Pupovac. Pupovac is a professor of linguistics at the Philosophical Faculty in Zagreb and since 1989 has been a well-known political activist in Yugoslav-reformist and democratic socialist organizations in Croatia. The SDF has from its very beginning stressed its non-partisan character and did not take part in elections, although it was defined as a political organization. Originally, the SDF sought to establish an all-embracing framework outside the arena of party competition for all Serb political orientations in Croatia. The rationale was that an intra-Serb dialogue in Croatia should be conducted prior to competing for power so that a Serb national political program could be formulated to serve as the basis for Serb-Croatian negotiations and agreement. The activity of the SDF was consequently much more focused on organizing dialogue among Croatian Serbs and maintaining links to Serb political organizations in "Krajina" and to Serbia itself.

The SDF strongly opposed the claim of the SNS to function as the only political representative of Serbs in Croatia. However, it could not achieve the objective of becoming a real "forum" for all-Serb national coordination and articulation in Croatia. In October 1994 this fact was acknowledged by the caucus of the SDF: its leader Pupovac resigned from his post as president and turned to the task of establishing a new party, the Independent Serb Party (Samostalna srpska stranka—SSS). At the same time, the SDF would concentrate on general improvement of Serb-Croat relations, human rights protection, and research and publishing activities.[46] After the military action in western Slavonia in May 1995, a well-known moderate Serb leader from this region, Veljko Džakula, became the new president of the SDF.

Milorad Pupovac succeeded in founding the SSS by late 1994, but he was not able to register the party until after the October 1995 elections. He nonetheless succeeded in entering the *Sabor* as a candidate of the leftist Action of Social Democrats of Croatia, receiving 17,639 votes or 15.7 percent of Serb ballots. It is likely that the existence of a second Serb party in Croatia will increase the quality of Serb political representation, for, although the existing Serb political organizations originally strongly opposed one another, at least in their public statements, their programs and activities necessarily have had much in common. Particularly because of the numerous violations of Serb human rights, they have all been forced to engage in elementary human rights protection, thus performing functions of citizens' groups beyond the political arena that were largely absent. With the subsequent establishment of non-political Serb civic associations concerned with these issues (as well as cultural and informational activities), programmatic distinctions among parties competing for Serb votes should begin to emerge more clearly.[47]

The most important Serb civic organization to emerge is the Community of Serbs in Croatia (*Zajednica Srba u Hrvatskoj—ZSH*), established in Zagreb on September 16, 1992. Its program defines it as a "social organization" established to secure the identity and development of Serbs in Croatia, develop Serb education and culture, contribute to multiculturalism in Croatia, both at the national and regional levels, cooperate with other minority and citizens' associations, and organize international contacts. Although officially non-partisan, the president of ZSH, Borislav Arsenijeviç, was nominated as a candidate for the SNS in the February 1993 elections in Primorsko-goranska County (Rijeka), which contains the highest regional concentration of Serbs apart from Zagreb. The ZSH has not yet established a strong network of local organizations, although it claims to have about ten regional and local branches outside Zagreb. In fact, however, a separate organization, the Community of Serbs of Rijeka, Istria and Gorski kotar (*Zajednica Srba Rijeke, Istre i Gorskog kotara—ZSRIGK*), established in Rijeka on December 14, 1992, and headed by Zdravko Radoviç, an engineer from Rijeka, essentially covers at the regional level the activities performed by the ZSH on a statewide basis. The practical emphasis of both the ZSH and the ZSRIGK remains human rights protection.

In order to preserve and develop Serb cultural identity in Croatia, the cultural association *Prosvjeta* has been re-established. *Prosvjeta* was an important center of Serb educational and publishing activities in the post-World War II period, although it focused its attention primarily on rural areas and was subjected to strict communist control. It was dissolved in the early 1970s (along with the analogous Croatian cultural organization) during the communist repression of the Croatian national movement. While the revived *Prosvjeta* would be a natural candidate to play a significant role in designing autonomous Serb educational programs and organizing the publication of school books, whether it will do so appears to be largely dependent on the uncertain future course of official cultural policy towards the Serb minority.

Prospects

The events of 1995 caused a sharp, and probably irreversible, decline in the power and status of Serbs in Croatia. Due to continued emigration from Croatia since 1991 and especially the mass exodus from "Krajina" in August 1995, the number of Serbs has been dramatically reduced and their official standing downgraded to that of a small minority. The historical novelty of this situation can hardly be over-emphasized. While their proportion of the total population fell to a little less than 20 percent at the beginning of the twentieth century from a high of 30 percent in the mid-nineteenth century, all estimates say that Serbs currently account for less than 4 percent. Of course, Serbs from eastern Slavonia should be added to this figure after the process of reintegration of this region into the Croatian state has been completed. It might be expected that in the future this region would remain the last part of Croatia with a significant concentration of Serb population, in which at least some mechanisms of inter-ethnic balance and power-sharing could develop.

The remarkable ineffectiveness of Serb political representation in Croatia is not, however, solely the result of political pressure from nationalist Croatian forces and the impact of the war. Rather, it is also a necessary consequence of splits among Croatia's Serbs themselves—the most important of which occurred at the conflict's outset between urban Serbs and rural voters in "Krajina" over the question of loyalty to the new Croatian state. Indeed, the ultimate result of the politics of extreme Serb nationalism and its conflict with reactive Croatian nationalism is that Serb political articulation in Croatia has historically never been so weak and contradictory. The rebellion, defeat, and exodus of the "Krajina" Serbs increased the vulnerability of the Serb minority as a whole, and the remaining Serbs are left to face the daunting challenge of defining a viable political program for the future. Whatever its final shape, it now seems clear that it will be more concerned with promoting Serb-Croat reconciliation and especially with preserving Serb cultural identity. Earlier demands for territorial autonomy or power-sharing at the national level have become as irrelevant as they are unwinnable.

Notes

This chapter was completed prior to the January 2000 parliamentary election. The election's outcome heralded the accession of a new government promising democratic and economic reform, as well as closer cooperation with the West. However, it did not mark any change in the framework for ethnic minority representation analyzed here. On the contrary, as the discussion of the election in Carlos Flores's chapter in this volume demonstrates, the main features of that framework were reinforced.

1. Drago Roksandic, *Srbi u Hrvatskoj* (Zagreb: Vjesnik, 1991), pp. 7-54.

2. Ivo Banac, *The National Question in Yugoslavia: Origins, History, Politics* (Ithaca: Cornell University Press, 1984).

3. Drago Roksandic, *Srpska i hrvatska povijest i 'nova historija'* (Zagreb: Stvarnost, 1991), pp. 99, 134.

4. Roksandic, *Srbi u Hrvatskoj*, pp. 151-154.

5. *Statistički godišnjak SR Hrvatske 1987* (Zagreb: Republički zavod za statistiku, 1988), p. 84; Republic of Croatia & Republic of Bosnia and Herzegovina: Ethnic Map, Zagreb (s.a.).

6. Roksandić, *Srbi u Hrvatskoj*, pp. 79-116; Roksandic, *Srpska i hrvatska povijest i 'nova historija'*, pp. 93-143; Mirjana Gross and Agneza Szabo, *Prema hrvatskome gradanskom društvu* (Zagreb: Globus, 1992), pp. 150-156, 181-189, 265-278, 437-464, 496-501; Aleksa Djilas, *Osporavana zemlja. Jugoslavenstvo i revolucija* (Belgrade: IK Književne novine, 1990), pp. 37-76.

7. Josip Horvat, *Politička povijest Hrvatske* (Zagreb: August Cesarec, 1990), vol. 1, pp. 276-286; Djilas, *Osporavana zamlja. Jugoslavenstvo i revolucija*, pp. 59-61.

8. Ferdo Aulinovic, *Jugoslavija izmedu dva rata* (Zagreb: Izdavački zavod JAZU, 1961); Banac, *The National Question in Yugoslavia: Origins, History, Politics*, Horvat, *Politička povijest Hrvatske*, vol. 2; Roksandić, *Srbi u Hrvatskoj*, pp. 121-132; Hrvoje Matkoviç, *Suvremena politiăka povijest Hrvatske* (Zagreb: MUP Hrvatske, 1995), pp. 76-150.

9. Matković, *Suvremena politička povijest Hrvatske*, pp. 151-162; Djilas, *Osporavana zemlja. Jugoslavenstvo i revolucija*, pp. 181-191.

10. Roksandić, *Srbi u Hrvatskoj*, pp. 133-146; Djilas, *Osporavana zemlja. Jugoslavenstvo i revolucija*, pp. 168-178.

11. Djilas, *Osporavana zemlja. Jugoslavenstvo i revolucija*, pp. 225-247. For a comprehensive overview, see Dušan Bilandžić, *Historija SFRJ* (Zagreb: Školska knjiga, 1985).

12. Ottmar Nikola Haberl, *Parteiorganisation und nationale Frage in Jugoslawien* (Berlin, 1976).

13. Matković, *Suvremena politiăka povijest Hrvatske*, pp. 231-238.

14. Branka Magaš, *The Destruction of Yugoslavia* (London: Verso, 1993), pp. 3-73, 105-155, 159-177.

15. *Ibid.*, pp. 241-246, 260-265.

16. Mirjana Kasapović, "Strukturna i dinamička obilježja političkog prostora i izbori," in Ivan Grdešić, et al., *Hrvatska u izborima '90.* (Zagreb: Naprijed, 1991), pp. 15-48.

17. Nenad Zakošek, 1991, "Polarizacijske strukture, obrasci političkih uvjerenja i hrvatski izbori 1990," in Grdešić, et al., *Hrvatska u izborima '90,* pp. 131-187.

18. Ivan Šiber, "Nacionalna, vrijednosna i ideologijska uvjetovanost stranačkog izbora," in Grdešić, et al., *Hrvatska u izborima '90.,* p. 100.

19. Željko Sabol, ed., *Sabor Republike Hrvatske 1990-1992* (Zagreb: Sabor Republike Hrvatske, 1992).

20. *Ibid.*

21. Mirjana Kasapović, *Izborni i stranaäki sustav Republike Hrvatske* (Zagreb: Alinea, 1993), pp. 64-72.

22. Magaš, *The Destruction of Yugoslavia,* pp. 327-345.

23. For a comprehensive description of the war's dynamics and outcome, see Božidar Javorović, *Velikosrpska najezda i obrana Hrvatske* (Zagreb: Defimi, 1995).

24. Ivan Lajiç, "Demografski razvitak Hrvatske u razdoblju 1991 do 1994," in *Revija za sociologiju,* vol. 26, no. 1-2 (1995), p. 60.

25. See *Draft Agreement on the Krajina, Slavonia, Southern Baranja and Western Sirmium,* mimeo, p. 43.

26. Ozren Žunec, "Država i pobunjenici. Operacija 'Oluja' i njene posljedice," *Erasmus,* no. 13 (October 1995), pp. 4-10.

27. International Helsinki Federation for Human Rights, *Izvještaj OSCE-u: Medunarodna Helsinška federacija za ljudska prava, Misija IHF-a iz Beča za Krajinu 17.-19. kolovoz 1995,* mimeo, Vienna, August 25, 1995, p. 2.

28. *Vjesnik,* February 28, 1996, and March 2, 1996.

29. See *Basic Agreement on the Region of Eastern Slavonia, Baranja, and Western Sirmium,* mimeo, 2.

30. *Principal State Acts. A Collection of English Translations of the Principal State Acts of the Republic of Croatia* (Zagreb: Sabor Republike Hrvatske, 1993), pp. 9-20.

31. *Ibid.,* p. 37.

32. *Ibid.,* pp. 45-52; *Narodne novine,* September 21, 1995, p. 1833.

33. *Principal State Acts,* pp. 71-88; *Narodne novine,* September 21, 1995, pp. 1833-1836.

34. *Ustav SFRJ/SRH* (Zagreb: Informator, s.a.), p. 212.

35. *Principal State Acts,* p. 9.

36. Temporary establishment of a Provisional Court was provided for, with a majority of judges to be appointed by countries of the European Union.

37. *Narodne novine,* September 21, 1995, p. 1836.

38. See, for example, *Amnesty International Report 1993* (London, 1993), pp. 106-108; International Helsinki Federation for Human Rights: *Annual report of activities 1993/1994* (Vienna), pp. 38-44; Damir Grubiša, "Ljudska prava u Hrvatskoj: Studija slučaja," in *Erasmus,* no. 13 (October 1995), pp. 26-36; numerous contributions in *Naš glas* (monthly journal published by the Community of Serbs in Croatia [Zajednica Srba u Hrvatskoj]).

39. *Izvještaj OSCE-u and Izjava,* br. 28, October 5, 1995 (Zagreb: Hrvatski helsinški odbor za ljudska prava).

40. *Vjesnik,* February 3, 1995; *Globus,* February 2, 1995.

41. See also Lajić, "Demografski razvitak Hrvatske u razdoblju 1991. do 1994," p. 60. A considerable number of residents of these territories appear to have fled to Serbia and western

countries even before the Croatian military operations of May and August 1995.

42. *Službeni rezultati izbora zastupnika u Zastupnički dom Sabora* (Zagreb, 1995).

43. For the election results, see Izborna komisija Republike Hrvatske, *Izvješće,* no. 30 (August 11, 1992) and no. 32 (August 12, 1992).

44. Only three of the eight SDP deputies remained members of this party throughout the electoral term, while the others became independents.

45. Izborna komisija Republike Hrvatske, *Izvješće o provedenim izborima za zastupnike u Županijski dom Sabora Republike Hrvatske.*

46. *Vjesnik,* October 30, 1994.

47. In this article it was not possible to present the political developments of 1996 and 1997. It should be only briefly noted that in 1997 Pupovac's SSS merged with the local Serb activists from Eastern Slavonia into a new party, Independent Democratic Serb Party (Samostalna demokratska srpska stranka—SDSS). SDSS took part in the 1997 House of Counties county and local elections and won a significant number of mandates in county assemblies and city and municipal councils (e.g., 6 mandates in the assembly of Osječko-baranjska county and ten mandates in the Vukovarsko-srijemska county, an absolute majority in the Beli Manastir city council, etc.), while its president, Vojislav Stanimiroviç, became a member of the House of Counties in the Croatian *Sabor.*

9

EMIGRATION AND THE POLITICS
OF IDENTITY:
THE TURKISH MINORITY IN BULGARIA

Ivan Ilchev

Following the demise of communist rule in 1989, many observers feared an imminent explosion of communal violence between Bulgaria's ethnic Bulgarian and Turkish populations. As with many bold predictions concerning post-communist outcomes, this one has so far proven to be unfounded. On the contrary, while anti-Turkish sentiment continues to be an important part of public life and the potential for localized conflict remains, ethnic Bulgarians have not supported extreme nationalist parties or policies, while the judicial system has repeatedly asserted its independence by issuing key decisions protecting the Turkish minority's political rights. Equally important, the realization of a radical or separatist ethnic Turk political agenda has been constrained by persistent emigration to Turkey, internal divisions, and the uncertain identity of key groups. As a result, the Turkish minority's main political party, the Movement for Rights and Freedoms (DPS), has become dependent for its survival on electoral and political cooperation with ethnic Bulgarian parties.

This chapter examines Bulgaria's post-communist management of ethnic pluralism, arguing that communal conflict has been successfully contained within democratic institutions because the political salience of the ethnic cleavage has declined, particularly since 1994. The chapter first outlines the historical context of the contemporary situation of Bulgaria's Turkish minority, and then assesses the organization, behavior, and development of the DPS.

Demographic Background

The last census in Bulgaria was conducted in December 1992, following a protracted political debate over its implementation. According to its results, ethnic (Slav) Bulgarians comprise by far the most numerous group within a total population of almost 8.5 million. Ethnic Turks, numbering 822,000, or 9.7 percent of the population, constitute the largest national minority. The Roma, with 288,000 (3.4 percent) members, are the third largest minority. However, many demographers have argued that a large but unspecified number of Muslim Roma and probably around 30,000-35,000 Bulgarian-speaking Muslims (Pomaks) chose to declare themselves as Turks in the census.[1] Of the overall population, 7.3 million (86.2 percent) are Orthodox. Muslims, 90 percent of whom are Sunni, number 1.1 million (12.7 percent). These include virtually all the Turks (only a tiny fraction are Orthodox), 174,000 ethnic Bulgarians, and 113,000 Roma.

Ethnic Bulgarians are also the predominant ethnic group in almost all of the country's 26 districts. The exceptions are the Razgrad region in northeastern Bulgaria, where the population is almost equally divided between ethnic Bulgarians and Turks, and the Kurdzhali region in southeastern Bulgaria, where ethnic Turks outnumber ethnic Bulgarians by two to one. The Turkish minority is concentrated in five regions of the country (Razgrad, Kurdzhali, Shumen, Burgas, and Silistra), where roughly one-half of their total number now lives.[2] While a majority of ethnic Bulgarians live in cities, rural dwellers still outnumber those in urban centers among ethnic Turks. There is no significant Turkish presence in the largest cities, with the possible exceptions of Shumen and Ruse.

The Bulgarian Turks and the Bulgarian State

The ancestors of the present-day Bulgarian Turks came to Bulgaria between the 14th and 16th centuries, establishing an empire that lasted almost six hundred years. However, even before that time, the Balkans had long been the site of several smaller Turkic influxes, which resulted in permanent settlement by some members of invading Turkic tribes. Turkish colonization—massive on the peninsula as a whole—was particularly significant on the territory of present-day Bulgaria. As conquerors, the colonists settled along the main trade routes, around strategically important points, and on the most fertile land. Gradually, thousands of Slavic Bulgarians converted to Islam—most of them probably forcibly. Some maintained their language, but the surrounding Turks assimilated others.

There are no reliable statistics on Bulgaria's Turkish population in the 19th century, but it seems relatively certain that on the eve of Bulgarian independence in 1878, a sizable proportion of the population was Turkish, and an even larger share was Muslim. In 1881, three years after independence and after hundreds of thousands Turks had emigrated from the newly-established Bulgarian state, almost half the population of northeastern Bulgaria remained Muslim. Nevertheless, Bulgarian independence greatly altered the situation of the Bulgarian Turks, reducing them to the status of an ethnic and religious minority. Those Turks responsible for the worst excesses during the struggle for Bulgarian national liberation prudently chose to leave. The emigrants' land was divided among ethnic Bulgarians, and even those who eventually decided to return generally preferred to sell their land to the new inhabitants and leave permanently.

Following the establishment of the new state, Bulgarian Turks shared the same formal rights as those granted to other Bulgarian citizens, and Turkish deputies were among those who voted for the liberal Turnovo Constitution of 1879. Yet, while deputies of Turkish origin consistently sat in Bulgarian parliaments (in the last two parliaments before 1989 they numbered approximately twenty), they have just as consistently been excluded from the highest ranks of executive power. Never in the 120-year existence of the modern Bulgarian state has a Bulgarian Turk been a minister (although some were members of the State Council in the last years of the communist regime and many more were members of the Bulgarian Communist Party's Central Committee). Turkish voters were considered to be pliant, easily manipulated by their leaders, and a rightful "dowry" for deployment in the electoral frauds regularly perpetrated by whatever government was in power.

The Turnovo Constitution took heed of some of the traditional structures of ethnic Turkish society. The Bulgarian Treasury paid the salaries of the twelve Muslim Muftis, and the Muslim religious courts were preserved within the new legal structure. Turkish military recruits were allowed to take their oath in Turkish rather than Bulgarian. More than 1,300 Turkish schools—most of them religious—existed at the beginning of the century and were supported by both local communities and the government. From 1878 to 1934, more than eighty Turkish language newspapers and journals were published in the country, and a thin stratum of intellectuals appeared.

Post-independence relations between ethnic Bulgarians and Turks were strained first by the Balkan wars of 1912-1913 and then by the propaganda of Kemalist Turkey. The influence of the Kemalist regime, which successfully promoted a secular Turkish national identity, was substantial among Bulgarian Turks. In the years following the First World War, a number of organizations with nationalist and Pan-Turkish goals sprang up in the country. The most influential of them in the inter-war period, the Varna-based *Turan*, encompassed some fifty separate organizations with almost 10,000 members, predominantly students, teachers, journalists, and other professionals, within ten years of its establishment in 1924 as a cultural society of young Turks. Their contacts with Kemalist Turkey created suspicion on the part of the Bulgarian government that Ankara was using *Turan* for intelligence purposes and that the organization sheltered activists striving to establish autonomy for the Bulgarian Turks. Indeed, one of the organization's professed goals was to inculcate Bulgarian-speaking Muslims with Pan-Turkish sentiments.[3] *Turan*, along with all ethnic Bulgarian political parties and movements, was disbanded after the *coup d'état* of May 19, 1934, and its leaders were imprisoned.

The most severe problem confronting Bulgaria's Turkish population prior to the communist period was its relative economic backwardness. The predominantly Turkish areas were among the least prosperous in a country that was itself underdeveloped. Urbanization and industrialization in northeastern and southeastern Bulgaria lagged behind other regions. The local economy was (and remains) primarily dependent on tobacco farming, a highly labor-intensive enterprise requiring large families but affording levels of health care and education that were appalling in comparison with the rest of the state. Throughout this period, therefore, the Bulgarian Turks developed apart from, and more slowly than, the mainstream of Bulgarian political, economic, and cultural life, as they were characterized demographically by higher birth rates, lower household incomes, shorter life expectancy, and lower literacy.

The Bulgarian Turks in the Post-War Period

Following the Second World War, the situation of the Bulgarian Turks was conditioned by two factors: the ideological stance of the newly established communist regime and the geo-strategic confrontation between the Warsaw Pact and NATO. The participation of Bulgarian Turks in the wartime activities of the Bulgarian Communist Party had been negligible, and the only political party that had any influence among Bulgarian Turks in the years immediately after the war was the peasant-based Bulgarian National Agrarian Union (BANU). From the very beginning of this period, therefore, the new rulers energetically pursued measures designed to alter the traditional patterns of life followed by Bulgarian Turks, creating in the process a wide array of benefits, most of which were maintained until 1984. Steps were taken to break the hold of religious leaders, particularly among the young, while Turkish pedagogical institutes were created to provide a new cohort of teachers. Several newspapers and journals were founded, state publishing houses began issuing books by previously ignored Bulgarian Turkish authors, and three Turkish theaters were opened. The number of Turkish-language schools increased rapidly, and their graduates were encouraged to continue their education. Many Bulgarian Turks in fact benefited from a quota system that exempted them from university entrance examinations.

By 1958, there were already 1,156 Turkish primary and secondary schools in the country, in which about 112,000 students were enrolled. Almost 97 percent of Turkish children attended school—a profound increase over the pre-war years. In 1952 a chair of Turkish philology was established at Sofia University, and almost four hundred young Bulgarian Turks were sent to the Soviet republics of Central Asia to study.[4] Yet, throughout this period, strong emphasis was placed on Bulgarian-language education as well, and Bulgarian Turks became much more conversant in the language of the ethnic majority.

The communist regime's effort to create a Turkish intelligentsia imbued with a secular, socialist worldview registered significant successes. The Turkish nomenklatura, although not numerous, was privileged on a par with its Bulgarian counterpart. By the end of the 1950s, 4,000 Bulgarian Turks were members of the Bulgarian Communist Party (BCP), and 18,000 ethnic Turk bureaucrats were employed in the state administration.

The living standard of the Turkish population as a whole also rose, contributing to greater compliance with the policy and leadership of the BCP. While the forced collectivization of agriculture interrupted this tendency for a short period, by the beginning of the 1960s, Bulgarian Turks were not faring badly in comparison with their ethnic kin in Turkey, given the general trend toward improved living conditions for all Bulgarians and Turkey's severe economic crisis at the time. The success of this policy, however, led to misgivings among communist party leaders concerning the potential for ethnic Turks' alienation from the rest of Bulgarian society and—what was considered far more dangerous—from the Bulgarian state. These fears were encouraged by the domestic security apparatus, which claimed to have found evidence of a tendency among Bulgarian-speaking Muslims and some of the Muslim Roma to associate themselves with the Turks. Consequently, the official attitude regarding the "Turkish problem" changed, with the BCP Central Committee eventually adopting a new policy that stressed the amalgamation of Bulgarians and Turks rather than the independent development of Turkish culture.[5]

During the 1960s and 1970s, however, official policy towards the Bulgarian Turks remained in a state of flux. While cultural provision for the Turks continued, research into the history of the Bulgarian lands under the Ottoman Turks was encouraged, and at the same time assertions began to appear in Party documents that Bulgaria was becoming ethnically homogeneous. These latter developments reflected a general shift in BCP policy away from the internationalism prevalent in the sixties to a kind of moderate nationalism exemplified by the activities of General Secretary Todor Zhivkov's daughter, a member of the Politburo who began preaching national pride and revived interest in Bulgarian history.

Even so, while changes in the BCP's orientation toward the Turkish question became steadily more apparent, a clear break with previous policy did not occur until the end of 1984, when the names of all Bulgarian Turks were changed administratively to the Bulgarian form. The background, overall rationale, supporting arguments, and moving forces connected with the decision to pursue a campaign of forcible assimilation remain shrouded in mystery. Most of those believed to have been leading participants now deny any knowledge of either its formulation or the frequently brutal enforcement measures taken by the police in northeastern and southeastern Bulgaria.[6] The truth probably consists in a combination of causal explanations that have been suggested in recent years, with each at varying degrees of temporal and conceptual proximity to what was officially called the "revival period."

The first explanation revolves around the alleged danger to national security posed by Islamic fundamentalism, which, whatever the actual extent of the threat, may very well have been perceived by the BCP as a serious ideological challenge meriting a sharp and decisive response. (The Soviets' treatment of Afghanistan beginning in 1978 stands as an important precedent in this respect.) This fear was reinforced by the finding that, despite three decades of atheist propaganda, Bulgarian Muslims retained a more religious worldview than did Orthodox ethnic Bulgarians. Viewed from the regime's perspective, the development of modern mass media allowed no hope that the Bulgarian Turks could be entirely isolated from the proselytizing of well-organized religious activists, who could count, moreover, on the material support of foreign states.

Second, the living standards of Bulgarian Turks rose considerably in the 1960s and 1970s as their income from tobacco-growing and building construction grew, while the state granted additional privileges to the population living close to the Turkish border. Almost one-third of all Bulgarian Turks lived in this area and thus received higher salaries than ethnic Bulgarians who held comparable jobs in the interior. The Turkish villages changed—new houses were built, modern amenities became standard, and the appearance and style of the younger generation became indistinguishable from that of ethnic Bulgarians. Yet the birth rate of the Turkish population in the country increased while that of ethnic Bulgarians decreased. This demographic trend, combined with restrictions on emigration to Turkey, meant that the number of ethnic Turks in Bulgaria would soon surpass 10 percent of the population. Since the beginning of the twentieth century, this figure had held extraordinary symbolic significance as an indicator of the state's national character, and the danger that the proportion of Turks might soon exceed it, particularly given rising living standards, gradually came to be acutely perceived by the authorities.[7]

A third factor in the regime's decision appears to have been the example of Cyprus. The "inevitable" danger from Turkey, exemplified by the events of 1974, steadily became a common propaganda weapon, and the diplomatic behavior of Turkey, which at the time strove to assert itself as the dominant regional power, did not help to dispel suspicions of a threat to Bulgaria's territorial integrity.

Fourth, by the early 1980s, the BCP leadership had been deeply entrenched for several decades. Its world was a stable one that moved slowly and changed little. Even in its most catastrophic scenarios, the Party could not conceive of changes as radical as those that would occur only a few years later. The decisive shift to a policy of forced assimilation of the Bulgarian Turks was an act conceived in this atmosphere, and it is unlikely that its perpetrators expected immediate results. Rather, while short-term resistance would have to be overcome, the ultimate goal was to transform gradually the consciousness of younger ethnic Turks and their successors.[8]

Fifth, Bulgaria's contemporary international prestige was at its lowest level following allegations of Bulgarian participation in the shooting of Pope John Paul II. BCP leaders may have judged that the country did not have much to lose in the eyes of the international community as a result of escalating domestic repression. Moreover, a hard-line ethnic policy could in no sense be considered an exception in the Balkans and vicinity. Official Turkish policy refused to recognize the existence of the Kurds in Turkey, forbade Kurdish-language education, and sponsored widespread human rights violations against the Kurdish population. Similarly, the existence of ethnic Bulgarian minorities in Yugoslavia and Greece was consistently denied by their authorities despite the fact that hundreds of thousands of Bulgarians lived in both countries prior to the Balkan wars of 1912-1913.

Finally, the least temporally proximate explanation suggests that forced assimilation became inevitable once the primary goal of Bulgarian foreign policy—the achievement of national unification by bringing the Macedonian and Thracian territories within the boundaries of the Bulgarian state—became unattainable with the consolidation of the post-war international and regional order. This view takes on greater causal significance in light of Turkey's behavior during and after 1974. At this point, BCP leaders were already possessed of a latent fear that a numerous, well-educated, and unified Turkish minority might constitute a threat to the country's territorial integrity.

The implementation of the policy in 1984-1985 took place in the context of a surprising lack of opposition among the Turks and even less among ethnic Bulgarians. On the Turkish side, initial demonstrations were put down immediately, with several hundred killed, injured, or arrested. Even bearing in mind the effectiveness of the secret police, however, the level of resistance was extremely low, primarily taking the form of attempts to smuggle information concerning the situation in the affected regions to western diplomats. In many places, ethnic Bulgarians refused to use the new Bulgarian names of their Turkish neighbors and friends, and, predictably, the name changes produced a wave of political jokes. Yet, following the initial shock, the only signs of open resistance appeared in the form of small clandestine organizations that resorted to terrorist acts, but whose members were quickly discovered by the secret police.[9]

The Emigration Problem

An "exit" option has existed for Bulgaria's Turks since the state's establishment, when hundreds of thousands left in the months following the Russo-Turkish War of 1877-1878. Probably another 100,000 or more followed over the next several years as it became clear that a restoration of Ottoman power could not be expected, and a steady trickle of emigration continued up until the Second World War, regulated by several agreements with the Turkish government. Reaching an understanding with Ankara had not been easy, however. On one hand, the Bulgarian authorities did not have a clear policy towards Turkish emigration. Some politicians were in favor of promoting it, while others were afraid of losing a labor force whose economic contribution was obvious. On the other hand, Turkey encouraged would-be emigrants, but was also concerned that a sufficient number of ethnic Turks remain in Bulgaria so that political pressure could be brought to bear on Sofia should the need arise.

Serious problems emerged after World War II, however, when the BCP sealed the borders and no Bulgarian citizens were allowed to leave. In 1947, Turkey declared that it was ready to accept new immigrants from Bulgaria. The communist government hesitated, but eventually decided to take Ankara at its word. The confrontation between the two states was approaching new heights with the onset of the Cold War, and the existence of a significant population with sympathies toward an adjacent ethnic motherland was already regarded as potentially harmful for Bulgaria. In addition, the European experience of the immediate post-war years seemed to speak in favor of permitting Turkish emigration, as millions of ethnic Germans, Hungarians, Poles, and Ukrainians had by that point already been "transferred" to their respective kin states.

In the summer of 1950, the two countries' ministries of foreign affairs engaged in prolonged negotiations over the number of Turks to be allowed to emigrate to Turkey. However, despite its declarations in favor of ethnic Turkish emigration from Bulgaria, Ankara continued to harbor doubts. Not only was it reluctant to forgo completely an effective instrument for exerting political pressure, but it feared (with good reason) that the Bulgarian intelligence apparatus would smuggle active Communists and spies into Turkey among the emigrants. As the negotiations lagged, thousands of Bulgarian Turks gathered at border checkpoints awaiting permission to enter. Several hundred managed to break through the border, and with the situation in danger of erupting into chaos, the Turkish side opened the border on December 2, 1950. During the eleven months that it remained open, more than 150,000 Turks left the country, although another 111,000 who had applied for exit visas were not permitted to leave.[10]

A number of agreements were concluded in subsequent years in order to reunite divided families, and another 120,000 Bulgarian Turks left between 1968 and 1978. There was virtually no emigration in the early 1980s, but Ankara exerted constant pressure on Sofia to allow it after 1985. Events culminated in the spring of 1989 when the Turkish government asserted its readiness to accept all immigrants from Bulgaria and President Zhivkov proclaimed the opening of the border. By August 1989, when Turkey closed the border unilaterally (claiming an inability to accept any more immigrants), roughly 360,000 Bulgarian Turks had left the country. More than one-third of these returned to Bulgaria, however, after the ban on Turkish names was lifted at the end of the year. In 1990-1991, an additional 150,000 left voluntarily, and this outflow has continued to the present, fueled by Bulgaria's economic decline, which has been especially sharp in the ethnic Turkish regions as a result of low tobacco prices, the loss of Soviet bloc markets, and the collapse of the construction sector. In 1992 alone, according to its regional governor, 32,000 people left the Kurdzhali region for Turkey. In the area surrounding Ivailovgrad, some villages have been left completely uninhabited. While more than 40,000 people lived in the small Krumovgrad region in 1992, a local census conducted the following year revealed that the number of inhabitants had declined to just over 20,000. As a whole, almost 60,000 left the region in the period from 1989 to June 1993, and 45–50 percent of Kurdzhali's seven municipalities had left by June 1995.[11] Alarmed by the size of the influx of Bulgarian Turks, the Turkish government began imposing what it called "informal" visa requirements on Bulgarian citizens in 1994 in order to target ethnic Turks, and Turkey has also intermittently expelled illegal immigrants. However, neither of these measures has halted the outflow from Bulgaria's depressed eastern regions.

Ethnic Bulgarian Perceptions of the Turkish Population

Substantial differences exist between the image of the Turk living in Turkey and that of the Bulgarian Turk, and it is important to recognize that until 1989, the Bulgarian Turks were virtually invisible outside the regions they inhabited, particularly given the absence of a substantial Turkish presence in Sofia, the country's political, economic, and cultural metropole. Their depiction in the mass media before 1984 was minimal, and with the advent of the "revival period," they vanished from public view altogether. Thus, it is necessary to distinguish to some extent between two large groups of ethnic Bulgarians: those who have everyday contacts with Bulgarian Turks, and those who do not.

The attitude of both groups is shaped to a large extent by the historical and cultural heritage of the country. Slavic Bulgarians lived for almost five centuries under the Ottoman Empire, and their historical memory is often bitter and uncompromising. The Empire is blamed for its barbarity, for its lack of opportunities for the development of national culture, for brutally suppressing armed revolts by ethnic Bulgarians, and for Bulgaria's relative backwardness (a denunciation that is particularly popular now). Whether explicit or not, anti-Turkish sentiments form the basis for the education of ethnic Bulgarian children and can be viewed as the foil against which Bulgarian national identity has taken shape. The view of history as it is presently constructed and taught is thus to a large extent a Manichaean one. Equally important, it has carried over to perceptions of current Bulgarian Turk leaders.

A high school history textbook published in 1997, for example, described the ethnic Turk political leader Ahmed Dogan, a former dissident, as a terrorist during the "revival period."[12]

The unfavorable image of the Turk in the minds of ethnic Bulgarians was captured in a 1993 public opinion survey, which suggested that a majority believe the Bulgarian Turks represent a threat to national security, wield too much influence in Bulgaria's power structure, and are religious fanatics. Only 14 percent of ethnic Bulgarians were prepared to accept a marriage with a Turk (among the Turks the percentage of those who would accept a marriage with a Bulgarian was 32 percent). However, other measurements of the social distance between the two groups were less discouraging, possibly reflecting the actual accommodations of daily life in ethnically mixed communities. For example, most ethnic Bulgarians are prepared to live in the same town, village, or quarters with Turks, to befriend them, and to work alongside them.[13]

A poll on national and ethnic identity conducted in 1996 confirmed the dichotomy between social and political perceptions. Ethnic differences were revealed to be much less of a social concern than unemployment, inflation, and crime, but deep rifts appeared on questions concerning political status and representation, especially in the three ethnically mixed areas (Kurdzhali, Blagoevgrad, and Razgrad) that were surveyed. Only one-half of the respondents in the nationwide sample supported the right of ethnic minorities to form organizations to preserve their cultural identity, while 59 percent of those surveyed in the mixed regions opposed permitting the establishment of ethnic minority political parties.[14]

The Resurgence of Religion?

Confessional factors have, perhaps inevitably, played a considerable role in shaping inter-ethnic relations over the past several years. Under the *ancien régime*, the religious sentiments of all Bulgarians were stifled by the state's official atheist policy. However, while it is difficult to render a decisive judgment as to whether Islam or the Eastern Orthodox Church was the more persecuted, it seems evident that the plight of Islam was relatively more severe. Given that Orthodoxy, the religion of an overwhelming majority of Bulgarians, received state subsidies to maintain its clergy and property, and that Islam was the officially sanctioned religion of Ottoman rule, national traditions easily combined with the BCP's increasingly chauvinist policy to make the practice of Islam particularly difficult.

Many observers believed that the establishment of democracy in 1989-1990 would inevitably lead to a surge in religiosity. This proved to be only partly true. The Orthodox Church, accustomed to being a semi-official, fully co-opted, and financially dependent element of the state system, emerged from communism quite apathetic and unprepared for engagement with society. The Islamic community, however, responded more vigorously. According to a 1993 survey, 86 percent of Turks consider themselves religious, and three-quarters of the respondents declared that they believe firmly in the existence of Allah. Among the Orthodox, the percentage of those who firmly believe in God was only 30 percent. As elsewhere, there is an inverse correlation between religiosity and educational attainment. Significantly, however, the level of religious belief among the youngest cohorts of Bulgarian Turks does not differ substantially from that of their Orthodox counterparts, with the differences between the two groups instead concentrated among the older generations. Nor does a higher level of religiosity necessarily mean that Muslims are more inclined to engage in organized worship—only 15 percent (again, mostly the elderly) frequent the mosques, and only 30 percent pray more or less regularly.[15]

Still, it is evident that Islam plays a greater role in the life of Bulgarian Muslims than in past years. One ubiquitous sign is the construction or renovation of mosques in most Muslim villages, with 945 mosques and 1,148 mufti districts established by 1996, according to the Supreme Theological Council of Muslims.[16] Similarly, religious leaders have attempted to restore forgotten traditions. One of the first manifestations of their growing self-assurance was the refusal of many local imams to sanction religious burials for Muslims who had not changed their Bulgarian names to Islamic ones. The imams have also frequently insisted on removing headstones with photographs of the deceased from Muslim burial tombs, regarding these as contrary to Islamic religious practices, while some parents have demanded that their daughters wear traditional head coverings to school.[17] In 1990, a religious secondary school was opened in Shumen, soon followed by similar institutions in Momchilgrad and Ruse.[18] Koranic schools have been organized at mosques in many towns and villages, although it appears that after a period of initial enthusiasm, interest in such schools among children has not remained high.[19]

Reports of the arrival of Islamic preachers from Arab countries have also come from different parts of the country, generating widespread alarm among ethnic Bulgarians, whose Orthodox faith is enshrined in the 1991 constitution as "the traditional religion in the Republic of Bulgaria."[20] In some places, either these missionaries or various Islamic religious foundations have donated substantial sums for the construction of new mosques and the restoration of old ones. The fear, basic to Bulgaria given its history and geography, is that these emissaries constitute an advance team of propagandists for religious fundamentalism, and that the country will be used as a springboard for Islamic penetration into "Christian" Europe.[21] However, notwithstanding the fears such episodes have provoked and the symbolic constitutional privileging of Orthodoxy, free exercise of religious rights has received strong protection and is unlikely to constitute an immediate source of political instability in the foreseeable future. Rather, it is in the field of politics itself that long-held and deeply rooted animosities have been most clearly and directly expressed.

The Emergence of the Movement for Rights and Freedoms

In view of the political perceptions of ethnic Bulgarians captured in the surveys cited above, the most important aspect of post-communist transformation that accentuated negative views of the Turkish minority was the creation of the Movement for the Rights and Freedoms of the Turks and Muslims in Bulgaria (now simply the Movement for Rights and Freedoms, or DPS). Again, it is important to emphasize that the purely confessional elements of the party's identity have not been primary to its self-definition. Even many leaders of the DPS, which in general is a secular organization, have declared their opposition to religious proselytizing by foreign Islamic clerics and organizations.[22] Nevertheless, the establishment of the DPS caused considerable controversy in Bulgarian public life: never before had a political party so explicitly and unequivocally based on ethnicity operated in the country.

The DPS was founded in Varna on January 4, 1990, with its official establishment taking place at a meeting on March 26, 1990, in Sofia, at which the philosopher Ahmed Dogan was elected its chairman. The DPS considered itself the successor to the traditions of the illegal Turkish National Liberation Movement in Bulgaria, which was created in 1985 and destroyed by the secret police the following year. Under the slogan "Struggle without blood," the Liberation Movement had opposed violence and limited itself mainly to establishing contacts with foreign journalists and embassies to convey reports on human rights violations during the "revival period." Dogan (at that time named Medi Doganov) was sentenced as one of its leaders to ten years imprisonment, and was released at the end of 1989.[23]

It remains exceptionally difficult to determine precisely how the DPS was legally registered in 1990. The latent distrust of ethnically based parties, and perhaps hostility toward the Turkish minority in particular, was later reflected in Bulgaria's post-communist constitution and electoral law, both of which were adopted in 1991 and expressly forbid the creation of political parties based on religious or ethnic grounds. However, the DPS was legalized on April 26, 1990, only days after it filed for registration. The process took place behind closed doors and is not documented. The first step in this direction, however, was a decision taken by the BCP's leadership on December 29, 1989, under severe pressure from public protests, to renounce officially its own actions during the "revival period." In fact, it is likely that the leadership of the BCP's legal successor, the re-named Bulgarian Socialist Party (BSP), agreed to the existence of the DPS in order to divide the electorate in ethnically mixed regions, in which the opposition Union of Democratic Forces (SDS) was expected to triumph. However, the SDS itself supported the decision to grant legal recognition to the DPS, as it considered the Bulgarian Turks to be one of the main victims of communist rule.

In the short run, the BSP's decision turned out to be a shrewd tactical move, for it did indeed lead to a divided vote in the predominantly or partially Muslim regions. However, BSP leaders soon realized that it would be difficult to put the genie back in the bottle, and they began to challenge the DPS's right to exist on constitutional grounds, simultaneously blaming it for regional ethnic unrest in the winter and spring of 1990. Although the DPS's right to compete in Bulgarian elections was upheld by the Constitutional Court in April 1992, the Socialists were thus able to present themselves as the defenders of the majority ethnic Bulgarian population and of the country's national interests. The newly emergent democratic opposition, meanwhile, stood squarely behind the Turkish minority's rights to free association and political organization.

DPS leaders claim that even they were surprised by the party's swift legalization. In the spring of 1990, the party lacked both a disciplined national organization and active local branches. However, in the first free elections to the Grand National Assembly in June 1990, the DPS nonetheless managed to win 6.02 percent of the vote, gaining the support, according to some estimates, of 61 percent of Bulgarian Turks.

The DPS's deputies were quite active in the National Assembly in addressing issues related to the new constitution, particularly its human rights guarantees. They also worked relentlessly to create a statewide organization comparable to those built by the BSP and SDS. In 1990 and 1991, the influence of the DPS among the Turks and among Muslims as a whole increased (although not among Bulgarians or other ethnic groups), and reached its peak by the second parliamentary elections of October 1991, when the party captured 418,000 votes (7.55 percent of the total). As only three political parties managed to surpass the 4 percent electoral threshold, the DPS received 10 percent of the National Assembly's 240 seats. Its success at the local level was also substantial. In regions where Turks and Bulgarian-speaking Muslims were not in the majority and where the ethnic Bulgarian vote split among different parties, DPS candidates were elected. The DPS won 10.57 percent of the mayoral contests in larger communities and 13 percent of those in smaller villages, and gained almost 12 percent of all communal council members.[24]

In the parliamentary elections, the DPS received 50,000 more votes than in 1990, yet its political strength continued to be overwhelmingly concentrated in those districts with the largest Muslim populations: Kurdzhali (66 percent in 1991 versus 65 percent in 1990), Silistra (27 percent/27 percent), Turgovishte (27 percent/20 percent), Shumen (24 percent/21 percent), Smolian (12 percent/3.5 percent), Dobrich (11 percent/11 percent), and Blagoevgrad (11.7 percent/8.5 percent). The new votes came mostly from regions with high concentrations of non-Turkish Muslims. In districts with few Turks or Bulgarian-speaking Muslims, the DPS received barely any support whatsoever: Vidin (0 percent), Vratza (0 percent), Kjustendil (0 percent), Mihailovgrad (now Montana—0 percent), Pernik (0 percent), and Sofia (0.2 percent).

Hence, it is clear that the DPS quickly managed to mobilize most of the ethnic Turkish vote and a significant share of the Bulgarian-speaking Muslim vote. However, the question of the Bulgarian-speaking Muslims' political identity is more complex. At the outset, the DPS's leaders paid them little attention, tacitly relying on their own bitter memories of the "revival period" and thus taking their support for granted. As a result, substantial non-Turkish Muslim support for the DPS came only from those living in the communities of the Western Rhodopes (ranging from 43.8 to 73.2 percent), where, surrounded by Orthodox Bulgarians, the excesses of forced assimilation had been most profound. In the rest of the country, the Muslim vote was split more evenly among the BSP, the SDS, and the revived Bulgarian Agrarian National Union (BANU). Generally, no more than one-quarter of the Bulgarian-speaking Muslims voted for the DPS.

The 1991 election results not only confirmed the DPS as a viable political force, but its relatively modest presence in the National Assembly belied its political influence, as neither the BSP nor the SDS managed to obtain sufficient support to form a government. Not surprisingly, the DPS pledged its support for a SDS government, which was subsequently formed by its leader, Philip Dimitrov. Given the legacy of communist-era policies directed against the Turkish population, an alliance with the Socialists was, at least for the moment, out of the question.

However, the DPS continued to be viewed with suspicion by an over-whelming majority of ethnic Bulgarians. Even the SDS seemed uncomfortable with having the DPS as a coalition partner. The main obstacle to accepting the DPS as a legitimate political force remained its status as an ethnically based party, and efforts to have it banned on constitutional grounds were reinitiated after the BSP took power following the December 1994 parliamentary elections. In its statutes, the DPS defined itself as "an independent socio-political organi-zation established with the aim of promoting the unity of Bulgarian citizens by respecting the rights and freedoms of all ethnic, religious and cultural entities in Bulgaria."[25] However, at its second congress in December 1993, Dogan called the DPS "an ethnic party of a national type or a national party of an ethnic type"—a definition that clearly contradicts the constitution's prohibition of parties established "on ethnic, racial or religious lines."[26]

The DPS went still further at its 1996 congress, amending its statutes to include a provision calling for Bulgarian Turks to be declared a national minority. On the initiative of the Socialist-allied Nationwide Committee for the Defense of National Interests, 94 BSP deputies petitioned the Constitutional Court to ban the DPS on the grounds that the constitution defines Bulgaria as unitary national state.[27] There is probably considerable truth to DPS accusations that the BPS was attempting to divert mounting popular hostility caused by its gross mismanagement of the economy, which culminated in a wave of protests in January 1997 that quickly brought down the BSP government.[28] Nevertheless, while the Constitutional Court rejected the petition, citing its 1992 decision, it also pointed out that the law on political parties authorizes the prosecutor-general to ask the Supreme Court to disband a party found to be operating in violation of the constitution.[29] As a result of this implied threat, the DPS has continued to insist on official recognition of the term "national minority," but it has subsequently couched this demand in language that attempts to dispel suspicions of separatism. As the DPS's deputy chairman, Kemal Eyup, put it in a 1998 interview, "Bulgaria is a uni-national state compris-ing all its citizens as the single Bulgarian people."[30]

Notwithstanding such statements, and despite its own claims to the contrary, the DPS has remained predominantly Turkish, with ethnic Turks comprising roughly 90 percent of its members and 90 percent of its voters and the remainder composed of Bulgarian-speaking Muslims, Roma Muslims, and a few ethnic Bulgarians. There is no sign that Jews or Armenians have been attracted to the DPS, or that it has ever succeeded in broadening its appeal to ethnic Bulgarians, despite placing several, including former Deputy Prime Minister Evgeni Matinchev and Bulgaria's ambassador to Finland, Stoyan Denchev, on its candidate list in 1994.[31]

The apex of the DPS's political influence was reached following the 1991 elections. For one year it supported Dimitrov's SDS-led government. At the end of 1992, however, it withdrew its support, forcing the government to resign. The new government led by Prof. Lyuben Berov was constructed according to the mandate given to the DPS and received the conditional support of the BSP. The DPS was careful to consider the prevailing mood in Bulgaria and did not press for the appointment of ethnic Turkish ministers, preferring to rely on ethnic Bulgarians who could be considered political allies. Thus, the new cabinet consisted mainly of SDS deputies, including two ministers from the previous government. However, the relationship between the DPS and the SDS became steadily more acrimonious, undermining continued cooperation between the two parties and pushing the DPS to accept closer cooperation with the BSP. After Berov decided to resign in September 1994, citing the absence of stable parliamentary support, the DPS declined the mandate to form a new administration and precipitated a parliamentary crisis that eventually led to new elections and the BSP's return to power with a majority government.

The sources of the SDS's growing hostility toward the DPS are not difficult to identify. Throughout the 1991–1994 period, the DPS had been at the center of several political controversies that deeply embittered ethnic Bulgarian voters. First, on every important issue where Bulgaria's state interests conflicted with those of Turkey, especially in 1991–1992, DPS leaders adopted pro-Turkish stances, thereby rekindling the suspicion of foreign meddling in Bulgaria's affairs. A second point of contention was (and continues to be) Turkish-language education, an issue that has recurred with the advent of each school year. The DPS claims that the legal framework does not permit Turkish children to learn their mother language, because it provides only for voluntary rather than compulsory instruction. Ethnic Bulgarian politicians, for their part, retort with charges of undue influence exercised by the DPS over teachers in municipalities it controls.[32] So far, however, the DPS leadership's advocacy of compulsory Turkish-language education has been unsuccessful, in part because it has run counter to the preferences of many Turkish parents, who, in order to improve their children's eventual employment opportunities, prefer that they study Bulgarian and western languages.

Leadership of the DPS

To a large extent, Ahmed Dogan epitomizes the DPS, a characterization supported by virtually all public opinion surveys. While he is well educated and speaks Bulgarian fluently, the media follow his statements and actions closely and with considerable animosity, searching for even the smallest hints of disloyalty to the Bulgarian state. In June 1993, for example, his assertion that Bulgaria's road to the West passes through Turkey and the Arab states provoked a vigorous and bitter reaction in the mass media.[33] Yet he is pragmatic and alters his positions quickly, adapting well to changes in the political situation. In November 1991, he asserted that he was ready to propose a ban on the activities of the post-communist BSP, yet only six months later he proclaimed that in looking for a way out of the SDS-led government's crisis he was prepared to accept even a BSP-led cabinet.[34]

At the same time, however, he is not immune to political blunders. A serious scandal erupted in 1992 surrounding a list of Bulgarian spies in Turkey which, it was claimed, Dogan himself had turned over to the Turkish embassy in Sofia, dealing a severe blow to his carefully crafted image as a national, rather than an ethnic, leader interested in the well-being of Bulgaria as a whole. Whether these allegations were true or not remains unclear, but his unwillingness or inability to deal with them forthrightly meant that for almost two years they re-emerged in periods of heightened political tension.

Similarly, in 1994, when the National Assembly debated a draft law that would make Bulgarian the official language in the Bulgarian army, Dogan declared that if the law was adopted, Turkish recruits would boycott military service. This produced an uproar that did not subside when he added that Bulgaria's national security might be jeopardized if the question of lifting his parliamentary immunity were raised. Even in Smolian, where the DPS wields considerable influence, two thousand people subsequently signed a petition to ban the party.[35]

More problematically, while Dogan speaks eloquently about the dire socio-economic predicament of the Bulgarian Turks, his personal life is by no means modest. He enjoys expensive and fashionable clothes, restaurants, and nightclubs. In October 1993, Dogan, then almost 40, married a 19-year-old woman. The wedding ceremony was supposed to symbolize the important role of the DPS and its leader in Bulgarian politics. Instead, its lavishness, at a time when many DPS voters found it difficult to feed their families, tarnished his image.[36] Similarly, he paid in cash for a large apartment in one of Sofia's most fashionable districts that cost far more than his deputy's salary would indicate he could afford.[37]

These episodes signify more than Dogan's personal shortcomings, for they indicate the large dose of charismatic authority and patrimonialism that characterize his leadership. In 1994, the former chairman of the DPS's Haskovo organization spoke openly about corruption among the leadership.[38] Partly as a result of such malfeasance, the DPS's financial situation has steadily deteriorated, reducing its organizational effectiveness (its newspaper, *Prava i svobodi,* quit publishing in 1994 due to a lack of funds). Indeed, it is precisely this style of leadership that has been an important source of internal party opposition, impeding the DPS's smooth institutionalization.

Rifts in the Movement

From the outset, the DPS appeared to be a monolithic organization devoid of any internal problems and strongly united behind its goals. While some of the most important political parties in Bulgaria, including the SDS, splintered into a myriad of factions during the first years of democratic rule, the DPS remained intact. However, the first, albeit weak, symptoms of rifts within the DPS appeared as early as the convocation of the National Assembly in 1990, where one of the DPS's founders, Adem Kenan, voiced strategic aims that were far more radical than Dogan's. Kenan was promptly expelled from the DPS, and he hastened to form the Turkish Democratic Party (TDP). Although Bulgaria's courts have never legally recognized the TDP, Kenan made the most of the media's interest in him. He claimed that he would struggle to win for the Turkish population the official status of "national minority," accused Dogan of betraying the interests of the DPS electorate, and boasted of his alleged contacts among Turkish diplomats and Turkish government officials.

Predictably, this radical stance was welcomed by ethnic Bulgarian nationalist groups, who saw in Kenan, a poorly educated worker from a village in northeastern Bulgaria, a more attractive opportunity to clamor against the demands of "the Turks" than that offered by the refined and politically talented Dogan. It was initially unclear whether Kenan had significant popular support or was merely a creature of the media. Yet the DPS leadership continued to ignore him, and, perhaps more importantly, Turkish diplomats and government officials denied that they had established, or intended to establish, any contacts with him.[39] With no organization and few resources, Kenan and the TDP quickly faded from the political scene.

However, factional tendencies continued to appear in the DPS's parliamentary club. In June 1993, one of its deputies, Emil Buchkov, announced his departure. He was then followed by Professor Dimitur Sepetliev.[40] On February 2, 1994, two more deputies left the club, followed a week later by yet another, leaving the DPS with only nineteen MPs. The decision of Sherife

Mustafa—the only woman in the leadership—to remain in the parliamentary club but to resign from her position as its deputy chairperson was considered a particularly painful blow. As she was long considered to be close to Dogan, her departure was inevitably interpreted as a tacit criticism of his leadership.[41]

Wider conflicts within the DPS leadership had already become evident at the party's second congress in December 1993. After lamenting that their pleas for increased attention to Bulgarian Turks' social problems were not being addressed, the members of the Kurdzhali organization—one of the party's strongest because it represents the only region where Turks out-number ethnic Bulgarians—walked out. The move had been precipitated two months before when Dogan severely criticized the local leadership.[42] The Kurdzhali deputy Mehmed Hodzha subsequently emerged as the leader of those who sought to change the DPS's leadership and political style.

The reasons for the split have never been made entirely clear. Prior to 1984, Hodzha had been a teacher of Marxism-Leninism in local schools. When the "revival period" began, he was an active participant in the official propaganda campaign, but then became a victim of the repression and was imprisoned. According to Dogan's supporters, the Hodzha faction was reacting against the decision of the DPS's congress to expel from leading positions those who had previously been BCP secretaries (Hodzha himself had been deputy secretary of a local BCP organization until 1984). As a result, according to this view, those leaders whose positions were threatened decided to strike first. Hodzha's supporters, however, claimed that Dogan's loyalists were themselves active participants in carrying out the BCP's aims during the "revival period," and they continued to insist that the party was neglecting the plight of its constituents and that its leaders had separated themselves from the rank-and-file membership.

Both explanations contain some truth. The number of former party secretaries and active participants in the "revival period" within the two factions was not substantially different.[43] Moreover, the rebellion of the DPS's organization in Kurdzhali—the region from which Dogan himself had been elected in 1991—made it true by definition that the leadership had lost touch with an important constituency. Yet it is equally evident that the DPS followed the path already taken by most of the country's political parties, with leadership rivalries, vested local interests, and prodding by the SDS, which had a substantial interest in attracting at least a part of the Turkish vote, all playing a role.

Indeed, it seems quite probable that Hodzha's supporters hoped to make use of the SDS's established mechanism of absorbing other parties' splinter groups, a move that, by mending the bridge to the relatively well-institutionalized

SDS, would assure them of political survival. Subsequent events seemed to corroborate this explanation. From the very beginning of the DPS's internal conflict, the SDS's newspaper followed the development of Hodzha's group sympathetically. Hodzha announced the formation of a separate political party, the Party of Democratic Change, and declared that he would begin seeking contacts within the SDS in order to agree on a joint pre-election strategy for the December 1994 elections.

It is also likely that problematic relations between two main groups of Bulgarian Turks have manifested themselves in the DPS's internal conflicts, especially since 1993. Ethnic Turks living in northeastern Bulgaria tend to exhibit condescension toward those in the southeastern Kurdzhali region. In the words of one: "We are also Turks but we are not on speaking terms with that lot—the Kurdzhali Turks are fanatics, they speak with a Turkish accent, they are conservative, they are more devious and we here are easygoing."[44] While the extent to which such intra-ethnic tensions have provided a basis for political splits and maneuvering has never been openly discussed within the DPS, the existence of distinct regional identities probably contributed to weakening the party's purchase on its ethnically defined constituency in subsequent elections.

The DPS and Local Politics

The DPS's ability to represent its constituency has, however, been affected by factors that go beyond internal rifts. Following the first post-communist local elections in 1991, 653 mayors and 1,144 councilors represented the DPS, holding majorities on 27 local councils. In the Shumen region alone, the DPS dominated five of ten local councils. In the Ruse region, Güner Tahir became deputy regional director—the first Bulgarian Turk to hold such a powerful position.[45] However, the DPS did not have nearly enough members who were adequately prepared for their responsibilities as elected officials. More than 9,000 university-educated Bulgarian Turks had emigrated in 1989/1990, leaving their communities with few trained leaders. Indeed, even local DPS activists and mayors discouraged by the economic and social crises in Bulgaria left for Turkey. In the Kurdzhali region, 25 mayoral by-elections to replace emigrants had already been conducted by mid-1994.[46] At the party's second congress, Dogan stressed that overcoming the problem would require 10-15 years, and he confirmed the widespread impression that in many cases DPS mayors and councilors were poorly qualified and had gained office either by chance or because nobody else was willing to assume such positions.[47]

Moreover, many of the party's local leaders have not been immune to the temptations of power: financial scandals, bribes, and nepotism are commonplace in villages and towns under DPS control (in this respect, however, they are not an exception).[48] But the more fundamental problem is that even those DPS officeholders with the best of intentions have been in no position to cope with the profound social, economic, and infrastructural crises afflicting their constituencies. While modest local successes have been achieved even in the midst of Bulgaria's deepening economic crisis, none has been in an area under DPS control. Indicative of the overall situation is the small town of Ardino in the Rhodopes, where the DPS voluntarily gave eight council seats to ethnic Bulgarians from BANU who were regarded as more knowledgeable and experienced in addressing local problems.[49]

Bearing out the findings of the opinion surveys described earlier, while social relations between ethnic Bulgarians and Turks in municipalities where DPS representatives hold power are stable, communal tension arises over questions of political status and identity. Bulgarian public opinion, shaped as it is by a traditional view of Turks as second-class citizens, still tends to take notice of ethnic appointments in public employment only when Turkish officials replace ethnic Bulgarians. In several cases, moreover, local officials have aroused considerable media attention, particularly by attempting to replace Bulgarian names of villages, streets, and cultural institutions with Turkish ones. Thus far, however, the courts have repudiated such initiatives.[50]

At the same time, local political control by the DPS has occasionally provoked serious disputes with both the BSP and the SDS at the national level. The BSP government challenged the results of the mayoral election in Kurdzhali in November 1995, alleging serious irregularities. A district court upheld the challenge, overturning the election of the DPS's Rasim Musa, who won by a mere 600 votes with 50.7 percent support over an independent candidate supported by the Socialists. However, the Supreme Court reversed the lower court's decision and confirmed Musa's election, ruling that the voting irregularities in Kurdzhali were no greater than those in five other municipalities (all with overwhelming ethnic Bulgarian majorities) and held that they did not affect the election's outcome.[51]

Although the SDS supported the DPS's demand that the Kurdzhali election result be upheld, its position on the region's status changed markedly after it regained power following the April 1997 parliamentary election. Since then, local SDS officials have joined with BSP leaders at the national level in calling for a referendum on changing the Kurdzhali region's boundaries so that the more prosperous, ethnic Bulgarian-dominated town of Kurdzhali itself may be separated from the poorer, ethnic Turkish villages that surround it.[52]

In addition to this initiative by local SDS officials, the national government itself intervened in the municipal affairs of the eastern Bulgarian village of Tranak in September 1998, ordering the removal of a plaque commemorating three ethnic Turks executed in 1985 for carrying out a series of bombings. The interior minister in the SDS government, Bogomil Bonev, stated that, "We respect the victims of the 'revival period,' but we cannot allow that terrorists are honored." Dogan responded to the order by laying a wreath at the site in violation of a court injunction, calling the plaque's removal "an act of vandalism and a display of the incumbents' barbaric attitude to the value system in Bulgaria."[53]

The Failure of the DPS's Ethnic Strategy

The DPS never again achieved the degree of electoral success and political influence it enjoyed after the 1991 parliamentary elections. The splits that followed, the gradual erosion of Dogan's unrivaled leadership position, and the party's flirtation with the BSP in supporting the Berov government, all contributed to a fall-off in popular support in the 1994 elections, in which the DPS gained only 5.4 percent of the vote. In addition, both the Socialists and the SDS had by this point taken care to attract ethnic Turk voters, and their success, although not initially spectacular, has become increasingly evident.[54] A local BSP organization, formed mainly by ex-BCP members but also including some new recruits, was established even in the radical Adem Kenan's native village. Nor was the DPS alone in parliament with the BSP and the SDS any longer, as two other parties, the People's Union and the Bulgarian Business Bloc, had also cleared the 4 percent electoral threshold, which meant that the party received only 15 seats.

However, two factors in addition to internal splits and a shift in party allegiances by a portion of the Bulgarian Turk population underpinned the DPS's decline in the 1994 election. The first was the steady emigration of the DPS's electoral base to Turkey. While two parliamentary seats were removed from Kurdzhali as a result of the decline in the region's population, the DPS clearly expected to benefit from Bulgaria's electoral law, which, unlike many postcommunist states, allows absentee voting. Yet, despite the DPS's appeals to the *émigrés* to vote, the turnout in Turkey was extremely light, with only 466 Bulgarian citizens voting in Ankara and 755 in Istanbul.[55]

Second, confronted with the long-term perils associated with demographic factors, the dynamics of the party system, and the crystallization of party identification, the DPS had begun in 1993 to focus more attention on the problems of Bulgarian-speaking and Roma Muslims. However, rather than modifying or expanding the party's self-understanding as an ethnically-based organization, the DPS attempted to influence non-Turkish Muslims to define themselves as "Turkish." For example, the DPS insisted on having Turkish taught as the mother tongue of the Bulgarian-speaking Muslims, although most of them did not possess even a rudimentary knowledge of it. Similarly, in a sad reversal of the "revival period," Slavic endings of family names began to be changed administratively by local DPS activists and office-holders in order to promote the more "authentic" Islamic form.[56]

Not surprisingly, this strategy heightened inter-ethnic tensions, for, while Bulgarian public opinion had generally become reconciled to the fact that many ethnic Turks chose to be represented by the DPS, it regarded the DPS's efforts to attract Bulgarian-speaking Muslims as an attempt to "alienate" yet another portion of the country's population. The fears that this perception generated were exacerbated by Dogan's provocative tone whenever he discussed the Western Rhodopes. At the DPS's second congress, he declared:

> As far as the status quo of the Western Rhodopes is concerned, I want to state firmly that we are not going to allow anybody, including the parliament, the president, the government, the executive, and the political parties, to dictate our rights and freedoms in this region. I state this quite firmly. Let someone try… to decide the fate of this region… If we will have to choose in this problem between national security and human rights we shall choose human rights notwithstanding the consequences… The chain reaction might be so unexpected and sharp that Europe will have to read Balkan history for a long time before attempting to help us.[57]

However, one of the most significant factors affecting ethnic politics in Bulgaria, and the main political problem confronting the DPS, is that the ethnic identity of a high proportion of Bulgarian-speaking Muslims is currently in flux. The DPS evidently sought support for its strategy in ethnographic theories emanating mainly from Turkey and the Arab countries which assert that the Muslims of the Rhodopes are descendants of Turkish tribes that settled in the region before the arrival of the Slavs. Yet the vast majority of them appear to consider themselves ethnic Bulgarians who practice Islam.

At the same time, however, some Bulgarian Muslims claimed that until the Balkan wars of 1912-1913 they spoke Turkish.[58] One Bulgarian Muslim leader, Kamen Burov, even claimed the existence of a separate "Pomak" nation. This may have been a reaction to the continuing neglect of Bulgarian-speaking Muslims' social demands by all political parties, but it outraged the ethnic Bulgarian public. Especially alarming to Orthodox Bulgarians was the fact that Burov, a mayor of one of the Muslim villages in the Rhodopes, had recently returned from a trip to the United States, where he attended a seminar organized by the United States Information Agency (USIA). The link appeared logical to a suspicious public: the DPS, the Americans' tool, had not been entirely successful in attracting the Bulgarian-speaking Muslims, so the Americans had tried to influence their less-educated local elites by promising them prosperity as leaders of a separate ethnonational group. Support for this conspiratorial view grew when Burov founded a political party, the Democratic Party of Labor, to defend the interests of the Bulgarian-speaking Muslims.[59]

Unable to engineer a unified Bulgarian-speaking Muslim identity, the DPS's strategy of "deepening" its ethnic base proved to be a dismal failure in the 1994 elections. The DPS not only failed to win the Muslim Roma vote, which has generally benefited the BSP, but it even lost one of its two seats in the Western Rhodopes, a region it had considered secure. Thus, on the one hand, the DPS had heightened the deeply ingrained suspicions of ethnic Bulgarians toward its aims and goals,[60] while, on the other hand, the structural pressures confronting the party due to continued emigration to Turkey threatened to shrink its electorate below the 4 percent electoral threshold and deplete its already small contingent of qualified leaders.

Abandoning Ethnic Exclusivity

Consequently, the DPS reached a strategic impasse. It could continue to pursue a strategy that merely alienated the ethnic Bulgarian public by stepping up efforts at recruitment among Bulgarian-speaking Muslims. Yet, while the DPS has never abandoned this aim, its electoral debacle in 1994 indicated that it would be able to increase its support among non-Turkish Muslims only by addressing their social and economic problems rather than appealing to an artificial and unconvincingly construed ethnic identity. Alternatively, the party could support measures taken by both the Bulgarian and the Turkish governments to discourage the ethnic Turks from emigrating. However, this would carry the obvious risk of setting the party against its own constituency, a large part of which regards the "exit" option as its economic salvation and many of whom want to be reunited with family members already in Turkey. It would also contradict the DPS's longstanding opposition, on ethnic grounds, to Turkey's visa requirements. According to Dogan, many ethnic Turks have changed their names to the Bulgarian form in order to receive a visa.[61] Indeed, by its own admission, the DPS has assisted illegal emigration, evidently preferring the loss of current voters—which may, after all, be temporary should the economic situation improve—to the permanent loss of their ethnic identity.[62]

In any case, neither of these options promised to improve the DPS's electoral fortunes over the short term, and this became an increasingly important consideration as popular pressure on the BSP government mounted over the course of 1996 and early 1997. Ethnic Turks quickly joined the large demonstrations in January 1997 calling for the government's resignation, and the DPS supported the appointment of a caretaker cabinet to guide the country to early elections in April.[63] The DPS had opposed the BSP government in principle since its establishment following the 1994 elections. For example, the DPS was sharply critical of Ilcho Dimitrov's appointment as education minister, as he had filled the same post during the "revival period" and had chaired a coordinating committee on implementing the assimilation plan at the Bulgarian Academy of Sciences.[64] By the beginning of 1997, however, the party's constituency, like the rest of the country, had been mobilized by the threat of Bulgaria's imminent economic collapse.[65]

A new leadership split within the DPS quickly appeared over whether to rejoin the United Democratic Forces (ODS), an opposition coalition that had been formed with the SDS and the People's Union prior to the appointment of the caretaker government in February 1997. Those who supported contesting the upcoming election within the ODS were led by Güner Tahir and were mainly concentrated in the northeastern cities of Veliko Turnovo, Dobrich, and Rozgrad, where local organizations established an Initiative Council for the Reform of the DPS.[66] Tahir was strongly supported by the SDS, which had consistently made a point of blaming DPS leaders, rather than rank-and-file members, for those policies with which it disagreed, thereby steering clear of implicit ethnic appeals and keeping the door open for future cooperation. However, Dogan opposed re-joining the ODS, while Kemal Eyup accused the SDS of attempting to form "a second DPS." With Dogan unsatisfied by the prospect of being a junior partner within the ODS, the DPS formed the Alliance for National Salvation (ONS), which included the Nikola Petkov Bulgarian Agrarian National Union, the Green Party, the liberal New Choice, the monarchist Kingdom of Bulgaria federation, and the Democratic Center Party.

The ONS received 7.6 percent of the popular vote and 19 seats in the National Assembly and supported, but did not join, the new ODS government, which won 52.2 percent of the popular vote and 137 seats. The 25 members of the Initiative Council, including Tahir (who was the chair of the DPS's Rozgrad organization), were expelled from the DPS the following month.[67] However, notwithstanding the split—the most serious faced by the DPS so far given that it neatly divided the northeastern and southeastern regions— the party had decisively abandoned its exclusive ethnic orientation. This remained true even after the DPS withdrew its support for the ODS government at the end of 1997 following Dogan's inclusion on a list of 23 alleged collaborators with the communist-era secret police that was read by Interior Minister Bonev in the National Assembly.[68] Indeed, the ONS itself was subsequently replaced by a more ideologically coherent inter-ethnic coalition, the Liberal Democratic Union (LDU), including the DPS, New Choice, the Liberal Democratic Alternative, and the Free Radical Democratic Party.[69]

Conversely, the DPS's increasingly strong cooperation with ethnic Bulgarian parties has been underpinned by the failure of Bulgarian extremist nationalism. Even in the heated atmosphere of the 1991 elections, when ethnic relations were a paramount political issue, groups such as the Bulgarian National Radical Party, led by Dr. Ivan Georgiev, received a combined total of around only 100,000 votes throughout the country. Even if these parties, which based themselves almost exclusively on anti-Turk (and anti-Roma) rhetoric, had formed a single electoral organization, they would not have gained parliamentary representation. In the December 1994 elections, Bulgarian nationalist parties fared even worse, drawing only about one-third the number of voters they attracted in 1991. By the April 1997 election, their combined total was less than 20,000 voters.

Instead, Bulgarian nationalists focused primarily on the domains of culture and identity. Beginning in 1993, the Movement of St. John the Precursor, led by Father Boian Saruev, attempted to combat the DPS's influence among the Bulgarian-speaking Muslims in the Rhodopes by performing baptisms of those he has persuaded to "return" to Orthodox Christianity. The number of Bulgarian Muslims who initially embraced Orthodoxy is unknown, but Father Saruev's claim of 50,000 converts is surely a gross exaggeration.[70] In any case, more typical of the region is Love of the Motherland, led by Branko Davidov, who asserts that his organization maintains chapters throughout the Rhodopes. Unlike Father Saruev, Davidov's group is based on an ecumenical form of ethnic loyalty and patriotism, consciously pursuing an integrated membership of Muslim and Orthodox Bulgarians.

Conclusion

The imminent danger of violent ethnic conflict following the collapse of Bulgaria's communist regime is the proverbial dog that didn't bark. Yet, although relations between Bulgaria's two major ethnic groups seem calm, especially in comparison with other Balkan states, they have not been without tension. Bulgaria's mass media, particularly print media, do not always behave responsibly and to a considerable extent incite conflict, particularly at the local level. A 1994 study, for example, found that only 11 percent of all publications treating problems of compatibility and incompatibility among different ethnic and religious groups regularly cover instances of inter-ethnic cooperation, while 89 percent regularly report on conflicts.[71]

However, the activities of small nationalist groups notwithstanding, it is also clear that neither Bulgarians nor Turks have politicized religion in pressing their ethnic agendas. To be sure, anti-Turkish or anti-Bulgarian slogans occasionally appear on the walls of churches and mosques, and ethnic Bulgarians became indignant in the spring of 1993, when on St. Cyril and Methodius day—a national holiday commemorating the arrival of Christianity—Bulgarian flags were not raised in DPS-controlled Momchilgrad.[72] Yet all surveys indicate that religious tolerance prevails in the country. Intolerance is a comparatively rare phenomenon (3–5 percent among the Muslims and 10 percent among the Orthodox), and religious fundamentalism is abhorrent to both groups. Even more importantly, the suspicion that the "other" is a religious fanatic has gradually lost ground.[73]

Bulgarian ethnologists, sociologists, and political scientists pin their hopes for prolonged ethnic peace on *komshuluk*, a Turkish word denoting the traditional good relations between neighbors. In fact, negative perceptions of Turks among ethnic Bulgarians living near Turks have to some extent declined. Virtually an equal number of Turks and ethnic Bulgarians consider the forcible assimilation of the "revival period" a crime, and everyday contacts have begun to correct perceptions created by history, popular culture, education, and mass media.[74] Of course, as Balkan observers are quick to point out, the problem is that the same had once been true in Sarajevo. In Bulgaria, too, acceptance of the other on an individual level remains much higher than acceptance of the group as a whole, placing much of the burden for maintaining ethnic peace on the political elite.

In this respect, the current ODS government's careful distinction between the DPS and the Bulgarian Turkish electorate has been critical to undermining ethnic radicalism. Indeed, in June 1998, the SDS-led cabinet launched a concerted effort to address the country's ethnic and demographic problems and to integrate members of ethnic minorities into all levels of state administration. It subsequently enacted a new media law permitting unrestricted Turkish-language broadcasts, and, in an important symbolic gesture, leading government officials have repeatedly apologized to ethnic Turks on behalf of Bulgaria for the abuses suffered during the "revival period."[75]

To the extent that ethnic Bulgarians still do not accept the presence of ethnic Turks at higher echelons of power, two factors appear to be at work. first, emigration to Turkey raises the suspicion that ethnic Turks' ties to the "mother state" are stronger than their identification with Bulgaria.[76] However, the fears that this arouses may subside gradually given the profound improvement in bilateral relations since 1997, marked by the signing of several agreements on economic, political, and cultural cooperation.[77] Second, and somewhat less importantly, the DPS has never completely abandoned its political strategy of ethnic recruitment among the Bulgarian-speaking Muslims, thus fueling similar suspicions of disloyalty. Nevertheless, the persistence of emigration and the failure of the DPS's strategy to compensate for it without surrendering an ethnically exclusive agenda are likely to continue forcing it to develop into a responsible force within the Bulgarian political framework.

Notes

1. The term "Bulgarian-speaking Muslims" denotes Slavic Bulgarians living mainly in the Rhodopes and parts of the Balkan mountain range who practice Islam. They are commonly called Pomaks, although they consider this to be a pejorative term. The Bulgarian Turks, of course, are also Bulgarian-speaking Muslims, so the term is inevitably somewhat artificial, but it will be used here to maintain a distinction that has played an important role in Bulgaria's ethnic politics.

2. P. Bozhikov, "Etnodemografska harakteristika na bulgarskoto naselenie," *Guven*, vol. 3, nos. 29-30, July 27, 1994.

3. U. Memishev, *Uchastieto na bulgarskite turtzi v borbata protiv fashizma i kapitalizma, 1919-1944* (Sofia, 1977).

4. *Prava i svobodi*, September 3 and September 9, 1993.

5. O. Zagorov, "Vuzroditelnijat protzes. Teza i antiteza," *Otritzanie na otritzanieto* (Sofia, 1993), p. 21.

6. *Rabotnichesko delo*, December 30, 1989; *Literaturen front*, June 7, 1990; G. Milushev, *Po koridorite na vlastta* (Sofia, 1991).

7. M. Beitulov, *Zhivotut na naselenieto ot turski proizhod v NRB* (Sofia, 1975); I. Tatarliev, "Kulturnata revoliutzija sred turskoto naselenie," *Narodna republika Bulgarija - nasha rodina* (Sofia, 1964).

8. This tendency already existed to some extent among young Turks, who often placed a Bulgarian name alongside their Turkish names when in mixed company.

9. On these events, see the following memoirs of Bulgarian secret police agents: G. Sotirov, *Turskite teroristi i az edin ot Shesto* (Sofia, 1991); A. Musakov, *Shesto. Spomeni na poslednija nachalnik na VI upravlenie v Durzhavna sigurnost* (Sofia, 1991); N. Krusteva, B. Asenov, *Poturchvane II* (Sofia, 1993). Numerous descriptions of the situation in northeast and southeast

Bulgaria in the 1980s and early 1990s are provided in the monograph *The Ethnic Situation in Bulgaria 1992* (Sofia: Club 90, 1993).

10. J. Baev, N. Kotev, "Izselnicheskijat vupros v bulgaro-turskite otnoshenija sled Vtorata svetovna voina," *Guven*, vol. 3, no. 23-24, June 15, 1994.

11. *24 Tchasa*, January 4, 1993; *Prava i svobodi*, September 24, 1993; *BTA*, June 19, 1995. It should be added that over the same period, some 300,000 ethnic Bulgarians left the country for Western Europe, North America and South Africa.

12. *24 Tchasa*, December 4, 1997.

13. Zh. Georgiev, I. Tomova, M. Grekova, Kr. Kunev, "Niakoi rezultati ot izsledvaneto 'Etnokulturnata situatzija v Bulgarija,'" in *Sotziologicheski pregled*, no. 3 (1993), pp. 68, 72.

14. *BTA*, March 1, 1996.

15. P. Mitev, "Vruzki na suvmestimost i nesuvmestimost vuv vsekidnevieto mezhdu hristijani i mjusjulmani v Bulgarija," *Sotziologichesko izslledvane. Vruzki na suvmestimost i nesuvmestimost mezhdu hristijani i mjusjulmani v Bulgarija* (Sofia, 1994), Table 1-10.

16. *BTA*, August 9, 1996.

17. The media quoted hundreds of examples during the first years of democracy. See, for example, *Prava i svobodi*, Nov. 19, 1993; *24 Tchasa*, June 21, 1993; *Demokratzija*, May 11, 1993; *Duma*, April 20, 1993.

18. *Prava i svobodi*, December 24, 1993.

19. The regimen faced by children in some villages is extremely grueling. They must study at school for six hours a day, including lessons in Russian and a west European language, and many Muslim children are then expected to study Turkish for three hours per week. At the same time, they must help their parents in the tobacco fields. It is little wonder, then, that initial enthusiasm for attending Koranic schools to learn Arabic was short-lived.

20. *Constitution of the Republic of Bulgaria*, art. 13 (3).

21. In 1996, for example, reports appeared that the Turkish emigrant organization Pulgyoc had sent missionaries to establish Muslim "colonies" in the Pomak areas of the Pirin and Rhodope regions, with Orthodox inhabitants warning that "Islamicization" would be the first step to Muslim autonomy in Bulgaria. See *Standart*, August 4, 1996. Similarly alarmist reports of Islamic proselytizing in the Pirin and Rhodope regions by foreign missionaries—allegedly including members of Middle Eastern groups such as Hamas and Hezbollah—dating back to 1992 have continued to appear in the Bulgarian press. See, for example, *Monitor*, February 1, 1999.

22. *24 Tchasa*, May 29, 1993; *Demokratzija*, May 12, 1993; *Trud*, September 5, 1994; interview with DPS deputy Ivan Palchev in *Kontinent*, February 24, 1993; *Zora*, January 26, 1993.

23. P. Gocheva, *DPS v sianka i na svetlina* (Sofia: Impress, 1991).

24. B. Gjuzelev, *Electoralni naglasi i electoralno povedenie na maltzinstvata v Bulgarija (1990-1992)* (Sofia: Centre for Democracy, 1993), p. 21.

25. *Prava i svobodi*, December 10, 1993.

26. *Prava i svobodi*, December 3, 1993. Constitution of the Republic of Bulgaria, art. 11 (4).

27. *Standart*, December 6, 1996.

28. Dogan had already accused the BSP of provoking ethnic tension after its candidate in the 1996 presidential election, Ivan Marazov, claimed on national television that the DPS and the SDS had a secret agreement that would allow the "Islamicization" of the Rhodope mountains by giving Muslims there greater power. *Standart*, October 16, 1996. Marazov lost the election to the SDS candidate, Petar Stoyanov.

29. *BTA*, December 21, 1996.

30. *Pari,* September 27, 1998.

31. *BTA,* December 12, 1994.

32. See, for example, *Standart,* September 6 and 10, 1994; Demokratzija, January 6, 1994.

33. *Kontinent,* June 18, 1993.

34. *Debati,* Nov. 12, 1991; *Trud,* May 23, 1992.

35. *24 Tchasa,* Aug. 23, 1994, Sept. 1, 1994; *168 Tchasa,* Aug. 22-28, 1994, pp. 9-12.

36. More than four hundred guests were invited to a reception dinner in the most expensive restaurant in Varna. In the northeastern city of Isperih, 15,000 people were entertained at the city stadium with more than six hours of music, folk dances, and wrestling matches. *Prava i svobodi,* Nov. 5, 1993. The marriage lasted six months.

37. Dogan's salary for the three years that he was a deputy up to that point was 342,000 leva, while the apartment cost two million. See *Trud,* July 25, 1994, *Standart,* August 25, 1994.

38. *Trud,* September 7, 1994.

39. *24 Tchasa,* June 25, 1993, June 29, 1993.

40. *24 Tchasa,* June 17, 1993.

41. *Duma,* February 2, 1994; *Demokratzija,* February 14, 1994.

42. *Prava i svobodi,* November 5, 1993.

43. *168 Tchasa,* August 15,1994.

44. K. Stoilov, "Muslim Stereotyped Forms of Behavior," *The Ethnic Situation in Bulgaria* (Sofia: Club 90, 1993), p. 99; see also D. Madjarov, "Adaptation—Reality and Images," *Ibid.,* p. 106.

45. *Prava i svobodi,* May 21, 1993, November 5, 1993.

46. *Standart,* August 1, 1994.

47. *Prava i svobodi,* December 3, 1993. Recently one of the leaders of the movement asked that the old system of privileges for the Turks be reintroduced.

48. *24 Tchasa,* June 28, 1993; *Demokratzija,* September 10, 1994.

49. *Duma,* June 16, 1993; *Standart,* May 31, 1993.

50. *Duma,* February 17, 1993; *Kontinent,* June 22, 1993; *Standart,* June 17, 1993, and August 8, 1994.

51. *BTA,* November 23, 1995; *Pari,* April 25, 1996.

52. *Kontinent,* May 17, 1998.

53. *Standart,* September 11, 1998; *BTA,* September 9, 1998.

54. See the persuasive analysis by Konstantin Subchev in *Kontinent,* May 23, 1998.

55. *BTA,* December 20, 1994. Many potential voters in Turkey are illegal immigrants who may have been deterred from voting by fears that casting a ballot would bring them to the attention of the Turkish authorities.

56. A special parliamentary commission confirmed such allegations against local DPS leaders in 1993. See *Duma,* May 22, 1993; *Kontinent,* May 22, 1993; *Demokratzija,* May 22, 1993; *Trud,* April 10, 1993; *Standart,* May 31, 1993. The DPS representative on the commission refused to sign the joint statement.

57. *Prava i svobodi,* December 3, 1993.

58. P. Gocheva, "Koi vkarva vulka v balkanskata koshara ," *Duma,* June 30, 1993.

59. *Duma,* June 29, 1993; *Standart,* June 28, 1993; *24 Tchasa,* June 28, 1993; *Demokratzija,* April 28, 1993; interview with Burov in *Standart,* June 25, 1993.

60. See the first part of the multi-faceted research carried out by the Centre for Minority Studies in Sofia, supported by the PHARE program, especially V. Mutafchieva, "Obrazut na turtzite, evreite i tziganite," *Vruzki na suvmestimost i nesuvmestimost mezhdu hristijani i mjusjul-*

mani v Bulgarija (Sofia, 1994), pp. 5-34, and D. Dimitrova, "Etnicheskite plashila v pechata i traditzionnite modeli na obshtuvane mezhdu hristijani i mjusjulmani v Bulgarija," *Ibid.*, pp. 176-188.

61. See, for example, the interview with Dogan in *The Turkish Daily News*, November 16, 1998.

62. On the DPS's active support of illegal emigration, see the statement by Idris Mehmed, chair of the party's Kurdzhali municipal organization, in *Pari*, July 21, 1998.

63. *Standart*, January 18, 1997.

64. *BTA*, January 26, 1995.

65. Bulgaria's economy contracted by 10.9 percent in 1996, while the value of the leva depreciated by around two-thirds, causing monthly inflation to exceed 200 percent by the beginning of 1997.

66. *BTA*, March 28, 1997.

67. *Standart*, May 6, 1997.

68. *BTA*, December 10, 1997. Dogan has never confirmed or denied the allegation.

69. *Pari*, November 30, 1998.

70. *Standart*, June 24, 1993; *Demokratzija*, June 12, 1993. Interview in *24 Tchasa*, April 30, 1993.

71. D. Dimitrova, *Etnicheskite plashila*, pp. 176-187.

72. *Kontinent*, February 9, 1993, and August 25, 1994; *24 Tchasa*, January 18, 1994.

73. P. Mitev, "Vruzki na suvmestimost i nesuvmestimost vuv vsekidnevieto mezhdu hristijani i mjusjulmani v Bulgarija," pp. 217-218.

74. Tzvetlana Georgieva, "Suzhitelstvoto kato sistema vuv vsekidnevnija zhivot na hristijanite i mjusjulmanite v Bulgarija," *Vruzki na suvmestimost*, pp. 142-143, and pp. 148-150.

75. *Standart*, June 11, 1998; *BTA*, August 1 and November 16, 1998.

76. Although ethnic Bulgarians also continue to leave the country for western Europe, North America, and South Africa for economic reasons, their emigration has not, in the absence of ethnic kinship, raised analogous concerns about *political* identity and loyalty.

77. For details of the agreements, see, for example, *Standart*, December 4, 1997.

10

MANAGING ETHNOPOLITICS
IN EASTERN EUROPE: AN ASSESSMENT
OF INSTITUTIONAL APPROACHES

Jack Snyder

Since the French Revolution, a rise in nationalism has often coincided with the collapse of an autocratic regime and a burst in popular participation in politics, especially where democratic institutions for constructively channeling those popular energies remain weak.[1] As Jonathan Stein's introduction points out, post-communist eastern Europe embodies many of the risk factors that would seem to make it ripe for ethnic political mobilization: a sudden transition from an autocratic system that left a weakly organized civil society, no legacy of democratic political parties, and a yawning gap between the demand for mass democracy and the carrying capacity of nascent democratic institutions. In the past, demagogic nationalist ideology and cultural alignments in politics have often filled such institutional gaps. Thus, it is not a surprise that ethnic politics has been a common feature of the east European landscape over the past decade, except in those countries where strong democratic institutions and practices were rather quickly consolidated.

This decade of experience, richly described in the chapters of this book, presents an opportunity to study how ethnopolitics has been managed—or mismanaged—in the varied states of central and eastern Europe. In some of these states, dilemmas of management remain very much unresolved. In concluding this book, I will consequently examine a few of the most common approaches to managing ethnic rivalries in light of that post-communist European experience.

Although some very knowledgeable social scientists have developed sophisticated solutions for harmonizing ethnic pluralism with stable democratic institutions, each of the most commonly proposed approaches has as many drawbacks as benefits. Thus, debate over their relative merits still rages not only in academic journals like the *American Political Science Review*, but also in pragmatic magazines read by policymakers, such as *Foreign Affairs*.[2] I do not propose any solutions that are new in principle. However, my arguments about democratization and ethnic conflict suggest ways of sequencing and adapting these strategies which run counter to common practices.

Hegemonic Control By the Majority

One strategy that often gets left off the list of "solutions" to ethnic conflict, due to its unpalatability to a liberal audience, is hegemony. In many multi-ethnic societies, one ethnic group monopolizes the power of the state and uses it to dominate other groups. In some cases, this is accomplished by outright repression; in other cases, by stratagems that divide minorities in order to conquer them. Repression can sometimes be effective in preventing ethnic conflict, but only if the power of the dominant group is so overwhelming as to preclude rational resistance. This worked for decades in the Soviet empire, for example. On balance, however, political repression and economic exploitation tend to be associated with a greater risk of ethnic conflict.[3] Repression *per se* is not a very reliable long-term strategy of ethnic conflict management.

Domination works more reliably when those who are deprived of power tolerate it because they calculate that the benefits of being second-class citizens outweigh the costs of being first-class rebels. Ethnic minorities may thus be co-opted if they are granted benefits smaller than those of the dominant group, yet greater than their next-best alternative. As Neil Melvin's chapter notes, for example, Russians in Estonia and Latvia compared their situation to that of Russians in Russia, and decided to favor independence from Moscow, despite the prospect of dramatically unequal citizenship rights in their new states.

Such hegemonies work best when tangible side-benefits are reinforced by ideological justifications of ethnic subordination. Sometimes this is accomplished by the fiction that status inequalities are based on neutral legal criteria, not on ethnic ascription. For example, the measures that initially excluded most Russians from Estonian citizenship were based not on ethnicity per se, but on one's ancestors' citizenship in the inter-war Estonian state (before most Russians arrived), and on knowledge of the official language of the state, which happens to be Estonian. Insofar as this seemingly civic justification for ethnic exclusion has helped to create an opening for more inclusionary outcomes, many Russian-speaking Estonians have found the ideology to be one they can work with.[4] As Melvin points out, the selective yet progressive inclusion of Russians in Estonian political life served to co-opt a stratum of Russian-speaking loyalists to the ethnonational Estonian state.

Though majority hegemonies or "ethnic control regimes" may be quite effective in moderating ethnic conflict, they nonetheless have some major drawbacks if they are implemented in too harsh a manner.[5] The systematic deprivation of equal civic rights to ethnic minorities creates an ideological climate in which the democratic rights of the majority are also held to be less than absolute.[6] If the collectivity is held to count for more than the individual, this insidious principle can be, and often is, used to undermine the rights of individuals of the majority ethnic group as well.[7] In places like contemporary Armenia and Croatia under Franjo Tudjman, for example, it was a short step from the expulsion of ethnic minorities by the government to the abrogation of democracy and journalistic freedom for ethnic majorities as well. Ethnic hegemonies would be less objectionable as temporary expedients than as permanent vehicles for civic inequality. Insofar as Estonia, for example, continues to gradually infuse real content into its nominally civic principles, its long run prognosis as a liberal democracy will be good.

Unfortunately, few dominant ethnic groups are far-seeing enough to soften their own hegemonic position voluntarily through gradual civic reforms. Melvin points out that Latvia has not been nearly as astute as Estonia in regularizing the terms under which Russian-speakers can participate as individuals and as groups in local politics. Instead, Latvia could successfully count on the relative disorganization of its Russian-speaking community in sustaining a system of high barriers to participation. In so doing, it was much slower than Estonia in seizing the opportunity to create a class of Russophone loyalists, which would provide insurance against the emergence of a Russian "fifth column" inside Latvia in the event of future tensions with a more nationalist regime in Moscow.

One lesson from the Baltic experience is to place quasi-democratic ethnic control regimes under moderate, but relentless pressure from the international community to gradually breathe life into the nominally civic provisions of their constitutions. As Melvin notes, the Council of Europe pressed Estonia to loosen its initially draconian law on resident aliens, while Latvia's eventual admission to the EU was strongly conditioned on liberalizing its citizenship provisions for Russophones. This influence was successful because it was exercised discreetly, and because it was backed by the perceived incentives of economic integration into the West and a future security guarantee against Russia. As a counterpart to such pressure, tolerance should be shown for ethnic hegemonies if their reforms are heading in the right direction, even if slowly. At the same time, the international community should be supporting the development of the institutional infrastructure that will be needed when the disadvantaged minority is finally allowed to play a full role in the civic life of the state. This means, for example, training ethnic minority journalists to take over responsible positions in mainstream media serving an ethnically mixed audience. It does not, however, mean jump-starting the creation of ethnic opposition media to give voice to the demands of excluded minorities. That only exacerbates the segmentation of the marketplace of ideas, making it easier for ethnonationalists to sow myths unchallenged.

Ethnic Partition

Another unattractive but important strategy is ethnic partition. One does not have to hold primordialist theories of ancient hatreds to believe that, once popular identities are mobilized to fight along lines defined by cultural differences, it will be difficult to erase fears and hatreds rooted in the memory of those conflicts. Once intermingled cultural groups have fought, it is likely that their subsequent cohabitation in the same state will be wary, and consequently that they will be prone to fight again in the future. Any of a number of triggers—retreat of the imperial order-keepers, democratization, economic changes, shifts in the demographic balance of power—may touch off a revival of violent conflict. For this reason, a number of scholars have been making the case for ethnic partition as the best solution for certain cases of very highly mobilized nationalist enmities.[8]

Among the objections to this strategy, the most obvious is that the creation of ethnically homogeneous states in places like the former Yugoslavia, Rwanda, Burundi, and the Transcaucasus would require the resettlement of huge numbers of unwilling people. Yet the history of many ethnic conflicts shows that homogenization happens anyway, but through the vilest kind of warfare rather than through internationally supervised, preventive operations in peacetime. One reason for ethnic peace in much of Eastern Europe today is that the two world wars occasioned a vast "unmixing of peoples" through what today's Serbs would term ethnic cleansing.[9] Even such civilized folk as the Czechs expelled over two million Germans—with the blessing of the victorious Allies—in the immediate aftermath of the end of the Second World War in 1945.

In the present period, expulsions have accompanied many ethnic conflicts. During the breakup of the Soviet Union, hundreds of thousands of Armenians and Azerbaijanis were hounded from each other's countries through pogroms and other forcible measures.[10] Fighting and intimidation in the former Yugoslavia has, as Nenad Zakošek's chapter shows, sharply eroded the social base underpinning an array of cosmetic measures initially adopted in Croatia to protect the Serb minority. Many less consolidated regions of the former Yugoslavia have likewise been made more homogeneous and thus more amenable to partition. Indeed, in light of the *de facto* partition of Bosnia-Herzegovina into Serbian and Muslim-Croat areas, the international community's insistence on maintaining the Dayton Accord's *de jure* fiction of political integration seems almost perversely designed to prevent the acceptance of an inevitable equilibrium. In future cases of this type, the UN High Commissioner for Refugees might be wise to make a preventive offer of low-interest mortgages to fearful individuals stranded in minority enclaves who wish to purchase housing in their ethnic home republic.

Opponents of this strategy argue, however, that partition rarely resolves conflicts, largely because populations often remain somewhat intermingled. In part for that reason, endemic conflict persists despite partition in Ireland, Palestine, Kashmir, and other cases. Most important, however, partition— and the anticipation of partition—may itself be a cause of heightened conflict. Many more died in communal violence in the aftermath of partitioning India and Pakistan, as a result of the turmoil and insecurities of migration, than before it. Indeed, plans to divide the former British Raj may have acted as a self-fulfilling prophecy, creating needless fears and uncertainties about the status of religious minorities that were to be abandoned in the "wrong" state.[11] For these reasons, while preventive partition should not be regarded as unthinkable, neither should it be viewed as a preferred strategy applicable to a wide range of cases.

Federalism

A related approach is federalism. Instead of partitioning ethnic communities into separate sovereign states, this strategy would divide an existing state into partially autonomous territorial sub-units whose boundaries are designed to coincide with ethnolinguistic concentrations. This method has a terrible track record, yet it remains popular with liberal problem-solvers, in part because it seems to allow national self-determination without the nasty fuss and bother of full-fledged partition. In fact, ethnofederalism is frequently a recipe for subsequent partition, and often needlessly so. In the wake of communism's collapse, the only states to break up were the three ethnofederal systems—

Yugoslavia, the Soviet Union, and Czechoslovakia—the former two with violent consequences. Arguably, in each of these states ethnofederalism was a strategy of rule actively chosen by its communist rulers, not a necessity forced upon them by the irresistible demands of ethnic groups. As numerous studies have demonstrated, ethnofederalism tends to heighten and politicize ethnic consciousness, creating a self-conscious intelligentsia and the institutional structures of an ethnic state-in-waiting.[12] When mass political participation expands, these ethnofederal structures channel it along an ethnic path. This process has played itself out even in Quebec.[13] As Janusz Bugajski's chapter demonstrates, it is the fear of a slippery slope to ethnofederalism—and beyond—that makes central governments in contemporary central and eastern Europe so wary of any proposals for group rights or local autonomy for ethnic minorities. For these reasons, ethnofederalism should be regarded as at best a last resort, which risks fueling rather than ameliorating the politicization of ethnicity.

One of ethnofederalism's very few success cases is India, which reluctantly acceded to demands to reorganize some of its provincial boundaries after 1956 to coincide more closely with linguistic divides. Nehru and the Congress Party, at this point still at the height of their authority, were adamant secularists. Thus, the central government kept a tight rein on the process of ethnofederal reorganization. Rules of thumb guiding this process were that no concessions would be made to secessionist groups, that demands for redrawing boundaries along religious lines would be rejected out of hand, that large-scale popular support for the change had to be demonstrated, and that reorganization had to be requested by all the affected linguistic groups.[14] Most observers credit these controlled boundary adjustments with redressing a reasonable grievance without compromising the basic principles of the centralized, secular, communal-blind state. Subsequent problems leading to heightened communal mobilization in Indian politics were caused by the breakdown of the Congress system at the center, not by ethnofederalism *per se*.

Assimilation

The opposite strategy is the assimilation of ethnic minorities to the cultural identity of the ethnic majority. This is possible for groups that are culturally similar, like Russians and Ukrainians, or for minority cultures that are assimilated before they achieve a literary consciousness or political organization beyond the kinship level.[15] In fact, as Erin Jenne's chapter on the Roma suggests, it is likely that both conditions must be fulfilled, especially where cultural differences reproduce, and are reinforced by, widespread socio-economic discrimination. Thus, for most groups that are already involved in sustained ethnic conflicts, even those where a coherent collective consciousness is largely absent, the window for cultural assimilation to the foe's ethnic identity has already closed. In such circumstances, attempts at coercive assimilation almost always backfire, heightening the political salience of ethnicity.

Power Sharing Versus Cross-Ethnic Alliances

This leads us to the two opposite strategies of ethnic conflict prevention that have stimulated the most academic debate: power sharing between ethnic groups, and institutional engineering to foster integrative, cross-ethnic political alliances.[16] The power-sharing approach theorized and advocated most prominently by Arend Lijphart takes the politicization of ethnic groups as a given in deeply divided societies, and offers guidelines for elite-led pacts between the contending groups that will allow them to live in peace and mutual security.[17] In contrast, the integrative approach developed most notably by Donald Horowitz seeks to depoliticize ethnic identity by means of institutional arrangements that create incentives to forge political alignments on the basis of cross-cutting cleavages.[18] The link between democratization and ethnic conflict underscores the problems with elite-managed ethnic power sharing regimes, for the construction of such systems cannot precede the consolidation of a democratically legitimated elite. More promising, therefore, are integrative approaches like Horowitz's, though these must be embedded in a broader context of supportive institutions than the constitutional and electoral schemes that Horowitz himself emphasizes.

Lijphart lists the central characteristics of power sharing as joint control of executive power of the state, substantial autonomy of ethnic groups to regulate their own internal affairs, a minority veto on important issues, and proportionality of parliamentary representation, bureaucratic appointments, and state financial benefits.[19] Underpinning these arrangements is a system of bargaining between leaders of the participating ethnic groups that is supported by deference to those leaders on the part of each group's ethnic rank-and-file. Lijphart lists nine factors as conducive to power sharing: the absence of a single majority group; no economic disparity among the groups; a balance of power among the groups; a small number of groups; a country with a small total population; the existence of an external threat common to all groups; overarching loyalties that reduce the exclusiveness of ethnic attachments; prior traditions of compromise; and geographic concentrations of ethnic residence. However, he adds that power sharing is always the best approach in deeply divided societies, even when these supporting conditions are absent.[20]

Among the numerous criticisms of the power sharing approach, I will focus only on the points that are most relevant to the context of democratizing societies. Power sharing, as Lijphart conceives it, depends on mass groups deferring to the judgments of moderate elites that represent their ethnic segments. However, deference can hardly be taken for granted in democratizing societies. Mass groups clamoring for a greater say in politics will use any available argument, especially the argument that traditional or incumbent elites are selling out the nation's interests by being too accommodating toward an out-group. In this context, elites jockeying for power within the ethnic group often have an incentive to be immoderate. Institutionalized power sharing exacerbates this by defining all politics as ethnic politics. As mass groups enter the political process, anyone who wants to participate must go through ethnic channels. Carlos Flores's chapter states the problems for democratizing societies attendant upon this approach very succinctly: "Facilitating electoral competition by ethnically-based parties or granting them parliamentary representation *ex ante* encourages the creation of such parties, indirectly promotes confrontation rather than alliances with parties representing non-ethnic ideologies, tends to reduce the presence of ethnic minority candidates in non-ethnically-based parties and thus the latter parties' interest in problems pertaining to ethnic minorities, discourages political pluralism within ethnic minority communities, and generates a perception of ethnic minorities and their representatives as exogenous and problematic elements of a country's political life." In such conditions, mobilizing support by definition means making sectarian appeals. Cross-ethnic politicking is reserved to elites, who are very likely to be too pressured from below to be accommodating toward elites of the opposing community.

Nor, unsurprisingly, is the empirical record very favorable to power sharing. Lijphart points to Belgium and Malaysia as textbook cases of successful power sharing in ethnically divided societies. Setting aside the (increasingly problematic) example of Belgium, a rich country in the heart of a peacefully democratic continent, Malaysia hardly counts in Lijphart's favor. Rather than a "consociational democracy," it is an example (like Indonesia until very recently) of a successful ethnic control regime, erected by suppressing democracy and free speech and with side-payments to the Chinese business elite. Lijphart also counts India as an example of successful power sharing.[21] However, while limited legal self-regulation by Muslims and linguistic federalism can be counted as power-sharing elements in the Indian political system, the main principle of the Congress system in its heyday was secularism, the opposite of representation along religious or communal lines. Congress's success in containing ethnic and religious conflict was based precisely on fostering cross-cutting cleavages and thereby encompassing all cultural groups, rather than permitting communal groups to be mobilized in competition with each other. Finally, Lijphart used to claim Lebanon as the premier example of power sharing, but since the outbreak of the bloody civil war there in the 1970s, he now stresses the flaws in Lebanon's consociational arrangements.[22] In fact, Lebanon, along with Yugoslavia, underscores the dangers of the consociational approach itself: by locking in an ethnic definition of politics, it courts disaster when the prospect of rising popular participation undercuts the moderation of elites, or when demographic shifts alter the ethnic balance of power.[23]

Horowitz's integrative approach pursues exactly the opposite strategy: it tries to depoliticize ethnicity by creating institutions that reward cross-ethnic alignments. For the most part, he suggests encouraging this through constitutional and electoral provisions. In federal systems, for example, he suggests that boundaries should not coincide with ethnic patterns of settlement, but cut across them or break them up into smaller units. He notes that Nigeria's three-province system, which corresponded with ethnic lines, broke up into bloody ethnic warfare. Afterwards, the new regime imposed a twelve-province scheme that successfully politicized local identities and subcleavages within the broader ethnic categories.[24] For similar reasons, Horowitz recommends electoral rules that require winning candidates to get at least some of their votes from voters of a different ethnicity. As several chapters in this book demonstrate, mere proportional representation by itself accomplishes little, even where appropriate electoral thresholds are in place, since the handful of minority representatives in parliament will still be outvoted on every issue unless some incentives are created for cross-ethnic alliances, whether in general elections or in parliamentary coalition-making. This can be done by requiring that successful candidates receive a number of "second-preference" votes, or by requiring legislative supermajorities larger than any single parliamentary group could provide. Horowitz notes that such a scheme was instituted in Sri Lanka in 1978, but that by then politics was so polarized that electoral rules were insufficient to induce moderation.

Horowitz is on the right track, but his institutional schemes are too mechanistic and insufficiently embedded in a broader supportive context. It should be noted, for example, that the prevalence of large ethnic majorities and a single politically mobilized minority in most central and east European states can easily block the moderating influence of his proposed electoral rules and parliamentary voting requirements. Thus, cross-ethnic institutions are needed on more dimensions than just electoral and constitutional rules. Segmental boundaries in the marketplace of ideas need to be effaced by the development of media institutions that serve as a common forum for the presentation and rigorous evaluation of ideas for all the communities that comprise the state. That is, in addition to Horowitz's "vote pooling," multiethnic societies also need "idea pooling." Integrative institutions are also needed in the administrative realm. Whereas Lijphart favors strict ethnic parity in representation in state bureaucracies, what is really needed are highly professionalized, ethnic-blind courts, police, and armed forces which are capable of carrying out state policy equally toward all individuals, regardless of ethnicity.[25]

The commitment to the creation of a dense web of such ethnic-blind institutions can serve as the basis for civic patriotism, based not on the coexistence of ethnic groups but on the civic rights and duties of individuals. Unlike the strategy of ethnic assimilation, the promotion of civic nationalism does not require citizens to alter that aspect of their identity which is rooted in traditional culture, but simply to depoliticize it. Thus, Genevans do not need to speak German or eat sauerkraut to be fully Swiss.

As a practical matter, a civic national identity can emerge in a number of ways. In the case of Switzerland, a long history of cross-cultural cooperation against outside threats created powerful civic myths to underpin collective action. In a society of immigrants from many cultures, such as the United States, loyalty to state institutions based on equal individual rights can serve as a strong foundation for a common identity. In many states, however, civic nationalism is based on a broadened redefinition of a core ethnic identity.[26] British civic nationalism, for example, grew out of a redefinition of English patriotism that stressed the centrality of individual liberties and common struggles against foreign foes, in which the Scots and the Welsh could be full participants. French national identity, though based partly on the ethnic core of the Île de France, was broadened through the experience of the French Revolution to include civic principles of equality and the rights of man. As a result, immigrants have been able to become French by integrating themselves into French civic life much more easily than has been the case for outsiders living, for example, in Germany, whose conception of citizenship is more ethnic and exclusionary.[27]

A number of contemporary states stand at the cusp of developing civic national identities through one or another of these pathways.[28] Most may do so by making a core ethnic identity more inclusionary, whereas some may have to forge entirely new loyalties to a multiethnic territorial state. Russia and Ukraine, for example, have formed around a central core ethnic group, but apart from establishing the core group's language as the official medium for state business, they are not attempting to impose an ethnic stamp on the political system. The rhetoric of top government officials stresses inclusionary loyalty to the state rather than exclusionary loyalty to the ethnic group. Over time, and given prolonged regional stability, it is quite possible that Estonia and Latvia will likewise broaden the core of their ethnic self-definition to take on a more civic character. Civic identity in Kazakhstan, on the other hand, seems less likely to emerge from the gradual broadening of a core ethnic identity, since two core ethnic identities, Russian and Kazakh, are regionally concentrated, numerically equally balanced, and culturally too distant for easy assimilation. Any successful civic identity would have to be bicultural and based on loyalty to an administratively successful state. In light of this consideration, full democratic participation should probably wait until Kazakhstan's state has been able to demonstrate its effectiveness and thereby generate an enthusiastic mass following.

Yet, as this book's focus on the more politically advanced central and eastern European post-communist states demonstrates, democratization can coincide with the emergence of civic nationalism. Ivan Ilchev's chapter points out the various factors that have prevented the hardening of political boundaries between ethnic Bulgarians and Bulgarian Turks: internal divisions within the Turkish community, appeals by political parties to socioeconomic interests that cut across ethnicity, and the option of voluntary emigration for the most dissatisfied Turks. In such a case, it is surely preferable to pursue civic political identities, which blur lines of ethnic cleavages, than to unnecessarily reify them through a strategy of group power sharing.

Despite the advantages in principle of the civic solution, some caveats are in order. In some cases, as in the recent regime of the Slovak nationalist prime minister, Vladimír Mečiar, the argument that group rights can be best guaranteed through the protection of individual rights is a rhetorical fig leaf rationalizing a policy of ethnic majority hegemony. While touting civic rights, Mečiar tried to ban Hungarian street signs, gerrymandered districts to reduce the political clout of the Hungarian minority concentrated in southern Slovakia, and channeled economic investment to the ethnically Slovak north. Even in such cases, however, the best strategy is not to promote minority group rights to defend against such encroachments, but to insist that the majority regime implement its putative adherence to civic principles in an even-handed way.

However, the promotion of overarching civic identities is not a short-term possibility in circumstances where the mobilization of ethnic cleavages is already extremely intense. Civic nationalism is a non-starter in Bosnia today, no matter how much the promoters of the Dayton Accord cherish that ideal. Nonetheless, short-run choices should, wherever possible, avoid expedients that make civic outcomes more difficult in the long run. Power sharing and ethnofederalism, by locking in ethnic identities, are in this sense a step in the wrong direction. Moderate, balanced ethnic control regimes, which constrain ethnopolitical mobilization of the majority as well as minorities, may be a better strategy in the long run, so long as they are combined with the gradual fostering of civic institutions.

Combating Nationalist Myths in the Marketplace of Ideas

Finally, another strategy emphasizes intellectual solutions to ethnic conflict.[29] Some argue, for example, that the root cause of ethnic conflict resides in the false historical myths that nationalists sow about the alleged perfidies of the ethnic foe.[30] From this standpoint, mechanical gimmicks like power sharing or electoral alliances are unworkable until these myths are exploded, and unnecessary once that is achieved. Consequently, textbooks, not electoral laws, should be reformed. However, while intellectual combat against falsifiable myths is indeed a key instrument for containing ethnic conflict, such combat can be waged effectively only in a well-constituted marketplace of ideas. Thin liberal solutions based on free speech and the spontaneous emergence of truth will be trumped every time unless they are placed within a thickly supportive web of norms and institutions. Thus, civic identity; scrutiny of myths; Horowitzian electoral incentives; professionalized bureaucracies; and high-quality journalism must be developed in tandem. None works effectively in isolation from the other components, and the development of the whole package may take time.

Democratization and free speech can be made compatible with ethnic harmony and the moderation of nationalist sentiment only if the marketplace of ideas is well-institutionalized and appropriately self-regulating. If these conditions do not exist, they need to be created before, or at least along with, the unfettering of speech and political participation.

For example, ethnically segmented media markets should be counteracted by the promotion of civic-territorial conceptions of national identity. Inclusive national identities can be fostered through an integrative press, which expresses a variety of outlooks on the same pages. All too often, international aid goes to the opposition press in democratizing countries, regardless of its journalistic quality, on the grounds that creating a pluralism of voices is the essential objective. In Romania, for example, the U.S. Agency for International Development has subsidized anti-government newspapers that fail to meet even the most minimal standards of accuracy in reporting.[31] Instead, aid should go to forums that present varied ideas, not a single line, in a setting that fosters effective interchange and factual accuracy. In post-1945 Germany, for example, American occupiers licensing newspapers showed a strong preference for editorial teams whose members spanned diverse political orientations.[32] The international community should encourage this kind of idea-pooling through integrative public forums to break down the intellectual boundaries between ethnically exclusive "imagined communities."[33]

For this reason, NGOs and other aid donors should reconsider projects to provide ethnic minorities with their "own" media.[34] Instead, support should go to media that strive to attract a politically and ethnically diverse audience, invite the expression of various viewpoints, and hold news stories to rigorous standards of objectivity. This can be done by expanding existing NGO programs, such as those of the International Press Institute in Vienna,[35] to train journalists from newly democratizing countries and by providing quality news organizations with equipment, subsidized newsprint, or other logistical support. Special efforts should be made to encompass the regional and local press in these efforts. In case after case—from Weimar Germany to contemporary Russia—a key vehicle of nationalist mythmaking has been face-to-face networks and rough-hewn periodicals. To provide an effective alternative to these, media projects should focus on the inclusion of local journalists in the activities of state-wide media associations, mid-career training sabbaticals for grassroots journalists, and financial subsidies to make a high quality local press independent and affordable.

Idea-pooling can also occur outside of formal journalistic institutions through face-to-face interactions of citizens. A study comparing Indian cities with low and high rates of inter-communal rioting shows the crucial role played by voluntary inter-communal civic organizations and even less formal communication channels in refuting myths that cause conflict spirals. Where such channels existed, rumors about inter-communal rape or desecration of a temple were nipped in the bud; otherwise, a cycle of retaliation was likely.[36] Thus, instead of partitioning a society into segmented communities that communicate only with themselves, an integrated forum for discourse and information sharing, whether through media or voluntary organizations, should be promoted.

Major efforts should be made to promote the institutionalization of effective, accommodative norms of elite discourse, journalistic professionalism, and independent evaluative bodies before the full opening of mass political participation. Whenever possible, market imperfections should be counteracted by decentralized institutions, not centralized regulatory directives, and by the promotion of norms of fair debate, not by restrictions on the content of speech.

Conclusions

The moment of transition from autocracy toward the beginnings of expanded democratic participation is fraught with peril, not least stemming from the heightened potential for ethnic conflict. This is especially true when, as Bugajski argues, "clientelist-authoritarian" parties enjoying residual strength left over from the autocratic *ancien* regimes try to maintain their power by appealing to nationalist sentiments. As a rule, those in the international community or in the transitional state itself who would resist the tide of ethnopolitics would be well-advised to avoid half-measures that seek to compromise between the principles of civic democracy and in-group favoritism. Nationalism and ethnic tension have been weakest in those East European states that have most thoroughly institutionalized civic principles in their political life. Thus, wherever possible, building the institutional foundations for individual rights-based civic regimes, rather than locking in group-rights expedients, ought to be the goal of international efforts in this realm. At the same time, however, in cases where the moment for the construction of a civic identity has already passed, partition should be seriously considered. And where the civic moment is not yet ripe, toleration of ethnically even-handed regimes that lack a popular base of support may be preferable to the promotion of more populist, yet more ethnically self-aware political movements.

Notwithstanding the intensity of ethnic violence in the former Yugoslavia, the mobilization of ethnic nationalism elsewhere in central and eastern Europe has been remarkably tepid in the past decade. This is in part due to the success of democratization, but it has also been due in part to the residual strength of neo-socialist parties in places like Bulgaria and Romania, to the disorganization of ethnic minorities themselves in places like Latvia and weak unification in cases such as the Roma, and to the debility of political mobilization in general in socioeconomically backward regions like Albania and Macedonia. These latter regions remain especially at risk for increased ethnic tension in the future, as their populations become more mobilized into politics, as their downwardly mobile elites face incentives to play the nationalist card, and as the Balkan region's seemingly chronic instability continues to produce a litany of real and perceived external and internal threats. In this respect, they resemble most closely many of the post-Soviet successor states, as well as the state- and nation-building experiences in post-imperial Africa, Asia, and elsewhere. As I have argued here, the clearest lesson that can be drawn from these cases is that those who would avert ethnic conflicts in the future should begin laying the institutional groundwork for civic patriotism—emphasizing both inclusive politics and civil public discourse—now.

Notes

1. This chapter adapts ideas found in Jack Snyder, *Nationalism in the Age of Democracy* (New York: Norton, 1999). See also Jack Snyder and Karen Ballentine, "Nationalism and the Marketplace of Ideas," *International Security* 21:2 (Fall 1996), pp. 5-40; Edward D. Mansfield and Jack Snyder, "Democratization and the Danger of War," *International Security* 20:1 (Summer 1995), pp 5-38; Edward Mansfield and Jack Snyder, "Democratization and War," *Foreign Affairs* 74:3 (May/June 1995), pp. 79-97.

2. Arend Lijphart, "The Puzzle of Indian Democracy," *American Political Science Review* 90:2 (June 1996), 258-268; Radha Kumar, "The Troubled History of Partition," *Foreign Affairs* 76:1 (January/February 1997), p. 26.

3. Ted Gurr, *Minorities at Risk* (Washington, DC: United States Institute of Peace, 1993), ch. 2-5.

4. Toivo Raun, "Ethnic Relations and Conflict in the Baltic States," in W. Raymond Duncan and G. Paul Holman, Jr., eds., *Ethnic Nationalism and Regional Conflict* (Boulder: Westview, 1994), 155-182; David Laitin, "National Revival and Competitive Assimilation in Estonia," *Post-Soviet Affairs* 12:1 (January-March 1996), pp. 25-39.

5. Ian Lustick, "Stability in Deeply Divided Societies: Consociationalism versus Control," *World Politics*, vol. 31, 1979; Kenneth McRae, "Theories of Power-Sharing and Conflict Management," in Joseph Montville, ed., *Conflict and Peacemaking in Multiethnic Societies* (New York: Lexington, 1991), pp. 93-106.

6. Liah Greenfeld, *Nationalism: Five Roads to Modernity* (Cambridge: Harvard University Press, 1992).

7. Michael Specter, "Drift to Dictatorship Clouds Armenia's Happiness," *New York Times*, January 3, 1997, pp. 1, 12.

8. Chaim Kaufmann, "Possible and Impossible Solutions to Ethnic Civil Wars," *International Security* 20:4 (Spring 1996), pp. 136-175.

9. Rogers Brubaker, *Nationalism Reframed* (Cambridge: Cambridge University Press, 1996), chapter 6.

10. Barbara Anderson and Brian Silver, "Population Redistribution and Ethnic Balance in Transcaucasia," in Ronald Suny, ed., *Transcaucasia, Nationalism, and Social Change*, 2d ed. (Ann Arbor: University of Michigan Press, 1996), 490-491.

11. Radha Kumar, "The Troubled History of Partition," *Foreign Affairs* 76:1 (January/February 1997).

12. Brubaker, *Nationalism Reframed*, ch. 2.

13. Karen Ballentine, Columbia University Ph.D. dissertation in progress.

14. Paul Brass, *The Politics of India since Independence* (Cambridge: Cambridge University Press, 1990), pp. 169, 172-173.

15. Karl Deutsch, *Nationalism and Social Communication* (Cambridge: MIT, 1966), ch. 6; Lars-Erik Cederman, *Emergent Actors in World Politics: How States and Nations Develop and Dissolve* (Princeton: Princeton University Press, 1997), pp. 157-161.

16. Timothy Sisk, *Power Sharing and International Mediation in Ethnic Conflicts* (Washington D.C.: US Institute of Peace, 1996), chapter 3.

17. Arend Lijphart, *Democracy in Plural Societies* (New Haven: Yale University Press, 1977); Lijphart, "The Power-Sharing Approach," in Montville, ed., *Conflict and Peacemaking in Multiethnic Societies*, pp. 491-510.

18. Donald Horowitz, *A Democratic South Africa? Constitutional Engineering in a Divided Society* (Berkeley: California, 1991); Horowitz, "Making Moderation Pay," in Montville, ed., *Conflict and Peacemaking in Multiethnic Societies*, pp. 451-476.

19. Lijphart, "The Power-Sharing Approach," pp. 494-495. See also Eric Nordlinger, *Conflict Regulation in Divided Societies* (Cambridge: Center for International Affairs, Harvard Studies in International Relations, 1972), pp. 21-33.

20. Lijphart, "The Power-Sharing Approach," 497-8; note also the list of conditions in Joseph Rothschild, *Ethnopolitics* (New York: Columbia University Press, 1981), pp. 162-164.

21. Lijphart, "The Puzzle of Indian Democracy," pp. 258-268.

22. Lijphart, "The Power-Sharing Approach," pp. 507-508.

23. Ivo Banac, *The National Question in Yugoslavia* (Ithaca: Cornell University Press, 1984), p. 414, notes that the conditions for successful consociational power sharing were also absent in Yugoslavia.

24. Horowitz, "Ethnic Conflict Management for Policymakers," in Montville, ed., *Conflict and Peacemaking in Multiethnic Societies*, pp. 122-123.

25. Horowitz's own recommendations on the ethnic composition of military forces in South Africa are complex, taking into account both professionalism and representativeness. *A Democratic South Africa?*, pp. 227-231.

26. Anthony Smith, *The Ethnic Origins of Nations* (Oxford: Blackwell, 1986).

27. Rogers Brubaker, *Citizenship and Nationhood in France and Germany* (Cambridge: Harvard University Press, 1992).

28. Ian Bremmer, ed., *Understanding Nationalism* (forthcoming).

29. Rothschild, *Ethnopolitics*, pp. 80-84.

30. Stephen Van Evera, "Hypotheses on Nationalism and War," *International Security*, 18:4 (Spring 1994), pp. 26-33.

31. Thomas Carothers, *Assessing Democratic Assistance: The Case of Romania* (Washington, DC: Carnegie Endowment for International Peace, 1996), pp. 80-89.

32. Richard L. Merritt, *Democracy Imposed: U.S. Occupation Policy and the German Public, 1945-1949* (New Haven: Yale University Press, 1996), pp. 291-315, esp. 296, which emphasizes the effectiveness of this strategy.

33. Horowitz, *A Democratic South Africa?*, chapters 4 and 5; Arend Lijphart, *Democracy in Plural Societies*. On a common media as a precondition for an integrated national consciousness, see Benedict Anderson, *Imagined Communities* (London: Verso, 1983).

34. Stephen Harold Riggins, *Ethnic Minority Media* (Newbury Park, CA: Sage, 1992).

35. Larry Diamond, *Promoting Democracy in the 1990s* (New York: Carnegie Corporation, Report to the Carnegie Commission on Preventing Deadly Conflict, December 1995), pp. 24-25.

36. Ashutosh Varshney, "Postmodernism and Ethnic Conflict: A Passage to India," *Comparative Politics*, October 1997. For similar findings, see Sherrill Stroschein, "The Components of Coexistence: Hungarian Minorities and Interethnic Relations in Romania, Slovakia, and Ukraine," in John Micgiel, ed., *State and Nation Building in East Central Europe* (New York: Columbia University, Institute on East Central Europe, 1996), pp. 153-176.

INDEX

For Product Safety Concerns and Information please contact our
EU representative GPSR@taylorandfrancis.com Taylor & Francis
Verlag GmbH, Kaufingerstraße 24, 80331 München, Germany